The External Environment of Business:
Political, Economic, Social and Regulatory

Second Edition

by

Anthony M. Pagano, University of Illinois at Chicago

and

JoAnn Verdin, Northwestern Memorial Hospital, Chicago, IL

Copyright © 1995, 1997
Anthony M. Pagano and JoAnn Verdin

ISBN 0-87563-682-9

Cover design by Lisa M. Ruffolo

Published by

STIPES PUBLISHING L.L.C.
202-204 West University Avenue
Post Office Box 526
Champaign, Illinois 61824-0526

DEDICATION

To the memory of our colleague and friend, Bert Elwert. From him, we have learned important things about the issues under study in this book.

TABLE OF CONTENTS

		Page
Chapter 1	Introduction	1
	How Important Is the External Environment?	2
	Why Study the External Environment?	4
	Management Functions	5
	Integrating the External Environment with Management Functions	8
	Managerial Implications	22
	Overview of the Book	23
	Questions	24
	Key Concepts	25
	Case Analysis: Pullman Standard	26
	Case Questions	28
	Case References	29
	References	30
Chapter 2	Theoretical Foundations: Prices, Markets, and Management	33
	The Interrelationships of the Major Elements of the External Environment: A Model of Change	33
	The Nature of the Market System	39
	The Role of Prices in a Free Enterprise System	56
	A Model of the Market System	64
	Environmental Analysis and Forecasting	66
	Summary	73
	Questions	75
	Key Concepts	76
	Case Analysis: An Example of Authoritarian Socialism before the Breakup of the Soviet Union	77
	Case Questions	82
	References	83
Chapter 3	The Public Sector Response and the Political System	85
	The Role of the Public Sector in a Free Enterprise System	85
	Problems of Government	92
	The Public Sector and the Private Sector Compared	97

i

        The Structure of Government in the
           United States 98
        The Public Policy Process 107
        Strategies for Impacting the Political Process .. 116
        Proposals for Reform 124
        Summary 125
        Questions 127
        Key Concepts 128
        Case Analysis: The American Trucking Associations
           and the Motor Carrier Act of 1980 129
        Case Questions 134
        Case References 134
        References 135

Chapter 4   **Corporate Social Responsibility – Introduction** 137
        What Is Business Social Responsibility? 138
        What Actions Are Socially Responsible? 140
        Arguments Favoring Social Responsibility 142
        Arguments Against Social Responsibility 146
        A Model of Business Social Involvement 148
        Determinants of the Level of Social
           Responsibility 150
        Relation between the Societal Element Changes
           and the Level of Social Involvement 156
        Business Response and Managerial Implications 162
        Summary 171
        Questions 173
        Key Concepts 174
        Case Analysis: Playskool Inc. 175
        Case Questions 179
        Case References 180
        References 181

Chapter 5   **Business Ethics – Introduction** 183
        What Is Business Ethics? 184
        Concepts of Ethics 185
        Choice among Ethical Concepts 193
        Ethical Tests 194
        Ethical Dilemmas in Business 197
        Managerial Implications 205
        Summary 212
        Questions 214

                Key Concepts 215
                Case Analysis: Polaroid In and Out of
                    South Africa 216
                Case Questions 223
                References 224

Chapter 6 **Government Regulation of Products, Prices
                and the Workplace** 227
                Scope of Government Regulation 228
                Reasons for Government Regulation:
                    Public Interest Theory 240
                Reasons for Government Regulation:
                    The Interest Group Theory of Regulation .. 243
                Why Regulation? 243
                Methods of Government Regulation 245
                A Typology of Regulation 247
                Traditional Regulation: Interstate Commerce
                    Commission 250
                The Consumer Movement 256
                Occupational Safety and Health Regulation ... 265
                The Benefits and Costs of Government
                    Regulation 269
                Alternatives to Regulation 272
                Managerial Implications 282
                Summary 286
                Key Concepts 287
                Questions 287
                Case Analysis: Manville Corporation 289
                    Chapter 11 291
                    Corporate Maneuvers 292
                    Outlook 294
                Notes 295
                Case Questions 296
                References 297

Chapter 7 **Energy and the Physical Environment** 299
                Government Policy and the Energy Crisis 300
                The Future of Oil Prices 309
                The Physical Environment 315
                A Model of Environmental Goals 316
                Federal Environmental Policy 321

    Benefits and Costs of Federal Environmental
      Policy 327
    Alternative Approaches to Pollution Reduction . 332
    Acid Rain 340
    Hazardous Wastes 342
    Managerial Implications 343
    Summary 345
    Questions 347
    Key Concepts 348
    Case Analysis: Union Carbide and the Disaster
      at Bhopal 349
    Case Questions 358
    Case References 360
    References 361

Chapter 8 **Regulation of Markets and Competition** 363
    Monopoly 364
    Social Waste in Practice 368
    Government Monopolies 370
    Oligopoly 370
    Contestable Markets 374
    Sources of Market Power 375
    Measures of Industrial Concentration 379
    Federal Antitrust Policy 384
    The Future of Antitrust Regulations 392
    Managerial Implications 394
    Summary 396
    Questions 398
    Key Concepts 399
    Case Analysis: The Union Pacific-Southern
      Pacific Railroad Merger 400
      Railroad Industry:
        An Economic Policy Overview 400
      The Current Railroad Market Structure ... 400
      A Competitive Strategy 402
      Reactions to Proposed Union Pacific
        and Southern Pacific Merger 403
      The UP-SP Oral Arguments Before
      Surface Transportation Board 405
    Case Questions 405
    Case References 406
    References 407

Chapter 9 **Factors Affecting the Employers of the Future** 408
    Underlying Forces 409
    Societal Element Changes 414
    Public Sector Response 423
    Government Regulation of Employment
        Practices 432
    Managerial Responses 437
    Summary 443
    Questions 445
    Key Concepts 446
    Case Analysis: Discrimination and Texaco 447
    Case Questions 455
    References 455

Chapter 10 **Impact of New Technology on the Workplace** 458
    Major Technological Breakthroughs 459
    Overall Impacts of Technological Change 462
    Automation in the Factory 468
    Automation in the Office 469
    Future Changes Resulting from Shifts in
        Technology 470
    Public Policy and New Technology 478
    Relationship to the Major Elements of the
        External Environment of Business 481
    Managerial Implications 484
    Summary 491
    Review Questions 492
    Key Concepts 493
    Case Analysis: Home Work—Mountain
        Climbers 494
        No More Party Lines 495
        The Dark Ages 496
        Windfall From Apple 498
        Pie in the Sky? 499
        Going Wireless 499
        Bigger Pipelines 500
    Case Questions 502
    References 503

Subject Index 505

Name Index 511

CHAPTER 1

INTRODUCTION

Businesses are not managed in a vacuum. Even the best managed in the traditional sense can run into substantial problems because of many factors outside the confines of the organization and beyond the direct control of managers of the firm. These factors constitute the external environment of business.

The external environment can be defined as *all of the regulatory, technological, economic, social and political factors outside the direct control of business managers, but having a profound influence on the success or failure of a firm.* The external environment can affect costs and profits. It can influence or even control prices that can be charged, markets that can be entered and products that can be produced.

Not only is the external environment important, but it is growing increasingly complex and is constantly changing. The external business environment is shaped by forces that were almost nonexistent only a few years ago: oil cartels and robotics, deregulation and environmental protection, equal opportunity and changes in social mores. Not only have technological advances changed the types of products being produced, but technology is beginning to shape the way business is conducted. The communication revolution has brought foreign buyers, suppliers and competitors within easy reach. Foreign goods appear in our stores and industry must compete in international markets. Business is deserting traditional locations and moving south and west, into suburbia, and out of the country. Government is playing an increasingly important role in the economy. Changing demographic trends are shaping the present and may have ominous implications for the future.

The external environment includes a variety of factors such as government regulation, energy and the physical environment, technology, social responsibility and ethics, labor markets and the political system. A list of the major elements of the external environment appears in Table 1.1. Each of these elements will be described in greater detail in this chapter.

How Important Is the External Environment?

There are several ways in which the importance of the external environment can be assessed. One is the impact on costs of production. It has been estimated that the costs of complying with regulations concerning the physical environment alone totaled $91.456 billion in 1991.[1] The cost of all federal government regulation of business has been estimated at $66 billion per year (Weidenbaum, 1979). One company, Occidental Petroleum Corporation, estimated its costs of meeting local, state and federal regulations at between $125 to $137 million (Jones, 1979).

Monitoring the external environment also involves managerial time. George Steiner, a prominent scholar of business and its environment, has observed:

> Top managers of corporations spend a preponderant part of their time today dealing with environmental problems. These include addressing social concerns of society, complying with new social legislation, communicating with legislators and government executives concerning new proposed laws and regulations, meeting with various self-interest groups concerning their demands and/or grievances, and administering their organizations in such a way as to respond to the new attitudes of people working in the organization. This is in sharp contrast to the top executive of a major corporation twenty years ago whose attention and decision-making was focused almost wholly on economic and technical considerations. The increased attention of top management time to social and political questions results, of course, in different allocations of time of lower-level managers than in the past. They, too, are spending more of their time on social and political issues and are being measured more and more on performance in these areas (Steiner, 1979, p. 13).

---

[1] Source: U.S. Department of Commerce, *Statistical Abstract of the United States*, 1994.

Table 1.1. Major Elements of the External Environment

Government Regulation
- Traditional Industry Regulation
- New Regulation
- Regulation of Markets and Competition

Energy and the Physical Environment

Labor Markets
- Development of Labor Unions
- Public Policies Restricting Labor Supply

Technology and the Workplace

Welfare and the Provision of Public Services

Inflation, Unemployment and the National Output

Regional and Local Issues

Global Trade and International Issues

Social Responsibility and Ethics
- Corporate Responsibilities
- Business Ethics

The Political System

Rogene A. Buchholz (1992), who has authored a study of the external environment of business, has estimated that the chief executive officer spends between 20 to 75 percent of his or her time on external matters. The noted economist Murray Weidenbaum (1979), who was at one time chairman of the President's Council of Economic Advisors, notes that many chief executives spend one third or more of their time on governmental and public policy matters.

Changes in the external environment can also affect the ultimate success or failure of a firm. The case at the end of this chapter concerns Pullman Standard Corporation. This company was at one time the largest railcar manufacturer in the world. In 1980, it had sales of over $800 million and employed over 5,000 employees. By 1982, however, its total production was zero. The case documents a variety of changes in the external environment which had both direct and indirect impacts on Pullman's problems. It also provides an important lesson regarding the importance of the external environment in determining business success or failure.

Why Study the External Environment?

The external environment seems so far removed from everyday business practice, that students frequently ask why they should study this subject. They compare this area with accounting, statistics, human resource management, marketing, computer science, etc., and ask what job skills are being developed.

Unlike other courses in business administration, study of the external environment leads indirectly to better managerial performance and job related skills, not directly. Study of the external environment leads to an increased awareness and understanding of the complex of factors which affect business at every turn. This increased awareness is important for managers at all levels. The chief executive has to be concerned with the regulations affecting the enterprise, but so does the first line supervisor. Changes in technology, labor markets, energy, etc., all have important implications for all levels of management.

In addition to becoming a better manager, study of the external environment can result in a better understanding of how business relates to the rest of society and how business can be conducted in a socially responsive manner. The Committee for Economic Development, a well known business group, has noted that:

> Today it is clear that the terms of the contract between society and business are, in fact, changing in substantial and important ways. Business is being asked to assume broader responsibilities to society than ever before and to serve a wider range of human values. Business enterprises, in effect, are being asked to contribute more to the quality of American life than just supplying quantities of goods and services. Inasmuch as business exists to serve society, its future will depend on the quality of management's response to the changing expectations of the public (Committee for Economic Development, 1971, p. 16).

Finally, study of the external environment is important if managers are to be good citizens. The course of public policy, international events, social changes, etc., should be evaluated in our decisions in the voting booth. Good government has as it basis a well informed electorate.

Management Functions

The external environment can affect management at all levels in an organization. It does so by affecting the management processes or functions which are carried out in all organizations. In order to understand how the external environment affects business, these functions need to be defined.

There are numerous ways to describe the management functions which take place in a business organization. In this book, the approach of the classical management school will be utilized and expanded to include the human resource function. The classical management school has outlined the functions of planning, organizing and controlling. An integration of this approach with other ways of looking at management activities suggests four primary functions which exist inside organizations: planning, organizing, controlling, and staffing/rewarding.

Planning

The planning function is most often carried on by the top managers or owners of the business. The focus is on the future, with the aim of setting goals, evaluating and selecting among various alternative strategies, and establishing general time frames and plans for implementation and evaluation. Planning is concerned with the analysis of the entry of the firm into new markets and the possible exit from others. It is concerned with analysis of product lines, plant locations, and mergers and acquisitions of other businesses. The planning function involves making decisions as to what new technology may be adapted into the production process and developing a distribution system for the products and services being produced. It also involves decisions regarding divestitures of existing units or subsidiaries of the firm. Finally, planning is concerned with developing strategies for implementation of the decisions made, considering timing, financing and relations with suppliers and labor. Both short term and long term planning is done.

Important inputs into the planning process are forecasting and environmental scanning. Forecasting involves developing estimates of future sales by product line, as well as the prices and availability of materials, labor and capital. Environmental scanning is the process of analyzing changes in the external environment and examining the impact of the environment on the business.

In addition to top management, managers at all levels may be involved with the planning process. Sales forecasts often come from the various units of the organization as well as do other analyses of the external environment. In fact, environmental scanning must be done continuously and at all levels of the organization to be effective (Stoffels, 1982).

In addition to environmental scanning, tools available to the planner include econometric forecasting techniques, computer simulations, benchmarking, interviews with experienced managers, and information from government agencies regarding the future supply and demand for labor, as well as the outputs of the production process. In addition, numerous consulting firms provide technical assistance to firms regarding their specific planning problems.

Organizing

The second management function is organizing. The organizing function is defined as the process of job design and task identification as well as placement of these tasks within the overall organizational structure. The organizing function is concerned with the creation of divisions, units and subunits within the business and the determination of the chain of command (that is, who reports to whom). Organizing also involves determining which jobs should be done (managerial, supervisory as well as production) and what are the responsibilities of each job.

The process of reengineering and job design is carried out using workflow and job analysis techniques such as interviews with incumbents, questionnaires, and supervisory analysis of the work. The human resource management area often directs these efforts. Changes in the external environment can impact this process, as will be explained in the next section of this book.

The determination of the overall organizational structure may involve managers at all levels. Planning decisions such as mergers, acquisitions and divestitures, as well as product and market entry and exit, usually lead to some changes in the organizational structure. Since the location of a job in the organizational structure involves determining supervisory responsibility, areas of decision-making responsibility, and staff versus line status, this function can have impact throughout the organization.

Staff versus line status refers to two types of managerial positions. Line positions are in the direct chain of command. Responsibilities can be traced through the line positions from the chief executive officer to the vice presidents, to the middle managers to the first line supervisory and production workers. Individuals in line positions have responsibilities directly related to the output of the firm. The responsibilities of staff positions, on the other hand, cannot be traced through the chain of command. Staff positions exist as adjuncts to the chain of command and are responsible for providing inputs into the decision making process. Thus, staff positions are of an advisory nature. The external environment can affect both line and staff positions.

Controlling

The controlling function involves budgeting as well as the measurement of output and efficiency, and the ongoing evaluation of productivity and quality. Essentially, it is the overseeing of the smooth functioning of the business on a day to day basis. Controlling involves monitoring of the efficiency of the production process and the quality of the products or services produced. It involves evaluation of the productivity and efficiency of the workforce. Raw materials and equipment suppliers and the specialists which are used to distribute the products or services to customers are also appraised and monitored in the controlling function.

Since the evaluation of productivity, efficiency, and quality occurs at all levels of an organization, the controlling function is carried out by managers throughout the chain of command. Managers throughout an organization often have some involvement in the budget planning process as well, by allocating the budget under their control.

Both budgeting and performance appraisal must be done within the framework established by company policies. Thus, some of the controlling procedures are often designed by accounting and human resource specialists, but the implementation is the responsibility of line managers throughout the firm.

Controlling on an organization-wide basis also involves the determination of productivity levels. A great deal of emphasis has been placed on increasing productivity in recent years. This is especially true in the office setting and in firms in the service industry. These efforts require the development of efficiency and productivity measures by specialists and the ongoing monitoring of productivity at all levels. This increasingly has involved the use of computerized evaluation techniques both in the factory and the office.

Staffing/Rewarding

The staffing/rewarding function is a part of human resource management and involves the selection of individuals for various jobs, movement of people and promotions within an organization. It also involves training and retraining the workforce for various jobs and the development of managerial and technical skills. The design of the compensation system, i.e., the pay levels for various jobs, and the design and administration of the benefit programs are also a part of this function. Staffing and rewarding also includes negotiation of union contracts.

Human resource policies are developed by specialists (especially in large firms) and are implemented throughout the organization. However, since the responsibilities of managers and supervisors include hiring subordinates, appraising their performance, and recommending salary increases, the staffing and rewarding function is carried out throughout the organization.

This function has been directly affected by the external environment of business through laws passed beginning in the 1960s. Because firms are liable for fines, back pay and other penalties if it is ruled that their staffing and rewarding procedures are not in compliance with the laws, these areas have become very important. Managers in all areas of the organization must be aware of shifts in the external environment regarding the staffing and rewarding functions. The four functions of management are shown in Figure 1.1.

Integrating the External Environment with Management Functions

The model presented in Figure 1.2 shows the relationships between the four management functions and the elements of the external environment outlined in Table 1.1. The inner circle represents the organization and its internal functions while the outer circle indicates which external elements are related to each of the four areas.

PLANNING	ORGANIZING
• Short Term, Long Term • Markets • Product Lines • Plant Location • Mergers and Acquisitions • Divestitures • New Technology Evaluation • Distribution System Development • Implementation Strategies	• Divisions, Units and Subunits • Chain of Command • Job Creation • Job Design • Reengineering
CONTROLLING	**STAFFING/REWARDING**
• Budgeting • Efficiency of Production Process • Quality Evaluation • Productivity • Performance Appraisal • Supplier and Distribution Evaluation	• Selection • Promotion • Training and Retraining • Compensation and Benefit Systems • Union Contracts • Career Planning • Succession Planning

Figure 1.1. The Four Management Functions

Throughout this book, it is assumed that organizations operate in a free market system. This means private ownership of the means of production. Decisions as to what to produce, what price to charge and how to produce it are primarily private decisions. This does not mean that government is not involved in these decisions. Rather, the primary decision making units are the individual firms, with some government inputs. In Chapter 3, the role of government in a free market system will be discussed in detail.

The four management functions must be carried out in a viable organization regardless of the size of the firm or the industry which it operates. Thus, the owner or top manager of a small business may

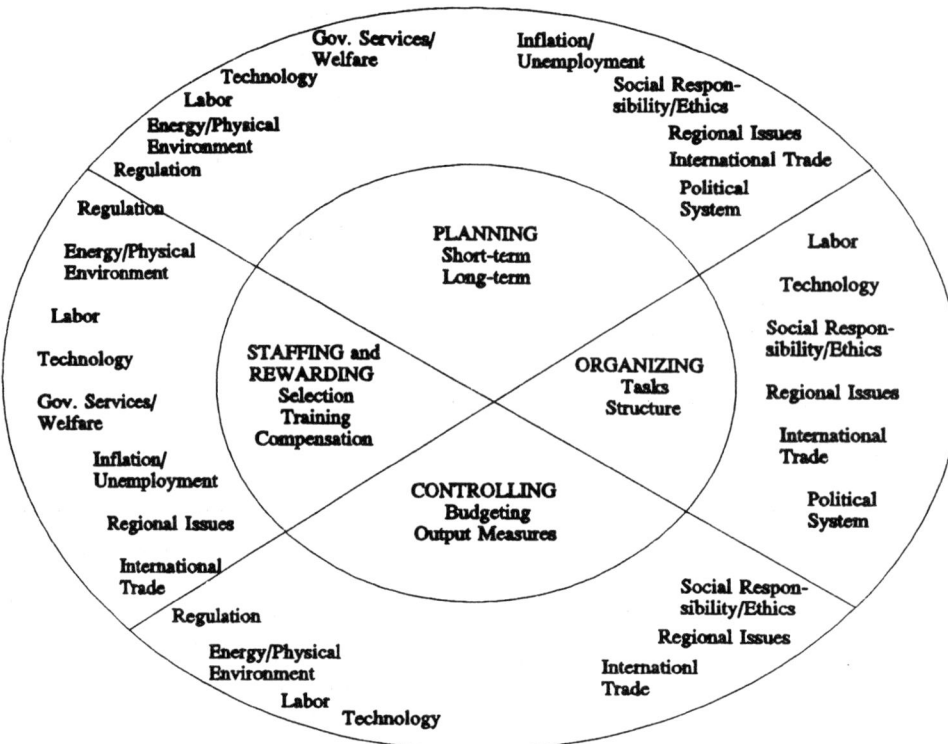

Figure 1.2. Integrating the External Environment of Business With Management Functions

perform all these functions, while in a very large organization, separate departments or managers may be involved. In either case, it is important for the relevant aspects of the environment to be considered by the manager or managers most directly affected. The elements are described below:

Government Regulation

Probably the most important element of the external environment is government regulation. Government regulation can be broadly categorized into three groups: 1) traditional industry regulation, 2) new regulation, and 3) regulation of markets and competition.

Traditional regulation concerns industry by industry regulation as exemplified at the federal level by the Interstate Commerce Commission

(ICC), the Federal Energy Regulatory Commission (FERC) and the Federal Communications Commission (FCC). The thrust of much of this regulation concerns economic regulation of prices and output, as well as entry and exit into an industry. This type of regulation has undergone major changes in the past several years, with emphasis on deregulation.

Unlike traditional industry regulation, the new regulation cuts across industries. It includes regulation of consumer products through the Consumer Products Safety Commission (CPSC); regulation of employment practices, industry pay and anti-discrimination provisions through the Equal Employment Opportunities Commission (EEOC) and the Office of Federal Contract Compliance; and regulation of the workplace itself through the Occupational Safety and Health Administration (OSHA).

Managers in traditionally regulated industries have dealt with regulation for many years. Lobbying, testimony before governmental commissions, and influence of the agencies which regulate a particular industry were often a part of management responsibilities. However, the new type of "across-the-board" regulation affects managers from all areas, in all industries.

Because of this widespread impact, it is much more difficult for individual firms in one industry to lobby against an inappropriate rule or argue for the merits of alternative proposals. Managers throughout an organization must devote much more time and effort to understand the ever growing number of regulations and agencies.

Although designed with specific social and economic goals in mind, regulation has affected business (sometimes adversely) in several ways. Government regulation affects the planning function directly through alterations of the costs of production and the costs associated with new plant and equipment. In addition, regulation affects the characteristics of new and existing products and in some industries, the prices that can be charged. Finally, regulation directly impacts the controlling and staffing/rewarding functions of the firm.

The output measures used for the controlling function are often specified by government regulators. For example, the Securities and Exchange Commission (SEC) requires certain financial data to be made available. Human resource decisions regarding selection of new employees and promotion of existing employees must rely on procedures which are both reliable and valid. Documentation of performance becomes very important when such decisions are questioned.

In general, the new regulation has had a profound effect on human resource management throughout an organization. As mentioned above, selection and promotion procedures must conform to guidelines of equal employment opportunity and affirmative action. The compensation system must insure equal pay for equal work. Training must be offered in such a way that discrimination does not occur. Thus, the human resource specialist plays a major role in designing and implementing company policies which meet the requirements of government regulation.

The regulation of markets and competition concerns government attempts to prevent monopolization and anti-competitive practices. An understanding of federal anti-trust policy and the workings of the Federal Trade Commission and the Justice Department is helpful in dealing with this set of laws and regulations.

Planners must consider the anti-trust laws when making decisions regarding acquisitions, mergers and divestitures. Expanding into similar markets may result in Justice Department action and merging with another firm in the same market may not be allowed. In addition, purchasing and advertising decisions must not be found to be anti-competitive.

The substantial deregulation of the airlines, railroads and motor carrier industries in the 1970's and 1980's, which will be discussed in Chapter 6, means that firms in these industries are now subject to anti-trust prosecution. Practices that were exempt from the anti-trust laws such as interorganizational price setting, in which several firms meet to agree on prices, are now grounds for Justice Department action. The need to understand the complexities of these laws has now become extremely important for these firms.

Energy and the Physical Environment

Until the first Arab oil embargo of 1973–1974, public policy concerning energy mainly involved protecting domestic production from cheap foreign oil. Since that time, gas lines, the entitlements program, the windfall profits tax and oil decontrol have entered the vocabulary of business. Energy costs have become important determinants of production costs and the overall performance of the economy. OPEC meetings have become the subject of national interest as well as proposals for natural gas decontrol, coal slurry pipelines, solar power, and expanded nuclear energy. The Gulf War was fought in part because of concerns over access to oil supplies. The future course of energy prices can have important implications for capital spending plans, conservation efforts, etc.

Regulation of the physical environment which includes air, water and noise pollution rests with the Environmental Protection Agency at the federal level. Individual states also regulate parts of the physical environment. The national debate on the physical environment concerns what level of cleanliness is desirable, when due consideration is given to employment and production cost tradeoffs, and what is the best means of achieving these goals. For example, effluent charges could be used instead of a regulatory approach. Managers need to monitor this debate, since costs of production, and relative costs of different products depend on the outcome.

The increase in regulation in this area has resulted in the need for energy and environmental specialists to be added to organizational staffs. In addition, all employees must be trained in new procedures and in the use of new equipment relating to pollution control. Planners also must consider the impact of energy supplies and emission standards when making decisions regarding plant location, possible plant closings, and new businesses to acquire or to begin. With regard to the controlling function, all managers must continually evaluate their decisions with regard to the impact on energy use and the physical environment. Environmental impact statements may have to be written and emissions and energy usage may require constant monitoring.

Labor Markets and Human Resource Management

Effective managers need to know about new approaches to labor relations both in the plant and in the office. Unions have demanded profit sharing plans and representation on boards of directors. Union attempts to purchase plants and entire enterprises have also occurred. The decline of the smokestack industries e.g., steel, automobiles, etc., and the growth of the service sector in which the product is an intangible such as financial services, computer programming, etc., means that white collar unions may be more important in the future.

Managers in the public sector or managers of firms which do a substantial business with the public sector should be aware of the trends in unionization here as well. Problems of determining public sector pay can affect the costs of providing public services, while the right of these unions to strike may mean disruption of services. Many people feel the long-term implications of the failed Professional Air Traffic Controllers Organization (PATCO) strike of 1981 was to accelerate the decline of unionization in the U.S. (The air traffic controllers are responsible for directing air traffic, and they struck in violation of federal laws. Participants in the strike were fired.)

Public policies which result in restrictions of the supply of labor available should be monitored in a good environmental scanning effort. These include minimum wage laws, professional licensing schemes and immigration policies.

Minimum wage laws keep the wages of some workers above a prescribed level. However, these laws also restrict the number of individuals who are selected for jobs, since business is unlikely to hire employees whose productivity is below a level sufficient to pay for their wages and benefits. Future prospects for increases in the minimum wage depend in part upon the political strength of organized labor. Proposals for a subminimum wage for teenagers, while creating job opportunities and training for youth, also provide opportunities for business to reduce labor costs and train personnel for less critical tasks.

In addition to establishing minimum education and competency requirements, professional licensing restricts the supply of professional employees. For example, the number of professional accountants would be greater if there were fewer requirements to become a CPA. Changes in licensing procedures can mean changes in the future availability of some types of professionals.

Immigration policy affects the supply of professional, skilled and unskilled workers. The future of immigration policy in the United States will have a profound effect on the skills distribution of potential employees. These changes need to be factored into capital expansion programs planned for the future.

The changes which occur in the labor area are important for all functions of management. Plant locations may be selected by planners in part due to the availability of skilled labor or the ability to attract new workers. Also, the prevailing wage may be too high to make expansion into a particular area feasible.

The labor supply also may impact how jobs are designed and how organizations are structured. This is a result of the price and availability of workers in a particular occupational category. For example, in health care, the growth in the use of physician assistants and nurse practitioners is attributable in part to the scarcity of physicians in some areas. As another example, computers today no longer require skilled, relatively expensive programmers or operators. Today's machines are designed for use by existing, nontechnical office staffs, greatly expanding the number of potential users and applications without a massive increase in the need for computer scientists.

Labor influences on the controlling and human resource functions may be direct through contracts negotiated between unions and management. Rules for layoffs, overtime, and grievances are often spelled out. Performance appraisal procedures may also be a part of the contract. Finally, increasing productivity requires both better measurement techniques by management and improved efficiency by labor.

Technology and the Workplace

One of the most recent, and quite possibly the most important changes concerns new technology, both in the factory and in the office. Automation is changing the shop floor. Not only are jobs being eliminated, but new technology is changing the relative costs of the determinants of plant location and size. With labor costs reduced, distribution, raw materials and inventory costs become much more important.

In addition, major changes have occurred in the office with the introduction of personal computers, voice mail, electronic mail, and the internet. These changes have resulted in increases in white collar productivity. Jobs are being redesigned and an elimination of clerical and secretarial positions may be anticipated. Perhaps even more interesting are the potential changes in middle management jobs as management information systems and personal computers are more common. The need for executive assistants and staff specialists has decreased due to the direct access to information by management through electronic-mail, facsimile machines, and voice-mail. Thus, changes in the office are taking place at the same time as changes on the shop floor.

Planners may be able to utilize technology to substitute for the high cost skilled worker. Thus, small firms may be able to enter industries previously closed to them due to shortages and the high cost of skilled workers. This change in the labor and capital mix will change the structure of business through changes in the skills distribution of jobs required.

The new technology is affecting both the controlling and staffing and rewarding functions as well. Measurement of performance and productivity will be easier. For example, the output levels of fully automated production systems can be easily determined. The need for new selection procedures, training and retraining programs and possible revision of compensation systems will provide new challenges in the future.

A variety of public policy issues have arisen. What role should the public sector play in retraining workers? How should publicly sponsored training programs be administered to provide workers in newly created jobs? What will happen to those workers who cannot be retrained? What will be the future role of the public sector in worker relocation? These issues will have both direct and indirect impacts upon business.

Welfare and the Provision of Public Services

The level of provision of public services can affect the costs of doing business. For example, adequate road systems are necessary for the distribution of finished products and raw materials. The highway system also affects the accessibility of a plant to the labor force. Poor accessibility can result in difficulties in attracting suitable employees. Lack of sufficient skills by potential employees because of inadequate education may require an organization to provide training and retraining of workers. The provision of a variety of municipal services from fire and police protection to garbage collection are also important determinants of the costs of locating in a particular area.

Government welfare programs include both cash and in-kind payments such as public assistance, unemployment compensation, food stamps, medicaid and public housing. These types of programs affect business in several ways. Welfare programs provide a safety net for workers who are laid off. Business can have less trepidation about reducing the work force in bad economic times or because of the introduction of new technology.

The manner in which welfare programs are devised can affect work incentives at the lower end of the economic scale. Wages for marginal workers must be sufficient to attract potential employees from the welfare roles. If a permanent welfare underclass is created, then the pool of potentially trainable workers is reduced.

Social security can also be considered a welfare program since it involves a transfer payment from one segment of the population to another. For example, a single worker retiring today will receive almost three times as much in expected benefits as the total amount that he and his employer contributed to social security. A married worker and spouse who never worked will receive an estimated five times the total employer, employee contribution. Future retirees are estimated to receive only a fraction of what they paid in.

Social security can change the costs of doing business directly through the level of taxation and indirectly by affecting the necessity of business to provide pension programs. Future long-term problems with the social security system may have ominous implications for business as well as society in general.

Inflation, Unemployment and the National Output

Probably no other element of the external environment has such a broad impact on almost all business as overall economic trends. These include cyclical fluctuations in economic activity, price level changes and the level of the rate of interest. The national economic debate among the traditional Keynesians, supply siders and monetarists should be carefully monitored. The policy prescriptions of each group involve different implications for the economy. However, the policy prescriptions of the theoreticians are usually not exactly what results from the political debate in Washington. The political economy of supply side economics is a case in point. It has been argued that Reaganomics was actually the policy that emerged from the political compromises that took place in the debate over President Reagan's original program, rather than being carefully planned.

Expected rates of inflation affect how business negotiates long-term contracts with suppliers and labor. Unemployment is an excess supply of labor and affects the price that business must pay for direct and indirect compensation. In general, overall economic conditions affect strategies regarding expansion and contraction of businesses, the location of new factories, and negotiation policies vis-a-vis suppliers and labor unions.

Inflation and unemployment impact the staffing and rewarding functions directly. Inflation affects the compensation required, particularly for those working under contracts negotiated with a cost-of-living adjustment (COLA) clause in which wages increase with rising prices. Other wages tend to follow this trend as well. Companies which must lay off employees also have costs such as those associated with higher turnover rates, training and retraining, and lower worker morale. There are also costs directly connected with plant shut down and start up. Demands on the public sector also increase during times of high unemployment, with associated increases in taxes or deficit spending.

Regional and Local Issues

Regional issues involve shifts in employment, incomes and population between regions of the country. The movement from the frostbelt to the sunbelt has implications not only with respect to the potential of future markets for products, but also with respect to access to pools of skilled workers and suppliers of business services. Government programs which encourage or stem this movement should be carefully monitored.

Local issues involve the changing economic complexion of the city, the growth of suburban development and the role of business in community affairs. The future of cities also affects the future of business, and government programs aimed at urban areas can have important effects on the businesses located there.

Planners' decisions to relocate to another region often are related to changes in product mix, labor costs and supplies; the availability of materials, tax incentives and distribution costs. Such movement has become more and more common in recent years.

As organizations decentralize, the controlling function may become more complex. New communication problems may arise and the need to formalize procedures may develop. Thus, the controlling function becomes more and more important.

The transfer of present employees is an expensive and complicated process, especially when the spouse's career must be considered. A move also may result in increased staffing and training requirements since new employees will be required. Finally, regional differences must be taken into account when designing the compensation plan for the new location. Thus, the human resource management function is affected during regional transfers of organizations.

Global Trade and International Issues

As the volume of U.S. imports and exports continues to increase, international trade issues loom larger in business decision making. Proposals for import restrictions on foreign imports may involve gains for some industries, but losses for others. The NAFTA agreement and the newest round of GATT agreements have major consequences for a variety of industries and their workforce.

Planners in the international firm must consider the political situation in foreign countries, import/export restrictions by other governments, as well as a possible take over by foreign companies or countries. In addition, the international competitiveness of organizations using (or not using) various technologies, joint venture agreements, and the fluctuation of exchange rates become important issues.

As organizations expand into the international arena, organizing issues also become important. Whole new divisions may be formed, foreign offices and plants must be managed, and specialists in international business may be required. Thus, both job design and changes in the organizational structure may be needed.

With this expansion comes the need for controlling in a decentralized environment. Also, different production standards and regulations may apply to the products made and/or sold in foreign countries. Thus, the role of environmental scanning as it applies to the controlling function becomes even more complex.

Finally, if a company expands internationally, special human resource problems arise. Paying American expatriates can be extremely costly and problems of families adjusting to new environments must also be considered. All managers in an international environment face many challenges in adapting to the ever changing situation.

Social Responsibility and Ethics

In order to be socially responsive, business needs to monitor the impacts of its decisions on society as a whole as well as on the organization's costs, revenues and profits. In addition, opportunities for positive social action need to be carefully evaluated. Socially responsive behavior may involve the development of a social audit and the integration of social considerations into corporate decisions.

Two issues are inherent in developing socially responsive behavior. One is to determine the level of resources to be devoted to these endeavors. Since some expenditures in this area involve positive impacts on long-term profitability and good will, the appropriate level of involvement may be greater than pure altruistic motives dictate.

The second issue concerns determining what constitutes socially responsive behavior. Is it to simply make a profit as Nobel Prize winner Milton Friedman contends or should public policy be a guide as other scholars such as Lee E. Preston and James E. Post discuss? One contributor to this debate, Thomas M. Jones argues that the concept is not easily applied in practice.

Issues regarding social responsibility also may impact which jobs will be retained and which will be changed. Commitment to programs for the hard-core unemployed, for example, may militate against wholesale replacement of low skilled workers by machines. Also, retraining programs may be constituted to allow employees to move within the organizational structure and to transfer their skills to the changing needs of the firm. Finally, plant closings and selling of businesses may be influenced by the overall responsibility to the community and to the employees.

Output and productivity goals may be altered due to social responsibility considerations. Special training programs may require some time periods during which productivity does not meet optimal levels. Also, plant productivity may be evaluated in light of the economic needs of the community as well as the "bottom line".

Ethical behavior is founded on traditional Judeo-Christian beliefs which have evolved over thousands of years. However, business frequently encounters situations in which ethical behavior is not clearly definable. Bribery is a way of life in some countries. Is it ethical to do business with countries that significantly violate basic human rights? Ethical dilemmas need to be examined and the implications of each type of behavior analyzed.

The Political System

All of the elements of the external environment of business have an important aspect in common. To a significant extent, the course of public policy is a determining factor (and for some elements the most important factor) in the future direction of the external environment. To manage effectively business must have a good understanding of how government operates and in which direction public policy seems to be heading.

If some functions are transferred to state and local governments or remain at the federal level, different implications for taxes and the level of public expenditure may result. Special interest government has grown substantially, so the political muscle of special interest groups needs to be understood in order to anticipate future directions of public policy.

The political system indirectly impacts the organizing function. Business has been involved in the political process through lobbying efforts, influencing public opinion and political action committees. PACs and other attempts of business to influence government often require specialists in the area of public relations and occasionally entire units to represent the firm in Washington. This results in these units and individuals becoming a part of the organizational structure. Thus, the organizational structure must be adapted to the changing external environment.

A variety of proposals have been suggested to change the political system including federal financing of elections, spending limitations for TV and radio ads, and national referenda. The passage of reform measures can alter the political balance of power, and the rules of influencing public policy. This could result in public policy taking a different course than would otherwise be the case. The implications for each of the elements of the external environment should be assessed.

Managerial Implications

The material presented above identifies four functions of management which occur in the business organization, the key elements of the external environment, and integrates the internal functions and the external elements. From this analysis a number of implications for management result. First, it is apparent that regardless of one's position in an organization, an awareness of the external environment is necessary. Top management is involved in strategic business planning and organizing and is ultimately responsible for the actions of the firm in areas such as workplace safety, fair employment practices, and correct accounting procedures. Middle managers are involved in controlling and staffing/rewarding and must become "experts" on the regulations, economics, technology, and demographic changes which impact their own area as well as related functions. Finally, supervisors and general employees are directly affected by and act as the implementors of these policies. Thus, in order to make effective decisions, managers at all levels must take the various elements of the external environment into account.

Second, there is some evidence that firms which engage in long-range planning (which indicates some process of environmental scanning) may enjoy greater financial success than those who do not. Studies of manufacturing and durable goods industries indicate that firms using formal planning techniques enjoyed greater financial performance [Thune and House (1970) and Fulmer and Rue (1974)]. Two other studies focused on banks [Sapp and Seiler (1981) and Wood and LaForge (1979)]. Both found that banks practicing formal planning outperformed those who did not. Because so many other factors are related to success such as size, general economic conditions, and overall management skill, it may be overly simplistic to credit planning with financial success. For example, Kudla (1980) found no such relationship. However, the importance of environmental scanning and general management awareness cannot be ignored.

Third, as an organization grows or becomes more decentralized, there may be an increased need for formal rules and policies and coordination among units. The environmental scanning activity may be placed under the purview of one department, or managers may be trained to continually monitor that part of the environment which is relevant to their area of responsibility.

Fourth, managers will be more likely to monitor the environment if both monetary rewards and positive feedback such as praise from superiors for such activities are present. In this way, the firm can combine scanning of the external environment with various management functions at all levels in the organization.

Finally, business firms may influence the environment through programs related to social responsibility and through the political system. The private sector may contribute to the social welfare through special training programs and direct donations and involvement in local affairs. Organizations do not exist in a vacuum, and the continued adaptation to the external environment is a necessary condition for their long-range success.

Overview of the Book

Chapters 1-5 establish the theoretical foundations which serve as the basis for analyzing the problems, processes and factors to be discussed in later chapters. How the free market works and the role of government in the free enterprise system are the topics of Chapter 2. Also included are management techniques for incorporating an external focus into the decision making process. By utilizing the framework described in Figure 1.2 and the analytical tools developed in Chapter 2, the issues discussed throughout this book can be analyzed.

The political system and the democratic form of government are described in Chapter 3. The federal system of governments, the growth of special interest groups, and the growth of bureaucratic government are discussed in this chapter. The chapter also deals with how business influences political decisions through lobbying and PAC's. Conflicts between corporate interest and public interest are discussed. Several proposals for reform of the system are examined.

Chapters 4 and 5 concern social and ethical issues. Corporate social responsibility is discussed in Chapter 4 while business ethics is the subject of Chapter 5. The issue of plant closings is addressed in a case study of Playskool, Inc. The ethics of doing business in countries which have major human rights abuses as exemplified by South Africa when it had a system of apartheid is the subject of a case at the end of Chapter 5.

Chapters 6–10 examine specific areas which impact business. Chapter 6 deals with government regulation of products, prices and the workplace. Traditional industry wide regulation and the new regulation are included in this chapter. Chapter 7 includes a discussion of energy and the physical environment. Both Chapters 6 and 7 deal with impacts of the current types of regulation, the reasons for regulation, and the deregulation movement. Emphasis is placed on understanding the ultimate effects of these regulations. The subject of Chapter 8 is government regulation of markets and competition. Measures of market power and government attempts to preserve competition through antitrust enforcement are dealt with.

Chapter 9 describes the major factors affecting employers of the future. These include an aging population, diversity in the workplace, immigration, increasing labor force participation of women, and changes in labor unions. Public sector factors include affirmative action, social security and Medicare. Government regulation of employment practices are then dealt with. The chapter ends with a discussion of approaches business has used to attract and retain a competent workforce.

Chapter 10 reviews the impact of technology on the workplace. The impact of technology on the labor market, the importance of education, production techniques in both the factory and the office, and the impact on productivity are discussed. Potential managerial responses to these changes are also included.

This book involves an examination of the key elements of the external environment. These are described and analyzed with respect to their impact on business organizations. Each will also be examined with regard to its interrelationship with other elements and its relation to the four management functions.

Questions

1. What is meant by the external environment of business?

2. Why is the external environment important to business managers?

3. Describe the four management functions.

4. Explain how each of the major elements of the external environment affect business managers.

5. Why is knowledge of the external environment important to all managers, regardless of their position in the firm?

Key Concepts

environmental scanning	controlling
forecasting	staffing
planning	rewarding
organizing	

Case Analysis: Pullman Standard

For over 100 years, the railroad freight and passenger car business has been dominated by the Pullman Standard Corporation. Founded by George Pullman, in the heyday of railroading in the United States, the name Pullman had become almost a generic term in the industry. In 1980, Pullman Standard had a production capacity of 25,000 cars per year, the largest in the industry. Its production facilities included two plants, one in Butler County, Pennsylvania, and another in Bessemer, Alabama. The Bessemer plant is the largest railcar production facility in the world, with 1.4 million square feet of space. Pullman had sales in 1980 of over $800 million and employed over 5,000 employees. In the late 1970's its stock sold for as much as $43.50 per share.

By 1982, all of Pullman's production facilities had been closed. Over 5,000 employees were discharged, with only around 25 remaining. Total sales and production were zero. Its stock sold for 1 5/8 per share.

How did this happen? How did the largest railcar manufacturer in the United States almost shut its doors in two years? Although a variety of factors can be used to explain Pullman's plight, including poor management decisions, changes in the external environment and managements' lack of perception of these changes explain much of the problem.

Pullman's problems can be traced back to 1972. In that year, President Nixon negotiated the famous Russian wheat deal in which grain was sold to the Soviet Union to help alleviate shortages there. The sale caused not only an impact in the grain markets, but in the railcar business as well.

Much of the grain was shipped by rail to Gulf ports. The ports could not handle the increased demand, resulting in railcars being backed up for miles waiting to be unloaded. The demand for the hopper cars used to haul grain skyrocketed, in part due to the larger amounts of grain being moved, and in part due to the poor utilization of the cars caused by waiting at the ports. Shortages of covered hopper cars began to appear.

At that time, the railroad industry was highly regulated at the federal level by the Interstate Commerce Commission. Small shippers began to complain about the lack of availability of hopper cars. In an effort to manage the shortage of cars, the ICC ruled that cars had to be shared with small shippers on the same basis as large shippers. The result was a worsening in the utilization of these cars with many trapped at branchlines and small grain elevators. The shortage was aggravated.

Shortages of other types of railcars occurred in the 1970's as well. The tax laws at the time encouraged investors to purchase boxcars as tax shelters, thus significantly increasing the demand for these cars. The Arab oil embargo and consequent massive increases in oil prices increased the demand for coal and for railcars to haul the coal.

The result of all these factors was a sustained increase in the demand for railcars in the United States. Pullman, and other manufacturers, expanded production to meet the demand. The railcar business was thriving, as was Pullman Standard.

The 1980's brought changes in the environment and consequent effects on the railcar business. Instead of a wheat deal, in 1980, President Carter embargoed grain sales to the Soviet Union. This was because of the Russian invasion of Afghanistan. The demand for covered hopper cars fell drastically.

The ICC removed its restrictions on the hopper cars resulting in a dramatic improvement in the utilization of these cars. The hopper car shortage had suddenly turned into a glut.

ICC regulation of the railroads was reduced substantially when Congress passed the Staggers Rail Act of 1980. This legislation had many far reaching impacts on the railroad industry including several provisions resulting in increased utilization of existing equipment. Increased utilization of rail cars, however, results in reduced demand for these cars, and thus demand for Pullman's output fell.

The boxcar shortage of the 1970's also turned into a surplus for several reasons. The tax laws were changed, and the rate of inflation was reduced making boxcars a less lucrative tax shelter. In addition, regulatory changes resulted in a substantial increase in piggyback traffic which is a truck trailer loaded on a rail flatcar. Many goods shipped by piggyback would have been transported by boxcar instead. Some rail experts feel that the 50 ft. boxcar has become obsolete and that another may never be built. By 1982, over 25% of rail boxcars were idle nationwide.

The recession of 1981–1982 had a direct impact on railcar loadings and an indirect impact on the demand for new railcars. The problems in the economy, and the end of massive increases in oil prices led to reductions in coal movements as well.

All of these factors resulted in a decline in freight car loadings and a decline in the demand for new railcars. In 1982, freight traffic on U.S. railroads was 12.3% below that of 1981. Cars placed in service in 1982 totaled 18,736, the lowest amount since 1938.

Pullman's problems did not end with declines in the demand for railcars. The company was also not cost competitive with other manufacturers. Pullman had a contract with the United Steelworkers and paid steel industry wages and benefits. The contract at the Butler, Pa. plant resulted in direct labor costs of $11 per hour plus $7 per hour in fringe benefits. An incentive plan allowed workers to draw 130% of an eight hour wage for 6 1/2 hours of work. Half the workforce was allowed 13 weeks paid vacation every five years. Direct labor costs and fringe benefits were twice those of competitors located in the sunbelt. Inefficiencies were introduced through an extensive job classification system. The Butler, Pa. plant had 160 separate classes of jobs.

As a result of all of these factors, including government wheat deals and international events, regulation and deregulation of the railroad industry, tax laws, energy problems, recession, inflation and Pullman's own labor problems, the company headed toward bankruptcy. The external environment has exerted a powerful influence on Pullman. No less significant is the influence that the external environment can have on other businesses as well.

Case Questions

1. Identify the elements of the environment which impacted Pullman Standard.

2. What changes in the environment will have to occur to allow Pullman to resume production?

3. What strategies are available to Pullman Standard's managers for the future?

Case References

Dorfman, John R., "Byebye, Boxcars," *Forbes,* June 7, 1982, pp. 135–138.

"Jack Kruizenga: Pulling Pullman Together Again," *Railway Age,* June 14, 1982, pp. 23–26.

Rail News Update, Association of American Railroads, January 12, 1983 and February 9, 1983.

Tamarkin, Bob, "What's Going on at Pullman?" *Forbes,* July 7, 1980, pp. 36–37.

References

Buchholz, Rogene A., *Business Environment and Public Policy* (4th edition). Englewood Cliffs, New Jersey: Prentice-Hall, 1992.

Committee for Economic Development, *Social Responsibilities of Business Corporations,* New York, 1971.

Friedman, Milton, "The Social Responsibility of Business is to Increase Its Profits," *The New York Times Magazine,* September 13, 1970, pp. 122–26.

Fulmer, R. M. and Rue, L. W., "The Practice and Profitabilities of Long Range Planning," *Managerial Planning,* vol. 22, May/June 1974, pp. 1–7.

Jones, C. Clyde, Rapporteur, "How Chief Executive Officers See the Impact of Social and Political Environmental Forces on their Managerial Tasks." In Lee Preston, ed., *Business Environment/Public Policy, 1979 Conference Papers.* American Assembly of Collegiate Schools of Business, St. Louis, Mo. pp. 69–74.

Jones, Thomas M., "Corporate Social Responsibility Revisited, Redefined," *California Management Review,* vol. 22, Spring 1980, pp. 59–67.

Kudla, R. J., "The Effects of Strategic Planning on Common Stock Returns," *Academy of Management Journal,* vol. 23, March, 1980, pp. 5–20.

Preston, Lee E., and Post, James E., *Private Management and Public Policy,* Prentice-Hall, Inc., Englewood Cliffs, New Jersey, 1975.

Sapp, Richard W. and Seiler, Robert E., "The Relationship between Long Range Planning and Financial Performance of U.S. Commercial Banks," *Managerial Planning,* vol. 30, September/October, 1981, pp. 32–36.

Steiner, George A., "An Overview of the Changing Business Environment and Its Impact on Business." In Lee Preston, ed., *Business Environment/Public Policy, 1979 Conference Papers.* American Assembly of Collegiate Schools of Business, St. Louis, Mo. p. 13.

Stoffels, John D., "Environmental Scanning for Future Success," *Managerial Planning,* vol. 31, November/December, 1982, pp. 4–12.

Thune, S. W. and House, R. J., "Where Long Range Planning Pays Off," *Business Horizons,* vol. 13, August 1970, pp. 81–87.

Weidenbaum, Murray L., "The Changing Nature of Government Regulation of Business." In Lee Preston, ed., *Business Environment/ Public Policy, 1979 Conference Papers.* American Assembly of Collegiate Schools of Business, St. Louis, Mo. pp. 77–86.

Wood, D. R., Jr. and LaForge, J. M., "The Impact of Comprehensive Planning on Financial Performance," *Academy of Management Journal,* vol. 22, September, 1979, pp. 516–526.

CHAPTER 2

THEORETICAL FOUNDATIONS: PRICES, MARKETS, AND MANAGEMENT

The external environment of business involves a complex of factors, institutions, activities, conditions, and laws. Each element of the environment can affect business firms in a variety of ways. Each may differentially affect firms in different industries, in different geographic locations and of different sizes. Some elements may be of crucial importance to some firms and of marginal consequence to others. Some may affect business planning decisions, while others may indirectly impact other management functions.

In this chapter, a theoretical foundation will be laid for the analysis of the external environment presented in the rest of the book. This will be done through the development of a model of the interrelationships of the major elements of the external environment. This model illustrates the process by which changes in the environment can affect business decision making. The role of prices and management decisions in the market economy will then be explored. The chapter concludes with an overview of a variety of managerial tools, techniques, and processes which are useful aids to monitoring and incorporating environmental change into the decision making process.

The Interrelationships of the Major Elements of the External Environment: A Model of Change

The manner in which changes in the external environment affect business is through a process by which key elements interact and interrelate. A model of these relationships is presented in Figure 2.1. In this model, the elements of the environment described in Chapter 1 are apportioned among systems and response categories which constitute the external environment. These are the societal elements and the responses of the public sector, marketplace and business responses. These responses are linked through the political system, the market system and the social involvement of business. The model in Figure 2.1 is one of change and interaction, rather than a static depiction of a balance of forces. Changes in one or more of the societal elements may result in

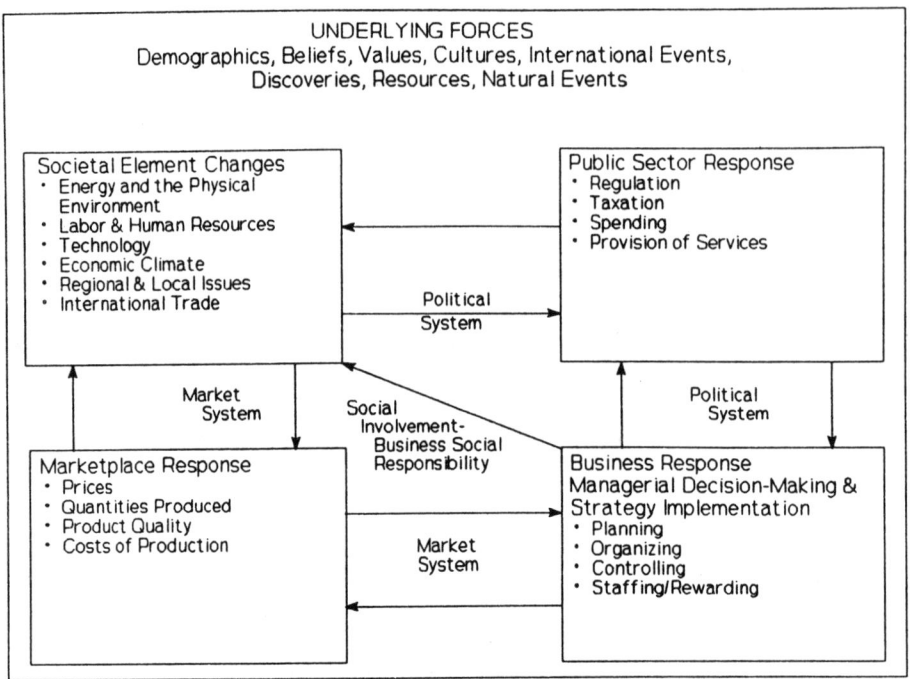

Figure 2.1. A Model of the Impact of Change in the External Environment on Business Decision Making

public sector and marketplace responses through the political and market systems. In turn, a business response may also result. The business response may affect the societal elements through the marketplace, the political system or directly through business social involvement. The business organization represents a particular enterprise in this environment. Management is involved and is influenced by each of the changes and responses to change. All of the elements of the external environment are affected and shaped by a variety of underlying forces.

Underlying Forces

These forces include demographics, social norms and cultures, beliefs and values, and international events such as wars, famines and agreements between nations. Other underlying forces include scientific discoveries, resource discoveries and depletions, and natural events such as the weather, floods, earthquakes and long-term climatic change.

Some of the forces are completely exogenous to the system described in Figure 2.1; that is, they are completely independent of and are not affected by the societal elements, the public sector, marketplace or business responses. Natural disasters are examples. Other underlying forces are in part determined by the forces depicted in Figure 2.1. For example, human fertility rates are affected by overall economic events as the drop in the birthrate during the Depression of the 1930's made evident.

The interactions among underlying forces are not shown in Figure 2.1 since they represent a more basic level of abstraction than what is needed in this book and would take us too far afield. It is of course possible to develop a more complete model illustrating the relationships and interactions of the external environment to these forces. In fact, a variety of attempts by researchers have been made to do exactly that. Jay Forrester's (1961) model of the world economy is an example.

Business, however, usually interacts with the environment at the societal element level, not at this more basic level. For example, changing social mores affect labor force participation rates of women. Business is not necessarily interested in the underlying cause of the change in participation rates, but the result. Thus, rather than developing a detailed theory of the workings of the world or the universe, the model described in Figure 2.1 was developed to better reflect the elements ultimately affecting business decision-making.

This does not mean, however, that these underlying forces are not important. Major changes in the business environment can be initiated by one or more of these factors. Thus, the relevant forces will be discussed to some extent in each chapter. However, the impact on business is usually through each of the elements of the environment.

Societal Elements

The societal elements are: energy and the physical environment, the characteristics of the labor force, new technologies, the overall economic climate, regional and local issues, and international trade. The societal elements thus include all of the changes in the external environment outside the political system and the public sector which impact business decision-making.

Each of the societal elements are interrelated in that change in one element can result in changes in others. For example, the introduction of new technology in the workplace will affect the demand for certain types of labor and thus result in changes in wages for various categories of workers. Overall economic conditions affect a variety of societal elements including international trade, energy use and unemployment.

The societal elements impact the public sector response through the political system and business through the market system. Both the market system and the political system affect the interrelationships among the societal elements. The societal elements are also altered by the policies and programs developed through the political system, the decisions of managers made through the market system, and the direct impact of business decision making outside the market system. The latter impact of business on the societal elements is called social involvement.

Linking the Societal Elements and the Public Sector Response:
The Political System

A change in a societal element, possibly initiated by a change in one of the underlying forces, will not directly affect business. Rather, its impact will be modified by a public sector response and/or a market response.

The public sector response can be initiated by either the federal, state, or local governments. A variety of policy tools have been and are utilized by the executive, legislative, and judicial branches of each of these three levels of government. These include regulation, taxation, spending, and public service provision. Regulation is instituted through legislation and rules promulgated by administrative agencies and/or court decisions. Government, through the executive and legislative branches, has the power to tax and to spend money on a variety of public programs. In addition, public services such as roads and streets, refuse collection, and school systems are provided directly.

The public sector response is determined through the political system. The political system includes the process through which issues are raised, coalitions of various groups are formed and public sector programs are proposed. It also includes the policy formulation process of agenda setting, legislation, and implementation. The political system is the mechanism by which broad public policy objectives are defined and evaluated and are translated into the appropriate public sector response.

A change in one of the societal elements will eventually elicit a response from the public sector. Such a response may involve regulation, taxation, spending or public production decisions. The public sector response will in turn alter the initial environmental conditions and may lead to changes in other societal elements as well. The arrow drawn from the public sector response to the societal element changes illustrates this point.

In addition, the public sector response can affect business directly. The public sector may establish additional rules and regulations for conducting business, impose taxes and purchase goods and services from firms. The response may also involve direct subsidy of business. All levels of government have subsidy programs aimed at particular industries or designed to encourage business location in particular areas. The arrow drawn from the public sector response to the business response highlights this direct public sector impact.

Linking the Societal Elements and the Business Organization: The Market System

The initial societal element change, modified by the public sector response, then affects the marketplace in which business is involved. In the marketplace, business interacts with competitors, suppliers of similar goods and services and the buyers and potential customers of its output. Not only does business interact in the marketplace for its products, but also in the marketplace for raw materials, labor, and capital. This set of markets is designated the market system in Figure 2.1. The market system determines the prices of goods and services produced, the quantity and quality of production, and the costs of production.

Business firms are primarily economic entities. Through the market system, business provides wages and salaries for workers, profits for owners of capital, and a flow of savings and investment. More importantly, business is the primary mechanism for organizing the productive activities of the economy. That is, most of the goods and services which are produced for consumption and investment are produced by business.

Since business is an economic entity, external environmental change ultimately affect business by altering marketplace prices, the quantity and quality of goods and services produced and distributed in the market and the costs of production. For example, technological change may alter production processes, unionization can affect labor costs, and the overall economic climate can affect the prices that can be charged. This is an important point that cannot be overemphasized. The process by which changes in the societal elements are transmitted to business is the market system.

The managerial response to environmental change involves adaptation of the functions of planning, organizing, controlling and staffing/rewarding. If many businesses in an industry or market adapt to these changes, then the marketplace variables can be further affected. For example, if many firms adapt to higher petroleum prices through conservation and substitution of alternative fuels, then oil prices may decline. Large surpluses of oil, as were present in the early 1980's, may also result. Thus, not only do changes in societal elements affect business most directly through the market system, but the most direct impact of the managerial response to the changing environment is also through these markets. The market system plays a critical role in transmitting managerial responses and environmental changes.

Business Impact on the External Environment:
Social Involvement and Ethics

Business, however, does not merely adapt to a changing environment, but its actions can also affect and influence the political system and the societal elements. Business can form political action committees (PAC's), contribute to candidates, lobby for particular pieces of legislation and influence public opinion. The public sector response can thus be altered by the anticipatory as well as the defensive response of business.

Management actions can also have a direct effect on the societal elements. Decisions to close plants in particular areas may have severe consequences for an entire regional economy. Air, noise and water pollution are the results of many types of production processes. Business can also take a proactive stance and institute socially beneficial programs such as training and creation of employment opportunities for the hard core unemployed.

Notions of social responsibility are necessary in evaluating the impact of business on the environment. It is not sufficient for business to merely gauge the effects of its actions on profits and losses. Rather, many actions will have consequences far beyond the plant gate or office door. Since business is part of society, it interacts with various elements of society. Thus, the impact of managerial actions on society need to be analyzed and taken into account.

Although not shown in Figure 2.1, ethics affects all interactions of business with the external environment. Whether business is dealing with the public sector, analyzing its impact on societal elements or responding to marketplace changes, management should be guided by notions of ethical behavior. As will be discussed in Chapter 5, ethical behavior extends beyond merely obeying the law, since laws have not been written to cover all possible situations. Concepts of ethical theory are sometimes helpful in deciding whether an action is correct.

As can be seen from the above discussion, the relationship of business with the external environment is quite complex. Understanding this relationship requires knowledge of the ways in which a constantly changing environment affects business decision making. It requires an understanding of the impact of the public sector response to environmental change and the marketplace response which results. The impact of the managerial response on the external environment also must be comprehended. This includes the impact on the marketplace, the impact on societal elements and business's relationship with the public sector through the political system.

The Nature of the Market System

Since the market system and the associated marketplace response is an important part of the relationship of business with its environment, a good understanding of the external environment requires a knowledge of how the market system operates. In this section, the American free enterprise system will be described and compared to other types of economic systems. In addition, the functioning of individual markets and the forces at work determining the marketplace response will be explained. The concepts which will be developed in this section will be utilized extensively in the remainder of the book as each of the societal elements are examined and potential public and managerial responses are evaluated. Although these concepts are somewhat abstract, they serve as important theoretical underpinnings to the study of the business environment.

Types of Economic Systems

Economic systems are not easily classified since the system present in a particular country is unique. Any classification scheme must recognize that systems vary slightly from one another so that most countries could be placed on a continuum reflecting the degree of government involvement in production decisions. Nevertheless, many economists have characterized four broad groups of economic systems (see for example Samuelson, 1995; McConnell, 1995; or Case & Fair, 1994). These systems are shown in Table 2.1. Each of these classifications differ as to the degree of private ownership of productive capacity, the extent of freedom of the marketplace and the degree of government involvement and interference with marketplace results.

Table 2.1. Types of Economic Systems

		Laissez Faire Capitalism	Modern Mixed Economy	Democratic Socialism	Authoritarian Socialism or Communism
Ownership	1.	Complete private ownership of means of production.	Mostly private ownership of means of production, some government ownership.	Mixed private and public ownership of means of production.	Public ownership and control of almost all industry.
Markets	2.	Totally free, competitive markets.	Emphasis on free, competitive markets, with some governmental production and regulation.	Emphasis on government control and operations of basic industry. Many markets remain competitive.	Severe restriction on individual choice and competitiveness.
Government Involvement	3.	No governmental planning control of marketplace results.	Some governmental planning and interference with market determined results.	Heavy government planning and interference with market determined results.	Heavy government planning and directions of industry, government dictated results.

At one extreme is <u>laissez faire capitalism</u>. This is an economic system which places heavy emphasis on the private sector. Government involvement in economic decisions is minimal or nonexistent. The factories, equipment, and resources used to produce goods and services are owned exclusively by the private sector. Final goods and services, raw materials, intermediate products and labor services are all bought and sold in freely competitive markets. There is no government planning or interference with marketplace results. For example, incomes are determined solely by the valuation of labor services by the market and on the basis of the ownership of productive capital.

This type of economic system does not exist today. If it did exist at all, it would have been during the late eighteenth and early nineteenth centuries in the United States and England, when there was little involvement of government in the activities of business. An understanding of the workings of this type of system, however, is useful to understand how modern economies operate. The marketplace of laissez faire capitalism operates independent of government involvement. Thus, it provides an "ideal type" or example of what outcomes may be expected if government is not involved in particular markets. Further, it provides a basis for comparison in understanding the impact of government involvement in markets today.

The <u>modern mixed economy</u> best describes the economic system which exists in the United States today. This system consists of mostly private ownership of the means of production. Government, however, is involved in economic decisions in a variety of ways. Some portion of productive capacity is owned by government. For example, in the United States, AMTRAK, the national passenger railroad, and TVA, the Tennessee Valley Authority which provides electricity to the southeastern United States, are owned and operated by the federal government. Although freely competitive markets are emphasized, government regulation of business and adjustments of marketplace outcomes occur. Government planning and overall management of broad economic aggregates such as interest rates, the overall price level, and unemployment is attempted. In the modern mixed economy, government frequently intervenes in the marketplace either to correct undesirable outcomes or to encourage favorable results. Some form of income redistribution from one segment of the population to another is also performed.

As the amount of government involvement increases, the modern mixed economy can gradually evolve into <u>democratic socialism</u>. Economic systems of this type have greater public ownership of the means of production than mixed systems. Government control and operation of basic industry and agriculture is a feature of such systems. Competitive markets are still present, but with heavy government regulation. Public sector planning and adjustments of market determined results are also carried out. Income redistribution programs are conducted on a large scale in this economic system. Sweden and Denmark are examples of democratic socialism.

Communism or authoritarian socialism carries government involvement in the marketplace to its logical conclusion. This type of system is at the opposite extreme of laissez faire capitalism. A hallmark of communism is state ownership and control of almost all industry. Individual choice of both consumers and producers is severely restricted. Government is extensively involved in planning, organizing, controlling and staffing/rewarding for most industry.

Since the demise of the Soviet Union, communism is all but extinct in the world. The few exceptions are Cuba, China and North Korea. Even in these countries, pressures continue to mount to abandon this economic system. Even in China a degree of free market capitalism has begun to make its presence felt. Cuba must more than likely wait for Fidel Castro to retire or die.

In Cuba for example, the state owns all land, transportation, natural resources, communications, most housing and retail stores and almost all industry. Agriculture is performed through government organized collective farms. Government bureaucrats plan the details of almost all economic activity. Production is assigned to different plants, goods and services are distributed on the basis of the central plan, and almost all facets of production are coordinated through the state.

The free enterprise system can best be characterized as either laissez faire capitalism or the modern mixed economy. Free enterprise means exactly that. The marketplace operates as a freely competitive system, albeit within the bounds established by government. Free enterprise does not necessarily imply only laissez faire capitalism, but a much broader concept. Indeed, some markets in a democratic socialism type of system may also be characterized as free enterprise.

In a free enterprise system, management carries out the functions of planning, organizing, controlling, and staffing/rewarding, relatively independent of government involvement. Government establishes the rules and regulations under which business operates and may indirectly influence certain markets. Consumers are free to make decisions as to which goods and services to consume, constrained only by their tastes and incomes. The model of the interrelationships between business and the environment presented in Figure 2.1 essentially describes a free enterprise system.

Throughout this book, it will be assumed that business is conducted under a free enterprise system. Accordingly, in the next sections, the role of demand, the role of supply, and the role of prices in a free enterprise system will be explored.

The Concept of Demand

The marketplace in a free enterprise system is governed by supply and demand. That is, prices and amounts of goods and services produced and consumed are determined by the separate and independent forces of supply and demand. Thus, of critical importance to understanding the functioning of the marketplace is knowledge of these two forces. We begin with demand.

An individual consumer's demand can be defined as:

A schedule of the different quantities of a good or service which the consumer is willing and able to purchase at each and every possible price.

This definition has within it a number of words and phrases the examination of which help to shed light on the nature of demand.

First, demand is a <u>schedule</u> which relates the quantity to be purchased at each of a number of different prices. It indicates not necessarily what a particular consumer may actually purchase, but rather his or her intentions to purchase goods and services at various prices. For each price there exists a unique quantity that consumers would purchase.

Second, the demand schedule shows the amount that the consumer <u>is willing and able to purchase</u> at a given price. It is not enough for the consumer merely to be willing to purchase a given amount of a good or service. Demand must also be effective. The consumer must have the ability, i.e. financial resources available, to purchase a particular product. One may have the willingness to purchase an expensive car, for example, but unless demand is effective and one has the ability to make the purchase, then the item will not appear on an individual's demand schedule.

For a given product, each consumer possesses a unique demand schedule. For any particular price, some individuals will demand a large quantity of a given product, while at that same price others may demand relatively little. For example, why do some individuals purchase 52 jars of peanut butter in a given year, while others only purchase 2 jars? The answer is that there are a variety of determinants of the demand for goods and services. Each consumer is a unique individual who faces a slightly different set of circumstances. This set of circumstances define the determinants of an individual's demand for a particular good or service. These determinants of demand are:

1. Income
2. Price
3. Price of substitute goods and services
4. Price of complementary goods and services
5. Attitudes and tastes

Income

A consumer's income affects the demand for individual products, although the relationship is somewhat complex. In most situations, as income increases, demand for a particular good or service increases, all other things staying the same. Goods whose consumption increases as income increases are called normal goods. Examples are clothes, steak, cars, and houses. Inferior goods are those whose consumption diminishes as income increases. These are commodities that are substituted by higher quality or different goods and services as incomes increase. Examples are beans, rice and second hand clothing and furniture.

Price

In general, as the price of a commodity rises, consumption will be reduced. There are two exceptions, however. First, the quality of some goods may be difficult to evaluate by the average consumer. In comparing one brand against another, some consumers assume that higher price implies greater quality. These consumers would tend to purchase greater quantities of the higher priced good under the assumption that it is of higher quality. An example is cosmetics. Unless one is a chemist, the quality of cosmetics is not easily discernable. Thus, it is possible for a business to increase the demand for its cosmetics by increasing the price. Of course, a question arises as to the responsibility of business in using price in this manner. Should price be used to manipulate consumption patterns, or should consumptions patterns (i.e., demand) be used as an input into determining the price of a good?

The second exception concerns inferior goods. In unusual situations of extreme poverty, it is possible that the consumption of inferior goods may actually increase as the price rises. This is because higher prices for inferior goods would lead consumers to reduce consumption of normal goods, and increase consumption of the inferior commodities, since they have less income available to spend. If the price of beans increases, for example, the poor in underdeveloped countries are unlikely to substitute steak. Rather, they would reduce consumption of the few normal goods purchased in order to have enough money to buy beans.

Price of Substitute Goods and Services

Goods and services are substitutes if they are competing. That is, they generally satisfy the same needs and desires of consumers. Butter and margarine are the classic examples of substitute goods. As the price of substitute goods and services increases, consumers use more of the cheaper good or service, and less of the higher priced substitute. Thus, as the price of butter increases, the demand for margarine will increase. The price of close substitutes therefore is a determinant of the demand for a good or service.

Price of Complementary Goods and Services

Complementary goods and services are those which logically "go together." Additional consumption of one leads to additional consumption of the other. Examples are peanut butter and jelly, cars and tires, bacon and eggs. If the price of one complement increases, its consumption will fall. Demand for the other good or service will likewise fall. For example, the demand for tires is reduced whenever automobile demand falls.

Attitudes or Tastes

Consumer attitudes and tastes are important determinants of demand. To some extent, these can be influenced through advertising. For example, the elimination of cigarette advertising on TV and the placement of health warnings on packaging has resulted in changed attitudes of consumers toward cigarettes and other tobacco products.

The Demand Curve

In order to understand the relationship of demand to each of the above determinants, it is usually assumed that, except for the factor being examined, all are fixed. If this assumption were not made, then, with everything varying simultaneously, it would be impossible to isolate the effect on demand of any one determining factor.

In order to isolate a demand schedule or demand curve, it is usually assumed that all factors are fixed, except for price. The demand schedule then relates quantity demanded of the good or service to price.

As an example, assume that we wish to examine an individual's demand for beer. It is assumed that the individual's income remains constant, that his or her attitudes and tastes stay the same and that the prices of complements (pretzels, for example) and substitutes (such as wine) do not vary. If the consumption patterns of this individual consumer are examined over a period of time in which beer prices are allowed to vary, the demand schedule shown in Table 2.2 may result. The demand curve D-D in Figure 2.2 is drawn from the information in Table 2.2. The demand curve slopes downward and to the right and illustrates the Law of Demand:

The lower the price, more of a good or service will be purchased. The higher the price, less will be bought.

The market demand curve is obtained by adding up the demand schedules for all individuals in the marketplace. Since the demand curves for all individuals slope downwards and to the right, the same is true for the market demand curve. A determinant of the market demand is the number of individuals in the marketplace. If new consumers enter the market, additional demand schedules will be added, increasing the market demand for the product or service.

Table 2.2. An Individual's Demand Schedule for Beer

Price per Glass	Glasses of Beer Demanded per Day
$2.00	1
1.60	2
1.20	4
.80	6
.40	8

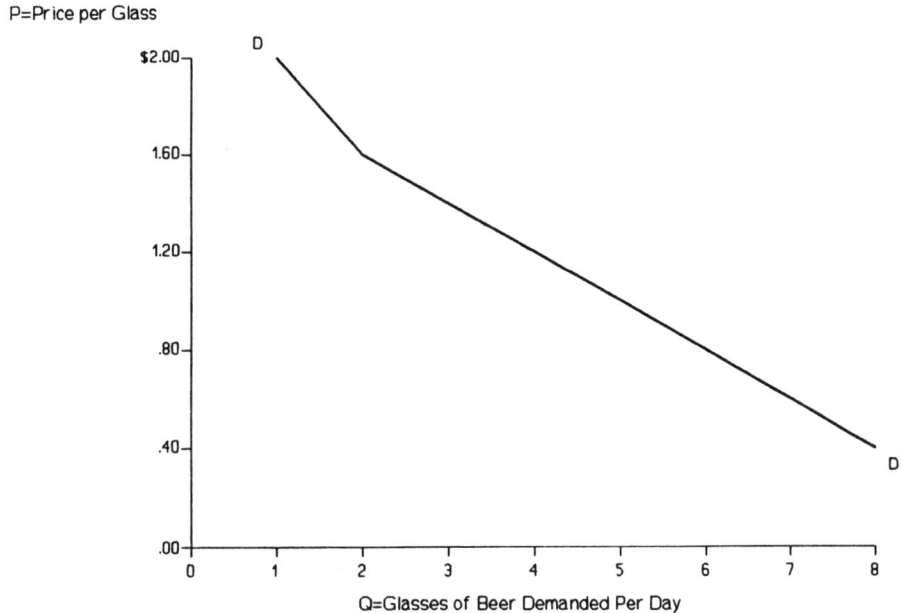

Figure 2.2. An Individual's Demand Curve for Beer

The Concept of Supply

Supply for one firm or seller of a good or service can be defined as:

A schedule of the different quantities of a good or service that the seller is ready and willing to sell at each and every possible price.

Like demand, supply is a schedule. It does not necessarily indicate what a seller will actually sell, but rather the firm's intentions to sell a good or service at various prices. For each and every price, there exists a unique quantity that the firm would sell. Supply curves usually slope upward. That is, at higher prices, producers are ready and willing to sell more than at lower prices. A supply curve S-S for a hypothetical firm is shown in Figure 2.3.

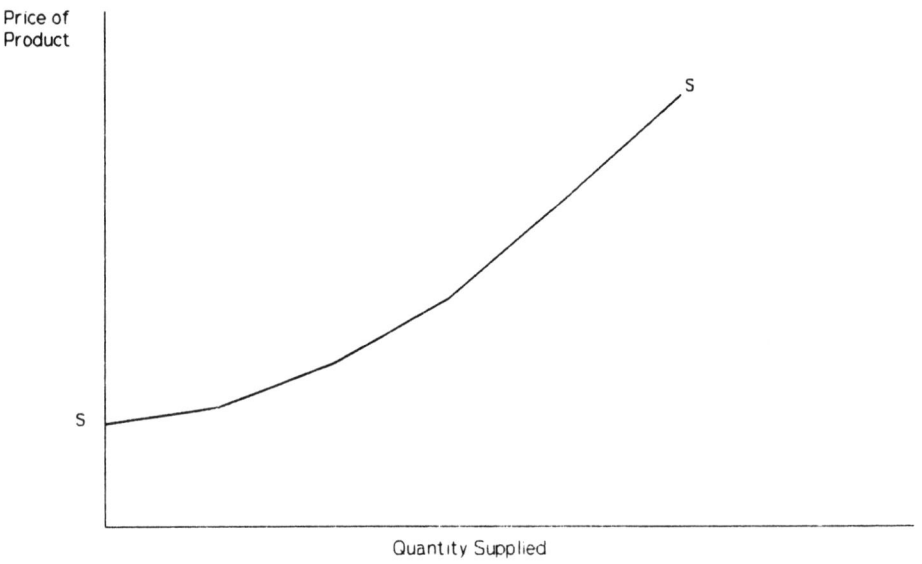

Figure 2.3. A Hypothetical Firm's Supply Curve

There are a variety of factors which affect supply in addition to the price of the good or service. These include resource prices, labor costs, taxes and subsidies and the particular production technique used. However, all these factors affect supply by influencing production costs. Thus, the key to understanding supply is a knowledge of costs.

An important cost concept is <u>marginal cost</u>. Marginal cost can be defined as:

The additional or extra cost incurred in producing one more unit of a good or service.

Marginal cost can also be thought of as the amount that can be saved by not producing one more unit of a product. A hypothetical firm's marginal cost curve is shown in Figure 2.4 and is labelled MC.

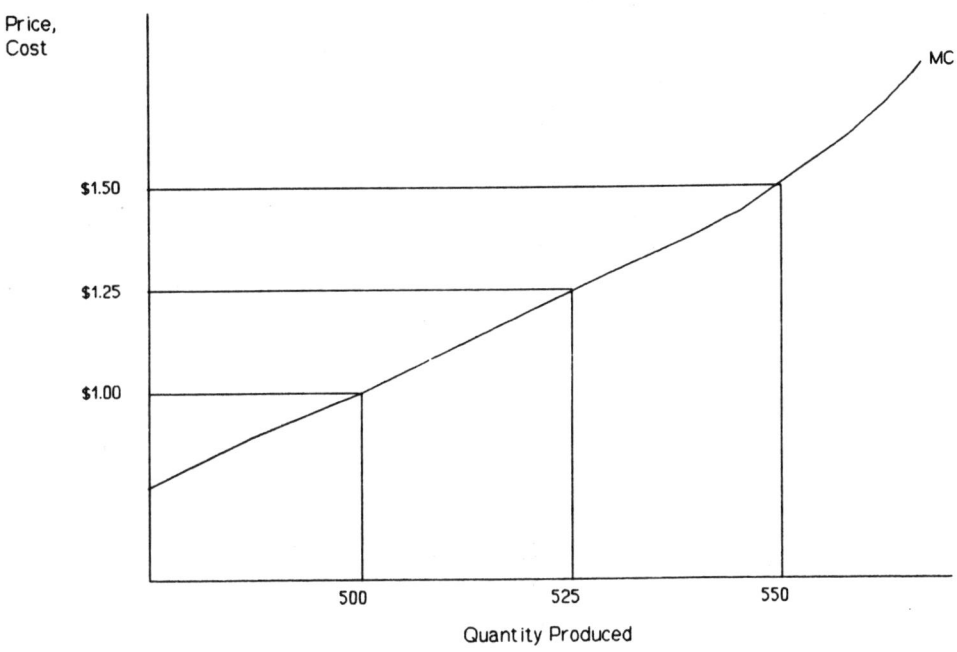

Figure 2.4. A Hypothetical Firm's Marginal Cost Curve

In the figure, the additional cost of producing the five-hundredth unit is $1.00. If the firm produces 525 units, the last unit would cost $1.25 to produce. The marginal cost of unit 550 is $1.50.

The marginal cost curve in Figure 2.4 is drawn upward sloping. This means that marginal costs increase as output of the good or service in question increases. Beyond some point, marginal costs will eventually increase for any plant or firm. This is because as output increases, overtime may be paid, workers may not be as efficient, older and less reliable production capacity may be used and bottlenecks may appear in the distribution system. In short, as long as the productive capacity of a firm cannot be increased instantaneously, increased production will eventually result in increased costs. These increased costs show up not only as increased per unit costs, but increased marginal costs as well.

The Supply Curve

Let us make two assumptions regarding the hypothetical firm of Figure 2.4. First, assume that the firm is so small that its decisions to produce will not appreciably affect the market price. That is, we are assuming that this firm has very little market power and cannot control prices on its own by withholding supplies or increasing production. Although there are many industries in which a few firms exercise a great deal of market power, there are many markets in which national and worldwide competition is sufficiently strong that an individual enterprise can do little but take the market price as given. In these markets, a small firm's decision to increase production will not swamp the marketplace with massive excess production. Likewise, a small firm's decision to cut production will do little to reduce total supply.

Second, assume that the firm attempts to maximize profits. Of course, firms in which ownership and control are separated (i.e., corporations) may not necessarily maximize profits. Other goals and objectives may be present. This may also be true for smaller enterprises as well. However, any firm, in order to survive, must eventually achieve some profitability level. Thus, profits are an important motivating force for any business, although not the only force.

Suppose that the price of the good or service being produced in Figure 2.4 is $1.25. How much should the profit maximizing firm produce? If the firm produced less than 525 units, say 500, then the costs of producing an additional unit would be less than $1.25. The additional revenue to be derived from producing each additional unit, however, is $1.25. It would cost the firm an additional $1.00 to produce the five-hundredth unit, but it could sell it for $1.25. Producing unit 500 makes a $.25 additional contribution to profit. Each additional unit produced up to unit 525 also results in additional contributions to profits, although by lesser amounts.

If the firm, on the other hand, produces 550 units of the good or service, then it would cost an additional $1.50 to produce the last unit. This unit could only be sold for $1.25. Profits would be reduced by $.25 by producing unit 550. Every unit produced above 525 would result in a reduction in profits since the additional or marginal costs of production of these units exceeds the additional revenue obtained from selling them.

Clearly, the profit maximizing firm would produce 525 units of this good or service if the price were $1.25. Suppose the price were $1.50, instead. The same sort of analysis would lead to the conclusion that in order to maximize profits the firm should produce 550 units. Likewise, a price of $1.00 would lead to production of 500 units. The marginal cost curve, then, shows the amount of the good or service that the firm would produce at each and every possible price.

Another way of saying the same thing is that the marginal cost curve is a schedule of the different quantities of a good or service that the seller is ready and willing to sell at each and every possible price. But, this is the definition of the supply curve! For the profit maximizing, competitive firm, the marginal cost curve is the supply curve.

The market supply curve is obtained by adding up the marginal cost curves of all the firms in an industry. Thus, the market supply curve represents the marginal costs of producing a good or service.

Market Equilibrium in a Competitive Marketplace

In order to understand how the forces of supply and demand operate in a free enterprise system, a simplistic market model will be analyzed. This is a purely competitive marketplace. Underlying this market model is the assumption that buyers and sellers are so many and so small that their decisions to purchase or produce a product will not affect the market price.

Another characteristic is that all firms in the industry produce a standardized or very similar product. Thus, the output of any firm is considered an extremely close substitute for the goods or services produced by other firms in the industry. Finally, new firms are free to enter and existing firms are free to exit the industry. There are few legal, technical or financial obstacles to easy entry and exit.

With these rather restrictive assumptions, a purely competitive market would not, on the surface, seem to be a very helpful model to understand the workings of the free enterprise system. There are few industries in the world which even approximate the conditions set forth above. There are, however, several reasons why this market model is in fact quite useful.

First, the manner in which markets operate under these conditions provides a standard or yardstick to judge other, less competitive market systems. The emphasis in the phrase "pure competition" is in the last term—competition. Competition between buyers and suppliers, each acting independently, determine prices and outputs. These competitive market forces reign supreme in this market model.

Second, the forces at work in a purely competitive market are present in most other markets in a free enterprise system, even if these other markets are not purely competitive. An understanding of market forces in a competitive framework provides knowledge of many of the forces at work in other market structures as well.

Third, the purely competitive market model provides a good approximation to the results of many real world markets. Some markets operate almost as if they were purely competitive. For these types of industries, pure competition provides a reasonable representation of the outcomes of the marketplace.

Characteristics of the Market Equilibrium

Price and quantity of output are determined by the intersection of the supply and demand curves as shown in Figure 2.5. In the figure, P_E and Q_E are the marketplace or equilibrium price and quantity. Neither supply alone (producers) nor demand alone (consumers) decide on price and amount of goods or services produced. Rather, the independent forces of supply and demand jointly determine prices and quantities.

The point E where supply and demand intersect, is an equilibrium point. This means that if price or quantity deviate from this point, forces will be set in motion to bring the marketplace back to that level. If price is above P_E, then supply would exceed demand. Firms would produce an amount greater than consumers would demand. This excess supply would cause the price to fall to P_E. On the other hand, if price were

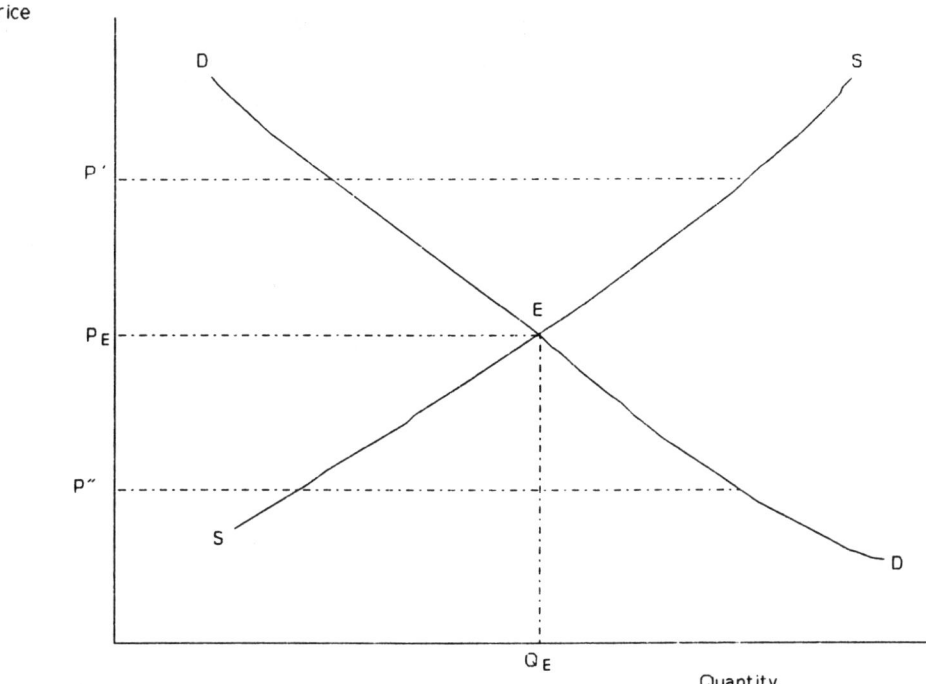

Figure 2.5. Price and Quantity Determination in a Competitive Marketplace

below P_E, then demand would exceed supply. Consumers would bid up the price and producers would produce additional amounts until price returns to P_E.

Another characteristic of this market equilibrium concerns the relationship between the amount of resources used to produce the good or service in question and the preferences of consumers. Since the supply curve is the sum of the marginal cost curves of the individual firms which produce a particular good or service, it represents the marginal cost of the industry. That is, any point on the supply curve represents the additional costs incurred by firms in producing one more unit of the particular product.

The demand curve, on the other hand, represents consumer's willingness and ability to purchase a good or service. But, if a consumer is willing and able to purchase a unit of a good or service at a particular price, then he or she must value that unit at or above the price.

Otherwise, the purchase would not be made. An individual demand curve, then, represents an individual consumer's valuation of the good or service in question. Since the market demand curve is the sum of all consumers' demands, it represents the marketplace valuation of the good or service in question. That is, any point on the market demand curve represents the value that consumers place on having one more unit of the product.

The significance of the equilibrium point, E, should be quite evident from this analysis. Since supply equals demand, the marginal cost of producing one more unit of the good or service is exactly equal to the value that consumers attach to it. In addition, price is equal to both marginal cost and to the valuation of the last unit produced. Thus, price reflects both consumers' value of a product and the cost of producing it. If consumers value the product by more than the marginal costs of production, more will be produced. If consumers value one more unit of the product by less than the marginal costs of production, it would not be produced. The marketplace allocates resources to the production of goods and services in such a way that consumer preferences and valuations are exactly met.

The Role of Profits

Profits, or rather the quest to maximize profits, plays an important role in a competitive market. Producers attempt to increase profits and in the process produce goods and services in line with the preferences of consumers. Firms that do not produce what consumers desire at the lowest possible price will not survive. If profits are being earned in an industry, existing firms will expand output. In addition, new firms will enter the industry. Prices will eventually fall, and output will expand. Profits will also eventually fall to a level similar to what can be obtained in other industries.

The hand held calculator industry is a classic example of how a competitive marketplace results in lower prices. Electronic calculators were first introduced in the late 1960's. A typical calculator which could only do basic arithmetic functions sold for $400–$500. By the late 1970's, not only had prices of a basic calculator fallen to $5–$10 range, but they were smaller and performed many more functions. Today, those $400 calculators of the 1960's are routinely given away free for promotional purposes. The advances in technology over this period had combined with increasing demand and a shift in the supply curve to reduce the price of a single unit.

The "Invisible Hand"

In a free enterprise system, the closer that individual markets approximate the ideal of pure competition, the more likely that resources will be allocated to production of goods and services to meet consumer preferences. Of course, many markets in a free enterprise system cannot be classified as approaching this standard. In these markets, the forces of supply and demand are still working. However, either because of government intervention, or the market power of either producers or buyers, substantial deviations from the efficient allocation of resources that are present in a purely competitive system may result.

The key to understanding the workings of the free enterprise system is the nature of the voluntary exchanges which take place. Each party to an exchange pursues his or her own self interest. Thus, the exchange will not take place unless both parties (buyers and sellers) feel that they will benefit. A Scottish philosopher, Adam Smith, in 1776 wrote a book entitled *The Wealth of Nations* which has led him to be described as the father of modern economics. In his work, Smith recognized the role of mutual exchange in a free enterprise system and observed that as individuals pursue their own self interest, the greater good of society is served. He stated that individuals seemed to be moved by an "invisible hand" to promote the social welfare.

The concept of the "invisible hand" can best be illustrated through an example. Consider how food is produced and distributed in the United States. Food is produced on farms, shipped to food manufacturers and processors who then send their production either to grocery wholesalers or to retail distribution centers. Food is then shipped to retail stores for final distribution to consumers. This food production and distribution process involves millions of farmers, processors, distributors and retailers. Every day millions of pounds of agricultural production makes its way through this system.

Consumers take this system for granted and seldom give it a second thought. Food is always available in grocery stores. Restaurants provide a finished product in millions of variations ready to eat. Without food, however, no one could survive. But yet it is always available.

All of the farmers, producers, distributors and retailers do not perform their functions for altruistic motives. Rather, they do so in the quest for profit. That is, they are pursuing their own self interest. But, in the process, a bountiful supply of foodstuffs is provided in the United States. This happens without government planning, coercion, or direction. The system of voluntary exchanges which is the hallmark of the free enterprise system directs the food production and distribution system to assure adequate supplies everywhere in the United States.

The Role of Prices in a Free Enterprise System

Price performs a variety of functions in a free enterprise system. These are:

1. Transmits Information
2. Provides Incentives
3. Allocates Resources
4. Affects the Distribution of Income

Each function will be examined in turn below.

Transmission of Information

Prices transmit information to producers, consumers, resource suppliers and labor. Prices provide signals to these groups to produce more or less, to consume more or to substitute another good instead. Information is provided to suppliers to distribute raw materials to the highest value in use. Producers receive information regarding costs of raw materials and labor.

Managers of businesses operating in a free enterprise system frequently use price information to decide on whether to enter new markets, use one production technique versus another, produce more of a particular product, etc. Failure to comprehend the information present in prices can lead to lost business opportunities.

Consumers use prices to make decisions as to which product to purchase, to increase or decrease consumption of different goods, and to allocate income between consumption and savings. Thus, information transmitted by prices is important to both business and consumers.

Suppose that the demand for a particular product, shoes for example, increases. An increase in demand is caused by a change in one of the non-price, underlying determinants—income, prices of substitutes or complements, and tastes. Such an increase in demand is represented by the shift in the demand curve from D-D to D´-D´ in Figure 2.6. A shift in demand tells producers that at each and every price, consumers are willing and able to consume more shoes. This information is transmitted to producers through an increase in the market price of shoes. This price information tells producers to expand production, which they do from Q_0 to Q_1. Price rises from P_0 to P_1.

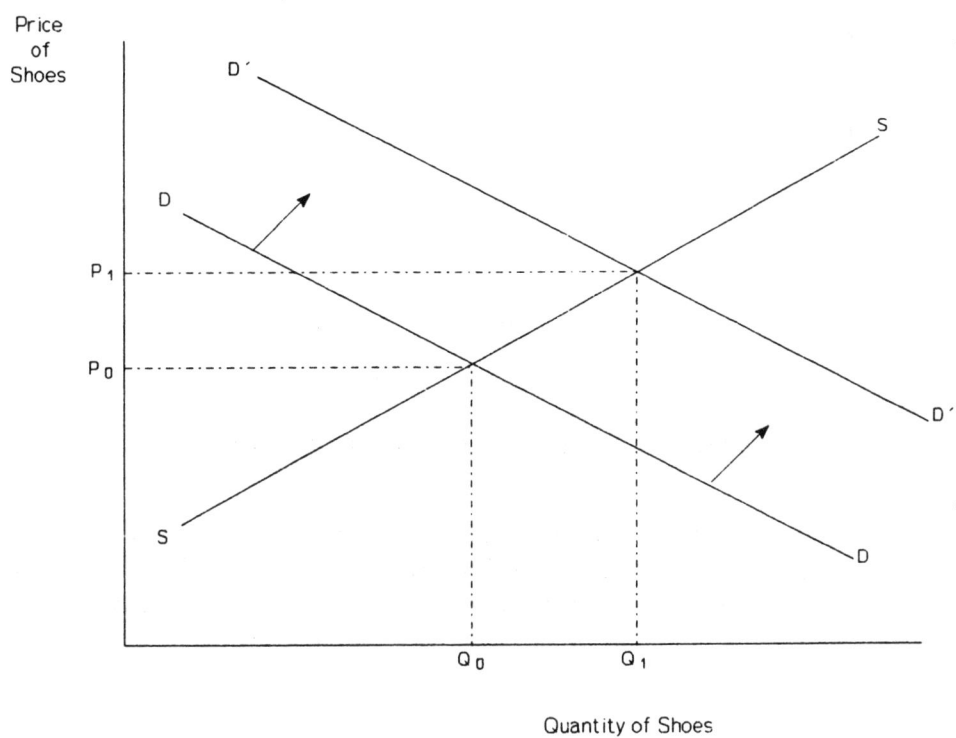

Figure 2.6. A Shift in the Demand for Shoes

On the other hand, suppose one of the underlying costs of shoe production increases. Possibly, leather costs may go up. The marginal cost of shoe production increases. An increase in marginal costs of production results in a shift in the supply curve as shown in Figure 2.7 to S´-S´. Consumers receive the information from prices and reduce their purchases of shoes. Price rises to P_2 and quantity falls to Q_2.

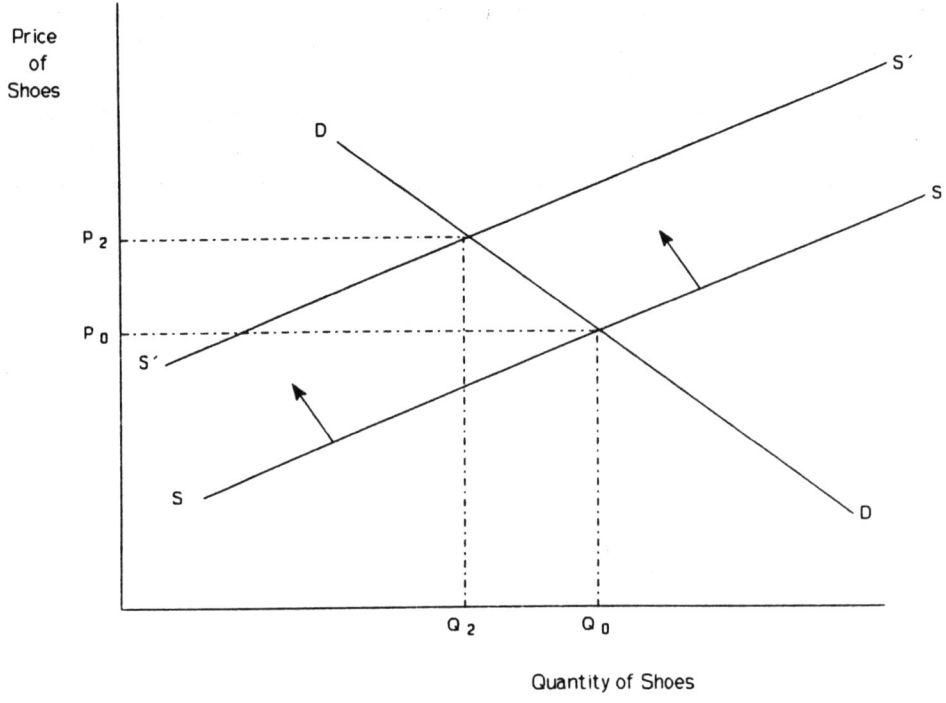

Figure 2.7. A Shift in the Supply of Shoes

Businesses also receive important information from prices in deciding which raw materials to use in production and from which source. An increase in the price of one raw material may lead to substitution of another cheaper material. Prices provide the information needed to make these decisions.

Market Power Distortions

The information transmission mechanism can be distorted through the market power of both suppliers and buyers. Monopoly producers can increase price above a free market level, giving consumers the wrong signals with regard to how much they should consume. Monopoly buyers of a good or service (called monopsony) can keep price artificially low resulting in lower levels of production than would be the case under competition.

Government Distortions

The greatest potential for distortion of the information transmission mechanism in a free enterprise system rests with government, however. As Milton and Rose Friedman (1990, p. 17) note:

> Important as private distortions of the price system are, these days government is the major source of interference with a free market system — through tariffs and other restraints on international trade, domestic action fixing or affecting individual prices, including wages. . ., government regulation of specific industries. . ., monetary and fiscal policies producing erratic inflation . . ., and numerous other channels.

As an example, suppose that government imposes price controls on a particular product. During the 1970's maximum prices for gasoline and oil products were set by government. Market clearing prices, however, had begun to move up beyond the maximum allowable price because of actions by OPEC, the oil cartel. Such a situation is depicted in Figure 2.8.

Had price controls not been present, domestic oil prices would have risen to the international market price. Consumers would have been given a signal to cut back consumption, while domestic oil producers would have been given a signal that production should be increased. Instead, regulation of the maximum price resulted in both consumers and domestic producers receiving the wrong information.

Consumers received the information that there was no need to cut back on consumption. Price was still relatively low. Domestic producers received the information that production should not be expanded. The result was a shortage of oil products, especially gasoline.

Inflation

Inflation produces what the Friedmans (1990) call <u>static</u> in the information transmission mechanism. Such static can lead to misinterpretations of information by both business and consumers. The job of interpreting price information becomes more difficult as inflationary price changes must be sorted out from the real changes in prices of goods and services.

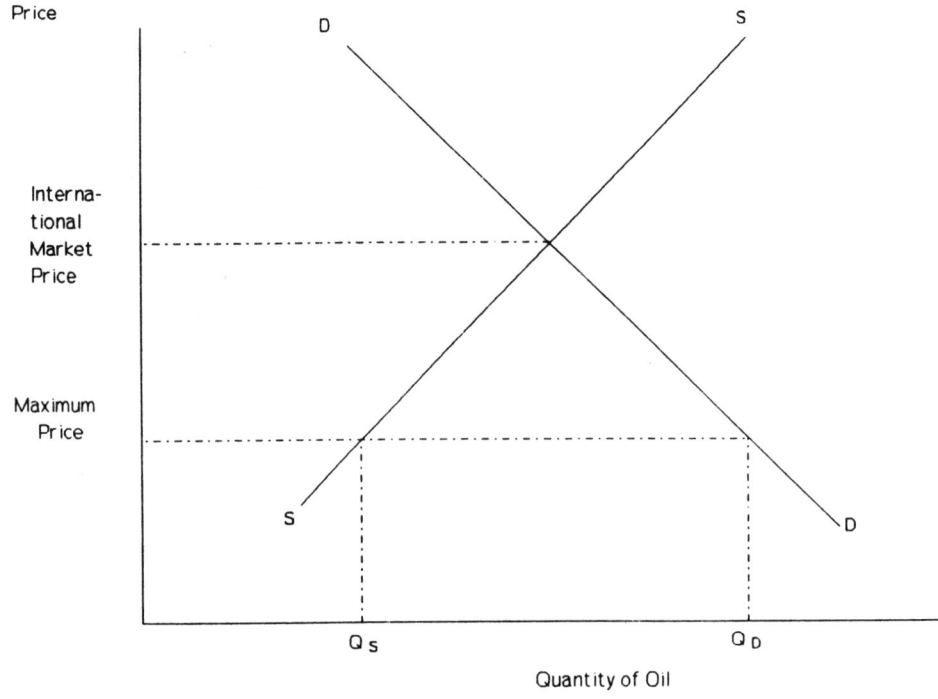

Figure 2.8. Effect of Price Controls on the Information Transmission Mechanism

Provision of Incentives

Prices also provide incentives to producers, consumers, labor and owners of productive resources. Prices provide incentives for business to expand or contract production. This incentive is through the potential to make additional profits or to minimize losses. Prices for raw materials, capital equipment and labor provide business with incentives to organize production as efficiently as possible. If production costs can be reduced, substituting lower cost productive factors for more expensive, increased profits may result.

The incentives provided by prices in a free enterprise system also result in new firms entering an industry and existing firms leaving. High prices and the potential for high profits provide incentives for firms to take chances and produce new products or enter new markets. It is not necessary for high profits to be sustained indefinitely. In fact, that would be a sign of some private or public distortion of the price mechanism. The incentives provided by prices are through increased profit potential. Such potential may not ever be realized. The quest to maximize profits will turn this incentive into new products, new markets or new and better production techniques.

Incentives are also provided to buyers of goods and services. If the price of one good rises, consumers have an incentive to substitute other goods and services instead. Consumers attempt to maximize their individual welfare through decisions as to what mix of goods and services to consume. Prices provide an incentive for consumers to choose that combination of goods that best matches their preferences.

Individuals, as suppliers of labor and owners of productive resources also are provided incentives through prices. Wages are really a price for labor services. Individuals respond to prices in their decisions to enter a particular trade or profession or to work longer hours. As owners of productive resources, individuals have incentives to supply their resources to the most productive activities, in which rewards will be the greatest.

Allocation of Resources

The information and incentives provided by prices provide the mechanism for scarce resources to be allocated to the production of goods and services. Through a system of prices, forces are unleashed to help determine which productive resources should be used to produce which goods and services. For example, electricity can be produced using several different energy sources. Although a variety of factors enter into this decision, including environmental concerns, the choice of nuclear versus coal versus oil versus natural gas depends in large measure on the relative prices of these different forms of energy. Prices thus create forces that help keep production costs as low as possible.

Prices help to allocate resources to the highest value in use. That is, if a resource is more productive in some activities than others, it would tend to be used in the most productive way. For example, airplanes could be used to ship coal. However, they are used to ship people and high value commodities since they are more productive shipping these instead of coal. Coal is shipped by rail, which is slower, but much more economical.

Goods and services are allocated to consumers through prices. We live in a world of scarce resources in which all the wants and desires of all consumers can never be fully satisfied. The system of prices determines which goods and services should be produced and how many should be distributed to each consumer. The way prices determine who gets what is through the effect on the distribution of income.

Affects the Distribution of Income

The market decisions that individuals make have an affect on their incomes. Decisions to save and invest, enter one field versus another, pursue an advanced degree, or work longer hours, all result in changes in incomes. The decisions of managers and owners of small businesses to produce a particular product, enter new markets or produce goods and services in particular ways using various combinations of labor and resources, all have an affect on their incomes.

The system of prices is a determinant of incomes through its effect on incentives. The only way that incentives can be relevant is by influencing the distribution of income. That is, if all incomes were the same, regardless of how hard one worked, how thrifty one became or how skillful one was at managing a business, how many incentives would there be to carry out these activities? Incentives for hard work, investment and saving are only created through the change in income which may result.

While a possibly larger income is the reward that the free enterprise system offers for hard work, saving and investment, income levels are not solely determined by these activities. Luck, inheritance, being born in the right place at the right time are also factors. There are many individuals in society who through no fault of their own would be relegated to extreme poverty if the free enterprise system by itself determined income levels.

Economic Goals of Society

A society has two primary economic goals (see Okun, 1975, for an exposition on these two goals). One is to increase incomes and living standards in general. The incentives provided by the free enterprise system are important to achieving this goal. As was discussed previously, incentives provide the mechanism for goods and services to be produced in the most efficient manner and to best match consumer preferences. Incentives also provide the fuel for the economic engine to steadily produce more and more at greater and greater levels of efficiency.

The second primary economic goal of a society is fairness and equity in income distribution. This goal says that economic rewards should be shared by all, not just those with superior ability, born into wealthy families, etc. Society attempts to achieve this goal through programs designed to equalize the distribution of income. The progressive income tax and welfare programs are examples.

Conflict Between Goals

There is a conflict, however, between these two economic goals. The more that incomes are equalized, the fewer incentives which exist to improve incomes overall. The incentives of the free enterprise system result in an unequal income distribution, since the greater rewards go to those who respond best. The more that incomes are equalized, the fewer the rewards from hard work, productivity and thrift. Many of the debates between liberals and conservatives really boil down to the importance placed on these two goals. Conservatives generally place heavier emphasis on the first, while liberals emphasize the second.

One possible way of resolving the conflict between these two goals is to examine an individual's income over time. The public policy debate between conservatives and liberals usually looks at the poor versus the rich or the number of people within a particular income bracket. The debate ignores changes in one person's income over time.

What may be most important is not whether a person is poor, but rather does he or she stay poor. Does the free enterprise system provide the mechanism for those at the bottom of the economic ladder to advance, or to stagnate in endless poverty. This line of reasoning suggests more than income redistribution as the way to achieve the second goal, and more than economic incentives to achieve the first. Individual job opportunities, continued economic growth, and availability of quality education are also required to achieve both improved standards of living and an equitable distribution of income.

A Model of the Market System

The market system is the two way link between the societal elements and the business organization. Through the interaction of supply and demand, prices, quantities and quality of goods and services produced, and costs of production are determined. A model of this two way linkage is presented in Figure 2.9. Business interacts with the market system on two fronts. It acts as a consumer of raw materials, capital goods and land, and hires labor. In return, owners of productive inputs receive incomes in the form of wages, interest, rents, and profits. Business also acts as a supplier and uses these inputs to produce goods and services which are consumed by members of society.

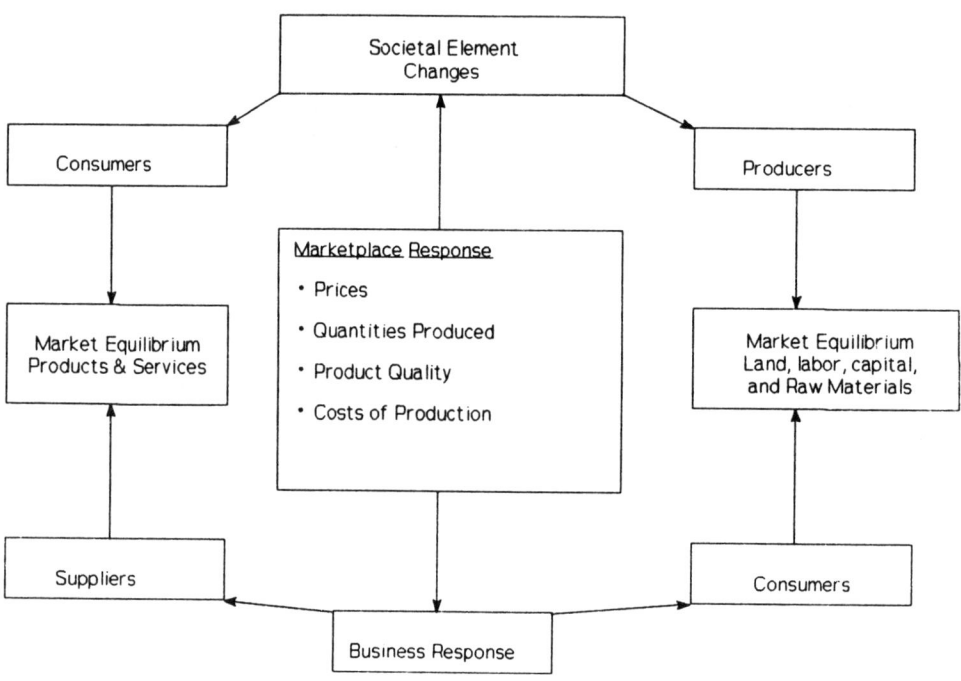

Figure 2.9. A Model of the Market System

Changes in societal elements can influence the demand for the products and services produced by business and the supplies of the inputs used in production. Changes in the societal elements impact consumers by affecting the determinants of demand for products. For example, the overall economic climate affects incomes of consumers, energy price changes impact the demand for small cars relative to large ones, and changes in technology affect the prices of substitute and complementary goods and result in the creation of new products competing for the consumer's dollar. For example, microwave ovens, once a luxury item are now commonplace, and home computers are rapidly increasing in numbers as a result of new technology.

Supplies of productive inputs are also affected by changes in the societal elements. The overall economic climate, changes in unionization and public sector programs and regulations affect the supply of labor. The supply of investment capital is influenced by the rate of interest. Energy costs and changes in environmental regulations impact resource and raw material supplies. All of these changes in turn affect production costs by influencing wages levels, the cost of capital and the cost of raw materials.

The managerial response of business to these changes in costs of production involves changes in planning, organizing, controlling and staffing/rewarding. These responses result in alterations in the supply of goods and services, which in turn affect market prices. Thus, changes in societal elements can result in changes in input costs which ultimately affect the prices that consumers pay for goods and services.

In addition, the changes in societal elements that affect the demand for the products of business also result in changes in business demand for raw materials, labor and capital. This can lead to changes in wages, interests, rents, and profits of input suppliers. Thus, societal element changes can impact the incomes of individuals who supply labor, capital and raw materials in the marketplace.

The marketplace response of changes in prices, quantities and quality of goods and services produced and costs of production can have a further effect on the societal elements themselves. For example, changes in technology allow the substitution of robots for unskilled and semi-skilled workers, resulting in changes in labor markets. Energy costs may affect plant relocation decisions and thus the regional economic climate. International competition can result in declines in various industries such as steel, automobiles and textile manufacturing resulting in regional, local, and labor impacts.

Environmental Analysis and Forecasting

In order to make effective business decisions, managers must anticipate societal element changes as well as public sector and marketplace responses. The process of environmental analysis and forecasting (also called environmental scanning) provides much of the information needed to integrate changes in the external environment into the business planning process. Environmental analysis focuses on:

> realistically and comprehensively describing the current environment, projecting future ones, foreseeing environmental changes so that unhappy surprises may be avoided, and preventing unanticipated consequences of strategies and actions.(Grant & King, 1984, p. 112)

Business responses must therefore be adjusted to take into account future contingencies. The functions of planning, organizing, controlling, and staffing/rewarding may be affected at various times by the results of environmental analysis and forecasting. For example, the implementation of a major environmental scanning effort may also require organizational changes, provide information regarding the performance of the organization vis-a-vis its competitors, and require new staff positions and modification of performance appraisal procedures to reward managers for continually monitoring the environment.

Guidelines for Environmental Scanning and Forecasting

The steps outlined in Table 2.3 provide basic guidelines for corporate environmental analysis and forecasting. Each step will be described below.

Step I – Define Areas

The first step in any effort to examine the environment involves limiting the scope of the study to areas which represent primary and secondary relationships between the business and the societal elements, the public sector, and the marketplace. Primary involvement as defined by Preston and Post (1975, p. 95) "is determined by the specialized functional role of the organization, the role that defines its nature and social purpose and that provides the basis for exchange relationships between it and the rest of society." Examples include relationships with

Table 2.3. Guidelines for Environmental Scanning

> I. Define area of corporate involvement with the external environment.
>
> II. Delineate external and internal topics and subtopics to be monitored.
>
> III. Determine the time frame and forecasting requirements for the scanning effort.
>
> IV. Design and implement a strategy to gather relevant information.
>
> V. Analyze the data for use by management.
>
> VI. Integrate the scanning process into the organization.

suppliers, customers, employees, labor unions, and stockholders. Secondary involvement includes "all those relationships, activities, and impacts of the organization that are ancillary or consequential to its primary involvement activities" (Preston & Post, 1975, p. 96). Examples are the use of a product by the customer, externalities such as pollution, hazards to the worker on the job, or the impact of company employment practices (e.g., new hiring or layoffs) on the labor market.

The number of factors stemming from these sources is virtually limitless, so the organization must focus only on those areas which impact the operations of the firm; are important to shareholders, employees, customers, suppliers and other interested groups; or which have been identified as important by top management in the planning process. A more detailed examination of limiting the scope of organizational involvement with the environment will be made in Chapter 4.

Step II—Delineate Topics

The second step is to delineate topics and subtopics to be monitored within the limits set in Step I. Many of these topics relate to areas external to the firm, including some of the underlying forces and societal elements discussed above. Factors relating to areas internal to the organization may also be selected. Information regarding corporate performance, plant and equipment, and employee productivity might be gathered.

Many companies have scanned the economic and technological environments to provide management with information regarding changes in interest rates, inflation levels, and competitive products and production processes. During the 1980's and 1990's, as the role of business has expanded and the internal operations have been increasingly regulated by government, examination of the political and social environments has also been included in the scanning process.

At Sears, Roebuck & Co., at least eight topics are monitored regarding the external environment (Barmeier, 1980). These include: demographics, values and lifestyles, technology, public attitudes, government, the economy, and the international scene. In a 1983 external environment scan completed by Honeywell, Inc., these eight factors were incorporated as well as regional/metropolitan characteristics (Honeywell, Inc., 1983).

In addition to the external environmental factors studied, Barmeier (1980) reports that four internal factors are continuously scanned. These are: sales, corporate income, capital expenditures, and facilities. When appropriate, analyses can be made of the relationships between the external and internal factors.

Step III – Determine Time Frame and Forecasting Requirements

The third step includes identification of the time frame to be utilized and the associated forecasting requirements. Depending on the situation, the time frame might range from 1 to 20 years. For example, a high technology company manufacturing microcomputer chips might only be able to market a product for a year before a better, less expensive substitute appears. On the other hand, a forest products firm may have a 20 year planning cycle for their product.

When long-term forecasts are needed, the manager must determine the appropriate methodology to use for making predictions. The area of economic forecasting is quite sophisticated, utilizing trend analysis, regression and curve fitting techniques which are beyond the scope of this book. (See Johnston, 1984 and Pindyck & Rubinfeld, 1991 for further information on econometrics.)

Much of the data regarding the technological, political and social environments, however, is qualitative rather than quantitative in nature. It may therefore be necessary to combine statistical forecasting methods with relatively non-quantitative methods such as the Delphi technique and analysis of scenarios.

The Delphi Technique. When long-range forecasts of qualitative areas are needed, it may be appropriate to use the Delphi technique to gather expert opinion. The process begins with the selection of an "expert" panel who respond to mail questionnaires which address the topics of interest with general questions. The results of these surveys are given back to the panel and a second, more specific questionnaire is completed. This feedback-survey process is repeated until a general consensus is reached by the panelists.

In practice, the results of a Delphi study may be biased by the composition and lack of continuous participation of the panel members. As with any forecast of the future, it is still necessary to continuously re-evaluate the results in light of unexpected events.

The Scenario Method. Using this method, the manager designs one or more scenarios or pictures of the future as related to the areas selected for study in Step II. Key factors may be varied such as the outcome of an upcoming Presidential election or the state of the economy. Business plans may then be developed which take into account the alternative scenarios (Tombari, 1984; Zentner, 1975).

Step IV – Design and Implement Strategy

The fourth step in the environmental analysis involves the design and implementation of a strategy to gather relevant information on the topics identified for the time frame chosen. Table 2.4 classifies various sources of information as external versus internal to the organization and as particularly useful for short-term versus long-term time frames. Each cell of the matrix is described in turn.

External/Short-term. Perhaps the most commonly used sources of external information are individual contacts with suppliers, customers and others outside the organization. These contacts may be on an informal basis, but a formal scanning approach would ensure systematic

Table 2.4. Sources of Information for Scanning the Business Environment

	External	Internal
Short-term	Individual contacts (suppliers, customers)	Organization's employees
	Publications (trade associations, business media, government documents)	Corporate reports (financial feasibility studies, market research)
Long-term	Delphi panelists	Strategic planning documents
	Aggregate economic forecasts	Financial planning reports
	Futures studies	Human resource plans

interaction with these sources to increase the probability of identifying key issues.

Other sources are publications from relevant professional and trade associations, newspapers, and "business" oriented periodicals. In some cases, government documents may also be important.

In order to maximize the usefulness of these sources, it is necessary to organize the collection and storage of information. A filing system should be set up which provides folders or computer files for each topic and/or subtopic being monitored. Further, it may be necessary to assign specific individuals the task of reviewing specific periodicals. These individuals should be users of the data, if possible, and be rewarded for their efforts by the organization.

Aaker (1983) outlines a specific strategy for organizing a strategic information scanning system (SISS). He proposes a matrix which identifies the information needs (topics) and likely sources of information (e.g., individuals, professional associations, or periodicals). Specific individuals are assigned to collect the data. The information gathered is then sent to a central location for storage and retrieval.

<u>External/Long-term</u>. Sources for long-term or future information regarding issues external to the organization include Delphi panelists and other experts in an area. The firm may also use aggregate economic forecasts, and studies of the future. It also may be necessary to develop forecasts from the information gathered regarding current trends.

<u>Internal/Short-term</u>. Employees of the organization can provide useful information regarding their attitudes toward company policies and products as well as their own expectations. In addition, standard financial reports can be used to measure performance, feasibility studies can be used to evaluate the costs and benefits of new programs as well as proposed acquisitions, mergers or divestitures. Finally, market research studies focus on the potential acceptance of customers to new or current product lines.

<u>Internal/Long-term</u>. Information from business planners can be used to determine future corporate or financial strategies. Human resource plans also are related to the future direction of the firm and will have a direct impact on long-term performance and its relation to the societal elements.

Step V—Analyze Data

Once the information is collected, it should be analyzed for use by management. This analysis step can involve summarizing the findings regarding each topic, forecasting trends when required, and prioritizing the areas of interest to the organization.

One approach that is useful in some studies is cross impact analysis. Cross impact analysis is a technique used to determine the interrelationships of the external issues among themselves as well as the relationship to the internal issues. Using this method, the probable impact of one event on another may be predicted.

An example of a cross impact matrix is shown in Table 2.5. In this example, three television technologies are examined. Each of the technologies are in various states of development or adoption. The matrix is used to predict the likely adoption of the technologies on a massive scale. The first technology is interactive TV in which viewers can play games, choose movies, order goods and services, etc. The second is digital TV. This technology involves extremely enhanced pictures, the

Table 2.5. An Example of a Cross Impact Matrix

	T_1	T_2	T_3
Television Technologies (Probability, Year)			
T_1 Interactive (.9, 2000)		Enhance 50% in 3 years	Enhance 50% in 3 years
T_2 Digital (.7, 2005)	-10% in 2 years		-60% in 2 years
T_3 HDTV (.8, 2008)	-10% in 2 years	Enhance 25% in 2 years	

video equivalent of digital audio. The last technology is high definition TV or HDTV. This approach also results in an enhanced picture. It involves adding a greater number of broadcast lines to the screen. It is a competitor to digital TV. For each of the three technologies, the probability of occurrence by the year indicated is shown in parentheses.

Above the diagonal, the effect if the earlier row event occurs is indicated. Here, the widespread adoption of interactive TV is expected to enhance the development and adoption of both digital TV and HDTV. It is expected that adoption of both technologies will be enhanced by 50% with a 3 year lag. Digital TV and HDTV are rivals, similar to when Beta and VHS were rival formats for video tape. The widespread adoption of digital TV will have a very negative impact of HDTV, resulting in a 60% reduction in adoption in 2 years.

Below the diagonal, the effect if the earlier column event does <u>not</u> occur is indicated. If interactive TV does not catch on, then both digital TV and HDTV will be negatively impacted by ten percent in two years. If digital TV does not happen, it is expected that adoption of HDTV will be enhanced by 25 percent in two years.

This method thus can be used to estimate the likely impact of one future event on another. Planners can use the information to adjust their strategies as events actually do or do not occur, and to make more refined estimates of the future.

Step VI — Integrate into the organization.

The final step in the environmental analysis and forecasting process involves integrating the program into the organization. Although not essential for a short-term, ad hoc study, this step should be taken if an on-going effort is planned.

In order to facilitate the process, some structural change in the organization may be appropriate. As suggested by Aaker (1983) and described above, participation by key individuals and the central storage of information is desirable. Thus, the organization must be willing to support the administration of the scanning effort.

As the effort grows in scope it may be necessary to assign a corporate staff professional to the project, perhaps initially part-time, but eventually full-time. In a very large scanning project, an entire department may be assigned this responsibility.

In addition to structural changes, it may be necessary to show top management the usefulness and importance of environmental scanning information for business decision making. The results of the effort must therefore be presented to managers in a usable and timely manner. Through dissemination of results of the environmental analysis, it is hoped that general management awareness of the key factors in the external environment will be increased.

Summary

This chapter presents a model of the impact of change in the external environment on business decision making. Underlying the change process are forces such as demographics, beliefs, values, cultures, international events, discoveries, resources and natural events. Changes in the societal elements described in Chapter 1 are related to responses from the public sector, marketplace and business. The processes impacting on business are the political system and the market system. Business, however, acts on the public sector through the political system and on the societal elements through social involvement. Important to understanding the market response are concepts of demand and supply.

Demand is a schedule of the different quantities of a good or service which the consumer is willing and able to purchase at each and every possible price. The determinants of demand are income, price, prices of substitute goods and services, prices of complements and attitudes and tastes. The marginal cost curve is a firm's supply curve.

In a competitive marketplace, demand equals supply. Price is equal to the marginal cost of providing a good or service which is in turn equal to the value that consumers place on consuming an extra unit of the product. Prices play several important roles in a free enterprise system. They transmit information, provide incentives, allocate resources and affect income distribution.

One method available to managers seeking to understand their firm's environment is environmental analysis and forecasting. The process of environmental scanning involves defining the areas of interest to the firm, delineating topics for study, determining the time frame and forecasting requirements, gathering information, analyzing the information, and integrating the scanning process into the ongoing operations of the organization.

Questions

1. Using the model presented in Figure 2.1, analyze the Pullman Standard Case described at the end of Chapter 1. Identify the societal element changes and public sector responses which impacted Pullman.

2. Using a company where you or a member of your family work, identify the societal elements most likely to affect the business in the next five years. What public sector and marketplace responses might be expected from changes in these elements. Given this situation, what business responses are likely?

3. What would the model presented in Figure 2.1 look like under authoritarian socialism?

4. What current changes in societal elements will affect the demand for products or services sold by the business analyzed in number 2 above.

5. Some consumers use price as a surrogate for quality of some goods. Is it ethical for business to raise the price of their product in order to increase sales?

6. How is marginal cost related to the supply curve?

7. What is the significance to managers of the concept of market equilibrium?

8. What is the role of profits in a free enterprise system?

9. At the present time the federal government has established a minimum wage for most workers. How does the minimum wage affect the four functions of prices in a free enterprise system?

10. Design an environmental scanning system for the company analyzed in number 2 above.

Key Concepts

market system

laissez faire capitalism

modern mixed economy

democratic socialism

authoritarian socialism

free enterprise system

demand curve

supply curve

marginal cost

market equilibrium

"Invisible Hand"

environmental analysis (scanning)

Delphi technique

scenario method

cross impact analysis

Case Analysis: An Example of Authoritarian Socialism Before the Breakup of the Soviet Union
Quid Pro Quo: Poles Survive Collapse Of Currency by Using Own System of Barter
by Frederick Kempe

Kartuzy, Poland — Marietta Dzoitek will wake up long before dawn at least one day this week and wrap herself in three thick layers of clothing. She will slip quietly out the front door, so as not to disturb her sick mother, and go out into the bitter cold to wait in line for hours outside the neighborhood newspaper kiosk.

Miss Dzoitek — a frail, 31-year-old hospital switchboard operator — will say little or nothing to those around her as she waits for the shop to open: Conversations in lines these days too often end in arguments.

She complains but endures the tedium for the reward at the end — cigarettes to use as barter. If she is lucky, she'll be able to buy four of the 12 packs her ration coupons entitle her to each month. She'll go through the same sort of ritual later in the week to buy her monthly half liter of vodka.

Miss Dzoitek herself rarely smokes or drinks, but such goods have taken on special significance in Polish society. "Tobacco and alcohol are the best currencies nowadays," Miss Dzoitek says wanly. "Money no longer matters."

Stock in Trade

This small northern town of 15,000, just 20 miles from the Baltic coast and 70 miles from the Soviet border, is surviving on barter. So, indeed, is all of Poland. If one has the right item to trade, he can bypass some of the other exasperating and ubiquitous lines and the frequently empty shop shelves.

This month, Miss Dzoitek wants to use her vodka and cigarettes to buy toothpaste, washing powder, and coffee. She also hopes to persuade a nurse to help find medicine, otherwise unobtainable, to treat her mother's asthma.

When Miss Dzoitek gets to work in the morning, there isn't any small talk about the weather or last night's television. Conversation takes the form of hard bargaining — a discussion of who has been able to get what items and what he wants in exchange for them.

"People won't help you anymore unless you can give them something in return," Miss Dzoitek laments. "Kartuzy was once such a happy place, but now all we do is bicker and suffer."

Pulling the Rug

Kartuzy is nestled between scenic lakes, and it is a place to which city dwellers from nearby Gdansk and Gdynia traditionally escaped for relaxation and a taste of country life. But now that the frustrations of everyday life have damaged friendships and disrupted society, the welcome mat to outsiders has been removed. Tourists are viewed as a drain on the town's short supplies.

The economic crisis that has so changed Kartuzy, has altered the life of villages, towns and cities throughout the country. Tension is building that many Polish economic experts feel could erupt in food riots before year's end. Strikes to protest food shortages are spreading and already have resulted in street skirmishes between citizens and police. Worthless money continues to accumulate in the hands of families who don't have enough to eat and who must face the daily, exhausting struggle to obtain necessities that money can't buy.

Finance minister Marian Krzak has warned: "The devolution of Poland into a barter society is our greatest problem. We must stop cigarettes from becoming money and money from becoming nothing."

The Worthless Zloty

Indeed, the Zloty, Poland's monetary unit, is one of the few things in Kartuzy that isn't in short supply. More than one-third of Polish wages aren't matched by goods in shops, and that gap grows every day. Incomes have increased more than 25% in the past year, but the supply of consumer goods has dropped by nearly as much. A general flight from money is taking place, and as a result the most desired and least available products — spirits, cigarettes, sugar, meat, washing powder, to name a few — have become the means of exchange.

People who can get those products most easily have become the new elite. They include the neighborhood butcher, the hardware-shop worker with access to washing powder, the candy-store manager who has chocolate, the doctor who demands cognac in exchange for treatment and the plumber who won't touch a drain unless cigarettes figure in the deal.

Miss Dzoitek's mother was amazed recently when the carpenter who replastered a hole in her ceiling rendered his bill: a pack of cigarettes and half a liter of vodka.

Tadeusz Ochman, 21, numbers himself among the new Kartuzy elite. He has only a basic education and earns a modest wage, but he sells washing powder—and he is all the rage.

"You have to be important enough or you are forgotten," he explains almost boastfully. "If I don't leave a package of washing powder during my next visit to the dairy store, I can be sure they will have no eggs for me the time after that."

Mr. Ochman also arranges deals for meat with the butcher next-door. Recently he traded 600 grams of washing powder for two kilos of pork. "Kartuzy is a small place," he says. "Everybody knows me. If they what some washing powder, they walk up to me on the street and offer me something in trade."

Barter's biggest plus is that it allows one to avoid some of the lines. On a recent stroll through town, one could see people spilling out of shops into the streets almost everywhere. They were waiting for sugar, butter, eggs and chocolates. The butcher shop had no line, the butcher explained, because he had no meat.

There was only one happy scene. Some 50 smiling teenagers waited patiently in front of an ice cream shop for their one scoop of vanilla. Ewa Hirsz, 16, giggled: "This is worth the wait. But I had to stand all night one day last week for school supplies. That made me angry."

Just down the street, her mother stands in a grim line of more than 200 people waiting to buy toilet paper. An emaciated old man struggles to drag a bag filled with 50 rolls of the coarse textured paper. He stops to catch his breath after each five or six short paces. No one in the line would risk losing position to assist him.

"At least he got what he wanted," comments Zenon Menard, 31, who works the night shift at the Lenin shipyard in Gdansk 30 miles away. "It might seem foolish to go through so much for toilet paper, but one must do this for any necessity," he laughs.

Mr. Menard and his wife divide line-standing duties. His wife stands in morning lines to allow him to sleep after his night work, and he takes the afternoon lines so she can stay at home with their two children. On Sunday evening, Mr. Menard's night off, he starts queuing at 8 o'clock for the meat delivery at the butcher shop the following morning.

Ration cards allow Poles to buy just three kilograms of meat each month, but shortages have made even that difficult. Because of such problems, ration coupons have lost their worth on the barter market. "You have to trade hard goods," says Mr. Menard. "The coupon is too much of a gamble."

No Trust Either

One local butcher admits that all-night lines could probably be avoided by some sort of a list system, but "people don't trust each other enough for that," he says. "Someone would cheat or alter the list."

Shop owners say that fights break out in lines with increasing regularity. "Things are starting to get ugly outside the store," complains Edmund Mazinowski, 48, a hardware merchant. "There is so much yelling and cursing. Even women are slugging each other."

The fights usually start when someone uses state-granted privileges to cut into the line. The law requires that every third spot be reserved for pregnant women, women with infants and persons officially recognized as handicapped or physically impaired.

The result has been a rash of applications from old people for state recognition of their incapacities. Men send their pregnant wives shopping. Women borrow infants from neighbors and shop where they aren't known. Mothers take children with them whom they normally would leave at home.

Hostile to Outsiders

The people of Kartuzy aren't just turning against each other; they are hostile to the city folk of Gdansk and Gdynia. The town passed a law two months ago prohibiting outsiders from coming here to buy big-ticket items such as refrigerators, ovens and carpets. Now Kartuzy is considering a law encompassing almost all products. "It has to be done," says Mr. Mazinowski. "We don't have enough for ourselves."

Kartuzy people are even more bitter about the farmers from surrounding villages who they feel exploit them. The farmers sell only what they must to the state at its artificially low prices. They opt instead to sell as much as half of their goods at places like the Tuesday and Saturday outdoor Kartuzy market for three times the state-controlled prices.

But what irks Kartuzy dwellers most is that these farmers also get state food coupons and can buy whatever remains in state shops at a cut-rate price while selling their own goods at the high prices.

"They have become the new elite," says Miss Dzoitek. "I really hate them. I see them walking by me on the street and I want to spit on them."

Paid in Potatoes

Many locals, however, have accepted the inevitable and now ask farmers for weekend jobs in exchange for goods. For example, Mr. Menard of the Gdansk shipyard worked at his brother's farm during the harvest this year and was paid a sack of potatoes.

So far, the government has insisted that steep price increases are the painful medicine needed to cure the economic crisis and to do away with the barter economy. It argues that increased prices will sponge up much of the excess Polish money while motivating farmers to produce and sell their goods to state suppliers.

The independent trade union, Solidarity, however, demands a price freeze until the union and government can agree upon a broader economic plan that includes price hikes as one element. It has threatened warning strikes if talks don't get under way and produce results.

Grzegorz Palka, the Solidarity presidium member who will lead negotiations with the government, warns: "We must immediately stop the return of Poland to a Stone Age society. The country will explode in food riots within four to six weeks if we don't act quickly."

But Miss Dzoitek in Kartuzy complains that Poles are doing too much talking that she doesn't understand. "All I know is that I'm not prepared for the winter ahead," she says. "I don't know how I'll get through it if things don't change soon."

Source: *Wall Street Journal*, October 23, 1981, pp. 1, 18. Reprinted with permission.

Case Questions

1. How does the situation in Poland described in the case compare to food distribution in the United States?

2. In Communist Poland, government control replaced the price system. Evaluate government control as a substitute for the price system.

3. What is the status of the Polish economy today?

References

Aaker, D. A. "Organizing a Strategic Information Scanning System." *California Management Review*, 1983, *25* (2), 76–83.

Barmeier, R. E. The Role of Environmental Forecasting and Public Issues Analysis in Corporate Planning. In L. E. Preston (Ed.), *Business Environment/Public Policy 1979 Conference Papers*. St. Louis, Mo.: American Assembly of Collegiate Schools of Business, 1979.

Case, Karl E. and Fair, Ray C. *Principles of Economics* (3rd edition), Englewood Cliffs, N.J.: Prentice Hall, 1994.

Forrester, J. W. "Industrial Dynamics." *Harvard Business Review*, July–August, 1958, *36*, 37–56.

Forrester, J. W. *Industrial Dynamics*. Cambridge, Mass.: The MIT Press, 1961.

Friedman, M. & Friedman, R. *Free To Choose: A Personal Statement*. New York: Harcourt, Brace, Jovanovich, 1990.

Grant, J. H. & King, W. R. *The Logic of Strategic Planning*. Boston, Mass.: Little, Brown and Company, 1982.

Honeywell, Inc. *Human Resource Trends, Implications for Human Resource Management*, 1983.

Johnston, J. *Econometric Methods* (3rd ed.). New York: McGraw-Hill, 1984.

McConnell, C. R. *Economics: Principles, Problems, and Policies* (13th ed.). New York: McGraw-Hill, 1995.

Okun, A. M. *Equality and Efficiency, The Big Tradeoff*. Washington, D.C.: Brookings Institute, 1975.

Pindyck, Robert S. and Rubinfeld, Daniel L. *Econometric Models and Economic Forecasts* (3rd edition). New York, N.Y.: McGraw-Hill, 1991.

Preston, L. E. & Post, J. E. *Private Management and Public Policy*. Englewood Cliffs, N.J.: Prentice-Hall, Inc., 1975.

Samuelson, P. A. *Economics* (15th ed.). New York: McGraw-Hill, 1995.

Tombari, H. A. *Business & Society*. Chicago: The Dryden Press, 1984.

Zentner, R. D. "Scenarios in Forecasting." *Chemical Engineering News*, October 6, 1975, 22–34.

CHAPTER 3

THE PUBLIC SECTOR RESPONSE AND THE POLITICAL SYSTEM

The linkage between changes in the societal elements of the external environment of business and the public sector response is the political system. The public sector response to a change in one of the societal elements is an important determinant in the ultimate effect of these changes on business. The public sector includes the institutions, bureaucratic structure and laws that make up the federal, state and local governments in the United States.

The political system is the process by which public sector actions are debated and acted upon. It includes the political party system, the power structure within government, interest groups and patterns of participation among the voting public. Through the political system, groups of individuals, including business influence public policy decisions. Politics and the political system influences almost every single step in the public policy process. Even the implementation of policy involves political considerations.

In this chapter, the reasons for public sector involvement in the free enterprise system will be explored. The problems engendered by public sector activities will then be examined. The chapter will then discuss the structure of the American system of government. The role of the political system and the manner in which political considerations influence decision making throughout government will be examined. The ways in which business can influence political considerations will be dealt with. The chapter then explores several political reform proposals. The chapter concludes with a case study of the attempt of the trucking interests to influence public policy decisions.

The Role of the Public Sector in a Free Enterprise System

In the previous chapter, several types of economic systems were described ranging from the laissez faire capitalism of the eighteenth century to the authoritarian socialism of modern day China, Cuba or North Korea. In each type of economic system, a distinct role for the public sector is implied. Laissez faire capitalism involves an extremely limited role for the public sector, while Communism places government in an all encompassing position.

In this section, the nature of the economic role of government in a free enterprise system will be explored. As was described in the last chapter, free enterprise does not imply only laissez faire capitalism. Instead, it implies a much broader concept which includes the modern mixed economy and some markets in democratic socialism as well.

Although the free market system produces a variety of desirable consequences which were described in the previous chapter, some undesirable results may also occur. The public sector role can be viewed as attempting to correct these shortfalls. The extent of government involvement in an economy for the purpose of correcting these shortfalls distinguishes the different types of economic systems.

The public sector has a variety of policy tools at its disposal. These include regulation, taxation, spending and direct provision of services. These tools are used to correct the undesirable consequences which may result in a totally free market system.

Legal Foundations — Establishing the Rules to Conduct Business

Government establishes and administers a wide range of laws and regulations. These include laws and an administration of justice which protect individuals from coercion from other individuals in society. (Friedman & Friedman, 1990, p. 29) Government also defines the legal status of business in a variety of forms. These include proprietorships, partnerships, and corporations. The definition of private property and the enforcement of contracts are other legal foundations established by government. The court system provides a mechanism for mediating disputes between individuals. The public sector is called upon to provide a system of standards of weights and measures, and to prevent fraud and deceptive claims in the provision of goods and services. In short, government establishes the legal 'rules of the game' to conduct business.

One shortfall of the free enterprise system is the tendency for some industries or markets to become concentrated so that one or only a few firms compete. Many of the desirable properties of free competition discussed in the previous chapter may not occur in these industries. Instead, inefficiency, high prices, less than optimal output levels and anti-competitive practices may result. One set of rules and regulations which government has established are the anti-trust laws. These laws have as their objective the prevention of concentration of economic power in a few firms and prohibition of a variety of anti-competitive practices such as price-fixing and agreements between sellers.

Some industries can be classified as natural monopolies. In these industries, only one firm can efficiently provide the good or service. More than one firm would involve higher costs of production. Public utilities such as electricity, natural gas, water and sewage are examples of natural monopolies. Government has taken a role in dealing with natural monopolies through regulation and through the public provision of services. Regulation is carried out at the federal, state, and local levels of government. Municipal water and sewer authorities are examples of public provision.

Adjustment for Externalities

An externality is a cost or benefit of an activity which falls on others who are not directly involved. Externalities are sometimes referred to as "third party" effects since individuals are affected who are outside the market transactions between buyers and sellers.

A negative externality is a cost imposed on others. Examples include the emissions of the factory which soils the laundry of the person living next door, and the abandonment of a building which lowers the values of the properties in a neighborhood. Another example is the closing of a plant which results in widespread unemployment and the subsequent deterioration of a region's economy.

Positive externalities are benefits of an activity which are imposed on others. One example is the beekeeper whose bees pollinate the orchard next door. A business which hires unskilled labor and provides training which raises the productivity and earnings potential of workers is another example.

The free enterprise system has a problem with externalities. That is, purely private exchanges will not necessarily take these third party effects into account. There is no mechanism for the market system acting on its own to require firms or individuals who create negative externalities to either compensate third parties or to not engage in such activities. The market system also has difficulty in encouraging the activities which result in positive externalities. The result is that the free market system does not on its own create the incentives for business and individuals to take externalities into account in production and consumption decisions. There is a role for government in correcting this shortfall in the free enterprise system. This role involves making adjustments in the outcomes of private production and consumption decisions so that the provision of positive externalities will be encouraged and negative externalities will be discouraged.

Although government has used regulation most often, the other policy tools of taxation, spending and public provision of services have also been used to correct for the externalities of the free market system. For example, government regulation has been used to require pollution control devices on plants to curb pollution of the air, streams and rivers. Regulation of rail line abandonments has forced railroads to take regional economic effects into account before closing a particular route.

An example of a non-regulatory policy tool used to correct for externalities is the deposit that some states require to be paid on beverage cans. This deposit is similar to a tax in that if the can is not returned, the deposit is lost. Another example is federal government subsidy of municipal sewerage treatment plants to encourage cleanups of the environment. Government production of education and highways are also examples of public policies aimed, at least in part, toward encouraging those activities which result in positive externalities.

Provision of Public Goods

Another shortfall of the free enterprise system concerns the provision of public goods. A public good can be defined as one which we enjoy in common and which if left to its own, the free enterprise system would not provide in socially desirable amounts. Examples of public goods are parks, roads and streets, national forests, and national defense.

Public goods have two characteristics which result in lack of free market supply in adequate amounts. The first characteristic is called non-exclusion. Individuals can be excluded from the consumption of private goods provided by the free market, if they do not pay for them. For example, if an individual does not pay for an automobile or a hamburger, the dealer or restaurant will not deliver the car or serve the food. Consumers of public goods, however, cannot be easily excluded from consumption of the benefits of the good if they do not pay for it. For example, individuals cannot be easily excluded from consuming the benefits of a natural area, roads and streets or even beaches. Public goods have a "free rider" problem. That is, people who consume the service can do so without paying for it.

The characteristic of non-exclusion means that if private business would attempt to supply public goods, they could not obtain payment from all consumers of the service. Although altruism may motivate some businesses, the lack of adequate revenues is a powerful deterrent to private provision of these goods and services.

The second characteristic of public goods is called <u>joint supply</u>. This means that if the good or service is provided to one individual it is jointly provided to everyone. The marginal cost of supplying one additional consumer is very low or zero. For example, police protection which is provided to one house in a neighborhood is provided jointly to all homes as well. National economic statistics collected for one business could be provided to other businesses at very low cost.

The joint supply characteristic of public goods means that the marginal costs of producing public goods for one additional member of society are close to zero. This does not mean that the total production costs are zero, however. As the large expenditures on defense make clear, total costs can be quite large. Rather, defense and other public goods are provided for all members of society. If the number of individuals in society increases, these expenditures need not increase.

Joint supply also means that the free market will not supply public goods in optimal amounts. One characteristic of the free market equilibrium discussed in the previous chapter is that the price of the product equals the marginal production cost which in turn equals the value that consumers place on the last unit produced. Since the marginal cost of supplying a public good to one additional member of society is approximately zero, optimal pricing requires that private producers charge a zero price for the product. But, what business would charge nothing for a good or service?

Since the free market system will not supply public goods in desirable amounts, government has taken on the role of providing these goods and services for society. Two policy tools have been used by the public sector to do so. The first is public provision. National defense, roads and streets and other public works projects are classic examples. The second, regulation, is also used by government to require the private sector to supply some of these goods. For example, some cities require that property owners pay for and maintain sidewalks. The sidewalks are used by all those in the community, not just by the adjacent property owners.

Reduction of Income Inequality

The incentives created by the free enterprise system also result in substantial inequality of income. The public sector has taken on the role of adjusting the distribution of income to mitigate some of the inequality that results.

All of the policy tools have been used by government in efforts to affect the distribution of income. However, the most important, by far, are tax and spending programs, especially at the federal level. Expenditure programs include a variety of transfer payments to individuals. <u>Transfer payments</u> are payments for which no productive activities are performed. Examples include welfare expenditures, food stamps, and medicaid which is a medical care subsidy program for low income people. Social security and medicare programs for the elderly are also forms of transfer payments.

The individual income tax at the federal level is progressive. This means that tax rates rise with increased incomes. At least on paper, higher income individuals should pay a greater proportion of their incomes than lower income persons. However, the income tax is not nearly as progressive as implied by the tax tables. This is because of a variety of loopholes and special provisions in the tax code which were created for a variety of reasons including special interest and public policy considerations.

Government attempts to affect the distribution of income also involve regulation and direct provision of services. Minimum wage laws can be viewed as government regulations which have a goal of keeping a floor under the incomes of people who work. However, there is a controversy over whether low income people on the whole benefit from the minimum wage. It is argued that the gains for those who continue working are offset to some extent by the jobs which are lost because of the minimum wage.

Direct provision of services to assist low income individuals include publicly run hospitals and housing projects. Although administered at the state and local levels, the federal government provides a variety of subsidy programs for these activities.

Stabilization and Promotion of Economic Growth

An additional shortfall of the free enterprise system is the tendency for cyclical fluctuations in output and employment to occur. That is, rather than the overall economy continuing to expand along a stable growth path, alternating periods of decline in economic activity and rapid advances may occur. The recessions and depressions which occur during periods of decline result in unemployment and lost production. Too rapid an expansion can lead to an overheating of the economy and inflation of prices. Over the past twenty years, simultaneous inflation and recession has also occurred.

While it is arguable whether many of the problems in the economy are inherent in the free enterprise system, or whether government intervention is primarily at fault, a goal espoused by the public sector is to promote economic growth, reduce unemployment and stabilize prices. Such goals are rarely if ever achieved, however. In fact, public policy may actually be counterproductive. For example, Milton Friedman has argued that the measures taken by the Federal Reserve actually exacerbated the Great Depression of the 1930's.

Government has a wide variety of policy tools at its disposal to deal with cyclical fluctuations in business activity and to stimulate economic growth. The use of taxation and expenditures to control economic activity is called <u>fiscal policy</u>. The set of policies aimed at regulating the money supply is called <u>monetary policy</u>. Together, fiscal and monetary policies provide the primary mechanisms through which the public sector attempts to exercise control over broad economic aggregates such as employment, interest rates and prices.

Several other policy tools have been tried or are being examined and debated as possible approaches to stabilization and growth promotion. During the early 1970's the federal government tried wage and price controls as a means to reduce inflation. These controls required strict regulation of all wages and prices in the economy. <u>National economic planning</u> and <u>industrial policy</u> are approaches which have been proposed and debated. Forms of national economic planning were attempted during the depression of the 1930's.

Both national economic planning and industrial policy involve the government in guiding the economy and developing strategies for individual industries. These include strategies for promotion of "sunrise" industries and for easing the decline of "sunset" industries. The two approaches differ in that national economic planning utilizes the coercive powers of government to implement strategies while industrial policy tends to rely on the incentives of the market system.

Problems of Government

The reasons for government involvement in the free enterprise system all concern real or perceived shortfalls in the system. However, just as the free enterprise system has shortfalls, so does the public sector. A number of problems are created whenever public sector actions are taken. These shortfalls do not mean that government should not intervene in the economy. Rather, it should be recognized that public sector action has costs as well as benefits.

Unintended Effects

Friedman and Friedman (1990, p. 81) argue that government measures have 'third party' effects similar to those which may result in the marketplace. These third party effects are many times unintended results of public sector actions. Some may be beneficial, but others can be harmful. For example, in the Pullman case discussed in Chapter 1, the public sector actions of a grain sale, tax loopholes and regulation kept the demand for rail cars artificially high. This unintended effect was later replaced by another unintended effect — collapse of the demand for rail cars.

Another example concerns the Consumer Product Safety Commission (CPSC). In the early 1970's, the CPSC required that children's sleepwear be flame retardant. This regulation resulted from a concern that children were needlessly burned in home fires. Manufacturers treated the sleepwear with a chemical called TRIS. However, TRIS was subsequently found to be a carcinogen. Children were exposed to a toxic substance as an unintended effect of public action.

Most unintended effects result from a lack of understanding of the complete consequences of government action. Many public policies are developed on the basis of someone's theory. Some theories are right, some are wrong. Most are untested, with all consequences unknown. The politician who gives a matter of fact solution to a difficult problem is many times expounding a theory that has yet to be proven. The unintended effects can be substantial.

Special Interests

Ostensibly, the primary goal of government is to promote the public interest. Many times, however, the public interest is promoted only if it coincides with the interests of a special group. Special interests are groups of like minded individuals who share common beliefs, goals and objectives. In addition, members of each group have similar social, economic and/or political ends. Special interests include union members, industry associations, government workers, farmers, minority groups, environmentalists, consumer groups, the elderly, and low income people. Everyone belongs to one or more special interest groups.

Frequently, special interests stand to gain or lose a great deal from public sector actions. Thurow (1981, p. 11) argues that there are gainers and losers from the implementation of almost any government program. He states:

> ". . . the gains and losses are not allocated to the same individuals or groups. On average, society may be better off, but this average hides a large number of people who are much better off and large number of people who are much worse off."

If the gains and losses can be attributed to identifiable groups, then a public policy may develop around an intergroup equilibrium that is established through a process of bargaining and compromise between the two groups. Preston and Post (1975, p. 68) give the example of two manufacturing industries, one which supplies materials to the other. The supply industry may seek tariff protection from the government to keep imports out and prices up. The consuming industry, on the other hand, would oppose protection since this would lead to higher materials costs.

The ultimate outcome depends upon the relative political power of the two affected groups.

Many times, however, the gains from government programs go to a few special interests while the losses are dispersed across many individuals. While in aggregate the losses may be great, spread over many people, they tend to be quite small for each individual. For those who gain, the benefits per person can be substantial.

For example, Friedman and Friedman (1990, p. 293), provide estimates of the cost of subsidizing the American merchant marine. Their estimate is $600 million per year or $15,000 per year for each person employed or actively involved in the industry. The costs are borne by the entire population and come to around $3 per person per year. It is worthwhile for the merchant marine industry to spend substantial amounts of money and effort to maintain these subsidies. On the other hand, individual taxpayers gain little if the programs are cancelled.

Those who gain from government programs have a powerful monetary incentive to lobby legislators, influence public opinion and contribute to candidates who support beneficial legislation. The losers, on the other hand, lose such a small amount that it is not worth a great deal of effort to actively oppose proposed programs. The result is that even if the losses from a program are larger than the gains, the program may still be implemented. If many public programs are like that, then in the aggregate, society may lose a great deal from government action.

Benefits First—Costs Later

One set of theories of representative government holds that a politician's objective is to maximize votes and get elected and reelected. One consequence of attempting to achieve this objective is that politicians have very short time horizons. That is, they will support programs that yield benefits no later than two, four or six years in the future, depending on their term of office.

An example is the Reagan economic program of 1981. This program consisted of tax reductions, tight money policy and reductions in government regulation to stimulate economic growth and lower inflation. One immediate consequence of this program was the recession of

1981–1983. The program, however, yielded benefits before the end of the president's term of office with lower inflation and interest rates, and an economic expansion well on its way by election day. Had the benefits of the program only begun after the presidential election of 1984, it would have been unlikely that President Reagan would have sought reelection.

Attempting to achieve the objective to get reelected means that politicians have an incentive to support programs that have benefits first and costs later. In addition, programs with clearly definable benefits and hidden, ambiguous costs are also favored by vote seeking politicians. Of course, the public interest may be well served by these programs. However, the pressures to be reelected result in programs with benefits in the distant future and immediate costs receiving low priority, even if these are very worthwhile. Conversely, high priority is given to less desirable programs if they yield immediate benefits and distant costs.

It is an unusual case where a politician ignores his or her own interest to get reelected if it is at odds with the public interest. In fact, such cases are so rare, that they prompted President John F. Kennedy, while he was a U.S. Senator, to write a book entitled *Profiles in Courage* (1955). In this book, Kennedy documented and highlighted several such examples throughout American history.

Inefficiency in the Public Sector

As was pointed out in the previous chapter, the price system provides the incentives for firms to produce goods and services as efficiently as possible. Competitive forces and the desire to maximize profits are the means by which these incentives are provided. In fact, in a purely competitive situation, only those firms which have maximized production efficiency can survive.

In the public sector, on the other hand, the incentives to achieve efficiency in the provision of public services are indirect. Incentives are provided through the political system by voters, legislators and appointed commissions. If efficiency in the provision of these services is not achieved, then this indirect process may take some time to make adjustments. In many situations, adequate adjustments may never be made.

This indirect process may involve voting a party or elected official out of office. However, many issues are usually involved in a decision as to which candidate to vote for. Waste and inefficiency in the provision of public services may be hidden under an array of other problems and issues.

The process may also involve legislatures passing laws which attempt to provide incentives for the efficient administration of government programs. However, dedicated public administrators must implement these laws and deal with an entrenched bureaucracy protected by civil service status. This bureaucracy may remain largely unaffected by attempts to streamline public programs.

Special commissions perform studies and make recommendations to produce government services more efficiently. However, most reports seem to end up on a bookshelf rather than being implemented.

The problem is that the direct incentives of profit, loss and competition in the private sector are not present. As Burkhead, Fox and Holland (1967, p. 4) note:

"However, in the public sector there is no reason to assume that there is an inherent tendency to maximize efficiency. . . . The stimulus of competition and the quest for profit and survival which are presumed to enforce efficiency in private markets are lacking here."

Another problem in the public sector is that government outputs are difficult to measure. How does one measure the amount of education received by the students, the level of national defense provided, or the degree of fire protection supplied? If outputs are difficult to measure, then how can it be determined if the cost of producing that output is too high?

The problem of measuring government output leads to a perverse relationship between the efficiency of a government program and the level of expenditures devoted to it. It has been argued that the public agency that has been inefficient may be given a budget increase. Peter F. Drucker (1969, p. 13) has observed: "Indeed, the typical response of government to the failure of an activity is to double its budget and staff." In the private sector, inefficiency would lead to losses and elimination of the wasteful activities.

Another source of inefficiency concerns the behavior of the government bureaucrats who administer the various public sector programs. Niskanen (1971) argues that bureaucrats attempt to maximize the size of the budget under their control. He argues that increasing the budget increases the prestige, power and emoluments of the bureaucrats and that larger budgets insure the continuing survival of the programs which they administer. The only constraint on the bureaucrat is that the total costs of supplying the service must not exceed the available budget.

This behavior leads to two possible outcomes. One is that public services would be overproduced. On the basis of his analysis, Niskanen (1971) concludes that the level of output produced by the public sector may be as much as two times as great as it would be if a competitive industry had produced it. The other outcome of his analysis is that rather than increasing the amount of services produced, the budget is spent on inefficiency and waste.

Finally, one special interest that has developed over the years is the group of bureaucrats who administer and run the various public programs. These individuals have a strong self interest in preserving the programs which they control. They can lobby effectively for public programs even if these are inefficiently run and largely ineffective. The result is a tendency to perpetuate waste and inefficiency in government.

The Public Sector and the Private Sector Compared

The free enterprise system is far from being perfect. It suffers from a number of shortfalls including the lack of adequate competition in some industries, failure to take externalities fully into account in private decisions, insufficient provision of public goods, an undesirable degree of income inequality, and a tendency for recessions and inflation to occur. The public sector, however, also suffers from a number of shortfalls. These include the unintended effects of public programs, the tendency for special interests to gain at the expense of the general population, programs which have benefits first and costs later to be emphasized, and a bias toward inefficiency and waste. The problem is that neither is perfect. The choice is between two imperfect institutions whose shortfalls are somewhat different.

There are some individuals who hold liberal views who would expand the role of government in the economy with only a token glance at the problems created by government programs. There are some conservatives who would do just the opposite and reduce the size and scope of government with little regard to the problems of the free enterprise system. This analysis suggests that neither approach is sufficient. There is an important role for the public sector in a free enterprise system. However, this role must recognize the shortcomings of both the private and public sectors and design public programs which seek to emphasize the positive aspects of both institutions and correct for the shortfalls of each. Whether public officials act in this manner depends in part on the government structure and the process by which public policies are conceived and implemented. These are the subjects to which we now turn.

The Structure of Government in the United States

The system of government in the United States is set forth in the Constitution. The Constitution expressly details the powers of the national government. It reserves to the states or to the people all powers not given to the national government or forbidden to the states. The system created in the Constitution is one of shared powers among levels of government. In addition, a system of checks and balances was developed for the national government through creation of three separate branches: the executive, the legislative, and the judicial.

The Executive Branch

The structure of the United States government is shown in Figure 3.1. By far the largest, and most visible branch of the government is the executive. The president is responsible for administering all laws, proposing legislation and suggesting taxation and spending proposals to Congress. The president oversees thirteen cabinet departments and over 400 offices, independent agencies, administrations, boards, foundations and government corporations (See U.S. Government Manual, 1994–95).

An example of the structure of a cabinet level department is shown in Figure 3.2. As illustrated in the figure, the Department of Commerce consists of a variety of agencies, bureaus and offices which are responsible for carrying out the policies of the government.

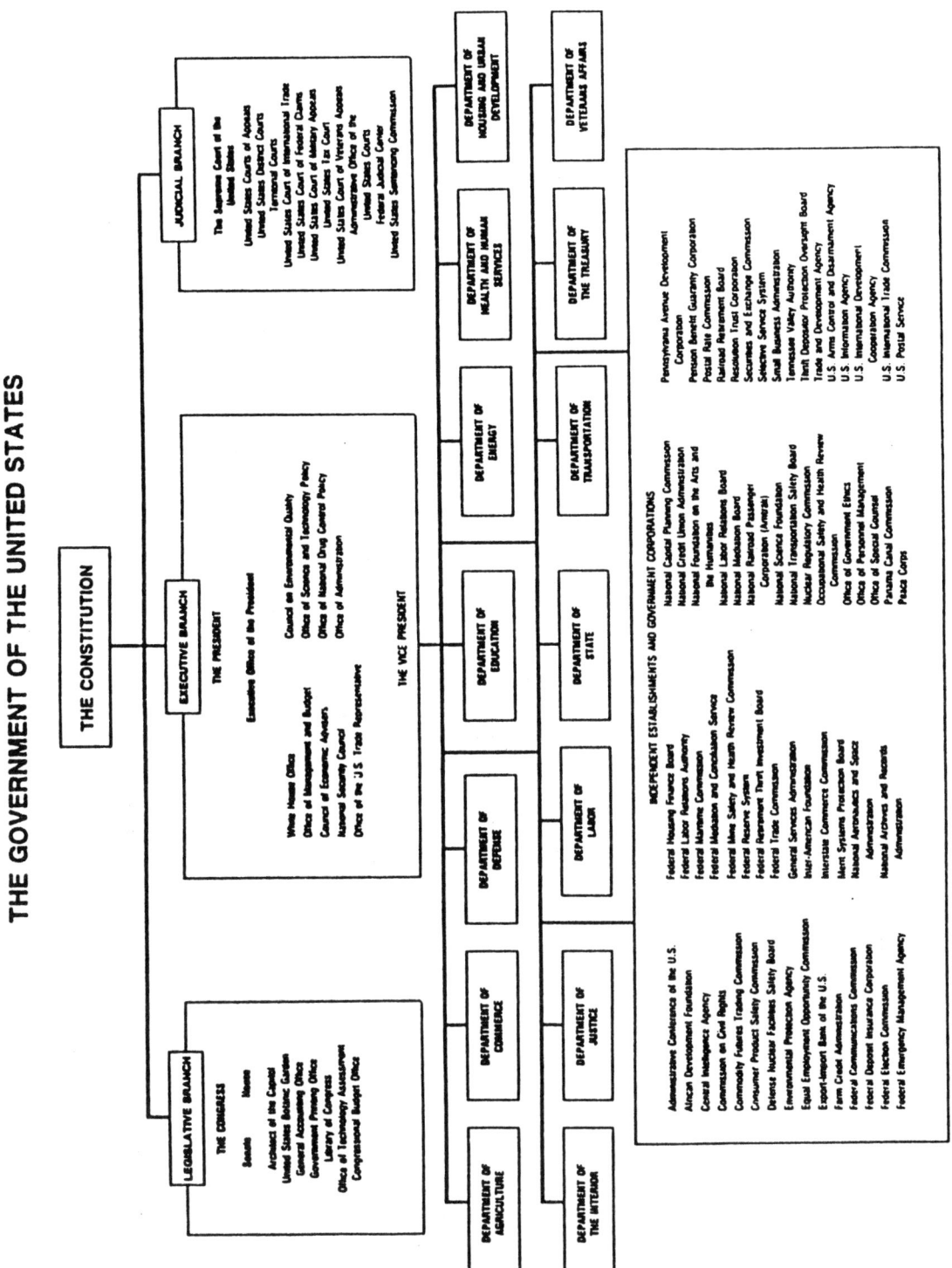

Figure 3.1: Structure of the United States Government
(Source: *U.S. Government Manual*, Office of the Federal Register, 1994–95)

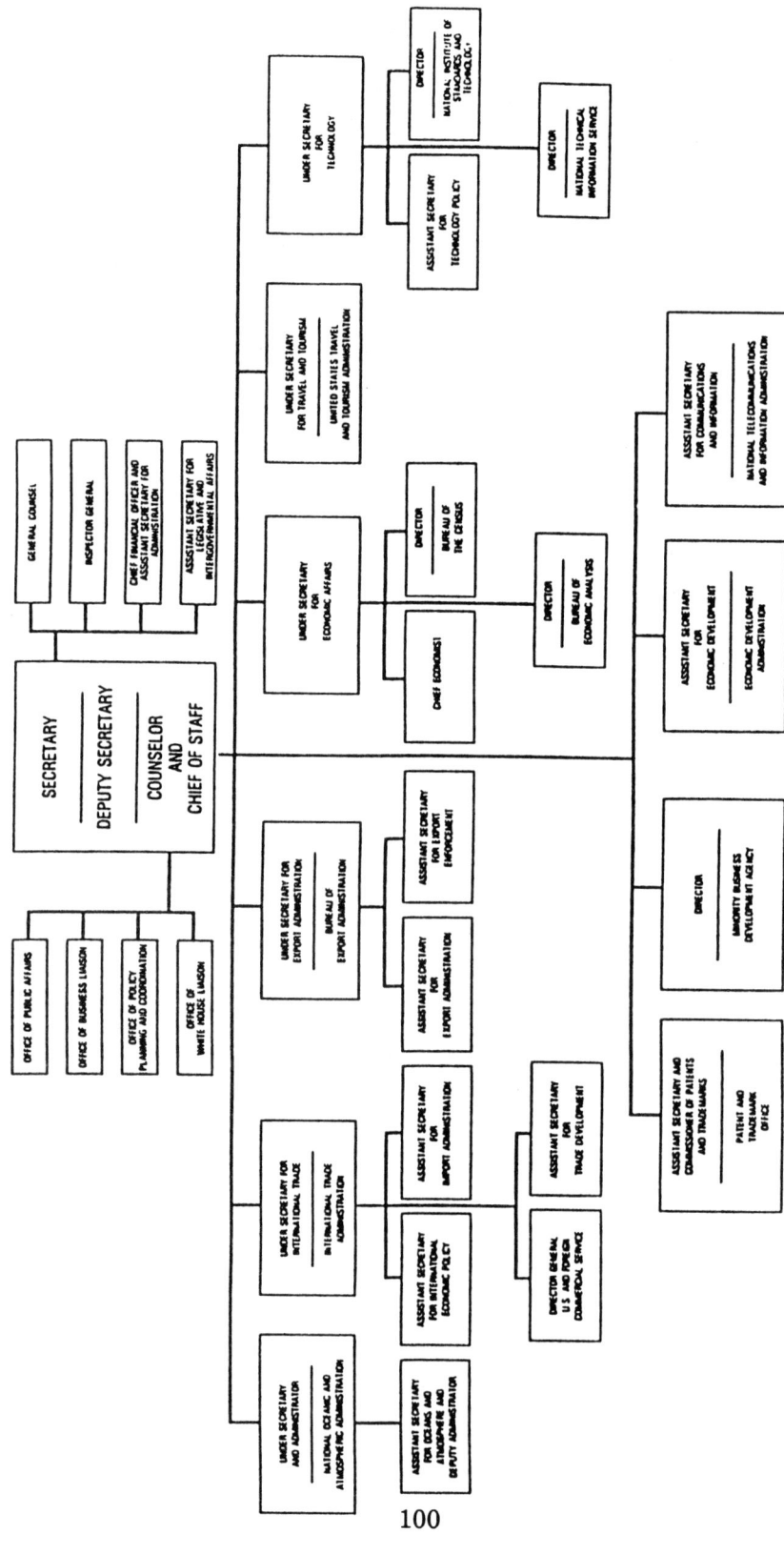

Figure 3.2: Structure of the Department of Commerce
(Source: *U.S. Government Manual*, Office of the Federal Register, 1994–95)

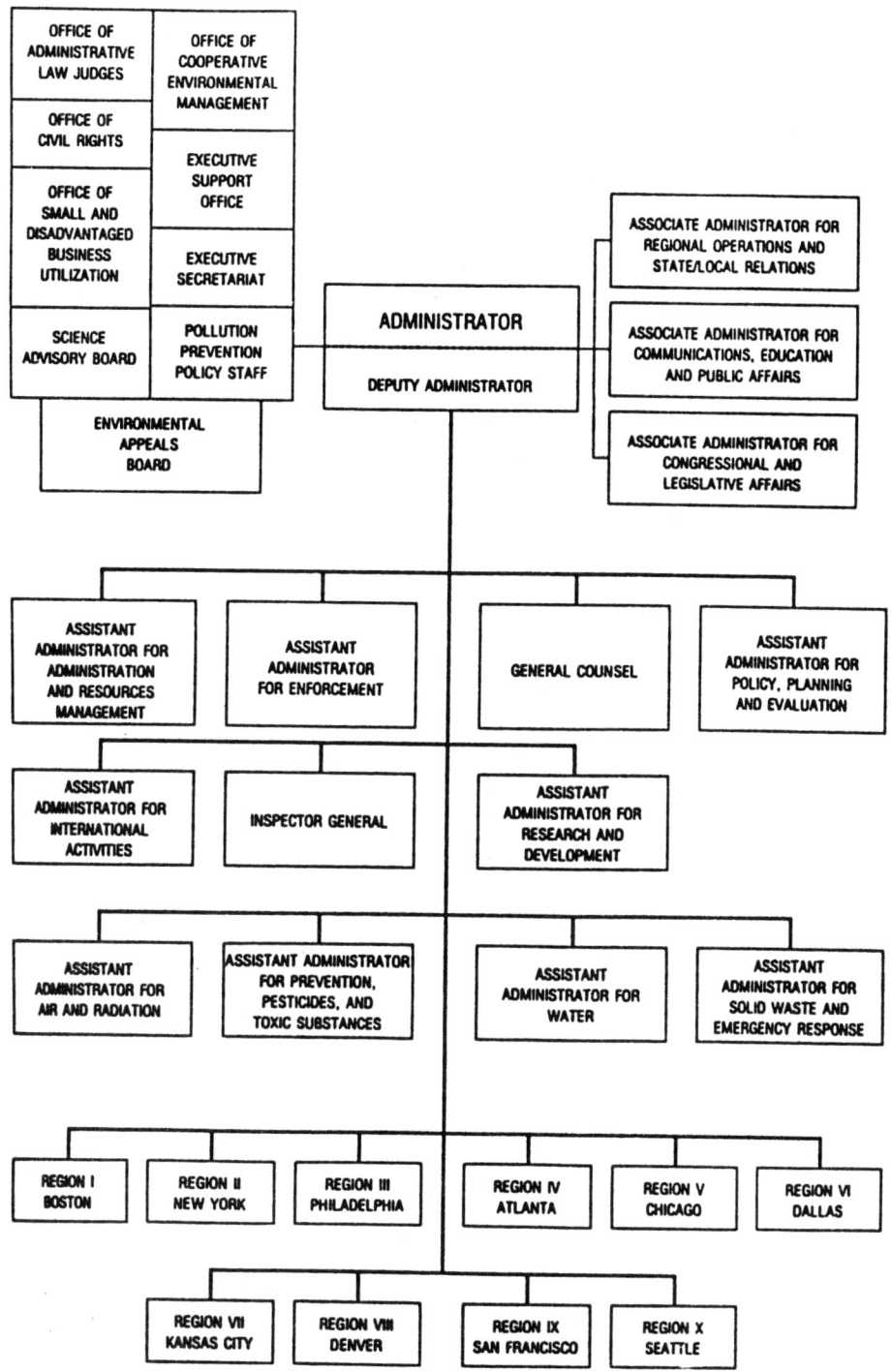

Figure 3.3: **Structure of the Environmental Protection Agency (EPA)** (Source: *U.S. Government Manual*, Office of the Federal Register, 1994–95)

A variety of agencies, independent of Cabinet level departments, are also under the purview of the executive branch. Many of these agencies were set up by Congress to administer laws and issue regulations in order to implement legislation concerning a particular area. An example is the Environmental Protection Agency, depicted in Figure 3.3. The agency is responsible for regulating and monitoring air, water, and noise pollution throughout the United States.

The Federal Home Loan Bank Board is another independent agency responsible for regulating the savings and loan industry. The agency issues regulations and oversees the workings of the industry. The number of regulations issues by these and other independent agencies and other regulatory bodies have increased dramatically during the 1970's and 80's.

The Legislative Branch

The legislative branch consists of the Senate and the House of Representatives. Congress has the power to pass all laws and can exercise some control over the administrative branch through the appropriations power. Each house of Congress has an elaborate committee structure with permanent committees and subcommittees each exercising jurisdiction over specific policy areas. A listing of the standing committees is shown in Table 3.1.

The committee system results in the Congress being susceptible to pressures from special interest groups. The political party having control of each house appoints committee chairmen through a seniority system. Committee chairmen exercise substantial control over the legislation under their purview. Thus, it is possible for special interests to prevent adverse legislation from being voted out of committee or to promote special legislation by influencing only a few congressmen and senators.

Because of the complexity of the regulations which the federal government administers, Congress has tended to pass laws which provide only general guidelines as to how regulations should be administered along with the overall intent of regulatory action. The details are usually left to the administrative agencies responsible for promulgating the regulations. The result is that Congress has transferred a considerable amount of power to these agencies.

Table 3.1. Standing Committees of the Congress

House Committee	Senate Committee
Agriculture	Agriculture, Nutrition, and Forestry
Appropriations	Appropriations
Armed Services	Armed Services
Banking, Finance and Urban Affairs	Banking, Housing, and Urban Affairs
Budget	Budget
District of Columbia	Commerce, Science, and Transportation
Education and Labor	Energy and Natural Resources
Energy and Commerce	Environmental and Public Works
Foreign Affairs	Finance
Government Operations	Foreign Relations
House Administration	Governmental Affairs
Judiciary	Judiciary
Merchant Marine and Fisheries	Labor and Human Resources
Post Office and Civil Service	Rules and Administration
Public Works and Transportation	Small Business
Rules	Veterans' Affairs
Science, Space and Technology	
Small Business	
Standards of Official Conduct	
Veterans' Affairs	
Ways and Means	

(Source: *U.S. Government Manual,* Office of the Federal Register, 1994–95)

Since the laws passed by Congress are subject to considerable interpretation, the agencies have great leeway in deciding how to administer a particular law. Thus, the president, in his power to appoint administrators of these agencies can exercise considerable control over regulatory activities.

The Judicial Branch

The third branch of the United States government is the judiciary. The courts interpret the statutes and provide a mechanism for appeal of decisions of state courts (if a question of federal law is involved) and the decisions of regulatory agencies. Thus, individuals and organizations not satisfied with a decision from a regulatory body can appeal the decision through the court system.

The role of the courts in interpreting the law can be crucial in altering the course of public policy. For example, in the famous 1954 Supreme Court Decision, *Brown vs. the Board of Education of Topeka*, the court struck down the concept of separate but equal and stated that separate school facilities for black children was inherently unequal. This decision served as a stimulus to the civil rights movement that resulted in numerous laws dealing with discrimination being enacted by the federal government and blacks advancing to a considerable extent in American society. Thus, the courts, especially the Supreme Court, play an important role in the public policy process.

Although the United States judiciary is not elected, it is not immune from political considerations. The president appoints the Supreme Court justices with the advise and consent of the Senate. These appointments to the court usually reflect the president's own political philosophy and thus it is expected that the justices will vote in a manner that is coincident with the president's ideas. However, this is not always the case. For example, Chief Justice Earl Warren was appointed by President Eisenhower and served until 1969. Although he was considered a conservative at the time, the court under his tenure has been regarded as one of the most liberal.

State and Local Government

The system of shared powers has resulted in the states retaining a variety of important functions including education, maintenance of the highway system, public safety, and administration of justice. The individual states also charter corporations and some banks. State laws govern legal agreements between individuals and organizations so that the laws pertaining to a particular contract depend on the state in which it was established. Local government powers emanate from the states. Local governments are concerned not only with police and fire protection, garbage collection, sewerage and other municipal functions, but also in attracting and keeping industry in their areas. Thus, local government (either city, township or county), may be involved in a variety of programs including area planning, issuance of industrial revenue bonds, special tax breaks, etc. to encourage business to locate in their areas.

Federal Grants in Aid

There has been a substantial erosion of state powers, with the national government exercising broad control over a variety of activities originally under the purview of the states. One policy measure that has contributed to this erosion of power is a system of grants in aid from the federal government to the states and cities. These grants are usually on a matching basis. The grants encourage states and cities to adopt policies and implement programs which have broad national objectives. For example, the interstate highway system was built by the states with the federal government contributing 90 percent of the cost through a grant in aid program.

Advocates of the grant in aid system argue that there are programs whose benefits accrue nationwide and not just within the borders of particular states or cities. In other words, certain public programs have externalities associated with them. A grant in aid program is viewed as a means to include broad national objectives into the policy making process at both the state and local levels. In addition, it is argued that states and cities cannot expand taxes to pay for many programs since they are constrained by the competition from other areas. If taxes are too high, industry and individuals may leave for lower taxing districts. Thus, the grant in aid system is favored as a means of assisting states and cities in developing public programs which could not be developed because of an overall revenue constraint.

On the other side, opponents of the system of federal grants in aid to the states and cities argue that it erodes the federal system established by the Constitution. One outcome of these grants is the transfer of effective control of programs to the federal government. It establishes the rules and regulations that must be followed by the states in order to receive grants. Less and less discretion is accorded the states in the administration of their own programs.

Further, it is argued that the grant in aid system is used as a stick to require states to subscribe to federal standards in policy areas that have only a vague relationship to the programs for which grants are designed. While these federal standards are largely worthwhile, it is argued that state control is again preempted by the national government. For example, in 1984, President Reagan signed a bill into law requiring that all states establish a minimum age of 21 years for legally drinking alcoholic beverages. The purpose of the legislation was to reduce drunk driving accidents by teenagers. States that did not comply would face a cut off of federal highway funds.

Finally, it is argued that the grant in aid system leads to waste and inefficiency in public programs. Public officials at the state and local levels are well aware of the income generating effects of government grants. The influx of federal money can have a positive impact on employment and incomes in a given area. These positive income effects may be sufficient to encourage states and cities to start programs and obtain federal aid even though there is little desire and few benefits in the community from the program. The obtainment of the grant becomes the benefit. Thus, states and cities are encouraged by the system to undertake new programs and expand existing ones even though few benefits may result.

Consolidation Movement

The federal system of government has also resulted in a number of overlapping and competing jurisdictions. In most metropolitan areas, residents and businesses receive services or pay taxes to a number of governmental entities. Typically, an individual or business would be under the jurisdiction of a general purpose local government (city, township, borough or village), a school district, a sewerage and water authority, a council of governments, and a variety of planning districts in addition to the county, state, and national governments. The Advisory Commission on Intergovernmental Relations (ACIR, 1973, p. 3) describes the extreme case of Whitehall, Pennsylvania in which residents were subject to 17 different governments or quasi-governmental units.

This hodgepodge of governments has provided impetus to the movement to consolidate governments at the local level. Consolidation is viewed as a way of reducing the confusion, duplication and overlap present when many governmental units are present. In addition, it is argued that small sized governments produce services inefficiently. If consolidation would be implemented, then the size of government could be increased and economies of scale could be achieved in producing government services.

Further, externalities may be present in the provision of many services at the local level. This is especially true, it is argued, for services provided by central cities. Residents and businesses located in the suburbs reap the benefits of city government programs without paying the cost. Consolidation is a means of assuring that all beneficiaries pay for the services which they consume.

On the other hand, it is argued that the framers of the Constitution were intent on establishing a compound republic with responsibilities and powers shared among a variety of governments. This compound republic was developed in order to assure that power would not be concentrated in the hands of a few, but rather dispersed over a large number of individuals. McKenzie (1980, p. 202) states:

> "Clearly, the democratic system established was intended to be a mechanism for the social control of government; its purpose was to permit maximum attainment of individual freedom by controlling government."

Consolidation of governments in this view would substantially diminish the social control of government and may lead to the erosion of freedom.

In addition, this compound republic leads to competition among governments which may be quite beneficial. If governments are forced to compete with each other, similar to businesses in a competitive environment, then services may be provided in a more efficient manner. In addition, the services that are provided would emphasize those that are most desired by the residents and businesses with the jurisdiction. Local governments which were inefficient, provided few services that were desired, and levied high taxes, would be subject to flight on the part of residents and business. That is, individuals and business can "vote with their feet" and choose a locality which provides services more efficiently or provides a package of services better tailored to their needs. Consolidation of governments, according to this line of reasoning, would result in diminished competition and thus reduced incentives for efficient provision of services in line with the preferences of those who reside in the jurisdiction.

The Public Policy Process

The public policy process is the mechanism by which public sector programs and policies are formulated, evaluated and implemented. The diverse and decentralized nature of the government system in the United States results in a process that is extremely complex at times and simplistic at others. The exact process depends on the issue being examined and can involve merely persuading the right public official or can require hearings by many committees of Congress. The process may differ for different levels of government.

Although it is quite complex, it is useful to examine the nature of the public policy process. This is because, even though there may be many exceptions to the process presented, an understanding of the typical process provides knowledge as to how the system works and why exceptions to the system exist. Many features of the policy making process are common to a variety of policy areas. Thus, it is useful to inquire into the nature of these common elements.

There have been a variety of attempts to model the public policy process including analyses by Preston and Post (1975), Dye (1995), Dolbeare (1982, 1992), and Tombari (1984). These attempts to model this process consist of both graphic depictions and verbal descriptions. The model that is developed in this section has been developed by synthesizing the work of these authors. Thus, it represents neither complete originality nor the product of one person's thoughts. The model does provide useful insights into the public policy process.

The model of the public policy process is presented in Figure 3.4. This model expands the linkage between the societal elements and the public sector response presented in Figure 2.1 of the previous chapter. In that chapter, it was stated that the political system links the societal elements to the public sector response. The model presented in Figure 3.4 illustrates how that linkage occurs.

Societal Elements

The first box in the figure contains the societal elements. The focus here is not with issues and problems, but rather with the social, economic and political leaders, the interest groups and the general public who are the members of society who represent particular points of view or are directly or indirectly affected by changes in one or more societal elements. These are the actors in the political process who lobby, influence public opinion and support candidates for office. These individuals attempt to influence public policy through the political system.

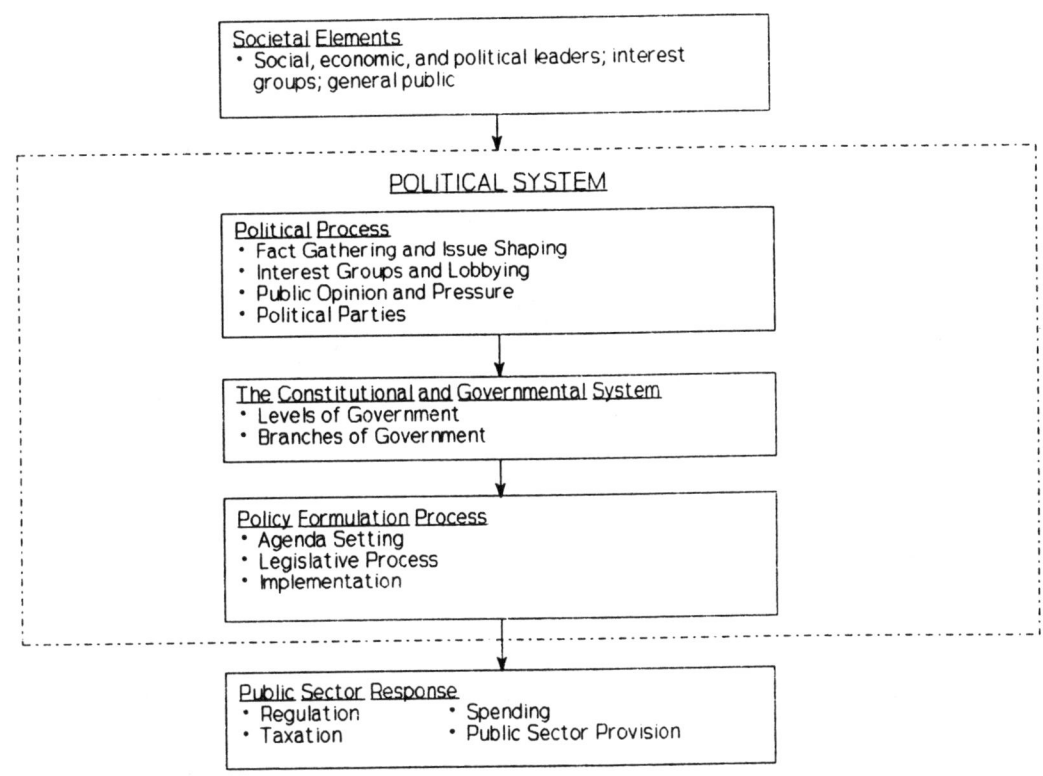

Figure 3.4. A Model of the Public Policy Process

Political Process

The political system consists of the political process, the constitutional and governmental system and the explicit policy formulation process. The political process many times begins with fact gathering and issue shaping performed by foundations, presidential commissions, private think tanks and government and university researchers.

Interest groups and lobbyists apply political pressure to legislators to introduce specific pieces of legislation or vote for particular bills. In addition, Dolbeare (1982) points out that these groups can also provide important sources of information to the political process. By clearly delineating their side of an issue, these groups furnish the political process with a set of ideas and policy recommendations which can be debated, discussed and revamped. The competition of ideas between interest groups can lead to better ideas being adopted by the political system, and poor ideas being put aside.

Dolbeare (1982) states that the general public may also participate in the process of policy choice, although less regularly than special interest groups. He mentions grass roots letter writing campaigns generated by industries adversely affected by policies under consideration as one mechanism through which the general public participates.

Attempts by business to mobilize public opinion include the efforts of banks and savings and loan associations in 1983 to stage a letter writing campaign to influence Congress not to pass legislation requiring income tax withholding of interest and dividend income. Although not subject to withholding, interest and dividends are still considered taxable income. These financial institutions contacted customers by mail suggesting they write their Senators and Representatives and urge them not to vote for the proposal. The legislation failed and income tax withholding of interest and dividends was not required.

Public opinion can also be affected by the news media or by political advertising. However, Dye (1995) argues that public opinion rarely affects public policy. Instead, he believes that public policy shapes public opinion. This is because few people have opinions on many policy questions, public opinion changes rapidly, and few policy makers have a clear perception of what mass opinion is.

As an example, during his term of office, President Carter was frequently criticized for making decisions based on public opinion. Frequently the decisions that were made did not seem to have widespread public approval. Ronald Reagan, on the other hand, during the 1980 presidential election did not seem to base his policy suggestions on public opinion. Yet, many of the policies which he proposed during that campaign had a clear appeal to the voters. His policy recommendations seemed to lead and shape public opinion.

Political parties are also part of the political process. However, Dye (1995) states that their impact on the public policy process is overestimated. He views political parties as "brokerage" organizations committed to winning public office instead of advancing policy positions. Indeed, political party labels are much less meaningful today than in the past with ticket splitting by voters taking on added importance.

Policy Formulation Process

The individuals, interest groups and the general population interact with the governmental system in the policy formulation process. (The structure of the governmental system is described above.) The policy formulation process consists of agenda setting and the legislative and implementation processes. Each of these are discussed in turn.

Agenda Setting

The issues which are raised in the political process may eventually become part of the public policy agenda. This is the set of issues that are perceived as important enough to be examined by the governmental system.

Of the many issues which are raised through the political process, very few become part of the policy agenda. Issues become part of the agenda through strong political action or wide public appeal. Dye (1995, p. 348) argues:

> "Creating an issue, dramatizing it, calling attention to it, and pressuring government to do something about it are important political tactics. These tactics are employed by influential individuals, organized interest groups, political planning organizations, political candidates and officeholders, and perhaps most importantly, the mass media. These are the tactics of 'agenda setting'."

Many times an issue becomes part of the public policy agenda because it has a person or a small group of people who become spokespersons for the issue. For example, Ralph Nader has become the spokesperson for many consumer oriented issues. Martin Luther King was the spokesperson for the Civil Rights movement of the early 1960's.

The Legislative Process

Once an issue becomes part of the policy agenda, it moves through the legislative process. At the federal level, a bill is introduced by a member of Congress and must make its way through several committees and be voted on by both the House of Representatives and the Senate. An illustration of how a bill eventually becomes law is shown in Figure 3.5. This process is similar in most state legislatures as well.

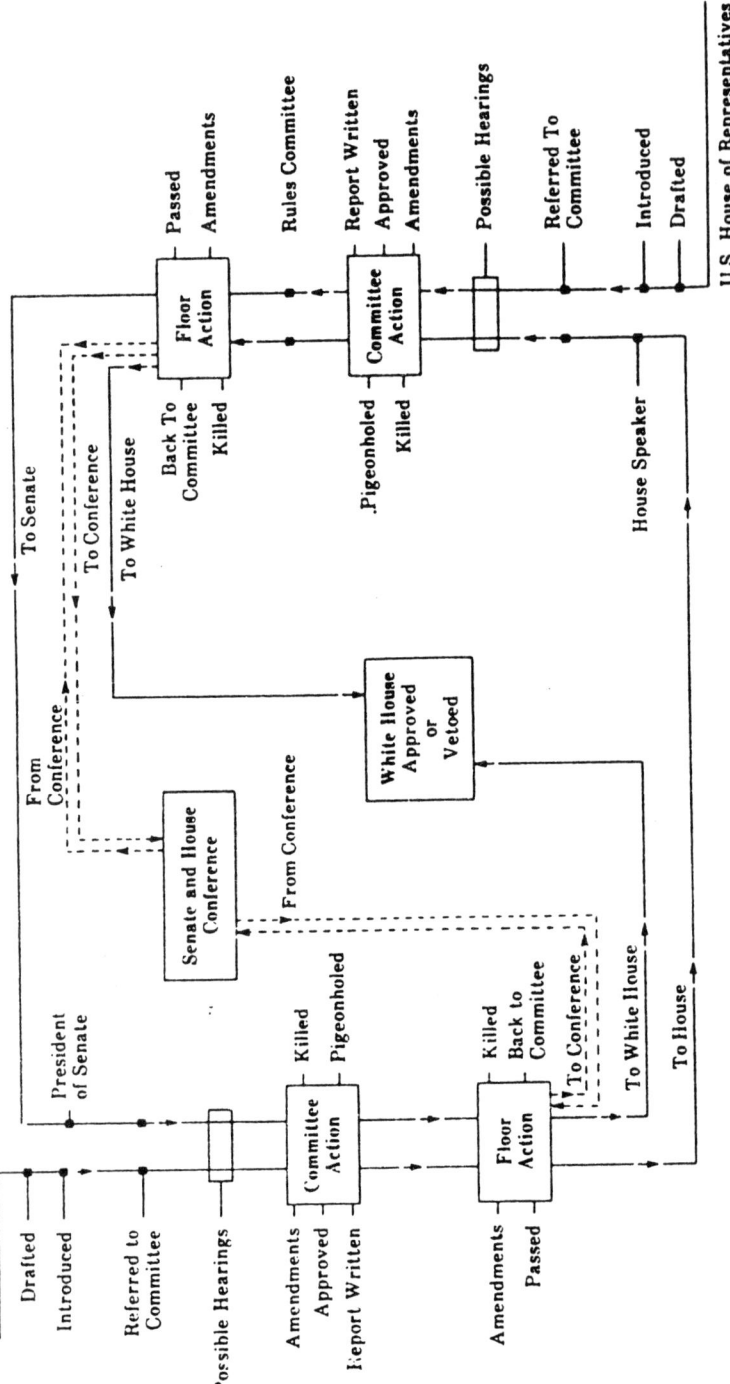

All phases of lawmaking do not lend themselves to lucid charting. For example—Bills are not always introduced by individual members of Congress; sometimes committees introduce them.

A bill approved by one chamber does not always go to a committee in the other. The chamber receiving the bill may have a similar one of its own ready for floor action. If so, and it acts affirmatively, it approves its own version, substituting its language for that of the other—under the latter's initials and number.

There may or may not be a House-Senate conference (dashed lines) to try to resolve the differences between the two versions. Often one chamber agees to the other's changes without a conference.

A bill need not be approved by the President to become law. If, under ordinary circumstances, he does not approve it within a specified time, it becomes law automatically. If he disapproves a bill, Congress can overrule him.

Source: "How A Bill Becomes A Law," Hon. Robert H. Michael, U.S. House of Representatives, *Congressional Record*, February 8, 1979.

Figure 3.5. How a Bill Becomes a Law

After a bill is introduced, it is usually referred to a committee which has jurisdiction over the policy area which the bill addresses. The committee may hold hearings on the proposed legislation, and in the process, amend the bill. The proposal is then either approved and forwarded to the full house, killed at the committee level or pigeonholed, which means it is tabled. In the House of Representatives, the bill must also make its way through the Rules Committee.

If the bill is sent to the floor for debate, amendments may be added and the bill finally voted on. If passed by one house, it would then be forwarded to the other chamber to undergo a similar process. If different versions of the bill are passed by both houses, the proposal goes to a joint Senate-House Conference Committee. Differences in the two pieces of legislation are then settled in that committee and the final version of the bill sent to both houses for approval. If approved by both House and Senate, the bill is sent to the President who can sign or veto it. If vetoed, the legislation can still become law by two thirds vote of both houses of Congress.

At each stage in the legislative process, Congress is vulnerable to the efforts of special interest groups to influence the proposal. Lobbyists can call on particular key Senators and Representatives such as those who chair or are members of the committees considering the legislation. Interest groups can also testify at the committee hearings and attempt to persuade the members that their position should be adopted. Interest groups can use the media to generate public pressure and stage letter writing campaigns to influence votes. Thus, each step in the legislative process represents a "pressure point" in which legislation can be altered, killed, or otherwise influenced by special interests, including business.

The legislative process is not complete, however, when a bill becomes a statute. Many public policies require the establishment of a new agency to monitor compliance, and money must be appropriated to implement the law. This is the appropriations stage of the legislative process. The President submits a proposed budget to Congress which is referred to the Appropriations Committees of both houses. The budget that is submitted and eventually approved by the Congress reflects changes in priorities and the extent to which the government is willing to enforce the letter as well as the spirit of the legislation. The appropriations stage is another "pressure point" in which special interests may influence public policy.

Implementation

The next step in the public policy process is implementation. As was discussed previously in this chapter, Congress tends to write laws which lay out broad principles. Details are left to the executive branch. Part of the implementation of these laws can be accomplished through executive order of the president in which the White House details the specifics of a policy based on legislation passed by Congress. Cabinet departments and independent agencies also make policy decisions in their interpretation of the statutes and in the manner in which they enforce provisions of the legislation. The president, through the appointment power, can influence the manner in which policy is shaped and administered by the various agencies in the executive branch.

For example, President Carter appointed Joan Claybrook, who was a key aid to Ralph Nader, as the head of the National Highway Traffic Safety Administration (NHTSA) in 1977. This agency is responsible for regulating the safety of vehicles on the highway system in the United States. In 1978, the agency made a decision to require air bags in all passenger cars by 1982. After the 1980 election, President Reagan appointed Raymond Peck as the head of NHTSA. Early in the administration, Mr. Peck rescinded the decision of Ms. Claybrook.

At the implementation level, pressure can be exerted by special interests, including business, to interpret legislation in a favorable manner. The political process is used by lobbying regulatory agencies, influencing public opinion and sponsoring studies which seem to confirm the validity of the particular interest's point of view. Dolbeare (1982, p. 47) argues: "The politics of implementation can be as bitterly fought as any other part of the policy-making process, and perhaps more determinative of the actual meaning of new public policy."

The politics of implementation continued in the air bag case described above. A variety of consumer oriented interest groups including the Center for Auto Safety and Public Citizen, Inc., headed by Joan Claybrook, pressured NHTSA and the administration to alter the air bag decision. Sensing a possible political problem in an election year, the Reagan administration changed its mind in 1984, and devised a complicated plan for auto safety which mandated air bags along with other "passive restraints" as part of the solution (Conte & Wautat, 1984).

Another example concerns the Federal Trade Commission (FTC) and a proposal to require used car dealers to post known defects on all used cars. This regulation was bitterly fought by the automobile dealers, arguing that the provisions would be unenforceable and would penalize "honest" dealers. In the end, the FTC did not adopt the proposed rule.

Congress is also involved in implementation of public policy. Congressional committees and subcommittees conduct an oversight function to assure that government agencies are conducting policy in a manner which is consistent with the intent of the enabling legislation. Both the appropriations committees and policy area committees conduct this oversight function. The General Accounting Office and the Congressional Budget Office both are utilized by Congress in this oversight function by tracing the use of funds and conducting studies of the problems that are dealt with by the government agencies.

The politics of implementation is also very much alive at the congressional oversight level as well. For example, when Anne Gorsuch Burford was head of the Environmental Protection Agency in the early 1980's, Congress conducted a long series of hearings into the manner in which the agency was run, especially its enforcement of the hazardous waste provisions of the environmental laws. The hearings led to widespread media attention and arguments by environmentalists that the agency was not enforcing the law properly and was being dominated by the interests of polluters. Ms. Burford subsequently resigned.

The court system also participates in implementation of public policy through the power of judicial review. Tombari (1984, p. 152) cites the example of the Occupational Safety and Health Administration (OSHA). The 1970 act establishing the agency made no provision for search warrants by inspectors. In 1978, the Supreme Court ruled that search warrants were required. However, it provided for easily obtainable warrants. As another example, minutes after the Reagan administration announced its air bag ruling in 1984, State Farm Mutual Insurance Co. and the National Association of Independent Insurers, who are strong air bag advocates, filed suit in federal court against the regulation.

The Public Sector Response

The ultimate outcome of this complicated and seemingly irrational process is the set of public policies which constitute the public sector response to changes in the external environment of business. This response can take the form of regulation, taxation, spending decisions, or public sector provision of goods and services.

Dolbeare (1982, p. 49) asks what does all of this complexity and uncertainty mean for public policy?

"The merits of issues are obviously buried under a heavy layer of ideology, interest, institutional complications, various conflicting priorities, and continuing struggle for political power. They are not lost or irrelevant, but they surely do not control the outcome of the policy making process. Power is parceled out to many participants in this policy making process, each with distinctive goals, and each seeks to gain as much as possible out of the end product."

Strategies for Impacting the Political Process

As described above, business and other interest groups attempt to influence the public sector response by directly or indirectly affecting the political system. During the agenda setting, legislative and implementation processes, various tactics are used to shape ideas, legislation, and the administrative structures set up to enforce the law. These tactics can be generally grouped under the first three elements of the political process: fact gathering and issue shaping, interest groups and lobbying, and public opinion and pressure.

In this section, each of these tactics will be discussed from the standpoint of how business and other interest groups go about influencing political decisions. Knowledge of these tactics serves two functions. The first focuses on the point of view of managers of organizations interested in influencing political decisions. Familiarity with tactics used by business and other interest groups will help managers influence the public sector more effectively. The second is from the broader societal perspective. Understanding of these tactics can help determine to what extent business should be involved in influencing political decisions.

There are a number of arguments both for and against business involvement in politics. Those advocating more business involvement stress the fact that it has the same rights of expression as other interest groups such as labor unions and professional associations. In fact, the involvement of business in the political process may be a strategy to offset similar activities of other groups. Further, business needs to be involved to make sure that information is provided to key administrators and legislators regarding the impact of regulations or taxes on economic goals and the long term viability of industry. The negative impacts of regulation, in addition, may indirectly affect other groups such as employees, local communities, and suppliers. These indirect impacts should be indicated as well.

Those opposed to business involvement cite management incompetence in political areas. The other side argues, however, that if this were true, then the average citizen may also be unqualified to participate. Another concern is with the potential power of corporations which take too active a role in politics. There is a potential danger of the public interest being replaced by business interests. Finally, too much political activity on the part of business may lead to increased public criticism which in turn may lead to more government control. Thus, it is argued that the business manager must evaluate the use of tactics to influence political decisions with regard to their potential benefit in changing public sector responses versus the risk of either increased government involvement in business or adverse public opinion (Frederick, Post and Davis, 1992).

Fact Gathering and Issue Shaping

The information gathering component of the political process may take the form of research studies sponsored or conducted by business, trade associations or other interest groups. The results of this research may be reported as technical reports, serve as the basis for testimony at congressional hearings, and provide background information for personal visits to legislators or legislative aides.

There is a fine line between objective research, in which fact gathering and analysis are used to reach conclusions regarding the appropriate public sector response, and propaganda. Many times, studies conducted by a particular interest group will purport to be objective, when in fact the group seeks to twist objective data to support a particular point of view. Such a tactic may lead to short term gains. However, in a free society, where ideas compete openly, this will only be at the expense of the organization's credibility. Over time, such propaganda may be taken less and less seriously by policy makers and legislators.

In order to utilize the results of objective, issue oriented research at the agenda setting stage, the organization must target relevant groups to be persuaded. These may include the media, legislators on key committees, or the public at large. The desired result will be a focusing of interest on issues identified as important to the organization at the present time and in the future. The agenda will thus be set to include areas of particular importance to the firm.

During the legislative process, the information available on a particular issue can be presented by expert witnesses at congressional hearings or to members of Congress directly. In this way, the position of the organization on an issue is known by relevant actors in the legislative process and can be incorporated into the proposals for legislation. At the implementation stage, research results can be used as testimony in the courts during any litigation in which the organization may be involved. Further, information can be made available to administrative agencies charged with implementing the legislation.

Interest Groups and Lobbying

Business managers who wish to influence the political system can join forces with others with similar interests and goals, open a Washington office, employ lobbyists or sponsor a political action committee (PAC). By using these strategies, the manager may influence the agenda being set, the legislative process, or the implementation phase.

Form Political Coalitions

As management identifies specific issues of interest, it may be beneficial to combine efforts to effectively influence the political process. One relatively inexpensive way for a single organization to increase its influence is to join a trade association. Typically, such an association provides information to its members on the status of legislation and rulings of regulatory agencies, pays for the services of lobbyists or other representatives in Washington, and provides expert witnesses for hearings. The association is an ongoing organization which adapts its specific strategies and goals to the changing political climate.

Sometimes, a coalition is formed around a specific issue, bringing together a variety of interested parties. Such an ad hoc coalition was formed in 1977 to defeat the Consumer Protection Agency Bill. Called the Consumer Issues Working Group, it was made up of 400 firms, business groups, and trade associations organized by Armstrong Cork Company (Guzzardi, 1978). The group was successful in influencing public opinion as well as the Congress and the bill was defeated.

Washington Representatives

A large firm may directly employ a group of people to staff a Washington office. One purpose of these offices is to supply information to the corporation regarding issues and policy changes which are being discussed and debated in Washington. This is essentially a fact gathering function. In addition, the staff can provide logistical support to company officials traveling to Washington to meet with legislators or to give testimony at Congressional hearings.

Firms which are government contractors may also use Washington representatives to market the company's current products or aid in the design of future ones. Finally, the individuals assigned to the Washington office may represent the company's views to the key actors in the political process. Technically, this function is not lobbying, but is more objective, information transmittal. Realistically, however, the purpose is still to influence the various stages of the policy formulation process (Weidenbaum, 1995).

Lobbying

Lobbying focuses both on the legislative process and the implementation phase of the public policy process. At the legislative level, the principle function is to provide factual information to legislators regarding the content of proposed legislation as well as to analyze the impact of a particular bill. Although pressure tactics are used, Aplin and Hegarty (1980) found that positive strategies such as political donations and provision of objective information have a significantly more favorable impact on legislators than do public relations tactics and direct pressure.

Lobbying also is used at the implementation phase. Here people in charge of regulatory and other administrative agencies and those who make appointments to key enforcement positions are the focus. Such lobbying is used to provide information to regulators regarding the impact of proposed rule changes and to influence appointment decisions.

Political Action Committees

The Tillman Act of 1907 prohibits corporations from making direct campaign contributions to candidates for federal office. In 1925, the Corrupt Practices Act broadened the definition of a contribution to include services for the candidate or anything else of value. These restrictions were extended to labor unions by the Labor-Management Relations Act of 1947. In 1955, the AFL-CIO's Committee on Political Education (COPE) began. COPE was established to provide a legal mechanism to conduct political activities which were otherwise prohibited. It was the first political action committee (PAC).

In the past, businessmen contributed individually to political campaigns, but there was relatively little disclosure of who gave how much to whom. During the Watergate era, a number of abuses were made public, including the large contributions to political candidates made by a few "fat cats." The Federal Election Campaign Act of 1971 and amendments to the Act in 1974 and 1976 attempted to address these abuses. The primary goals of these laws is to limit the impact of special interest groups and to promote disclosures of campaign finances. In addition, the laws provide a mechanism for corporations, labor unions, and other interest groups to legally support candidates for federal office.

The laws still prohibit corporations from directly contributing money to candidates. They can, however, use corporate funds to setup and administer political action committees. These PACs must be organized separately from the corporation, although they can solicit voluntary donations from a variety of sources including shareholders, employees, management, and their families. PACs may contribute a maximum of $5,000 per election to each candidate. An individual can contribute a maximum of $5,000 to a PAC per election. (Several states also place similar limits on direct corporate contributions to state level candidates.) In addition, the federal election laws limit an individual person's contributions to a total of $25,000 per year for all candidates for federal office and $3,000 per candidate per campaign ($1,000 each for the primary, runoff, and general election).

PACs can provide "in kind" assistance to candidates in addition to financial aid. For example, they may pay for political consultants to a particular campaign or send mass mailings in support of a candidate. In this way, the actual dollar amount spent for a given candidate for federal office may far exceed the $5,000 limit.

Unfortunately, PACs are also subject to abuse. According to Jackson (1984) the following means are used to circumvent the system:

> "Special-purpose accounts are being used by national political parties to accept donations that would be illegal if given directly to House, Senate or presidential campaigns."

For example, "Walter Mondale's campaign [in 1984] helped set up more than 130 'delegate committees' into which labor-union PACS poured about $400,000" (Jackson, 1984). In addition, both parties have established special building funds for which contributions are solicited to pay for the expenses of national party headquarters. Such funds are not subject to the limits imposed on campaign contributions by the federal election laws.

> "Tax-exempt foundations are being set up by parties and some political-action committees to take donations in excess of legal limits on direct giving."

The National Conservative Foundation has been set up by the National Conservative Political Action Committee (NCPAC). The foundation runs training programs for campaign managers as an educational rather than a political activity. Donors receive a tax deduction as well as protection from disclosure.

> "Creative accounting and 'independent spending' on behalf of favored candidates are being used by special-interest groups to skirt the $5,000 limit on what their political-action committees can give directly to federal candidates."

Unlimited mass mailings, paid television and radio advertising, and similar services can be provided for a candidate by a PAC if such activities are <u>not</u> coordinated with the campaign. Here the candidate does not have control over the content or timing of the message, so this could be either advantageous or harmful.

Another option (called bundling) is for supporters to mail their individual contributions (under the amount allowed by law) to a PAC which then collects and delivers them to the candidate. The total contributed amount in the bundle may greatly exceed the $5,000 limit. Neither the PAC nor individual campaign limits are violated. However, the PAC is recognized by the candidate as having supported their campaign.

> "Loose interpretation of credit rules is allowing bankers to lend their depositors' money to favored candidates without requiring full collateral. Wealthy businessmen may also advance credit on favorable terms."

Senator John Glen's campaign for president in 1984 was financed by $2 million from Ohio banks with a small fraction received as collateral. "Mott Enterprises" was a direct mail firm solely owned by Stewart Mott which gave $407,000 credit to the John Anderson campaign in 1980 when repayment was uncertain. In 1984, the same firm extended about $150,000 credit to Senator Alan Cranston for mass mailings during his presidential campaign.

> "Public disclosure of campaign donations, regarded almost universally as the best cure for vote-buying, is eroding rapidly as money moves underground and federal enforcement efforts wane."

At the grass roots level, money is spent for voter registration and turnout, field representatives, and in the case of unions, encouragement of members to vote for particular candidates. This "soft money" is not disclosed using normal processes. Finally, the Federal Election Commission has not been aggressively enforcing the laws, so that loose interpretations of the law are likely to continue. Thus, the original purpose of the 1971 Federal Election Campaign Act to limit the impact of special interests and promote disclosures has not been achieved.

Public Opinion and Pressure

Presenting a business's point of view to the public is an indirect approach to shaping issues and influencing the legislative and implementation processes.

Business managers may present their positions to community and professional groups, write articles for magazines, newspapers, and journals, and provide information to the media. Care must be taken that the position is correct and defensible, however, rather than only being in the interest of the organization.

The use of the media to educate the public regarding particular issues or the favored point of view is one tactic available. When corporations take a position on a public issue and present it through the media, it is called advocacy advertising. As with other attempts at influencing public opinion, care must be taken that the message is correct and credible.

A letter writing campaign (such as that described in the previous section aimed to defeat the passage of the bill to require withholding of taxes from interest income) is another strategy used to influence public opinion. Since such a campaign is closely tied to the company's image, some caution should be used in developing this strategy.

Advertising also may have the purpose of improving the image of a company or industry. Management expects indirect benefits through increased sales or better recruiting, due to improved public image. The extent to which these benefits occur, however, vary with each situation.

Managerial Implications

The strategies and tactics described above impact the planning, organizing, controlling, and staffing/rewarding functions of management. An overall business plan might include a strategy of influencing the public sector response through the political system. For example, Chrysler had as a part of its strategy for turning the company around in the late 1970's, obtaining guaranteed loans from the federal government. In addition, any large company attempting to merge with another firm in the same industry must convince regulators that the result will not be anti-competitive.

Establishing a Washington office, hiring a lobbyist, staffing a public relations department, or employing individuals to deal directly with government regulators or contractors involve changes to an organization's structure. New positions may be required and reporting relationships adapted to most effectively use these resources to impact the political system.

It may be necessary to select individuals with nontraditional business backgrounds for positions designed to provide the company with people who represent their point of view in Washington. Special knowledge of the political process or industry regulation may be most appropriate. Rewarding these individuals may require performance measures based on the success of the strategy to influence the political system.

In order to determine what is and is not a successful strategy, criteria must be established for both the short and long run. Success in stopping a particular bill may be reached at the cost of poor public relations in the long run. Managers must evaluate the strategies developed and implemented with both benefits and costs in mind.

Proposals for Reform

The political process allows the use of various tactics and strategies by business or other organizations. In order to offset the abuses which occur as well as to limit the influence of special interests, several proposals for reform have been offered.

First, federal financing of elections has been suggested as a means to reduce special interest influence. Such financing is currently done for presidential candidates who receive a certain percentage of the primary vote. Taxpayers are asked to check whether or not they want $1 to go to pay for presidential campaigns. The proposal would extend this financing to all candidates for federal office. However, if such funding were available to all candidates for federal office, there would be a problem determining who would be qualified to receive money and for what level of funding. Also, there is a public policy question of whether this is a proper use of tax monies.

Second, campaign spending limitations for all candidates for federal office have been suggested as a means of reducing abuses. Currently, such limitations are in effect for presidential candidates in order to qualify for federal funds. If candidates were prohibited from spending above a certain amount, then money would have less importance and thus less influence on elections. However, incumbents would be given an even greater edge in elections than they already have. Along with incumbency goes a professional staff, franking privileges from the post office, and public exposure. Incumbent office holders are usually not defeated unless their opponent has considerable financial backing.

In addition, it is doubtful that laws governing spending limitations could not also be circumvented. Iron clad laws which leave little room for abuse would probably also leave little room for the issues, qualifications, and personalities to receive a full public airing.

Finally, setting spending limitations on radio and television advertising or providing free television time to each candidate have been proposed. Very large expenditures are needed to finance TV and radio advertising. The logic of this proposal is that by limiting such advertising or providing such time free, less money would be needed to wage a successful campaign. Thus, money would not be as crucial to campaigns as it currently is. At the present time, television provides the well financed candidates an effective means for presenting their message to the public. Relatively underfunded candidates, such as Jesse Jackson during the 1984 Democratic presidential primaries, cannot afford to use this medium. Spending limits would be one method to put a ceiling on the exposure of each candidate.

Free television time presents a problem for the networks. The television and radio stations are profit-making organizations. Requiring donations of time to political candidates may or may not be in the public interest and may adversely affect a station's competitive position. Such a proposal would probably be vigorously opposed by the radio and television networks.

Although a number of alternatives have been suggested, each carries a new set of problems. Financing campaigns using traditional methods is likely to continue for the foreseeable future.

Summary

The free enterprise system has a number of shortfalls. These include the over-concentration of some industries, the existence of externalities, inadequate provision of public goods, undesirable income inequality, and unstable economic conditions. Thus there is a role for the public sector in a free enterprise system to correct these shortfalls.

The public sector, however, also suffers from a number of shortfalls. These include the unintended effects of public programs, the tendency for special interests to gain at the expense of the general population, programs which have benefits first and costs later to be emphasized, and a bias toward inefficiency and waste. The problem is that neither is perfect. The choice is between two imperfect institutions whose shortcomings are somewhat different.

The system of government in the United States is set forth in the Constitution. It consists of the executive, legislative and judicial branches of the government. In addition, state and local governments share power with the federal government in many areas. There has been a substantial erosion of state powers, with the national government exercising broad control over a variety of activities originally under the purview of the states. The federal system of government has also resulted in a number of overlapping and competing jurisdictions. This has led to a movement to consolidate government at the local level.

The public policy process is the mechanism by which public sector programs and policies are formulated, evaluated and implemented. It consists of the political process and the policy formulation process of agenda setting as well as the legislative and implementation processes.

There are a number of strategies that business can use to impact the political process. These include fact gathering and issue shaping, forming political coalitions, designating Washington representatives, hiring lobbyists, forming PACs, and influencing public opinion. PACs, an outgrowth of the election reform laws of the 1970's, have been used to enhance the ability of business, labor unions, and other interest groups to influence the political system. Unfortunately, they have also been utilized to circumvent the intent of these laws.

Proposals for reform of the political system include federal financing of elections, campaign spending limitations, limits on spending on radio and television advertising, and free radio and television time.

Questions

1. List several externalities that result from the closing of a large plant in a small town. Who gains and who loses from this business decision? What are possible public sector responses to this decision?

2. Suppose government turned over the construction and operation of roads and streets to the private sector? What problems would business have in providing these services?

3. The federal election reform laws had the intent to limit the impact of special interests and to promote disclosure. However, a variety of unintended effects have resulted from the laws. What are these unintended effects and what alternatives does government have to alleviate them?

4. Identify a current governmental project with respect to unintended effects, gainers and losers, and the distribution of costs and benefits over time. Based on this analysis, evaluate the desirability of the project.

5. Should government's role in the economy be expanded?

6. Identify the pressure points in the policy formulation process where a business might make an impact. What strategies are available to business managers at each of these points.

Key Concepts

externalities

public goods

non-exclusion

joint supply

special interests

budget maximization

federal grants in aid

consolidation movement

political process

policy formulation process

Political Action Committees

advocacy advertising

lobbyists

free rider

transfer payments

fiscal policy

monetary policy

national economic planning

industrial policy

special interests

compound republic

pressure points in the legislative process

politics of implementation

Case Analysis: The American Trucking Associations and the Motor Carrier Act of 1980

The Motor Carrier Act of 1935 was a Depression era solution to the economic problems which plagued the trucking industry at that time. It, and other subsequent legislation, legalized price fixing in the industry. Entry and exit into and out of the trucking business was also regulated. New trucking companies or existing carriers interested in expanding the geographic areas covered or commodities carried were required to seek authority from the federal government. Economic regulation of all interstate carriers was under the jurisdiction of the Interstate Commerce Commission (ICC). Collective ratemaking, the euphemism for price fixing, was accomplished through motor carrier rate bureaus. These were groups of carriers within a geographic area which met to agree on prices. Such collective ratemaking agreements were exempt from the anti-trust laws.

The question of deregulation of the trucking industry was largely confined to debates and discussions among academics until President Carter took office in 1977. He appointed several individuals to the ICC who were supporters of deregulation of the trucking and railroad industries. Under the influence of the Carter appointments, the ICC began to interpret the regulatory laws to ease a variety of restrictions on the trucking industry, including entry into the industry. For example, during the 1978 fiscal year, 96.7 percent of all applications for operating rights were granted by the ICC.

The largest, and most well known organization of trucking interests is the American Trucking Associations, Inc. The ATA is a national conglomeration of 51 state trucking associations which also includes the District of Columbia. In addition, the ATA is broken down into 12 independent conferences, each representing a different segment of the industry. These include associations such as the American Movers Conference, the Private Carrier Conference, the National Tank Truck Carriers and the Contract Carriers Conference. The ATA is organized under a tripartite structure of the national organization, the state associations and the 12 conferences. It has a 135 member executive committee and a 450 member board of directors.

The ATA decided to respond to what was termed "creeping deregulation" on the part of the Carter ICC. Bennett Whitlock, Jr., president of the ATA argued, "To combat this rising deregulation threat, the industry must move on the attack." The ATA decided to challenge the ICC decisions in court. Abe Fortas, former Supreme Court Justice was retained to advise on the proper court approach to curb ICC decisions. It also sought a congressional directive telling the ICC to cease and desist its administrative deregulation activities.

Interest in deregulation of the trucking industry was not solely confined to the Carter appointees to the ICC, however. The administration was considering the submission of legislative proposals to Congress to deregulate the industry. Deregulation of the airline industry was accomplished in 1978. With that law enacted, the administration began to concentrate on the railroad and trucking industries.

Advocates of deregulation were also present in the Congress, including Senator Edward M. Kennedy who was in the process of preparing his own legislative proposals. Several public interest lobbies also were deregulation advocates including the consumer interest groups which were directed by Ralph Nader. Common Cause, another public interest lobby, made deregulation of the trucking industry one of the top issues in 1979.

In response to this growing interest in deregulation, the ATA decided to move on the attack and change strategies. The organization was always very reluctant to have any type of deregulation bill be considered in Washington. They feared that even a very limited bill would end up as a springboard for opponents of regulation to pass tough legislation.

In what was characterized as a 180 degree change in thinking, the ATA developed its own deregulation bill which it entitled the "Motor Carrier Regulatory and Safety Improvement Act." The ATA proposal would allow limited rate setting freedom for existing carriers and remove certain operating restrictions. The anti-trust exemption on collective ratemaking was left intact, however.

The ATA proposal was overshadowed in 1979 when the White House, along with Senator Kennedy, introduced legislation in Congress to deregulate the trucking industry. The administration argued that its proposal would lead to lower freight rates, reduced inefficiency and better energy utilization by the industry.

In July of that year, the Senate Commerce, Science and Transportation Committee under the Chairmanship of Senator Howard W. Cannon (D. Nevada) began hearings on what was then called the Carter-Kennedy bill. At the Senate hearings, the ATA argued against deregulation. The Association stated that removal of entry restrictions on new trucking firms would lead to thousands of trucks flooding the highways making safety inspections impossible. The ATA also argued strongly for continuation of the anti-trust exemption for collective ratemaking. The Carter-Kennedy bill would have eliminated this exemption.

In addition to pushing its own proposal before Congress, the ATA continued its attack on deregulation. It undertook a multi-million dollar campaign to alert the public as to what they felt were the dangers of deregulation. NBC newsman Frank Blair was hired to anchor a film extolling the benefits of a regulated trucking industry. The film was entitled "If It Works – Why Fix It?"

A variety of reports on the regulated trucking industry were also sponsored by the ATA or written by its staff. These reports were distributed widely to Congressmen, Senators, administration officials, academics and individuals in the industry. The ATA had hoped to persuade the public and important officials with provocative titles such as "The Bare Facts About Rate Bureaus," "Countdown to Crises: The Threat to the Motor Carrier Rate-making System," and "Trucking Regulation: In the Public Interest."

In addition, Paul O. Roberts, a well known transportation expert from MIT was also retained by the ATA. Dr. Roberts was asked to study the effects of deregulation on the trucking industry, shippers and the economy as a whole. The ATA had hoped to use the results of this study as further ammunition against deregulation.

The attack against deregulation was taken to the partisan political arena as well. Persuaded by the many arguments against deregulation, the Republican Governors Conference which met in Austin, Texas in the fall of 1979 issued a resolution supporting regulation. The GOP governors felt that airline deregulation had failed and thus opposed it for the trucking industry.

John Connally, who was running for president, appeared at the ATA convention, also in the fall of 1979. Connally emphasized his disagreement with deregulation stating, "I am not the least bit interested in deregulating the trucking industry." Many truckers at the convention pledged their support for Connally's presidential bid. Two trucking leaders openly pledged $15,000 to his campaign.

The ATA also used the court system in their attack against deregulation. The Department of Transportation began mailings to public interest groups, state and local officials, and shippers, urging support of the Carter-Kennedy bill. The ATA condemned this lobbying effort and sought an order from a federal court in Washington to enjoin the DOT from any further efforts in support of the proposed legislation.

Although Bennett Whitlock and the national ATA organization felt that trucking interests should display a united front in opposition to deregulation, a rift in the ATA surfaced in January of 1980. The American Movers Conference openly advocated deregulation of the household goods shipping industry. The Contract Carriers Conference threw their support behind the Carter-Kennedy bill. Dissatisfied with portions of the ATA bill, the National Tank Truck Carriers also began to consider supporting the administration proposal. The Private Carrier Conference openly broke with the ATA on a variety of issues. In addition, the Minority Trucking Transportation Development Corporation endorsed the Carter-Kennedy bill. They stated: "The MTTDC has advocated that over-regulation of the trucking industry has stifled the business aspirations of minority truckers."

In March of 1980, the Senate Commerce, Science and Transportation Committee voted 13–4 in favor of the deregulation bill. The ATA did not give up, however. Attempting to reduce the impact of the proposed legislation, it tried to persuade Senators that the anti-trust immunity for collective ratemaking should remain.

The full Senate passed the legislation in April. This version included a compromise provision on collective ratemaking. The anti-trust exemption would continue. However, a commission was established in the proposal to review and study the trucking industry and make a recommendation to Congress on whether the immunity should continue.

Draft legislation, similar to that passed by the Senate, including the establishment of a ratemaking commission, was introduced in the House. In May, the House Surface Transportation Subcommittee under the Chairmanship of Representative James T. Howard (D. New Jersey) began deliberations on the proposal. The bill was quickly forwarded to the Public Works and Transportation Committee of which the subcommittee is a part. The full committee voted in favor of the proposal on May 22 and forwarded it to the Rules Committee. The proposal then became known as the Motor Carrier Act of 1980.

Sensing eminent defeat, the ATA made another 180 degree turn. The ATA Executive Committee voted unanimously to support, with reservations, the bill passed by the full House Committee. The ATA felt that at least the bill would put an end to the administrative deregulation which had been undertaken at the ICC. The resolution stated: "ATA supports — with reservations — HR6418, the Motor Carrier Act of 1980, and opposes any further substantive changes which will adversely impact the trucking industry."

In June, the Rules Committee gave a favorable ruling on the bill. The proposal was passed by the House and sent to the Senate. The Senate approved the House version by voice vote 24 hours later, thus eliminating the need for a joint Senate-House Conference Committee. President Carter then signed the Motor Carrier Act of 1980 into law.

The defeat experienced by the ATA was not confined to the Motor Carrier Act of 1980. The ICC continued its administrative deregulation efforts, despite President Reagan's appointment of a new chairman to the ICC in 1981. The new chairman, Reese Taylor, was a Nevada lawyer who represented trucking interests. It was felt at the time of his appointment that he would slow down the deregulation efforts.

The ATA objected to a proposal for complete deregulation made by the Department of Transportation after Reagan took office. However, it was the teamsters union, and not the ATA, who persuaded the administration to shelve the legislation.

The Motor Carrier Rate Making Commission, which the ATA fought for, voted against continuation of the anti-trust immunity for collective ratemaking. In addition, Congress passed steep heavy truck tax increases over the fierce objections of the ATA.

The ATA undertook a reexamination and hired the Hay Group, a management consulting firm, to examine its government relations operations and its organizational structure. It hoped that implementation of the recommendations would revitalize the organization and the political clout which it once had.

Some observers feel, however that the uncompromising tactics used by the ATA hardened reaction against the industry which led to the subsequent defeats. Senator Robert Packwood, who became chairman of the Senate Commerce, Science and Transportation Committee when the Republicans took control of that house in 1980 emphasized his displeasure over the ATA:

"I don't think truckers realize in what bad repute their lobbying organization is held. These fellows here [at ATA] do their industry no good service. They're devious. They'll go around you. They will mislead you deliberately. You cannot rely on the word of their lobbyists."

Case Questions

1. Who were gainers and losers from deregulation of the trucking industry?

2. What tactics were used to influence each of the stages of the policy formulation process?

3. What are the reasons for the failure of the ATA's efforts to block deregulation?

Case References

Butler, R. M. & Chapman, R. S. "ATA Shifts Gears to Counter Attack ICC on Its Drive for Deregulation." *Traffic World*, October 22, 1979, pp. 43–48.

Butler, R. M. & Chapman, R. S. "Trucking Industry Girds to Battle Deregulator; Preparing Own Bill." *Traffic World*, November 18, 1978, pp. 38–44.

Commercial Car Journal, July, 1979, pp. 19, 22; January, 1980, pp. 28, 30; September, 1983, pp. 16, 17.

Distribution, January, 1980, p. 14; April, 1980, p. 22.

Machalaba, D. "Trucking Associations, Powerful for Decades, Has a Load of Trouble." *Wall Street Journal*, February 21, 1984, pp. 1, 17.

Transport Topics, July 2, 1979; October 15, 1979; November 5, 1979; November 26, 1979; January 28, 1980; February 25, 1980, March 17, 1980; April 28, 1980; May 19, 1980; May 26, 1980; June 2, 1980; June 16, 1980; June 30, 1980.

References

Advisory Commission on Intergovernmental Relations (ACIR), *Substa Regionalism in the Federal System: Vol. 1.* Washington, D.C.: USGPO, 1973.

Aplin, J. C. & Hegarty, W. H. "Political Influence: Strategies Employed by Organizations to Impact Legislation in Business and Economic Matters." *Academy of Management Journal*, 1980, *23*, 438–451.

Burkhead, J., Fox, T. G. & Holland, J. W. *Input and Output in Large City High Schools.* Syracuse, N.Y.: Syracuse University Press, 1967.

Conte, C. & Woutat, D. "Rule on Airbags Won't End Safety Battle as U.S. Agency Plan Allows Alternates." *Wall Street Journal*, July 12, 1984, pp. 3, 22.

Dolbeare, K. M. *American Public Policy: A Citizen's Guide.* New York: McGraw-Hill, Inc., 1982.

Dolbeare, K. M. *American Ideologies Today: Shaping the New Politics of the 1990's* (2nd edition). New York: McGraw-Hill, Inc., 1992.

Drucker, P. F. "The Sickness of Government." *The Public Interest*, Winter, 1969, p. 13.

Dye, T. R. *Understanding Public Policy* (8th ed.). Englewood Cliffs, N.J · Prentice-Hall, Inc., 1995.

Frederick, William C., Post, James E. and Davis, Keith. *Business and Society: Corporate Strategy, Public Policy, Ethics* (7th edition). New York: McGraw-Hill, Inc., 1992.

Friedman, Milton and Friedman, Rose. *Free To Choose: A Personal Statement.* New York: Harcourt, Brace, Jovanovich, 1990.

Guzzardi, W., Jr. "Business Is Learning to Win in Washington." *Fortune*, March 27, 1978, pp. 52–58.

Jackson, B. "Loopholes Allow Flood of Campaign Giving by Businesses, Fat Cats." *Wall Street Journal*, July 5, 1984, pp. 1, 6.

Kennedy, J. F. *Profiles in Courage*. New York: Harper and Brothers, 1955.

McConnell, C. R. *Economics: Principles, Problems, and Policies* (13th ed.). New York: McGraw-Hill, Inc., 1995.

McKenzie, R. B. *Economic Issues in Public Policy*. New York: McGraw-Hill, Inc., 1980.

Niskanen, W. A., Jr. *Bureaucracy and Representative Government*. Chicago: Aldine, Atherton, Inc., 1971.

Preston, L. E. & Post, J. E. *Private Management and Public Policy*. Englewood Cliffs, N.J.: Prentice-Hall, Inc., 1975.

Thurow, L. C. *The Zero Sum Society*. New York: Penguin Books, 1981.

Tombari, H. A. *Business & Society*. Chicago: The Dryden Press, 1984.

U. S. Government Manual. Washington, D.C.: Office of the Federal Register, National Archives and Record Administration, 1994–95.

Weidenbaum, M. L. *Business and Government in the Global Marketplace* (5th edition). Englewood Cliffs, N.J.: Prentice-Hall, 1995.

CHAPTER 4
CORPORATE SOCIAL RESPONSIBILITY

INTRODUCTION

American corporations have engaged to some extent in social actions since their beginning in the late 1800s. Even though their primary focus is economic, many businesses engaged in philanthropy, community actions, and paternalism. For example, early business leaders such as Andrew Carnegie, gave large donations to educational and charitable institutions. In addition, Henry Ford developed personnel programs aimed at the recreational and health needs of his employees. More recently, efforts have been made by some companies to improve urban environments by locating offices and factories in low income areas, offering special training programs for the hard core unemployed and providing retraining programs for displaced factory workers. Such efforts are encouraged by the public sector responses of tax incentives and subsidy programs, and are in the economic interests of the companies involved. However, there is also a substantial component of socially responsible behavior in such activities. That is, many companies perform such actions, not necessarily out of short term profit potential, but often out of a sense of duty and obligation to those served by the programs.

The decisions made by managers have economic, political and social implications beyond the confines of the business. As has been discussed in Chapters 2 and 3, business interacts with the external environment through the market system and the political system. In addition, the organization has a direct impact on societal elements through social involvement. Resulting changes in these societal elements may then result in a public sector or marketplace response, ultimately affecting business through the market and political systems.

In this chapter, the background, definitions, and scope of social responsibility will be developed, arguments for and against business involvement in these areas will be made, and a model of business social involvement will be presented. In addition, possible managerial responses with regard to planning, organizing, controlling, and staffing/ rewarding will be discussed.

What Is Business Social Responsibility?

Definitions of social responsibility range from a narrow perspective advocating that the only obligation of business is to increase its profits to a general concern for the broader social system. The first major book devoted to the area of business social responsibility was written by Howard R. Bowen (1953) and was entitled *Social Responsibilities of the Businessman*. It provides the following definition of *social responsibility*:

> It [social responsibility] refers to the obligations of businessmen to pursue those policies, to make those decisions, or to follow those lines of action which are desirable in terms of the objectives and values of our society (Bowen, 1953, p. 6).

This broad based view is also found in McQuire's (1963) definition:

> The idea of social responsibilities supposes that the corporation has not only economic and legal obligations, but also certain responsibilities to society which extend beyond these obligations (McGuire, 1963, p. 144).

Milton Friedman, however, disagrees with the notion that business has a social responsibility beyond the economic and legal obligations of the firm. In his 1970 article entitled "The Social Responsibility of Business Is To Increase Its Profits," Friedman describes the responsibility of corporate executives as follows:

> In a free-enterprise, private property system, a corporate executive is an employee of the owners of the business. He has direct responsibility to his employers. That responsibility is to conduct the business in accordance with their desires, which generally will be to make as much money as possible while conforming to the basic rules of the society, both those embodied in law and those embodied in ethical custom (Friedman, 1970, p. 122).

The definitions proposed by Bowen and McGuire identify the broader responsibilities of business only in general terms. But how broadly should these general terms be interpreted? Should business become involved in the solution of all of society's problems? Or should it specialize in only some problems? If so, which problems? Should the majority of profits be diverted to non-economic, socially responsible activities, or is there in fact a primary responsibility to the stockholders? Further, how does a business know what is socially responsible, i.e. what are the objectives and values of society?

Friedman's view also presents problems to business managers. Because a firm may have many owners or stockholders, it is possible that there will be several, potentially conflicting "desires" or goals. Further, the "basic rules of society" are continually changing and must be monitored by management. Thus, the determination of what is appropriate management behavior, even within Friedman's relatively narrow purview, is a complex process.

In order to further refine the definition of social responsibility and to address some of the questions posed above, Preston and Post (1975) have developed the concept of *social involvement*. It is defined as:

> The view that the business organization and its larger host society are inherently interrelated and the scope of managerial responsibility extends to some activities not fully mediated by market contracts . . . (Preston & Post, 1975, p. 9).

The production processes of business result in interactions with many societal groups such as suppliers, customers, and employees. In addition, the existence of externalities, or costs and benefits of an activity which fall on individuals or groups who are not directly involved, is recognized by this concept. These "third party" effects are outside the market transactions between the business and their suppliers or customers. Managerial responsibility, according to Preston and Post, extends to these externalities. Thus, the notion of social involvement recognizes that externalities can result from the production process, but is neutral and does not suggest what specific actions business should take, only that management has some responsibility in these matters.

Bowman and Haire (1975; 1976) have developed a definition of social responsibility from the economic concept of externalities. Because the production process often produces "third party" effects, these authors suggest that it is the social responsibility of an organization to act to increase potential positive externalities or decrease potential negative externalities. This also can be seen as an attempt to increase social benefits and decrease social costs.

The definitions used in this book expand on the approaches of Preston and Post (1975) and Bowman and Haire (1975; 1976). Thus:

Social responsibility is the notion that business has an obligation to society which extends beyond economic and legal duties. It is the extent to which an organization acts to correct the negative effects and to maximize the positive effects associated with its production processes. In other words, it is the extent to which business voluntarily takes externalities into account in their decision making process. This may be through altruistic activities such as charitable contributions or through actions which directly impact the "third party" effects of production.

What Actions Are Socially Responsible?

The business manager must determine the specific actions which will correct negative and maximize positive externalities. First, it must be determined what externalities are being produced and which individuals and groups are impacted, both positively and negatively. Second, it must be ascertained which externalities have priority, i.e. which are most important to various societal groups or potentially have the greatest costs or benefits to society.

For example, many U.S. firms produce and/or sell goods in South Africa. The South African government had a policy of apartheid which limited black South Africans' rights regarding citizenship, land ownership, voting privileges, choice of place of residence, equal opportunity in employment, and freedom of expression. The white South African government utilized repressive methods, including arrest and detention, for anyone who opposed their policies.

Ironically, because of the cheap labor available, many companies found it economically beneficial to continue their relationships with South Africa. The manager of a business with operations in this area had two choices. First, he or she may have recommended the organization sever all relationships with South Africa because the government's policies of apartheid were reprehensible and in opposition to the basic tenets of human and civil rights. This action had the effect of eliminating the jobs held by black South Africans in this company as well as reducing the variety of consumer products and services available on the market.

The second choice was to continue doing business in South Africa, thereby providing jobs for black South Africans as well as other positive externalities such as scholarships or health care. This action could, however, be interpreted as an acceptance of the apartheid system. What should the company have done?

In order to determine what externalities are being produced and to identify and implement specific actions, Preston and Post (1975) have introduced the "principle of public responsibility." This principle limits an organization's economic and social activities to areas of *primary and secondary involvement*. Activities defined by the marketplace are called *primary involvement*. These include principle relationships with customers, suppliers, and employees. For example, an automobile manufacturer is responsible for ". . . the production process, marketing and advertising, procurement of components and inputs, employment and wages" (Preston & Post, 1975, p. 96). It is from these processes that externalities evolve.

Secondary involvement refers to the relationships and impacts ancillary to the use of products sold, and includes the consequences of production and sales activities, the indirect impacts of procurement, and neighborhood effects or externalities. Thus, the automobile producer might be responsible for the use of the cars and trucks produced, safety equipment, environmental pollution, and the implications of an expanding highway system. In addition, human resource issues of quality of worklife, special training for disadvantaged workers, equal employment/affirmative action policies and wage and hour laws may be of concern. Although far reaching, these impacts evolve from the primary, economic activities of the firm and do not necessarily include areas such as support of the arts, the condition of low income housing, or donations to charities for the handicapped.

Once the scope of an organization's involvement has been determined, the specific externalities of concern can be delineated. But what actions should then be taken? How does business know which actions are the most socially responsible and which are not?

The principle of "public responsibility" uses public policy as a guide. Preston and Post (1975) look to public policy to identify not only the objectives and priorities of society, but also the means of attacking the problems. For example, one goal of society may be to reduce unemployment. Public programs which support retraining not only attack a particular problem, unemployment, but suggest a specific solution as well. Also, the course of public policy with regard to South Africa would provide guidance to firms in deciding whether to close or continue operations there.

In addition, Preston and Post (1981, p. 61) suggest that in areas ". . . in which specific public policy is not yet clearly established or is in transition, it is legitimate — and may be essential — that affected firms participate openly in the policy formation." Methods such as lobbying, advocacy advertising, and political contributions (as discussed in Chapter 3) are examples of such behaviors.

Jones (1980), however, has identified several potential problems with using public policy as a guide to action. First, many issues confronting a particular firm may not be addressed by public policy. Second, conflicting statements of policy emerge at each level of government. For example, reducing pollution may result in closing old plant facilities while at the same time a conflicting goal of full employment may be stated. Third, local, state and federal governments often have conflicting policies. Which policy should the corporation heed?

In addition, the public policy process does not necessarily result in the "will of the people" being enacted into law. Rather, as was discussed in the previous chapter, the public policy process buries the merits of issues under a variety of special interests, conflicting priorities and uncertainties. Using public policy as a guide for action may lead business to act in a manner that may not benefit society as a whole, but rather serve the special interests of those groups having power in Washington.

Arguments Favoring Social Responsibility

The debate over social responsibility has raged over many years with proponents and opponents taking a variety of positions to support their points of view. Some of the proponents take a very broad view of social responsibility, while others stake out more narrow positions. Many of the opponents also argue against the broad conceptions of social responsibility while others focus on the more narrow aspects. Thus, the social responsibility debate itself is unclear, with individuals on both sides arguing for or against slightly different concepts.

The issue of whether business should be engaged in socially responsible behavior beyond that required by law and contractual arrangements may never be finally settled. However, in formulating a policy regarding social responsibility, it is helpful for management to be acquainted with the arguments, both pro and con.

On one side of the social responsibility debate are those who accept the view of organizations as entities which attempt to satisfy multiple goals and who are responsible for or impact several stakeholder groups. *Stakeholders* are those individuals or groups which have some type of "investment" or interest in the organization, such as suppliers, lenders, customers and special interest groups. *It is argued that managers must acknowledge the interests of multiple groups and attempt to reach legal, political, and social goals as well as economic objectives.* Socially responsible behavior is not only appropriate, but may be required to successfully achieve these objectives.

A second argument used to support business social responsibility spending is that *corporations are created by society and must meet the public's expectations or face a future loss of power*. To succeed over the long run, businesses must adapt to the changing norms of society with regard to their treatment of employees, the control of externalities, and their appropriate role in the market and political systems. The nuclear power industry in the United States, for example, has been severely limited as a result of public pressure resulting from a fear of accidents, changing policies regarding safety and construction requirements, and the failure of some contractors to meet standards.

A third argument presents *business as a source of both capital and human resources which should be used to improve the conditions in society*. Business is seen as having an active role to play in social betterment. Other supporters of this view feel the market system has failed to require business to act in a socially responsible manner. Therefore, constraints by legal, political, or other means should be enacted which force businesses to be socially responsible (Jackson & Aldag, 1980).

A fourth view suggests *business creates negative externalities and therefore is obligated to correct them*. Since businesses have "control" over the pollution produced or the working conditions provided, they should expend corporate resources to reduce pollutants and to improve worker safety. It should not be left to "third parties" who are not directly involved in market transactions with the firm to solve these problems.

A final argument supporting socially responsible behavior is that *it is a good investment*. It is argued (Bowman & Haire, 1976; Mintzberg, 1983) that investors respond positively to companies who are socially responsive and view companies which do not behave in this manner as riskier investments. In other words, socially responsive behavior may be positively related to profits or other financial outcomes.

The relation between financial performance and dollars spent on corporate contributions and other social actions has been examined by a number of researchers. One theory (Johnson, 1966) assumes that as a business increases its level of social responsiveness there will be an increase in spending in this area.

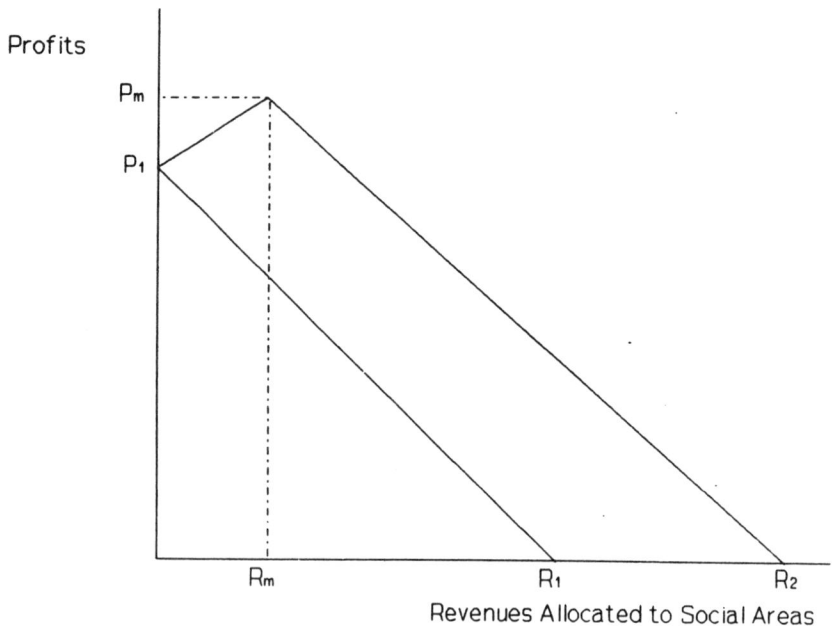

Figure 4.1. A Model Relating Social Spending to Profits

Adapted from Harold L. Johnson. "Socially Responsible Firms: An Empty Box or a Universal Set!" *The Journal of Business*, Vol. 39 (July, 1966), pp. 394–399.

In Figure 4.1, line P_1-R_1 represents a narrow view of spending on social responsiveness. This model says that dollars diverted from production to social areas would reduce profits by an equal amount. If this model is correct, then the profit maximizing firm would allocate zero resources on socially responsive behavior and managers would argue against business social responsibility spending.

However, a business may want to spend resources on socially responsive behavior in order to increase profits. This may be in response to pressures from stakeholder groups, because of altruistic motives of top managers, or because of an attempt to mitigate future negative impacts. That is, the business may decide that such expenditures are to their advantage in order to build good will. In addition, expectations of fewer government regulations or improved labor relations may be the underlying motives for social responsibility spending.

The relationship between profits and spending on social responsibility may look like line P_m-R_2 instead. Some level of expenditure may result in increased profitability. Eventually, however, profits will peak and then decline as more and more resources are diverted from production to social responsiveness. Profits are maximized at P_m with R_m spending devoted to social areas.

This theory is supported to some extent by studies of particular corporations. Bowman and Haire (1975) analyzed the annual reports of eighty-two food processing companies to determine the percentage of prose on corporate social responsibility. It was assumed by the researchers that the amount of space devoted to social responsibility issues in the annual report is a measure of the level of social involvement of the firm. The firms were then classified into six groups with respect to the percentage of prose on social responsibility. The median return on equity (ROE) was determined for each group. The results are shown in Figure 4.2. An inverted U-shape was found to exist, with the lowest ROE found for firms having the lowest and highest levels of social responsibility. The maximum ROE was reported by the fifteen firms with a moderate level of social responsibility.

Cochran and Wood (1984) reviewed fourteen studies which compared measures of social responsibility and financial performance. In all, nine studies found a positive relationship between financial performance and socially responsible behavior, three found no significant link, and one found a negative relationship. In addition, Cochran and Wood (1984) studied 39 firms in 29 industries from 1970 to 1974 and 36 firms in 28 industries from 1975 to 1979. They compared the reputation of the firms regarding social responsibility (classified as best, honorable mention, worst) to measures of financial performance. The results indicate there is some support for a link between corporate social responsibility and financial outcomes. Thus, from the manager's point of view, acting in a socially responsible manner may in fact be in the best economic interests of the firm.

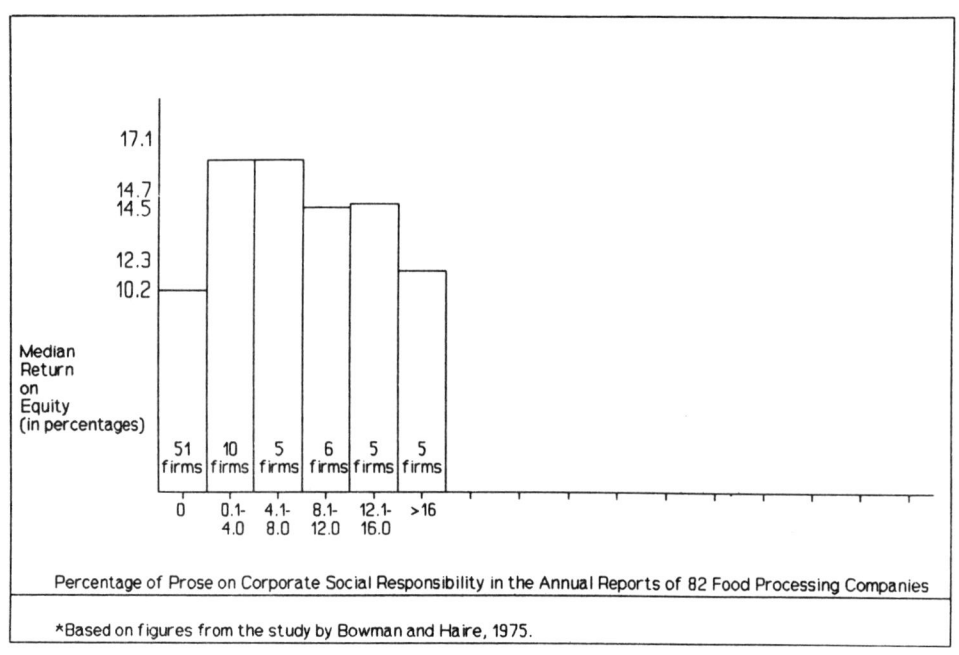

Figure 4.2. The Relationship Between Corporate Social Responsibility and Median Return on Equity

Adapted from H. Mintzberg, "The Case for Corporate Social Responsibility," *Journal of Business Strategy*, 1983 4 (2), p. 7.

Arguments Against Social Responsibility

Over time, a number of arguments against corporate spending on social responsibility have been set forth. In general, the assumptions underlying these arguments are: first, that an organization has a single goal, to make a profit, and second, it serves only one group, its stockholders or owners. Such a company would minimize its level of social responsibility spending.

Classical economic theory forms the basis of the first argument against corporate social responsibility. It is assumed that *social problems should be solved by the public sector if they are not solved by the free market system.* Taken to its extreme, proponents of this view feel that profit should be distributed to stockholders rather than being spent on social activities. The corporate executive's responsibility is to the stockholders, and expenditure of profits on socially responsible activities is in effect diverting these resources away from the owners of the firm. In fact, when managers spend the company's money on social areas, it has been interpreted as a tax on the stockholders. Since managers have no right to tax, the corporation has no right to pursue social goals (Friedman, 1970; Mintzberg, 1983).

A second argument deals with the nature of corporate goals. *Assuming a business's primary purpose is to make a profit, diverting attention to social or other noneconomic goals will reduce a business's efficiency.* Thus, management may not serve the stockholders' interest if part of their attention is on social matters. In addition, society is not served since goods and services are not produced in the most efficient manner possible.

A third argument is that *business managers do not have the required background or expertise to make decisions regarding the allocation of money to areas of social concern.* One problem is the nature of social problems, which require flexibility and political finesse rather than the efficiency and control found in business (Mintzberg, 1983). Another is that when dealing in social areas, managers are often making public decisions without being subject to the limits of either the market or the political process. Thus, there are no limitations on managers who make decisions regarding social spending.

Another reason cited for reducing business social responsibility spending is that *it is too expensive.* Spending on pollution control, special training programs, or extra safety equipment diverts resources away from improving the technology used in production or research and development of new products, and results in increased prices for the products produced. Thus, socially responsive companies may be at a disadvantage in international markets since the price of their products may be uncompetitive.

Managers are also unable to measure their social performance using traditional financial techniques. The benefits of controlling externalities such as pollution are not easily measured, and certainly not confined to one company's balance sheet. For example, a steel company which installs pollution control equipment may be able to measure the reduction in the number of particles in the air, but will have a difficult time in pricing the savings resulting from long term reduction in lung disease of the people living near the plant. Since social performance cannot easily be tied to profits, then it is outside the scope of management responsibility according to this view.

Some argue that *business corporations are currently too powerful within the economic, technological, and political arenas.* If their purview is increased to include social responsibility spending as well, then the balance between the public and private sectors would be upset. Proponents of this argument probably would like to see a shrinking of power rather than a broadening of the scope of corporate activities.

Another argument is that *it is difficult to determine what actions are socially responsible.* If a company tries to use public policy as a guide, as suggested by Preston and Post (1975; 1981) only those actions related to areas articulated by this process will be considered. In addition, conflicts may arise among the goals stated by a given level of government or between local, state and federal levels (Jones, 1980). Finally, if management judgment is used, then questions might arise as to the appropriateness of individual opinion.

Finally, some cynics feel that *corporate "concern" for social issues is simply a public relations campaign.* They feel that companies take on causes to improve their image, but that what is released to the general public is "rhetoric, not action" (Mintzberg, 1983).

A Model of Business Social Involvement

Given the definition of social responsibility as the correction of the negative effects and maximization of the positive impacts of the production process, then what explains the fact that some businesses go out of their way to minimize negative and maximize positive externalities, while others do little or nothing? A variety of factors influence business responses to the externalities created by the production process.

The model illustrated in Figure 4.3 shows the factors which influence these decisions. This model represents the direct and indirect impacts which business has on the societal elements as a result of the production of goods and services. Notice that these impacts occur outside the market and political systems. However, the scope of these impacts are defined by the primary and secondary involvement of business.

Before specific actions related to social involvement are planned or executed, the multiple goals of the organization and the pressures of various stakeholder groups must be considered. In addition, the

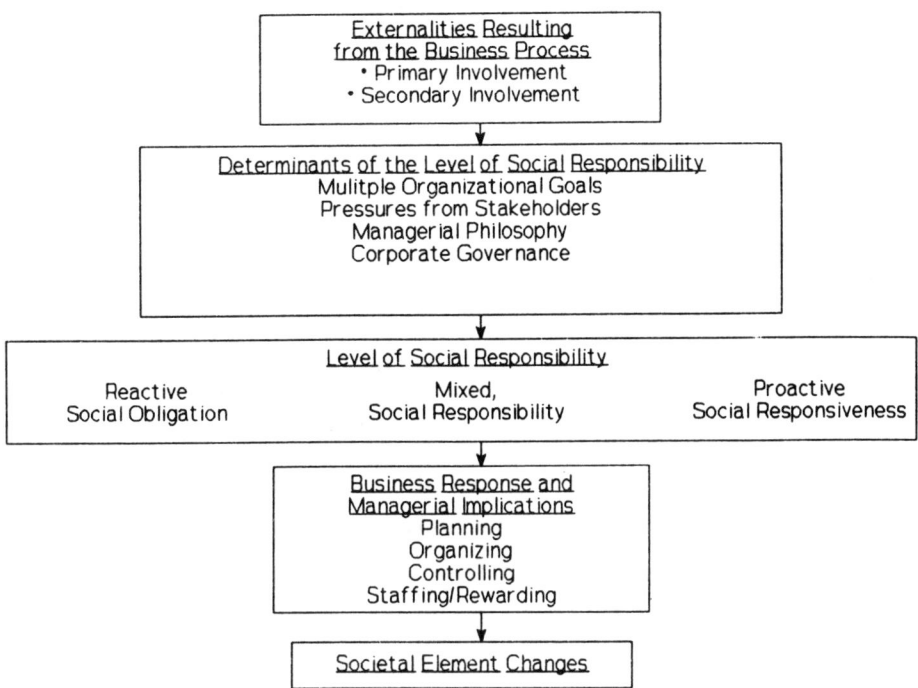

Figure 4.3. A Model of the Social Involvement of Business

managerial philosophy regarding the level of social involvement acts to define the activities which will be undertaken. Finally, the manner in which the corporation is governed reflects management's commitment to social responsibility.

Once these factors are combined, the level of social responsibility can be determined. It may range from a reactive, social obligation strategy to a mixed, social responsibility course of action to a proactive, social responsiveness approach. The level chosen then determines the actions of management in response to the externalities created by the business.

The implementation of management programs involves the functions of planning, organizing, controlling, and staffing/rewarding. It is the execution of these programs which results in changes in the societal elements.

Determinants of the Level of Social Responsibility

Multiple Organizational Goals

The business organization today must operate in an increasingly complex and constantly changing environment. An organization narrowly focused on maximizing profits in the short run at the expense of long run goals such as capital formation and investment in research and development may be short-lived. Successful organizations today must be multi-purpose, with goals set regarding social and political issues as well as the economic and legal. Government regulation and political interest groups may necessitate activities in certain areas such as pollution control, worker safety, and equal employment opportunity. For such organizations, managers often must take a strategic/policy making role within the restraints set by the market and political processes.

For example, before the Arab oil embargo of the mid-1970s, the oil industry mainly focused on producing and selling gasoline and related products. Political activities were confined to preserving the oil depletion allowance in the tax code. After the embargo, however, there were sharp price increases and localized shortages. Public opinion turned against the oil industry and negative publicity regarding "windfall" profits and hoarding of oil surfaced. Also during this period, the efforts of environmentalists increased, and the oil industry was one of the targets. Since this time, advocacy advertising and other attempts to improve the industry's image have become common. The industry could not afford to focus only on producing and selling oil, but needed to address pollution control and a perception that their profits were above the "fair" market price.

Stakeholder Interests

The traditional view of business defines the stockholder or owner as the individual or group of primary concern. A more recent view expands the scope of concern of the manager to consider many others including public interest groups, government agencies, unions, stockholders, employees, customers, and suppliers. In a broad sense, Freeman and Reed (1983, p. 91) see these stakeholders as ". . . any identifiable group or individual who can affect the achievement of an organization's objectives or who is affected by the achievement of an organization's objectives." Essentially, the stakeholders are those individuals and groups who are the recipients of the positive and negative externalities created by the firm as well as those having a direct interest in the corporation.

In developing corporate strategies of social responsibility, the interests and potential pressures from stakeholders may be considered as legitimate goals as well as the profits offered to investors (Halal, 1984). For example, in the late 1970s, Chrysler Corporation was headed for bankruptcy. Chrysler's management wanted givebacks from the United Auto Workers in the form of lower wages and benefits. In return, the union negotiated a place on the board of directors, occupied by the President of the UAW. This action could be considered as a response by management in which one group of stakeholders' goals were taken into account in future decisions.

Management Philosophy

The attitudes of top management toward social responsibility activities are crucial in developing an organizational culture which supports or avoids such issues. *Organizational culture* is the set of values, beliefs, and norms of behavior within an organization. For example, some organizations have a culture which supports and rewards only behavior leading directly to higher profits. Others, such as Hershey Inc., have long been involved in the local community and in philanthropic activities such as support of an orphanage and a medical school. Because company resources may need to be allocated to activities outside normal production processes, top management must have justification to commit to programs aimed at minimizing negative and maximizing positive externalities. This justification is sometimes developed through a management philosophy which stresses socially responsible spending. This philosophy will be reflected in the planning as well as the implementation of social programs.

In the mid-1970s Mead Corporation was one of 35 U.S. companies with a committee at the board of director level which dealt with questions of corporate social responsibility. The committee members included both directors and company employees. The chief executive officer encouraged the formation of this committee with the goal of bringing together the two groups to engage in a free flow of ideas. Issues such as plant closing policies and grievance procedures for nonunion employees were discussed, and consideration was given to expanding the membership of the committee to managers. Committees such as the one at Mead provide a formal mechanism for communication among various groups regarding social responsibility issues. However, their continued existence and effectiveness depend on the long term support of top management as well as a compatible organizational culture (Sturdivant & Robinson, 1981).

Corporate Governance

Another determinant of the level of social responsibility is the manner in which an organization is governed. The term governance generally refers to the process of internal control and decision-making. Who controls the organization? To whom is it accountable? For whom does it exist? Who are the owners?

Businesses today typically can be classified as proprietorships, partnerships, or corporations. The simplest form is a *proprietorship* in which a single individual holds the firm as his or her personal property. He or she maintains control of the organization and that individual is liable for taxes, legal suits, and debts.

A *partnership* has two or more members (partners) who share ownership and control of the business. Individual partners may be liable for debts incurred or other actions against the organization. Partnerships usually do not require large amounts of capital for plant and equipment, but are found in professional areas such as law firms, brokerage houses, accounting firms and advertising agencies.

The primary form of business, accounting for the vast majority of sales and assets, is the *corporation*. Corporations are chartered by individual states, issue stock, and are organized with a board of directors overseeing policy and serving to evaluate and give final approval to key management decisions. The owners of a corporation, however, are the stockholders while the operating duties lie with professional managers and are overseen by the board of directors.

The corporation is considered to be a "person" under the law and in many instances it is the organization which assumes liability rather than any individual or group. Recently, however, individual board members have been held liable in suits brought by stockholders for poor decisions. In addition, individual managers may be charged in price-fixing cases and other illegal actions taken on behalf of the corporation.

Thus, *corporate governance* may be defined as:

the process used by a corporation for decision-making and allocation of resources. The stockholders of the corporation are the legal owners while managers and the board of directors directly control the corporate resources and make decisions as required to operate the firm.

Key Issues — As the corporation has grown in importance and power, many people have questioned the effectiveness of the traditional system of corporate governance to meet societal goals in addition to the economic goals of the firm. Three primary issues have emerged: the focus and measurement of corporate performance, corporate power, and the professionalism of management (Dill, 1978).

The measurement of corporate performance is typically accomplished using the standard financial measures found in the annual report. Two problems are commonly cited. First, the measurement of social performance is often overlooked. It is not a normal part of financial reporting and the costs and benefits of social responsibility activities are difficult to measure. Second, the focus of most managers is on the short rather than the long run. Since many decisions regarding externalities, such as pollution control or employee retraining, have a long term payoff, socially responsible actions in these areas may be postponed or viewed as having low priority.

The second issue involves the increasing amount of corporate power as an influence on the marketplace and on the political system. Do corporations exert too much influence on the public sector through the political system? Does the vast wealth of corporations lead to control over regional or local economies? Do corporate policies shape public policies or vice versa? As mentioned above, some argue that corporations already have too much power and further activity in social areas would only serve to increase it.

The third issue involves the professionalism of management and potential vested interests of members of the board of directors. This is fundamentally an issue of separation of ownership and control. Critics argue that the idea of the separation of ownership and control is not always found in the modern corporation. They argue shareholders have only indirect control (through their voting rights at annual shareholder meetings) of the allocation of corporate resources and actions taken by managers. Individuals who are unhappy with the way a particular corporation is being governed will probably sell their stock rather than vote against management.

In addition, management has direct and sometimes unchecked control over corporate resources. The effectiveness of the board of directors to act as a balance to management's power is diluted by the fact that board members often are the managers of the firm or owe their positions directly to management. Further, both managers and board members may own large amounts of stock, narrowing the separation between ownership and control and reducing the probability that managerial decisions will be critically evaluated.

Possible Reforms — As a result of these concerns regarding the effectiveness of corporate governance, a number of reforms have been suggested. The issue of corporate performance measurement is addressed by the social audit, which is further described below. In the social audit, managers must consciously incorporate the measurement of their performance into the evaluation of social responsibility activities. Estimates of costs and present and future benefits are made, both quantitatively and qualitatively.

In order to control the power of corporations, increased disclosure to the stockholders and other interested groups has been suggested. This includes information on executive compensation and benefits, potential conflicts of interest of directors, and a 5-year history of financial statistics. It is hoped that this would increase public awareness of corporate activities.

Corporate power has also been questioned by shareholders who have become more active in their efforts to influence corporate decisions. It is possible for special interest groups to place resolutions on proxy statements which are sent to all shareholders. These resolutions cover issues such as doing business with South Africa, nuclear weapons and plants, community investment, and domestic political activities.

Finally, federal chartering of corporations has been suggested to reduce corporate power. It is argued that state charters are overly permissive in the granting of rights, powers and functions to corporations. In addition, firms conduct business across state boundaries and thus it is argued that chartering by one state is inappropriate. Those who favor federal chartering believe that corporations could be more readily held accountable at the national level for their social and economic actions.

The issue of the professionalism of management is addressed in proposals to open the governance process up to a wider group of people through changes in the structure of the board of directors. First, the addition of directors from outside the company is suggested. These new directors would include women, minorities and representatives from other stakeholder groups. Another special type of director, called a public director, would represent the general public. He or she would be responsible for monitoring corporate performance in social and public policy areas.

A second proposal is the addition of directors representing employee interests. This often occurs in employee buyouts when the union has representatives on the board. The addition of the president of the UAW on the Chrysler board is an example.

A third suggestion involves the formation of a special social responsibility or audit committee as part of the board of directors. Composed of members of the board, this committee may have responsibility for specific social action projects, overseeing the general level of social involvement, or auditing the financial and social performance of the corporation.

Levels of Social Responsibility

The multiple organizational goals, stakeholder interests, management philosophy, and corporate governance lead to various levels of social responsibility. These levels lie on a continuum ranging from reactive to proactive strategies as has been suggested by several authors.

Terms such as reactive, adaptive, social obligation, and defensive have been used to describe the lowest level of social involvement. Following this approach, an organization would meet minimum regulatory standards, provide a minimal level of benefits to employees, or give no notice of plant closings. Only actions required by law or governmental regulation are undertaken. Thus, the basic *social obligation* would be met, but no more.

A middle ground might be described as a mixed level where the organization may attempt to maintain the status quo or accommodate the situation by influencing the public sector response or changing stakeholder views to correspond with the organization's goals. The approach may be somewhat defensive, with a goal of minimizing future regulation or offsetting negative public opinion. Actions may be taken to mitigate possible negative impacts of the firm's activities beyond that required by law.

Companies using a mixed approach may go beyond required regulatory standards, provide additional employee benefits, or provide outplacement services to employees laid off as a result of a plant closing. The primary motive, however, is to reduce future government intervention, avoid unionization, or maintain the reputation of the firm as "a good place to work." The management of such firms may use a mixture of defensive and offensive strategies while acting in a *socially responsible* manner.

A third level uses a proactive approach toward social involvement. Described as interactive, socially responsive, or problem-solving, organizations using this approach may be considered industry leaders. Rather than simply reducing negative externalities, socially responsive firms may promote positive change and take actions which are anticipatory and preventive. For example, a company may not only act to reduce pollution, but may also develop any new technology needed. Quality of work life (QWL) programs as well as flexible benefit plans may be introduced. In addition, programs such as worksharing and retraining of displaced factory workers may be utilized. Also, notification of a plant closing may be given a year or more in advance and associated programs such as outplacement and relocation counseling begun. Such activities indicate the organization is using a *socially responsive* management philosophy to guide decisions regarding their level of social involvement.

Relation between the Societal Element Changes and the Level of Social Involvement

The three stages, social obligation, social responsibility, and social responsiveness, are applied to each of the societal elements of the external environment in Table 4.1. Examples of how corporate behavior is related to the elements of the environment are shown in the table.

Physical Environment

Social obligation with respect to the physical environment requires compliance with existing laws and regulations. Although the company may meet current standards, it risks failure to comply with future regulations. Social responsibility may require a clean up of pollution beyond what is required by law, reducing this risk but also reducing short term profits. This may still be in the shareholders interest, however, since future lawsuits may be prevented.

Socially responsive behavior could entail development of technology to reduce the production of pollution. On the surface, this expenditure of research and development funds does not appear to be in the best interest of the shareholders, but future profits from sale of this technology as well as avoidance of costly future clean-up and lawsuits may maximize the future stream of earnings.

Table 4.1. Corporate Behavior and the External Environment

Societal Elements	Social Obligation	Social Responsibility	Social Responsiveness
Energy and the Physical Environment	Comply with existing EPA, state and local laws.	Clean up pollution beyond required standards.	Develop technology to reduce production of pollution.
Labor Market	Comply with wage and hour laws and give minimum benefits.	Provide additional benefits to keep out unions or stop strikes.	Improve quality of work life through increased employee participation.
Technology	Meet minimum OSHA standard regarding video displays.	Provide special lighting for workers doing their original jobs.	Reevaluate jobs to minimize boredom and physical stress.
Welfare and Public Services	Provide only social security benefits for workers.	Provide additional retirement benefits to supplement base income.	Develop cafeteria benefits to meet the various needs of employees.
Economic Environment	Layoff people to the extent allowed by labor contracts.	Carry out layoffs only when absolutely necessary. Use seniority for decisions.	Utilize worksharing, retraining and relocation to minimize layoffs.
Regional and Local Issues	Close plants with only required notice when no longer profitable.	Give workers in closed plants a chance to relocate if needed.	Give substantial notice of plant closings, support employee buyouts.
Global Trade	Obey law regarding marketing infant formula in underdeveloped countries.	Provide educational information and eliminate in-hospital marketing of infant formula.	Support education and research on the pros and cons of formula feeding in underdeveloped countries.

Labor Market

The labor market operates to provide workers with appropriate skills for jobs which are available. The Fair Labor Standards Act specifies rules regarding wages and hours worked for many employees. An organization which merely meets the social obligation will comply with these laws, paying only what is necessary under various circumstances. Although a business following this strategy may maximize short term profits, turnover rates probably will be high and general labor relations poor.

The socially responsible firm may pay additional benefits or pay higher wages, with the goal of stopping strikes, reducing grievances, or keeping unions out, thus mitigating the negative impacts of their actions. The strategy may be successful over the near term, but worker productivity and commitment to the organization may not allow the organization to remain competitive over the long term.

The socially responsive firm, however, will raise the quality of work life and generally improve working conditions through changes in the system. Examples are election of employee representatives to the board of directors and implementation of profit sharing programs. The relatively high labor costs may reduce the level of short term earnings, but if productivity levels are high in relation to the industry, the organization may in the end be more competitive and show higher future earnings levels.

Technology

The introduction of new technology provides many opportunities for organizations to address social issues. One controversial area has been the prolonged use of video display terminals by workers. The company making minimal effort will meet current minimum government standards. This position is a high risk one, however, since it invites future government regulation as well as possible increases in worker compensation claims. Also, as offices begin to resemble the assembly line of the factory, problems of boredom and high turnover rates may emerge.

An organization which wants to reduce employee complaints about eye strain or back pain may install special lighting and adjustable furniture, but will assign workers the same repetitive tasks they have been doing. The problems of boredom, fatigue, and turnover will remain. There is also a continued risk of regulation of the number of hours spent in front of the VDT.

Finally, the firm which wants to develop an integrated office system will analyze and redesign the job to provide a higher quality work situation as well as a comfortable environment. This will result in more variety on the job, less physical strain, the development of higher skilled workers, and hopefully a more stable, productive workforce. Although there may be a higher initial capital investment, the increases in productivity and reduced turnover may offset it in the long term.

Welfare and Public Services

Welfare or transfer payments include social security benefits as well as benefits to the poor. A company meeting its minimum social obligations regarding the deferred income of its employees may only pay its share of their social security tax. Employees of this type of firm are probably part-time or short term, with little interest in retirement income. As businesses grow, however, it may be necessary to expand benefits to include deferred income in order to remain competitive.

Many companies also provide additional retirement benefits for their workers. Although this often is aimed at improving the ability to recruit high quality personnel, it also provides a higher quality of life for retired employees and is an example of a socially responsible strategy.

A socially responsive employer may also recognize the varied needs of the workers and develop a flexible or "cafeteria style" benefit plan. The administration of such a plan may cost more, but savings due to the reduction of undesired benefits and more efficient health insurance plans will probably offset the increase. In addition, employees are more conscious of the benefits they are receiving and may view them as an important part of their compensation package.

Economic Environment

The economic environment has unemployment as a major issue. When production is reduced, a firm may layoff as many people as possible, bound only by existing labor contracts. Although reducing labor costs in the short run, this strategy leaves the firm with a poor image and potential labor relations problems.

A more socially responsible company may try to keep layoffs to a minimum by shifting workers to new jobs or locations or encouraging early retirement when possible to open up career paths. Seniority may be used for all layoff decisions as stipulated in existing contracts. Questions regarding affirmative action plans may arise as a result of this strategy. Although the company's labor relations may remain on an even keel, the general image of the organization remains poor.

A socially responsive firm may utilize worksharing, retraining of current workers and outplacement to reduce the number of layoffs. Over the long-term, these alternative measures allow workers some continuous income and may in fact cost the company less than the traditional layoff approach. The long term costs of hiring and training new workers will be reduced and company image and employee commitment will be good.

Regional and Local Issues

Plant closings may severely impact the economic climate and general welfare at the local and regional level. The company which closes a plant with no notice to its workers except what is required by law is meeting its minimum legal obligations. However, it may be socially responsible to provide workers immediate outplacement services or offer the opportunity to relocate if jobs are available. The socially responsive firm would provide advanced notice of plant closing beyond the 60 days required by federal law and the opportunity and financial support for employees or other interested parties to purchase the business.

Global Trade and International Issues

As we move to international markets, issues regarding differences among cultures become apparent. One example is the infant formula controversy described by Sethi and Post (1979). Prior to 1970, multinational corporations engaged in a number of marketing efforts aimed at increasing the sale of infant formula in underdeveloped countries. A shift was occurring from breast-feeding to bottle-feeding in these countries as a result of sociocultural changes, changing attitudes of health professionals, and the promotional activities of infant formula manufacturers.

At that time, manufacturers produced literature on baby food, some of which implied infant formula was as good or better than mother's milk. They also engaged in media advertising and provided free samples of formula and bottles. Physicians were encouraged to make recommendations for specific brands to their patients. Nurses were trained (and paid by the manufacturers) to present products to new mothers while in the hospital, and the hospitals themselves engaged in direct sale of the products.

The United Nations Protein Calorie Advisory Group (PAG) found that these promotional activities led to misuse of the products and the possible perception that bottle-feeding was better than breast-feeding. They also found that poor women would dilute the product to make it last longer, leading to malnutrition of infants. In addition, sanitary conditions are needed as well as a pure water supply to avoid introducing disease to bottle-fed babies. These conditions may not be present in many underdeveloped areas.

Prior to 1970, the actions of infant formula manufacturers could be described as an example of social obligation. The companies continued their promotional efforts to the extent allowed in a particular area, with little concern for the proper use of the product by end users.

In 1973, several manufacturers participated in the UN Protein Calorie Advisory Group, although one company, Abbott Laboratories, took initial steps to mitigate the negative impact of bottle-feeding promotions in underdeveloped countries. In 1975, the International Council of Infant Food Industries (ICIFC) was formed. This socially responsible action was made in part as a result of public pressure. A code of marketing ethics was developed which included rewording advertising to emphasize the primacy of breast-feeding, increased precision of product-use information, and elimination of promotion and sales of infant formula in hospitals. Abbott felt this code was too weak and withdrew from the ICIFC.

In 1977 Abbott Laboratories took proactive, socially responsive actions. These included a $100,000 breast-feeding campaign as well as $175,000 for research in the area. Thus, the company had moved from actions which mitigated negative consequences to programs which increased the probability of positive externalities.

As can be seen from the examples above, companies which follow a social obligation strategy comply with existing regulations, laws, and contractual obligations. Little is done, however, to protect employees or the public from externalities not covered or which might pose future problems.

A socially responsible company goes beyond the law, and acts to correct the negative effects of the production process. The results are positive (less pollution, higher employee benefits, or unbiased advertising), but the motives may not be altruistic. Instead, actions may be taken to avoid negative consequences such as unionization and future increased regulation.

Finally, socially responsive firms develop new technology and innovative programs relating to various elements of the external environment. These may go beyond industry norms and practices, involve direct spending on basic research and focus on positive outcomes of the firm in the future.

Business Response and Managerial Implications

When multiple corporate and stakeholder goals surface and become an important part of the decision-making process, managers may need to integrate social responsibility activities with the functions of planning, organizing, controlling, and staffing/rewarding. A number of approaches are presented below to be used by managers to aid in the planning, implementation, and evaluation of business social responsibility activities.

Planning for Social Involvement

A large organization has several levels of strategic planning activities which can generally be dichotomized as macro and micro viewpoints. The macro view focuses on general questions such as the organizational purpose, which businesses to enter, and the relation of the organization to its environment. Thus, the top strategy level can be called "societal" and this level determines the role the organization will assume in society, the nature of corporate governance, the relation of the organization to the political system, and the tradeoffs between economic and social goals. It is thus at the very top levels of the organization that the development of social policy must begin, and it is here that it can begin to be integrated with the more traditional strategic areas.

The micro level of strategic planning deals with the functional or operational areas. It follows from the general policies set at the macro level and includes specific programs or areas of social involvement. Examples might include pollution control, worker safety, and equal employment opportunity programs established by the organization.

Important inputs to the planning of social involvement are the results from the environmental scanning and forecasting activities discussed in Chapter 2. Through this process, the areas of corporate involvement with the external environment and the external and internal topics and subtopics to be monitored are determined. The manager focusing on social involvement can gain important information by determining which social issues have already been identified as important to the organization and are being studied.

In addition to utilizing the results of existing scanning efforts, Jackson and Aldag (1980) suggest the social action model shown in Figure 4.4 as a guide to decision makers. By successively answering each of the six questions posed, managers can determine if a proposed social action is within the primary and secondary involvement of the firm, the extent to which multiple goals are satisfied, the relative costs, benefits and feasibility of a project, and its rating with regard to resource allocation.

The first two questions, (Does a social responsibility really exist in this case? and Does an assessment of all interests indicate that the act is desirable?) are from a macro viewpoint. The answers will come in part from the process described by the model of social involvement of business in Figure 4.3. The results of this analysis will be the general social policy of the organization set by top management.

The third question, Do benefits outweigh costs? calls for an evaluation of the benefits to society and the firm and a comparison to costs. Both short and long range costs and benefits should be considered. One problem of social responsibility activities is that the costs may occur in the short-term, as with investment in pollution control equipment, while the benefits from improved company image may only be seen over time. Likewise, the benefits of clean air and water may be felt by the entire region while the costs of increased prices may be spread out over a number of years.

Another approach to evaluating social programs is to establish a pilot project. In this way, the company can study the results of the project to determine if predetermined goals are met and to get a better idea of the costs involved. Also, changes in the administration and operations of the program can be made without involving the entire organization.

The fourth and fifth questions (Can costs of this action be acceptably distributed? and Do we possess the managerial competence to do the job?) deal with the micro viewpoint or operational questions. Although a social program may have specific goals, be well planned and look to be within budget constraints, it will be necessary to have appropriate staff

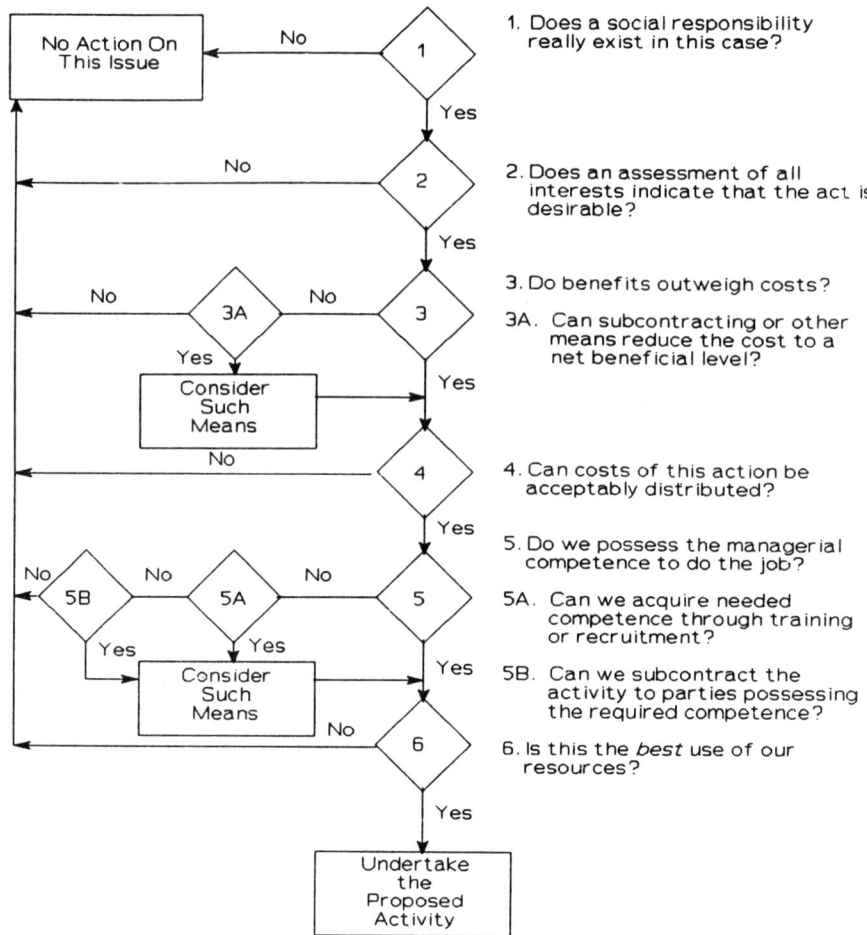

Figure 4.4. A Corporate Social Action Model

Adapted from D. W. Jackson and R. J. Aldag, "Planning for Corporate Social Actions," *Managerial Planning*, 1980, September/October, 28–33.

to run it and to be able to distribute costs among units or over time. Middle and lower level management typically is involved in the implementation planning phase.

The sixth question asks, Is this the *best* use of our resources? The social actions which maximize the use of the firm's capital and human resources while reducing negative and increasing positive externalities should be emphasized. Managers must continually make tradeoffs, however, since there are multiple, often conflicting demands placed on the organization by the various stakeholder groups. The social involvement activity which maximizes the firms multiple goals and satisfies a majority of the stakeholders may be preferable over a plan which is most efficient but meets only one goal or satisfies only one group.

Organizing

Ackerman (1973) studied two multi-divisional firms regarding the implementation of a pollution control system at one and an equal employment opportunity program in the other. He found implementation takes from 6 to 8 years and follows a three phase pattern. Phase I (called Policy) includes problem identification and policy formulation. Phase II is called the learning phase and involves developing experience in dealing with the programs and the development of staff specialists in pollution control and equal opportunity regulation. Phase III is the institutionalization phase and involves organizational changes, managerial role changes, and public affairs management.

Murray (1976) studied two banks with respect to their (voluntary) minority lending programs. Again, complete institutionalization through Phase III took approximately 8 years. In addition, he found policy formulation in Phase I and both technical and administrative learning during Phase II.

As organizations move from Phase I to Phase III of social involvement, different organizing strategies are appropriate. These are summarized in Table 4.2. During Phase I, the involvement of the Chief Executive Officer (CEO) and other top managers is crucial. Before issues can be identified and programs developed, the commitment of the top levels of the organization must be established and communicated throughout the firm. In addition, a task force focusing on social involvement activities may be established with members selected from appropriate areas in the company. The temporary nature of the task force is appropriate for the policy formulation and problem identification stage, but may impede implementation later on. The product of the task force may be a report describing policy and prioritizing the social issues to be used by managers in their decision-making process.

Table 4.2. Organizing for Social Involvement

Stage of Social Involvement	Organizational Structure
Phase I – Policy	Increased Involvement of CEO Task Force
Phase II – Learning	Public Responsibility Committee of Board of Directors Permanent Management Committee Development of Staff Specialists
Phase III – Institutionalization	Manager of Public Affairs Permanent Department or Unit for Social Activities

Once Phase II begins, a specific program or issue has been selected and attention must be turned to designing and implementing specific strategies for action. Permanent committees at the board and/or management levels may be formed to provide guidance and operational assistance for the program. Board committees provide a high level of status and authority, but must be well staffed and have access to organizational information to be effective.

A permanent management committee may be made up of line, staff, board members, and external interest group members. If run efficiently and not too large, such a committee may bring the required broad base of knowledge to a particular problem. Because the members also have other organizational duties, such a committee may not be able to quickly respond to changes in the environment. It may serve, however, as a bridge between top management and those lower in the organization responsible for the day to day operations of a particular social program.

As time goes on, staff specialists will develop in specific areas such as equal employment, occupational safety and health, and pollution control. Working with permanent committees and line managers responsible for the social programs, these specialists may play an important consultative role in the learning phase.

As the organization moves into Phase III, permanent departments or units in charge of specific social areas or public affairs in general may be formed. The specialists form an integral part of these organizations, and a manager of public affairs or social responsibility may be appointed. In addition, activities such as environmental scanning may be centralized and coordinated and communication of results enhanced. Such structures require a separate budget allocation and a high level of commitment on the part of the organization. Once in place, however, social involvement can become an integral part of the company.

Controlling

The primary mechanism for the measurement and evaluation of social responsibility and involvement is the *social audit*. Through this mechanism, it is possible to determine the impact of social programs on external groups and to evaluate their effectiveness in areas not usually covered in a financial report. Information used may come from the organization's environmental scanning process (as described in Chapter 2), special studies made in areas of particular concern such as equal employment opportunity or environmental conditions, and the normal financial and operating reports of the firm.

The results of a social audit may be reported as a simple descriptive summary or checklist of each relevant program, including major goals and achievements. Detailed statements may also be developed for each program, specifying the background, objectives, implementation strategies and evaluation procedures.

Some managers may also make estimates of the benefits and costs related to social programs. For example, the costs of a safety program may include equipment, developing training programs, and time spent at such programs. The benefits can be measured by the number of injuries per hours of exposure, the costs of medical and workmen's compensation claims, and the ratio of injuries to industry averages. Thus, for each program, the direct and indirect costs as well as specific outcome measures must be developed.

Another approach to measuring the overall social costs or benefits is outlined by Lee Seidler (1973). Table 4.3 shows a basic accounting statement which delineates the socially desired outputs not sold as well as the undesirable effects or externalities. By comparing these benefits and costs to the value added by the production of the firm, the net social profit or loss is calculated. Although assigning dollar values to the social outputs is difficult, this framework provides a starting place for managers developing the parameters around which a social audit will take place.

Table 4.3. Social Income Statement for Profit-Seeking Firm

Value added by production of the enterprise		$xxx
Add socially desirable outputs not sold		
Job training	$xxx	
Health improvement of workers	xxx	
Employment of disadvantages minorities	xxx	
Other	xxx	xxx
		$xxx
Less socially undesirable effects not paid for		
Air pollution	$xxx	
Water pollution	xxx	
Health problems caused by products	xxx	
Other	xxx	xxx
Net social profit (or loss)		$xxx

Source: Adapted with minor modifications from Lee J. Seidler, "Dollar Values in the Social Income Statement," *World* (Peat Marwick Mitchell & Co.), Spring 1973, p. 21.

A more detailed example of a socio-economic operating statement was developed by David Linowes and is shown in Table 4.4. Here social involvement programs are classified as relations with people, with the environment and with the product. The analysis points out that an organization must make trade-offs among social expenditures, with some programs being postponed in favor of others. In addition, socio-economic improvements are accumulated over time so that a long range picture of the costs and benefits of various programs can be developed.

Table 4.4. XXXX Corporation
Socio-Economic Operating Statement for the Year Ending
December 31, 1995

I.	*Relations with People:*			
	A. *Improvements:*			
		1. Training program for handicapped workers	$ 10,000	
		2. Contribution to educational institution	4,000	
		3. Extra turnover costs because of minority hiring program	5,000	
		4. Cost of daycare center for children of employees, voluntarily set up	<u>11,000</u>	
	Total Improvements			$ 30,000
	B. *Less: Detriments*			
		1. Postponed installing new safety devices on cutting machines (cost of the devices)		<u>14,000</u>
	C. Net improvements in People Actions for the Year			$ 16,000*
II.	*Relations with Environment:*			
	A. *Improvements:*			
		1. Cost of reclaiming and landscaping old dump on company property	$ 70,000	
		2. Cost of installing pollution control devices on Plant A smokestacks	4,000	
		3. Cost of detoxifying waste from finishing process this year	<u>9,000</u>	
	Total Improvements			$ 83,000
	B. *Less: Detriments*			
		1. Cost that would have been incurred to relandscape strip mining site used this year	$ 80,000	
		2. Estimated costs to have installed purification process to neutralize poisonous liquid being dumped into stream	<u>100,000</u>	
	C. Net Deficit in Environment Actions for the Year			$180,000 ($97,000)*
III.	*Relations with Product:*			
	A. *Improvements:*			
		1. Salary of V.P. while serving on government Product Safety Commission	$ 25,000	
		2. Cost of substituting lead-free paint for previously used poisonous lead paint	<u>9,000</u>	
	Total Improvements			$ 34,000
	B. *Less: Detriments*			
		1. Safety device recommended by Safety Council but not added to product		<u>22,000</u>
	C. Net Improvements in Product Actions for the Year			$ 12,000*
	Total Socio-Economic Deficit for the Year			($69,000)
	Add: Net Cumulative Socio-Economic Improvements as of January 1, 1995			<u>$249,000</u>
Grand Total Net Socio-Economic Actions to December 31, 1995				<u>$180,000</u>

*The starred items are summed to obtain the Total Socio-Economic Deficit for the year 1995.

Adapted from: David F. Linowes, "An Approach to Socio-Economic Accounting," *Conference Board RECORD*, November 1972, p. 60.

Although the approaches used above provide a framework for a social audit, the problem of actual measurement still remains. When beginning any social responsibility activity, careful thought must be given at the planning stage of what the actual direct and indirect costs are likely to be. Even more difficult may be the measurement of benefits, since these activities often affect individuals and groups outside the organization. By using multiple measures and incorporating the social audit into social responsibility planning and implementation, the outcomes of these activities may be reported.

Staffing/Rewarding

As an organization becomes more involved in social involvement, it may be necessary to integrate activities in this area into existing job descriptions and specifications. Eventually, separate positions may be developed under the office of the chairman to deal with specific issues or to consider various stakeholder group interests. The human resource manager will have to design and staff such positions as they evolve. Thus, a large corporation may have managers in the areas of government affairs, community affairs, employee relations, stockholder relations, consumer relations, and public relations. On the other hand, if the firm chooses to organize around individual issues, there may be a need for specialists in the areas of environmental protection, equal employment opportunity, and occupational safety.

In addition to changes in the positions found in the organization, changes in the compensation and reward system may be necessary. First, the performance of individual specialists must be assessed and appropriate compensation determined. What actions and outcomes regarding specific issues or stakeholder groups are desired? How much does the organization value the activities of these specialists? Will the organization reward individuals for actions which lead to the benefit of society or which result in mitigating possible negative consequences for the firm?

Second, the organization may want to reward all employees who engage in socially responsible activities. Involvement in community activities or participation in public education activities such as lectures at local schools might be given positive rewards. By incorporating such a service component in the company's performance appraisal and compensation system, the organization will be encouraging and supporting social responsibility at the individual level.

Summary

Social responsibility is the notion that business has an obligation to society which extends beyond economic and legal duties. It is the extent to which an organization acts to correct the negative effects and to maximize the positive effects associated with its production processes. One problem is to determine what actions are socially responsible. The principle of "public responsibility" is one approach to making this determination.

A variety of arguments supporting social responsibility have been made. These include: the need to acknowledge the interests of stakeholder groups and to reach multiple goals, the fact corporations are created by society and must meet public expectations or face a future loss of power, business is a source of capital and human resources which should be used to improve societal conditions, negative externalities are created by business and therefore should be corrected by these organizations, and social responsibility is a good investment. Arguments against social responsibility include: social problems should be solved by the public sector if they are not solved by the free market system, a business's efficiency will be reduced if attention is paid to social goals, managers do not have the required background or expertise to make decisions regarding social spending, it is too expensive, social performance is difficult to measure, business is already too powerful, it is difficult to determine what actions are socially responsible, and corporate "concern" for social issues is simply a public relations campaign.

A model of the social involvement of business develops a framework integrating the externalities resulting from the business process, the determinants of the level of social responsibility, the level of social responsibility, business response and managerial implications, and societal element changes. The determinants of the level of social responsibility are multiple organizational goals, pressures from stakeholders, managerial philosophy and corporate governance. Key issues in corporate governance include the measurement of corporate performance, corporate power, and the professionalism of management. A number of reforms in the way corporations are governed have been suggested. These include implementation of a social audit, increased disclosure to stockholders and other interest groups, stockholder resolutions in areas of social concern, federal chartering of corporations, increased representation of women, minorities, and employees on the board of directors, appointment of a public director, and establishment of a corporate social responsibility committee at the board of director level.

The three levels of social responsibility are social obligation, social responsibility, and social responsiveness. Companies which follow a social obligation strategy comply with existing regulations, laws, and contractual obligations. A socially responsible company goes beyond the law, and acts to correct the negative effects of the production process. Finally, socially responsive firms go beyond industry norms and practices and follow a proactive strategy in social areas.

Management responses may involve utilization of a social action model to evaluate planning strategies, reorganization to match the stage of development of social programs, development of a social audit to measure social performance, or modifications in staffing and rewarding to facilitate the implementation of social programs. In this way the organization may address the concerns of stakeholders and move toward meeting corporate goals.

Questions

1. How is the concept of social responsibility related to primary and secondary involvement? What role does public responsibility play in management decision making?

2. You are a shareholder in a copper smelting plant which is the major employer in a small town. Environmentalists want the company to install pollution control equipment at a cost of $20 million. What are the arguments for and against this expenditure? What actions should management take in this situation?

3. Using a company with which you are familiar, determine their level of social responsibility and actions in this area. Apply the model of the level of social involvement to this situation.

4. Identify the determinants of the level of social responsibility to the companies involved in the Infant Formula Controversy.

5. For each of the examples cited in Table 4.1 describe the externalities addressed. Do these deal with primary or secondary involvement? Hypothesize what the determinants of the level of social responsibility in each example might have been.

6. Examine the manner in which your university is governed. How are stakeholder interests taken into account? What suggestions would you have for reform?

7. You are a manager in a socially irresponsible company. After reading this chapter, you decide to try to incorporate social responsibility issues into the decision making process at the firm. How would you change the planning, organizing, controlling, and staffing/rewarding functions at the company?

Key Concepts

social responsibility

social involvement

primary involvement

secondary involvement

principle of "public responsibility"

stakeholders

levels of social responsibility

individual proprietorship

partnership

corporation

corporate governance

social audit

federal chartering

public director

social action model

stages of social involvement

Case Analysis: Playskool Inc.

Playskool, Inc., a maker of preschool toys and best known for its Lincoln Logs building sets, has had a facility in Chicago for almost 50 years. In 1968, Milton Bradley, another toymaker, acquired the firm and Playskool became one of its divisions. On September 10, 1984, Hasbro Industries, maker of Mr. Potato Head, GI Joe action figures, and toy robots called Transformers, acquired Milton Bradley. A new company was formed called Hasbro Bradley.

Less than two weeks later, on September 19, 1984, Hasbro Bradley announced that the Chicago facility of Playskool would be closed and the machinery and approximately 700 jobs would be moved to the company's facilities on the East Coast as of December, 1984. What factors entered into the decision to move the facility? Which stakeholders will be affected, both positively and negatively, by the decision? Did Playskool act in a socially responsible manner regarding the plant closing in Chicago?

In 1980, Playskool applied for City of Chicago sponsorship of a $1-million industrial revenue bond (IRB). These IRB's are low interest, tax exempt bonds available to Chicago businesses for the purposes of stimulating investment in the City of Chicago and retaining and creating jobs. Once approved by the city, private lenders, not the governmental agencies, provide the loan to the business. Governmental approval of the bonds only means that buyers of the bonds are exempt from paying taxes on the bond's earnings. This tax exemption means approximately 25% lower interest cost for the company borrowing the money.

Playskool's application for the IRB was approved by the City of Chicago on April 16, 1980 and the funds were used to buy automated equipment including injection and blow molding machinery, puzzle making equipment, painting and packaging machines, and children's blocks and lincoln log equipment. At this time, Playskool employed approximately 1,200 people in Chicago and predicted an increase of 446 workers if their IRB application was granted. Instead, the plant employment level decreased steadily since then, to approximately 700 workers as of September, 1984. No specific reasons had been given for the decline, but some observers felt it may have been due to increased productivity resulting from automation, a decrease in demand for Playskool products as a result of the recession, and an increase in the amount of overseas manufacturing by the company.

Milton Bradley Co. had been studying the possibility of closing the Chicago plant for some time. A study had been conducted prior to the acquisition discussions with Hasbro Industries, indicating the following reasons for a possible closing. First, there was significant underutilization of the plant, in part due to poor construction of a 1967 addition. In fact, early in 1983, Playskool won a $6.3 million judgment against Ragnar Benson Inc., the construction firm which built the addition because of the rapid deterioration of the concrete used. Second, there was reported to be some difficulty in attracting research and development staff in the toy industry to Chicago.

The Chicago workforce was praised in the Milton Bradley study, and an attempt to lower labor costs was *not* mentioned by Playskool as a reason for considering closing the plant. The workforce was 75% black and Hispanic and 60% women. They were represented by the Retail Wholesale and Department Store Union Local No. 20 and earned an average of $7 an hour.

According to Stephen Hassenfeld, Chairman of Hasbro Bradley Inc., "... the only reason the Playskool operation was profitable was because of goods brought in from overseas. That division was narrowly profitable last year[1]."

Until the official announcement of the plant relocation, Milton Bradley denied plans of the plant closure. For example, the president of Playskool, George Volanakis, received an anonymous letter from a plant employee who feared the plant was about to close. "He denied any movement was in the offing," said Mr. Lemonides of the Greater North Polaski Development Council, a highly respected neighborhood business development group. "He told me there was no reason to move a plant that was so profitable. It turned out the letter was prophetic[2]."

At the time of the announcement of the plant relocation, Charles Perrottet, vice president for corporate development at Milton Bradley, indicated Playskool management was developing an acceptable severance and job placement program for the Chicago employees. During September and October, 1984, Playskool's activities on behalf of the workers

---

[1] Quoted in *Crain's Chicago Business*, November 5, 1985, p. 70.

[2] Quoted in *Crain's Chicago Business*, November 5, 1984, pp. 2, 70.

to be terminated included posting of the names of potential employers in the area as well as specific job openings, conducting outplacement seminars on job search techniques for salaried employees, and offering transfers to other locations to 70 workers. In addition, a severance package worth more than $3 million was ratified by union members. In December, 1984 the Union offered outplacement seminars in English and Spanish for its members.

Despite these efforts by Hasbro Bradley, emotions surrounding the closing of the Chicago Playskool facility ran high. "This plant closing has stirred up as much sentiment as the U.S. Steel situation last year," said Economic Development Commissioner Robert Mier. "This corporation has shown no sense of responsibility[3]."

Several neighborhood and community groups also became involved. The West Side Jobs Network, a coalition of community groups seeking to retain or expand jobs on Chicago's west side, and the Greater North Pulaski Development Corporation utilized a number of measures to arouse public interest.

These community interest groups requested the decision to close the plant be reconsidered by Hasbro Bradley. They asked the City of Chicago to consider legal action against the company since the closing of the Playskool facility appeared to be in violation of the agreement made with respect to the Industrial Revenue Bond awarded in 1980. In addition, the community groups requested that the facility and equipment be left intact while employee ownership or a buyer for the plant was sought and ongoing maintenance of the plant be provided.

It was also pointed out that the majority of the Chicago plant workforce were Black or Hispanic. However, East Longmeadow, Mass., one proposed relocation site, is a nearly 100% White community and the other, Northvale, N.J., is the location of Hasbro's non-union plants. Thus, the move may have been considered discriminatory or an attempt to eliminate the union by some groups.

Public meetings were sponsored by the West Side Jobs Network to discuss the plant relocation with interested people from the area. On November 10, 1984 a rally was held at a Chicago area Toys-R-Us store

---

[3] Quoted in *Crain's Chicago Business*, November 5, 1984, p. 70.

selling Playskool and other Hasbro Bradley products. Speakers protested the plant relocation and called for a boycott of all toys and games made by the company. Another rally was held in downtown Chicago on November 23, 1984, the biggest shopping day of the year.

As a result of these community group efforts, both the local and national news media gave coverage to the controversy over the Playskool plant closing in Chicago. This included articles in the *Wall Street Journal*, *New York Times*, and reports on national news programs.

On December 4, 1984, Chicago Mayor Harold Washington announced the city had filed suit against Hasbro Bradley to block the closing. This was based on the violation of the agreement made when the approval was given for the 1980 $1 million IRB granted to Playskool, Inc. to buy equipment.

On December 6, 1984, Playskool paid over $1 million to purchase the Industrial Revenue Bond which had been issued in 1980. This action cancelled the bond, thereby voiding all provisions.

Hasbro Bradley then filed a motion to dismiss the city's lawsuit. A friend of the court brief was filed on December 21, 1984 by representatives of the Community Renewal Society, the Church Federation and the Jewish Council on Urban Affairs asking the Court not to dismiss the city's lawsuit against Hasbro Bradley.

During November, 1984, Mayor Harold Washington attempted to meet with Stephen Hassenfeld, chairman of the board and chief executive officer of Hasbro Bradley, to discuss the planned relocation. However, the meeting was not held until December 17, 1984.

On January 28, 1985, it was announced that an agreement had been reached between the City of Chicago and Hasbro Bradley. The city would drop its lawsuit against Hasbro Bradley, and Playskool would continue operations in Chicago with the approximately 125 employees remaining through most of 1985. In addition, job search facilities would be available at Playskool to all 700 employees layed off as a result of the closing of the Chicago facility. Five hundred dollars would be paid to employers for each Playskool employee hired, a $100 award would be given to employees who provided job leads, and a $300,000 advertising campaign including TV commercials and print ads featuring Gale Sayers (a former

Chicago Bears star) would be utilized to locate employment opportunities for the workers.

Stephen Hassenfeld, chairman of the board and chief executive officer of Hasbro Bradley, Inc. stated that he was offended by the appearance of a "deal." "We're doing all these things on our own initiative," he said. "Even if we had won the lawsuit, our ethical responsibility would have been the same. There is no deal here. I told everybody this, that this can't appear like a deal has been cut[4]."

The West Side Jobs Network also called off its boycott of Hasbro Bradley products. Although the plant would still close, considerable effort would be made to find jobs for all former Playskool workers desiring job placement services.

Case Questions

1. What stakeholder groups were affected by the decision to close Playskool's facility in Chicago? What were the impacts on each group?

2. What were the determinants of the level of social responsibility taken by the management of Playskool and later Hasbro Bradley?

3. How was Playskool's level of social responsibility affected by external factors? Did it change over time? If so, how?

4. If you were the manager of another plant in Chicago which was contemplating relocation, what lessons might be learned from Playskool's experience.

5. Was there a "deal" between the City of Chicago and Hasbro Bradley?

---

[4] Quoted in *Chicago Tribune*, January 30, 1985, Section 2, p. 2.

Case References

Chicago Tribune, September 21, 1984, Section 3, p. 1; October 22, 1984, Section 1, p. 1; December 15, 1985, Section 1, p. 5; January 29, 1985, Section 2, p. 3; January 30, 1985, Section 2, p. 2.

Crain's Chicago Business, November 5, 1984, pp. 2, 70, 71; November 19, 1984, p. 31; February 4, 1985, p. 68.

Greenhouse, Steven. "Toy Concern's Plan to Move Angers Chicago." *New York Times*, December 16, 1984.

Interviews with and materials provided by Playskool representatives.

Page, Clarence. "Hasbro, The Grinch Who 'Stole' Jobs." *Wall Street Journal*, December 9, 1984.

References

Ackerman, R. A. "How Companies Respond to Social Demands." *Harvard Business Review*, 1973, July–August, 88–98.

Bowen, H. R. *Social Responsibilities of the Businessman*. New York: Harper & Row, 1953.

Bowman, E. H. and Haire, M. "A Strategic Posture Toward Corporate Social Responsibility." *California Management Review*, 1975, *28* (2), 49–58.

Bowman, E. H. and Haire, M. "Social Impact Disclosure and Corporate Annual Reports." *Accounting, Organizations, and Society*, 1976, *1* (1), 11–21.

Cochran, P. L. and Wood, R. A. "Corporate Social Responsibility and Financial Performance." *Academy of Management Journal*, 1984, *27* (1), 42–56.

Dill, W. R. "Private Power and Public Responsibility." In *Running the American Corporation*, W. R. Dill (Ed.). Englewood Cliffs, N.J.: Prentice-Hall, Inc., 1978.

Freeman, R. E. and Reed, D. L. "Stockholders and Stakeholders: A New Perspective on Corporate Governance." *California Management Review*, 1983, *25* (3), 88–106.

Friedman, M. "The Social Responsibility of Business Is to Increase Its Profits." *New York Times Magazine*, September 13, 1970, pp. 122–126.

Halal, W. E. "Big Business vs. Big Government – A New Social Contract?" *Long Range Planning*, 1984, *17* (4), 30–37.

Heald, M. *The Social Responsibilities of Business, Company and Community, 1900–1960*. Cleveland, Ohio; Case Western University Press, 1970.

Jackson, D. W. and Aldag, R. J. "Planning for Corporate Social Actions." *Managerial Planning*, 1980, September/October, 28–33.

Johnson, H. L. "Socially Responsible Firms: An Empty Box or a Universal Set." *The Journal of Business*, 1966, *39* (July), 394–399.

Jones, T. M. "Corporate Social Responsibility Revisited, Redefined." *California Management Review*, 1980, *22* (2), 59–67.

Linowes, D. F. "An Approach to Socio-Economic Accounting," *Conference Board RECORD*, November, 1972.

McGuire, J. W. *Business and Society*. New York: McGraw-Hill, 1963.

Mintzberg, H. "The Case for Corporate Social Responsibility." *Journal of Business Strategy*, 1983, *4* (2), 3–15.

Murray, E. A., Jr. "The Social Response Process in Commercial Banks: An Empirical Investigation." *Academy of Management Review*, 1976, *1* (3), 5–15.

Preston, L. E. and Post, J. E. *Private Management and Public Policy*. Englewood Cliffs, N. J.: Prentice-Hall, Inc., 1975.

Preston, L. E. and Post, J. E. "Private Management and Public Policy." *California Management Review*, 1981, *23* (3), 56–62.

Sethi, S. P. "A Conceptual Framework for Environmental Analysis of Social Issues and Evaluation of Business Response Patterns." *Academy of Management Review*, 1979, *4* (1), 63–74.

Sethi, S. P. and Post, J. E. "Public Consequences of Private Action: The Marketing of Infant Formula in Less Developed Countries." *California Management Review*, 1979, *21* (4), 35–48.

Seidler, L. J. "Dollar Values in the Social Income Statement," *World* (Peat Marwick Mitchell & Co.), Spring, 1973.

Sturdivant, F. D. *The Corporate Social Challenge: Cases and Commentaries*. Homewood, IL: Richard D. Irwin, Inc., 1981.

CHAPTER 5
BUSINESS ETHICS

INTRODUCTION

In 1983, the Wall Street Journal commissioned the Gallop Organization to conduct a nationwide poll of a representative sample of the American public. The poll concerned the state of American ethics, especially business ethics.[1] According to the poll, 64% of the individuals in the sample thought that at least half of all business executives cheat on their taxes. Seventy four percent thought that at least half of all executives pad their expense accounts, and 28% thought that half or more of the business people in their own communities give bribes or favors to the police.

Since this poll was published, the newspapers and TV screens have featured the unethical exploits of Wall Street financial wizards, Chicago commodities traders, defense contractors, cattle futures traders, savings and loan executives and government contractors, among others. If that same Wall Street Journal poll were taken today, the 1983 opinions would look benign by comparison.

Is the state of business ethics really as bad as the public perceives? What can managers and future managers do to increase the level of ethics in business? What is ethical behavior and how can people in business deal with the ethical dilemmas that many frequently face?

This chapter is about business ethics. In it, we will explore a variety of ethical concepts which have been developed over time. The sources of values in society will be examined and several ethical tests developed which can be used to judge the appropriateness of alternative actions. Several ethical problems which are common in business will then be dealt with. The techniques that business can use to help raise the level of ethics within a company will also be examined. The chapter concludes with a case concerning the ethics of conducting business in South Africa.

---

[1] The results of the poll were reported in a series of articles in the *Wall Street Journal*, October 31, November 1, November 2, and November 3, 1983.

Ethics affects all the interactions that business has with the external environment. These include interactions with competitors, suppliers, customers, government, and society in general. The behavior of an organization's employees (whether ethical or not) can reflect on the firm in a positive or negative manner. Thus, ethics is an important ingredient in the relationship of business and the external environment.

What Is Business Ethics?

In their book *Business Ethics* Hoffman and Moore (1990, p.1) define ethics as ". . . the study of what is good or right for human beings. It asks what goals people ought to pursue and what actions they ought to perform." Buchholz (1992, p. 46) states that the study of ethics is ". . . a philosophical inquiry into various theories of what is good for people and what is bad or evil. . ." while Frederick, Post and Davis (1992, p. 52) believe that ethics ". . . is a conception of right and wrong conduct."

Two characteristics of ethics are evident from these definitions. First, ethics is an ought. That is, ethics tells people what they ought to do. It is a normative conception of what is right or wrong. Second, ethics is a set of principles or rules. It provides guidance to help differentiate moral or good conduct from immoral or unacceptable behavior.

Professional philosophers make a distinction between ethics or ethical theory and morality. Ethics is considered to be the study of moral principles, and morality refers to the principles themselves. The common notions of ethics embedded in the above definitions make no distinction between ethics and morality and use both terms interchangeably. This is the approach that will be taken in this book.

<u>Business ethics</u> is the application of general ethical concepts to the unique situations confronted in business. It asks what is right or wrong behavior in business and what principles or rules can be used as guidance in business situations. Ethics in business is no different than ethics in any other human endeavor, whether it be a profession such as medicine, law or engineering, or ordinary activities such as taking exams, buying groceries, or applying for credit. The same ethical concepts apply; only the situations differ.

There are two relationships which are important to understanding business ethics. One is the relationship of ethics to religion. The study of business ethics does not mean the study of religion. To be sure, religion can offer a great deal of guidance as to what is morally right or wrong. However, ethics attempts to develop a set of rules which are not dependent upon a particular religious belief.

A second relationship concerns business ethics and social responsibility. Both involve normative judgments as to what ought to be done. Frequently, topics in social responsibility appear in business ethics books. Some scholars even use the terms interchangeably.

In this book, however, a distinction will be drawn between the two concepts. Social responsibility will be considered a corporate or organizational concern. That is, social responsibility will be considered a managerial response to changes in the societal elements or other elements of the external environment. As discussed in the previous chapter, the degree of social responsibility is a business decision which concerns the level and type of social involvement.

Business ethics, on the other hand, has two different levels of concern. The first concern is on an individual level. That is, ethics at the first level involves the actions of a particular individual. Ethics provides guidance in what a manager or employee should or should not do. Thus, cheating, stealing, and lying are ethical concerns at the first level.

The second concern, like social responsibility, is at the corporate or organizational level. The difference between social responsibility and ethics at this level is that while the former analyzes the impact of business decisions on the societal elements through social involvement, business ethics involves all relationships that the business has with the environment. There are ethical considerations involving the relationship of business with the marketplace. Price fixing, false advertising, and dangerous products are examples. Ethics is involved with the linkage between business and the public sector. Bribery and payoffs are examples. Finally, many if not all social responsibility issues contain ethical considerations. Plant closings, training for the hard core unemployed and discrimination are a few instances.

Concepts of Ethics

There are a variety of concepts of ethics which have been developed by moral philosophers over generations. These concepts were developed to distinguish ethical from unethical behavior. Each views ethics in a slightly different light. Accordingly, the same action may be considered either ethical or unethical depending upon the concepts employed. Each concept also has its deficiencies. Thus, none stands out as the single approach which all individuals can use to decide the appropriateness of a given action.

Relativism

Ethical relativism is the belief that <u>there is no universal standard by which morality can be judged</u>. It is argued that an action may be ethically correct for one society or culture and morally wrong for another. Ethics and morality are relative.

In order to see how relativism and the other concepts of ethics can be used to decide on the morality of certain actions, an example will be utilized. This is the example cited in Chapter 2 concerning the use of price as a surrogate for quality.

In Chapter 2, it was mentioned that consumers frequently do not have a detailed understanding of every single product on the market. The quality of many goods may be very difficult for the average consumer to evaluate. In comparing one brand against another, many consumers assume that higher price implies greater quality. These consumers would tend to purchase greater quantities of the higher priced good under the assumption that it is of higher quality.

Suppose that you work for a cosmetics company. Most consumers are not chemists, so that in evaluating the quality of the cosmetics that your company produces against the products of other manufacturers, many of them assume that more expensive means higher quality. Marketing information indicates that if the company introduces another brand at a substantially higher price, sales will increase a great deal. The new brand would have the same chemical formulation and be exactly the same cosmetic as another brand that the company sells, but at a much higher price. The only difference would be the name and the shape of the container. Is it ethical to introduce this product?

If this action is evaluated according to ethical relativism, then it may be ethical to introduce the product. Since using price as a marketing device is widely practiced in our society, and many other firms do the same thing, then the standards of our society are not violated by this action. Even though the firm is technically deceiving the consumer, buyers are not forced to purchase the product. In other societies, however, if this practice is not widely accepted and practiced, relativism would lead to the conclusion that such pricing is not ethical.

Although relativism seems like a simple and straightforward approach to evaluating the ethics of a given action, it has problems. Hoffman and Moore (1990, p. 5) note that relativism says that what a society <u>believes</u> is right <u>is</u> in fact right for that society. However, "Several cultures throughout history have believed in slavery, for example. Yet most of us would argue that slavery is not only wrong now but was wrong then, in spite of cultural mores." Thus, there are in fact absolutes, such as prohibitions against slavery, murder, rape, and torture, that relativism would say would be ethical practices in some societies. Relativism leads to the conclusion that there are no such absolutes.

In addition, there is a problem in defining what is meant by a "society". Hoffman and Moore (1990) ask if a minority group holds ethical views different from those of the majority in a society, are those minority groups unethical? "Or should that group be viewed as a society in its own right, with an equally valid set of beliefs? If the minority is to be regarded as a separate society, ought not a dissenting group within the minority be seen in the same way? And should not each individual, as well, be looked upon as a society of sorts with a set of ethical beliefs which are right for himself or herself?" (Hoffman and Moore, 1990, p. 6)

Thus, ethical relativism leads to the conclusion that there cannot be disagreements about ethics, since each person's opinion is correct. ". . . if ethical relativism is correct, no comparative moral judgments are possible. We cannot say that any act or belief is better or worse from a moral perspective than any other" (Hoffman and Moore, 1990, p. 6).

Egoism

The concept of ethical egoism is <u>that one ought to act in his or her own interest</u>. Acting contrary to self interest is unethical, according to this point of view. This does not mean that others' interests should not be taken into account. Rather, the interests of other people should be considered, as long as this promotes ones own self interest in the long run. Beauchamp and Bowie (1988, p. 19) summarize the egoist's point of view:

> "... one should obey rules and laws only in order to protect oneself and to bring about a situation of communal living that is personally advantageous. One should also back down on an "obligation" whenever it becomes clear that it is to one's long-range disadvantage to fulfill the obligation. Thus, when confronted by a social revolution, the questionable trustworthiness of a colleague, or an incompetent administration at one's place of employment, one is under no obligation to obey the law, fulfill one's contracts, or tell the truth. These obligations exist only because one assumes them only as long as doing so promotes one's own interest."

How would the concept of egoism be used to evaluate the ethics of the decision to introduce the new cosmetic? The egoist would say that if this business decision results in greater profits for the firm, then it is ethical. However, if the decision to introduce the product results in consumers questioning the quality of the product, resulting in long run losses, then the product should not be introduced. Note that it is in the long run interest of the firm which is being evaluated, not the interests of the consumers.

Milton Friedman's concept of social responsibility, discussed in the previous chapter, that the only obligation of business is to increase its profits, is an egoistic statement. Adam Smith's notion of the "invisible hand" discussed in Chapter 2 is a conception of the results of egoistic behavior. If everyone acts in their own self interest, the greater good of all is achieved. Thus, it is possible to think of the market system in egoistic terms. The marketplace provides some vindication of egoism since it can lead to positive social benefits.

One of the shortcomings of the market system discussed in Chapter 3 also highlights an important shortcoming of egoism as an ethical concept. This is the presence of externalities. When externalities result from a market action, a conflict is created between two competing interests. The presence of pollution creates a conflict between the polluter and those who bear the costs of pollution. Egoism holds that both the polluter, in pursuing his or her interests to keep polluting, and the individuals who bear the costs are in a morally defendable position. Thus, egoism would hold that knowingly dumping toxic wastes and thus creating a cancer threat to individuals is ethical, provided the firm is not punished for such activities.

Further, egoism as an ethical concept, appears contradictory. This is because an egoist cannot advise others to be egoists. As Hoffman and Moore (1990, p. 9) point out, a true egoist would tell others to maximize the egoist's interests, and not their own. Urging others to pursue their own self interest may not be in the interest of the egoist.

Utilitarianism

Utilitarianism is an ethical concept <u>which holds that the morality of an action can be determined by its consequences</u>. Specifically, an action is ethical according utilitarianism if it promotes the greatest good for the greatest number. Beauchamp and Bowie (1988, p. 25) state that utilitarianism holds ". . . that an action or practice is right (when compared to any alternative action or practice) if it leads to the greatest possible balance of good consequences or to the least possible balance of bad consequences in the world as a whole."

Utilitarianism assesses the morality of an action by weighing the benefits and the costs, to whomsoever they accrue. If the benefits exceed the costs, the action is deemed moral. If the costs are greater than the benefits that accrue to all individuals, then the action is not moral. This concept is in essence a moral cost-benefit analysis.

Since utilitarianism attempts to maximize the greatest possible value for all individuals, the objective of maximizing economic efficiency is consistent with this concept. Greater efficiencies of production can lead to a larger variety and quantity of goods and services being available at lower cost to the consumer. Beauchamp and Bowie (1988, p. 26) argue that this is part of the traditional business conception of society. Thus, ". . . the enterprise of business harbors a fundamentally utilitarian conception of the good society." In addition, the concepts of utility, individual preferences and cost-benefit analysis in economics all have as their basis utilitarian concepts of what is good.

How would the decision to market a new cosmetic be viewed in utilitarian terms? One approach is to argue that consumers receive psychic value from purchasing this more expensive cosmetic. By making them feel better, consumer benefits are created that more than offset the additional costs that they must pay. If it were otherwise, consumers would not purchase the more expensive product.

On the other hand, it could be argued that consumers may have been able to spend the extra amount on other goods and services. They suffer a loss in utility since they could have consumed the cosmetic as well as other goods and services. This loss in utility, however, must be weighed against the benefit that the company receives in added revenue. The gain for the company can more than offset the losses of the individual consumers, depending upon how the gains and losses are weighted. Do the company gains carry a greater or lesser weight than equivalent consumer losses? If they carry a greater weight, then utilitarianism would approve of the action. If they carry a lesser weight, then this concept of ethics would judge the action as immoral.

This example highlights an important problem in implementing the concept of utilitarianism. This is the problem of quantifying and valuing the benefits and costs of a decision. Do all individuals' gains or losses count the same? Or are some gains more "valuable" if they accrue to some groups or individuals and less "valuable" if they accrue to others? Dollar values could be used. But how does one place a value on satisfaction, human life and health and other intangibles that may be affected by a particular decision? By what standard is utility measured and compared across individuals?

A second problem is that utilitarianism can lead to unjust consequences. Hoffman and Moore (1990) cite the example of a group of thugs who enjoy molesting small children. If the thugs received greater enjoyment than the pain inflicted on their victims, then utilitarianism would approve. They state: ". . . people have rights which ought not to be violated even when doing so results in a greater sum total of good. It is argued that utilitarianism is incapable of respecting such rights, because they can always be overridden in favor of an act or rule which maximizes total good." (Hoffman and Moore, 1990, p. 14)

Any restriction against the majority which protects a minority is not utilitarian. Thus, prohibitions against slavery which do not allow the majority to "own" members of a minority would not be approved by utilitarianism. In addition, individual protections in the Bill of Rights in the U.S. Constitution do not allow the majority to take advantage of an individual. Since the cost to the majority may exceed the benefits to the individual, utilitarianism may oppose these protections.

Deontologism

The term deontologism is derived from the Greek word for duty. This ethical concept is: "... <u>some actions are right or wrong for reasons other than their consequences. Factors other than good outcomes, then, justify at least some moral judgments and actions</u>" (Beauchamp and Bowie, 1988, p. 33). While utilitarianism asserts that the ends can justify the means, deontologism maintains that the means are what are important from an ethical standpoint.

Probably the best known of the deontological philosophers is Immanuel Kant (1724–1804). Kant developed the <u>categorical imperative</u> as means of formalizing this point of view. The <u>categorical imperative</u> states: "I ought never to act except in such a way that I can also will that my maxim should become a universal law." That is, Kant developed an ethical test which says that individuals should ask whether they would permit everyone to adopt an action which they are contemplating. If they are willing to permit universal practice, the action is moral. If the individuals want only to be an exception, then the action is immoral.

Kant called this ethical formulation the <u>categorical imperative</u> because it provides for no exceptions and is absolutely binding (categorical) and because it provides instruction as to how to gauge the morality of actions (imperative). It is duty based since the motive for acting is important in determining morality rather than the consequences. Thus, actions performed in self interest, even if they are beneficial to society, receive no special moral credit in Kant's view.

The categorical imperative provides guidance in dealing with other persons. Kant argued that people should never be treated as means to an end, but rather as ends in themselves. Hoffman and Moore (1990) argue that egoism and utilitarianism violate this principle. This notion of treating people as ends in themselves has developed into the principle of respect for persons. Beauchamp and Bowie (1988, p. 38) state: "To fail to respect persons is to treat them as mere means in accordance with our own ends, and thus as if they were not independent agents. To exhibit a lack of respect for persons is either to reject a person's considered judgments or to deny the person the liberty to act on those judgments."

Respect for persons thus leads to rejection of slavery and clearly deals with the difficult moral problems that utilitarianism and egoism seem to be unable to successfully address. The deontological point of view also provides guidance as to how employers and supervisors should deal with employees.

With regard to the decision to market the new cosmetic, the deontologist would argue that regardless of the justifications that are made, in the end, the decision involves a deception, which is morally wrong. The categorical imperative would state that one must be willing to allow universal deception of this type to make it morally acceptable. However, the reason that the cosmetic could be successful is because it is an exception and essentially fools consumers into thinking they are purchasing something which is more valuable. If all manufacturers of cosmetics practice this deception, then consumers may come to realize that more expensive may not mean better. There will then be no advantage in attempting to deceive them.

This example highlights an important dimension of ethical behavior. This is that such behavior builds security, friendliness, cooperation and trust in a society. If most individuals act in a moral or ethical fashion, then members of a society can feel confident that such behavior will govern most relationships with others. For example, consumers trust manufacturers to put more valuable contents into packages which cost more. This is especially true if consumers have difficulty judging the quality of certain items.

The security, friendliness, cooperation and trust which are outcomes of general ethical behavior are essentially public goods. That is, these are concepts and behavioral norms which we all consume in common. They are not subject to the exclusion principle in that a member of society cannot be excluded from them. They are subject to joint supply since consumption by one individual does not reduce the amount available for others.

These concepts and norms also have a "free rider" problem like other public goods discussed in Chapter 3. One or a few individuals can become exceptions and use the security, friendliness, cooperation, and trust to their own advantage. The cosmetic manufacturer essentially uses the trust developed by other producers and becomes a free rider, not adding to trust, but rather using it for personal or corporate advantage.

Kant's categorical imperative can be conceived as looking at ethics from a public goods standpoint. By focusing on the free rider problem, Kantian ethics attempts to preserve the public goods nature of widespread ethical behavior. The categorical imperative is thus a test to see if a particular action is in the nature of what a free rider would do, or whether it strengthens the concepts and norms of society.

Deontologism is not without its problems however. Hoffman and Moore (1990) note than Kant does not provide a framework for resolving conflicts between duties. How does one deal with a conflict between family and business? How about the example of the conflict between compensation of minorities and other disadvantaged groups for past discrimination, and the avoidance of discrimination against white males? Deontologism in general and Kantian ethics in particular does not provide a means of resolving conflicts between the duty to rectify past discrimination and the duty to avoid discrimination in general.

Second, Beauchamp and Bowie (1988) state that the utilitarians criticize deontologism for covertly appealing to consequences to demonstrate the rightness of actions. The utilitarians argue "... Kant's theory relies on a subtle but essential appeal to the utilitarian principle that if the consequences of the universal performance of a certain type of action can be shown to be undesirable overall, then that sort of action is wrong". (Beauchamp and Bowie, 1988, p. 41). Thus the utilitarians argue that Kantian ethics is not a separate ethical concept, but a disguised form of their concept.

Choice among Ethical Concepts

How should one choose among these competing ethical concepts? Which is correct? Is it relativism which holds that there is no universal standard by which morality can be judged, or egoism which contends that individuals should act only in their self interest? Is utilitarianism with its moral cost-benefit analysis the best concept, or deontologism with emphasis on duty the correct approach? The choice is all the more difficult because no concept is without its inconsistencies and defects.

Although ethical concepts can be quite helpful, in the end, ethics must remain a very personal decision. An individual's values and beliefs enter into the determination of the ethics of a particular action. In fact, the application of the various ethical concepts is not value free. For example, how does one value the benefits of a particular action if a utilitarian standard is used? Which outcomes should count as benefits and which as costs? How does one determine duty or justice? In the end it is the values of a society and of an individual which help shape perceptions of ethics and ethical behavior. This is not to suggest that ethics is relative. Rather, values and beliefs are important determinants of what is ethical behavior.

How do such values and beliefs develop? For any individual, the process of socialization over many years explains the inculcation of values. This socialization process has religion, the family, the schools, and the social environment, including the actions and beliefs of peers as inputs. The socialization process continues in a business setting. The ethical standards set by top management and actions of peers influence values and beliefs concerning what is ethical behavior.

This suggests that the study of ethics, the taking of a course at a university, or reading a book may not result in more ethical behavior. The study of ethics can, however, sharpen an individual's ideas of ethics and help to further develop a set of beliefs and values into a set of moral standards. In addition, the ethics of a given action are not always clear, so ethical concepts can be used to guide decision-making. Finally, management can play an important role in shaping the socialization process in the organization so that the ethics of given actions are considered.

Ethical Tests

None of the ethical concepts yields a clear cut, unambiguous test of the ethics of a given action. Accordingly, rather than rely on one approach, it is best to utilize several tests of the ethics of a particular action. If the action will pass several ethical examinations, then there is greater likelihood that the action is indeed moral. On the other hand, if a proposed action passes few tests, then it should probably not be undertaken. However, not all actions which are considered ethical will pass all tests.

1. Is it Legal?

The test of legality is an indication of whether an action is ethical, but it is not at all decisive. Henderson (1982) has developed a framework for classifying decisions as to their legal and ethical dimensions. He sees corporate decisions essentially going through a process of manifestation in which they are exposed to public scrutiny and codification in which they are determined to be legal or illegal, ethical or unethical. This codification process can yield four outcomes as shown in Figure 5.1.

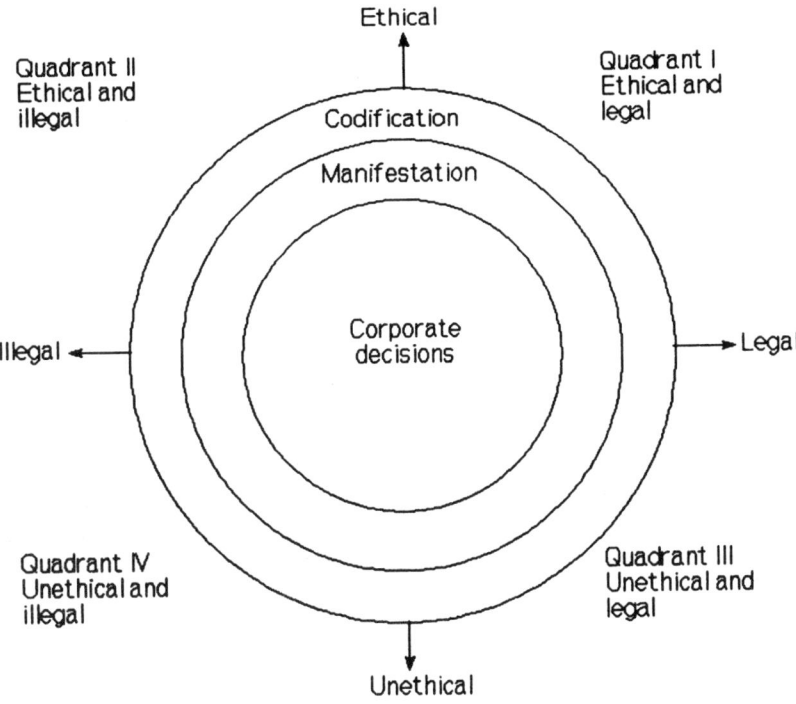

Figure 5.1. Classifying Ethical Decisions Using Henderson's Framework

Source: Henderson, V. E. "The Ethical Side of Enterprise." *Sloan Management Review*, 1982.

Corporate actions can fall in quadrant I and be both ethical and legal. Management would like all actions to fall within this area. At the opposite extreme is Quadrant IV. Such actions are unethical and illegal.

Most actions clearly fall in either of these two quadrants. These are the actions that are easily evaluated.

Some corporate and personal decisions may fall into quadrants II and III, however. Decisions falling in these quadrants are those that are either ethical and illegal or unethical and legal. These are the very difficult decisions that require much reflection and additional examination using several ethical tests.

2. The Benefit-Cost Test

This is the utilitarian test in which the benefits and costs of a proposed action are examined. All benefits and all costs, regardless as to who bears them, should be examined. Benefits and costs should be estimated as best as can be done. If the estimated benefits exceed the costs, the action passes the test.

3. The Categorical Imperative

In this test, an action should be evaluated from the standpoint of universal practice. If one is willing to allow everyone to practice the proposed action, then it passes the test. Alternatively, it should be asked whether the only reason that the action is undertaken is because the firm or individual desires to be a special case by taking advantage of general ethical behavior. If universal practice diminishes the value of the action, then it may not be ethical according to this test.

4. The Light of Day Test

Suppose that the decision or action that is contemplated became a featured story on the local news. Would you be proud, or would you fear public exposure? The light of day test asks to evaluate your reaction if the action were brought out into the open for public scrutiny. If you would want the proposal to stay hidden and not be brought out into the light of day then the action is probably unethical.

The light of day test is a way of incorporating the relativist point of view into the examination of the ethics of an action. Public scrutiny is a good test of whether the decision or action meets the ethical standards of society.

5. *Do unto others*

This is the "Golden Rule" that derives its name from the biblical admonition: "Do unto others as you would have them do unto you." Pattan (1984, p. 4) states: "Our actions are also moral if we act the way we would like everyone else to act toward us . . ." This test is quite simple. If one would like others to do the same to us, then the proposed action passes the test.

6. *Ventilation Test*

This test has been proposed by Carrol (1993). The essence of this test is that other person's views and criticisms should be sought out. An ethical problem should not be contemplated in isolation. If the proposed action is still looked on favorably after being exposed to others then it passes the test. Of critical importance to this test is the choice of individuals to discuss the proposal. These people should be objective and sufficiently knowledgeable to understand the complexities of the action under scrutiny.

In the course of the discussion, the results of the previous five tests can be considered. Thus, alternative opinions on whether a proposed action passes or fails each of the tests can be obtained through the use of these discussions.

Ethical Dilemmas in Business

A variety of ethical dilemmas and problems can occur in business. These can be both corporate and personal in nature. Ethical dilemmas can result from the relationship that a business may have with the public sector, from its interactions in the marketplace with suppliers, competitors and consumers, and its impact upon the rest of society.

In this section, four ethical dilemmas which occur frequently and transcend most types of businesses will be examined. These are conflicts of interest, whistleblowing, bribery, and the issues of bluffing and deception. These are not the only ethical dilemmas facing business. Ethical problems can occur with every interaction with the environment. Other ethical problems and dilemmas related to specific elements of the environment will be dealt with in the chapter in which the specific element is discussed.

Conflicts of Interest

Suppose you are the personnel director for a large corporation. Your brother in law has been out of work for the past eight months. His unemployment compensation is about to run out, and, when it does, he will not be able to pay the mortgage on his house. He and your sister have three children. There is an opening in your company for an individual with qualifications similar to your brother in law's. You know that he has not succeeded in previous employment and was fired from his last job. Your evaluation of him is that he is a lackluster performer who will do little damage but also will do little of anything positive in such a position. While you do not make the final decision, your recommendation carries a great deal of weight. Your sister asks you to recommend him for the job.

The above case is an example of a conflict of interest. In business, this is a situation in which an individual has two or more interests. If one is pursued, this may result in an unjustified effect on the other.

There are two types of conflicts of interest. The most common is when private interests conflict with corporate or social interest. Nepotism, receipt of gifts from suppliers, and insider stock trading are examples of this type. This conflict between private interests and other interests is what is commonly referred to as a conflict of interest. A second type occurs when the interests of the business conflict with the public interest. For example, the abandonment of a plant that leaves a large segment of a regional labor force unemployed poses a conflict between corporate and regional interests.

The perception of a conflict of interest can be just as damaging to a business or an individual as the revelation of an actual conflict. For example, Burt Lance who was President Carter's director of the Office of Management and Budget was forced to resign from office in an apparent conflict of interest involving a Georgia bank. He was later cleared of all wrongdoing. During the 1984 presidential campaign,

Democratic nominee Walter Mondale attempted to nominate Lance to a high campaign post. Lance subsequently turned down the appointment because of the public furor that was raised. The perception of a conflict of interest with the bank was still with him.

Whistleblowing

> You are in charge of quality control for a large manufacturing concern. The company makes parts that are used in automobile brakes, among other uses. You detect a microscopic defect in a part that has gone undetected for quite some time. This defect could cause the failure of automobile brake assemblies. Such failure, however, is not certain, and may take many years to develop. The vice president of production, who is your boss, tells you to overlook the defect. He argues that scrapping all the parts would have such a disastrous impact on profits that the firm may not be able to survive.

An employee is occasionally in a position to know about illegal, unethical or questionable actions on the part of others in an organization. Sometimes the employee is asked to participate. Whistleblowing is the act of disclosing such wrongdoing. "Like blowing a whistle to call attention to a thief, whistleblowing is an effort to make others aware of practices one considers illegal or immoral" (James, 1990, p. 332). Whistleblowing can be internal in which such actions are disclosed to others in an organization, or external in which outside groups such as reporters, public interest groups or regulatory agencies are contacted (James, 1990).

Whistleblowing can cause severe repercussions and problems within the organization and on the person who decides to reveal wrongdoing. Bok (1980) has observed that whistleblowing involves three elements which can produce bitterness. These are dissent, breach of loyalty and accusation.

With regard to dissent, whistleblowers must speak out and sometimes take great personal risks. Whistleblowers must evaluate the conflict between keeping quiet and taking risks. Such dissent may seem to be disloyal in most instances. The person who reveals questionable practices may be perceived as one who has violated a promise of confidentiality and loyalty to colleagues and the organization. But, Bok (1980) believes that it is the element of accusation that raises the strongest reactions. Whistleblowing singles out specific individuals as responsible for threats to the public or organizational interest.

These three elements mean that some form of retaliation is almost assured for whistleblowers. They can be fired, blacklisted, transferred to undesirable jobs and locations, receive poor letters of recommendation, etc. James (1990, p. 333) notes: "Their lifestyles, sex lives, and mental stability may be questioned. Physical assaults, abuse of their families, and even murder are not unknown as retaliation for whistleblowing."

Whistleblowing is dynamite that may blow up in the face of the person exposing the wrongdoing. On the other hand, failure to reveal illegal, unethical or questionable practices can lead to severe problems for society and for the organization if later found out. The would be whistleblower may even be implicated as an accessory before or after the fact.

The ethics of whistleblowing involves determining when revealing wrongdoing is ethical and when it is ethical to keep quiet. In addition: "What do you do when loyalties clash, when loyalty to your company or to your immediate boss conflicts with your duty to your family or to the values of the wider community of which you are a citizen?" (Wilson, 1983, p. 16).

A cautious approach to whistleblowing should consider a number of aspects:

1. <u>Make sure the situation involves an imminent threat to society or to the business.</u>

At this point, conflicting loyalties must be examined. The ethics of speaking out versus remaining silent need to be determined. The greater the risk to society of wrongdoing, the more importance should be placed on whistleblowing.

There are also situations where the impact of illegal, unethical or questionable practices fall only on the business. Embezzlement, fraud or the acceptance of kickbacks from suppliers are examples. Internal whistleblowing should be considered in these situations.

2. <u>Document all allegations</u>.

It is extremely important to get as much "hard" evidence as possible. Documents, recordings, computer output, etc. are all helpful. This evidence may be needed in court or in regulatory hearings.

Getting evidence will force a potential whistleblower to check and recheck facts to make absolutely certain that wrongdoing is involved and who the perpetrators are. In addition, careful documentation protects the whistleblower from being accused of slander or attempting to take the jobs of those who are engaged in these questionable activities.

3. <u>Examine internal whistleblowing first</u>.

The destructive effects of whistleblowing are much more severe when it is done external to the organization. Thus, it is best to explore internal avenues first. Where there is only an impact on the organization and not the general public, whistleblowing should be restricted to internal channels.

Find out if there are internal channels available for whistleblowing. Does the company have a policy regarding whistleblowing and a formal mechanism for doing so? What has happened to other whistleblowers in the past who have used the internal route? If it seems feasible, use the internal approach first, before going outside the organization.

In addition, the decision to remain anonymous needs to be explored. One problem with attempting to remain anonymous is that it gives the whistleblower less credibility. In addition, it is likely that eventually someone will find out who the whistleblower really is. Don't count on anonymity to be preserved for very long.

4. <u>Get another job</u>.

In order to minimize the retaliation that is almost certain to occur, it is best to find another job before blowing the whistle. Internal whistleblowing can be attempted by first asking for a transfer to another division, plant or department. Don't blow the whistle on your existing boss. If external whistleblowing is to be done, find another position in another organization. Then let go.

Bribery

Suppose that you work for a consulting firm that does a high proportion of its business overseas. The firm designs and supervises construction of hydroelectric power generating systems. You are told by a high government official in the foreign country in which you recently submitted a proposal that your design is far superior to that of any other firm and your bid is the lowest. In order to close the deal, the official requests a $250,000 fee to be deposited in his Swiss bank account. If you do not pay, the official states that the contract will go to someone else.

A bribe is a payment, usually to a public official, to induce that person to either do something improper or to influence that person's decisions or official actions in some way. Extortion is a situation where the recipient of the payment initiates the transaction. Bribery and extortion differ only with respect who initiates the activity. The end results are identical. Technically, the above example is one of extortion rather than bribery. However, the ethics of offering a bribe or becoming the payer of extortion are the same. Thus, this analysis will consider both possibilities together.

Bribery and extortion are clearly illegal and are generally felt to be immoral in the United States. This is not to say that these activities are not practiced here, however. Occasionally, a case of bribery or extortion involving a public official, usually at the state or local level, will surface in the news media. Some cities are legendary for the amount of corruption occurring in city hall and firms doing business in these cities must frequently compromise ethical standards to obtain contracts.

Arguments against offering bribes or paying extortion to obtain business stress the importance of free competition in providing government the most cost efficient services possible. Extortion and bribes are really in the end paid by the taxpayers. Bribery also takes advantage of competitors who do not offer such payments and places them at a disadvantage if they continue to compete solely on the basis of quality and price.

A more complex issue involving bribery and extortion involves payments to foreign government officials. In many countries, such payments are accepted practice. However, in 1977, Congress passed the Foreign Corrupt Practices Act. Payments from American corporations to foreign government officials for purposes of obtaining business or influencing decisions are illegal with the passage of this law. Grease payments, which are those made to government employees to facilitate decisions are not illegal under the act. Corporations can be fined up to $1 million and individuals can face up to five years in prison and/or $10,000 in fines for violations of the law.

Payments to foreign officials involve two related questions. Given that such transactions are illegal, the first question asks if it is not also unethical. In other words, are the paying of bribes to be classified in Henderson's Quadrant IV—unethical and illegal, or in Quadrant II—ethical and illegal. Secondly, does the Foreign Corrupt Practices Act provide social benefits greater than its costs and foster ethical behavior in American corporations, or is it another case of misguided legislation from Washington? The answers to both questions revolve around the same arguments, so they will be discussed together.

Those who argue against the Foreign Corrupt Practices Act[2] state that such payments are standard practice in many foreign countries. In some countries, these are required in order to do any business at all. If American firms are prohibited from making such payments, then lost business opportunities result with consequent adverse impacts on employment, stockholders' equity, and the balance of payments. This line of reasoning goes on to state that the prohibition against American firms has not stopped bribery and extortion in foreign countries. Instead, foreign officials merely accept bribes from non-American businesses. Finally, those who believe the act should be repealed believe that foreign countries are now worse off since they are more likely to purchase an inferior product with U.S. firms out of the bidding.

Arguments[3] in favor of continuation of the act stress that many American corporations have been successful in the international arena without resorting to bribery or the paying of extortion. Giving into extortion demands is not only morally objectionable, but also fosters corruption in the country in which it is paid.

---

[2] For a more complete exposition of these and other arguments against the Act see Pastin and Hooker (1980).

[3] Many of the arguments in this section are summarized in Alpern (1981).

This line of reasoning concedes that if American firms do not participate in such activities, foreign governments and consumers may end up with an inferior product since there are fewer bidders. However, the overall result of bribery and extortion payments is to increase the costs of goods and services to the foreign taxpayer who ends up paying the bribe indirectly. Further, much of the money spent on contracts with multinational firms is made available through loans and grants through the World Bank, USAID, and other international agencies. Since American tax dollars are used to partially or completely support those agencies, the U.S. taxpayer also ends up paying part of the bribe.

Additionally, it is argued that requiring American firms not to engage in bribery and extortion is not imposing our standards on the world. Alpern (1981) uses the analogy of a Muslim who, refusing to eat pork in England, does not impose his standards on the British. Finally, it is argued that even though bribery and extortion are practiced in other parts of the world, they are not necessarily held to be ethical or moral. Both are illegal in most countries.

Bluffing and Deception

You are negotiating a new labor contract with union officials. The contract covers a plant that has experienced operating losses over the past several years. It is unclear why these losses have occurred. You have decided to try to negotiate concessions from labor in order to reduce the losses. However, in the course of negotiations, labor seems particularly intransigent over the issue of givebacks. In order to reduce union opposition, you consider the possible strategy of telling them that the plant will be closed if no concessions are made. In reality, no such plans are contemplated.

Although it is generally believed in our society that lying is unethical and morally wrong, some argue that bluffing and deception in business is a special case. Albert Z. Carr (1968) in an often quoted article, maintains that bluffing and deception in business is simply game strategy, like bluffing in poker. He argues that all sides understand that the truth is not necessarily being spoken in all situations. Thus, bluffing and deception cease to be falsehoods and are not morally wrong. He cites the example of criminal court, where the criminal is not expected to be truthful when pleading "not guilty". Carr (1968, p. 428) states:

"Most executives from time to time are almost compelled, in the interests of their companies or themselves, to practice some form of deception when negotiating with customers, dealers, labor unions, government officials, or even other departments of their companies. By conscious misstatements, concealment of pertinent facts, or exaggeration—in short, by bluffing—they seek to persuade others to agree with them. I think it is fair to say that if the individual executive refuses to bluff from time to time—if he feels obligated to tell the truth, the whole truth, and nothing but the truth—he is ignoring opportunities permitted under the rules and is at a heavy disadvantage in his business dealings."

On the other hand, there are those who believe that bluffing and deception raise serious moral and ethical questions. They believe that bluffing is wrong since its intent is to deceive others.

Carr's argument that the executive who does not engage in these activities is at a disadvantage makes profitability a grounds for such behavior. But, this side of the issue would argue that if profitability can justify bluffing and deception, it could be used to justify an endless stream of unethical and immoral actions. Further, Carr's line of reasoning maintains that bluffing and deception are acceptable because they are standard practice in the "game" of business. But, the other side argues that just because something is standard practice or generally accepted, does not make it ethical. For example, slavery was once standard practice. This does not make it moral, now or when it was performed.

But, what about the situation in which others are trying to deceive you? There are those who feel that it is acceptable to bluff or deceive those who are attempting to do the same to you. Thus, in a negotiating situation, bluffing or deception are ethical, according to this perspective. On the other hand, it could be argued that two wrongs don't make a right. If for example, someone steals from you, you do not have the right to steal from them. Thus, according to this view, even in this situation bluffing and deception are not justified.

Managerial Implications

How serious is the problem of ethics in business? Do managers frequently encounter dilemmas of a nature similar to those described above, or are ethical problems mainly isolated instances? Brenner and Molander (1977) conducted a survey of managers and found that four out of every seven respondents had experienced a conflict between what was expected of them as efficient, profit conscious managers, and what was expected of ethical people. Carroll (1975), in another survey of managers, reported that almost 65 percent of those answering the questionnaire felt that managers are under pressure to compromise personal standards to achieve company goals.

Brenner and Molander (1977) also asked their respondents what factors influence managers to make unethical decisions. Their results are summarized in Table 5.1. As can be seen from the table, there are several factors which are directly or indirectly influenced by the business organization. Of highest rank is the behavior of a manager's superiors. Ranked second is the presence of a formal company policy dealing with ethics, or the lack thereof. In fourth rank is the behavior of a manager's equals in a company. The ethical climate in the industry, which was ranked third, can also be indirectly influenced by a particular business.

Table 5.1. Factors Influencing Unethical Decisions

Factor	Rank Order of Importance
Behavior of Superiors	1
Formal Policy or Lack Thereof	2
Industry Ethical Climate	3
Behavior of One's Equals in the Company	4
Society's Moral Climate	5
One's Personal Financial Needs	6
Adapted from Brenner and Molander (1977)	

These data suggest that there are a variety of programs, policies and actions which management can implement to help promote ethical behavior in a business organization. In this section, several of these approaches will be examined. Each one involves adapting one or more of the managerial functions of planning, organizing, controlling, and staffing/rewarding to stimulate ethical behavior.

Top Management Leadership

Promotion of ethical behavior in an organization should start with leadership from the top of the company. The Brenner and Molander study reported that the behavior of superiors is the highest ranked factor affecting unethical decisions. Thus, high level leadership is an extremely important factor in promoting ethical behavior.

Organizational theorists have developed the term organizational culture to define the set of values, beliefs and operating assumptions which permeate an organization. Although the culture of an organization is shaped by a variety of factors, one of the most important is the leadership and guidance provided by top management. Since the ethical standards and beliefs are part of the organizational culture, top management leadership can be an extremely important factor in encouraging ethical behavior throughout the business. Top management leadership can promote ethical behavior in a number of ways. First, high level people in the company can set a proper example by adhering to high standards of ethics themselves. In the words of one manager, "If the chief executive winks, some of his employees will wink back" (Cressey & Moore, 1983, p. 66). Second, in short and long term business planning, ethical factors should be considered. A business plan that ignores the ethical implications of alternative courses of action provides the wrong signal to everyone in the organization. Third, the encouragement and promotion of the specific actions, programs and policies outlined below will help to shape the culture of the organization to incorporate ethical considerations in all facets of the operations of the business.

Realistic Goal Setting

As part of the controlling function, management of many businesses set goals to be achieved by those individuals who report to them. If the goals are set too high, the subordinates may be put in a position where ethics may have to be compromised in order to achieve company goals. For example, in order to achieve extremely high sales goals, payoffs may be utilized. Those who achieve their goals through unethical means may be rewarded, while those employees refusing to compromise their ethics may be punished. Goal setting can provide a powerful incentive for good performance. It can also provide an incentive for unethical behavior if not established realistically.

Ethics Audit

In the previous chapter, the concept of a social audit was discussed. In a social audit, the annual financial statement is extended to include an audit of a firm's social involvement. The social audit becomes part of the controlling function.

The notion behind the ethics audit is to include an ethics component in the social audit. In the ethics audit, areas of concern for possible unethical behavior within the company are identified. Strategies are suggested for reducing incentives for unethical behavior. Incentives for ethical practices are also identified and evaluated.

The same problems which plague social audits also result in barriers to successful implementation of the ethics component. This is especially true of deciding what to measure and how to measure it. As this chapter has suggested, defining ethical behavior is not clear cut. Thus, measuring potential areas of ethical conflict is also not easy.

Code of Ethics

Another mechanism for promoting ethical behavior is an ethics code. A code can be developed by an individual company or by a trade or professional association. If a business develops its own code, it can be considered as part of the controlling function. Generally, the larger the business, the more desirable an ethics code becomes. This is because in large organizations, there is less opportunity for the chief executive to influence ethics through personal example. The code may take the place of this contact to some extent. Whether written by the business or an association, an ethics code becomes a specific statement of company policy and a guidepost for employees in dealing with ethical problems and dilemmas.

A good ethics code should contain a general policy statement with regard to ethics, specific discussion of matters of concern for the company, and a means of communication. The code itself should be communicated to each employee, and a system of periodic review and employee feedback should be established. Provisions for interpreting the code and an enforcement procedure should be implemented. A description of the most frequently prohibited employee behaviors incorporated in ethics codes is shown in Table 5.2.

Table 5.2. Fourteen Most Frequently Prohibited Employee Behaviors

Prohibited Behavior Variable	Ethical Dimension	Percent Firms Mentioning Variable within Ethical Dimension	Typical Treatment in Ethics Statements
1. Extortion, gifts, kickbacks	Employee's relation to firm / Firm's relation to suppliers	67%	
a) Extortion			Explicitly prohibited
b) Gifts		18	Generally prohibited with minor exceptions
c) Kickbacks			Explicitly prohibited
2. Conflict of interest	Employee's relations to firm	65	Generally prohibited with minor exceptions
3. Illegal political payments	Firm's relation to government	59	Explicitly prohibited
4. Violation of laws in general	Firm's relation to government	57	Explicitly prohibited
5. Use of insider information	Employee's relation to firm / Firm's rleation to shareholders	43 / 6	Explicitly prohibited
6. Bribery	Firm's relation to government / Employee's relation to firm	37 / 34	Explicitly prohibited
7. Falsification of corporate accounts Reporting full disclosure	Firm's relation to shareholders (both variables)	28 / 34	Explicitly prohibited
8. Violation of antitrust laws	Firm's relation to government	25	Explicitly prohibited
9. Moonlighting	Employee's relation to firm	25	Judgmental – usually tolerated if no conflict of interest
10. Legal payments abroad	Miscellaneous concerns	23	Some judgment
11. Violation of secrecy agreement	Employee's relation to firm	22	Explicitly prohibited
12. Ignorance of work-related laws	Firm's relation to government	22	Prohibited – employees to seek legal advice if in doubt
13. Fraud, deception	Firm's relation to customers	11	Explicitly prohibited
14. To justify means by goals	Miscellaneous concerns	10	Explicitly prohibited

Source: Chatov (1980).

Codes of ethics have several advantages. First of all, codes can provide guidance for employees in situations in which they are not completely sure what is the ethical course of action. Bowie (1990) points out that laws or codes of conduct provide more stable and permanent guidance than do human personalities. Secondly, ethics codes can help employees extricate themselves from possible unethical courses of action. "I'm sorry, but its against company policy" is a good closing statement. Finally, a code can provide an employee with a defense when ordered by a superior to do something unethical. Thus, the power of superiors over employees in condoning unethical behavior can be curbed (Bowie, 1990).

The major defect of codes of ethics is that they will not change behavior unless enforced. Brenner and Molander (1977) found that 61 percent of their respondents felt that others would violate a code whenever they thought they could get away with it. If business develops a code and then puts it on a shelf, it is unlikely to affect behavior. A consistent and visible enforcement program is essential to make a code operational.

Ethics Committee

One means of enforcing a code of ethics is through an ethics committee. This is a group of between three and seven people which should include both external and internal directors. The CEO should have at least an ex officio role in the committee. The ethics committee should have a variety of functions including communication of the code to all employees, review and revision of the code, investigation of violations and enforcement.

The enforcement function includes providing rewards to those who uphold the code. These rewards could include recognition, appreciation, commendation and money. The committee should have the power to discipline violators including the power of dismissal. Punishment of violators of a code of ethics is important to implementing a code. It provides evidence to all concerned that management is determined to uphold the provisions of the code.

Ethics Advocate

Another organizational change that could be made in addition to an ethics committee is the creation of the position of ethics advocate. This "angel's advocate" would have the responsibility of serving as an ethical catalyst by examining the ethics of proposed courses of action (Purcell, 1975). Such a person would probably not have the enforcement power of an ethics committee. Thus, he or she would not be involved in the rewarding function. Rather, the ethics advocate could serve as the conscience of the corporation.

Whistleblowing Mechanism

Either the ethics advocate or the ethics committee could serve as a means by which internal whistleblowing could take place. One problem with internal whistleblowing is the possibility of retaliation. Providing such a mechanism may reduce the possibility of repercussions on the person doing the whistleblowing. In addition, by providing a formal process, a corporation can deal with wrongdoing itself rather than through the press.

Ethics Training

Another idea is to establish an ethics training program as a part of management development. Both managers and other employees would receive such training. Weber (1981) mentions several advantages to having an ethics training program. These include:

1. Aiding management by reviewing the decisions made each day
2. Assisting managers in finding new and better ways to deal with ethical problems
3. The corporate ethics committee receiving suggestions for revision of the code
4. Helping to get ethical considerations formally and explicitly into daily business life

Although training in ethics may not make managers more ethical, it may help them to better understand the ethical implications of their actions.

Summary

Business ethics is the application of general ethical concepts to the unique situations confronted in business. It asks what is right or wrong behavior by managers and what principles or rules can be used as guidance in business situations. Business ethics has two levels of concern: the corporate and the individual.

There are several ethical concepts which have been developed by moral philosophers. Ethical relativism is the belief that there is no universal standard by which morality can be judged. The concept of ethical egoism is that one ought to act in his or her own interest. Utilitarianism is an ethical concept which holds that the morality of an action can be determined by its consequences. Deontologists believe that factors other than good outcomes determine the rightness of an action. The categorical imperative is one means of formalizing the deontological point of view. It states that an action is moral if one is willing to allow universal practice.

Since none of the ethical concepts yields a clearcut, unambiguous determination of the ethics of a given action, several tests are suggested. These are the legality, the benefit-cost, the categorical imperative, the light of day, the do unto others, and the ventilation tests.

A variety of ethical dilemmas and problems can occur in business. These include conflicts of interest. Private interests can conflict with corporate or social interests. In addition, the interests of the corporation conflict with the public interest.

Whistleblowing is the act of disclosing wrongdoing by others. It can be internal, in which such actions are disclosed to others in an organization, or external, in which outside groups are contacted. Whistleblowing can cause severe repercussions and problems within the organization and on the person who decides to reveal wrongdoing.

Bribery and extortion involve payments to influence decisions, especially those made by public officials. The Foreign Corrupt Practices Act prohibits such payments from American corporations to foreign government officials. The debate over the act has continued, with opponents arguing that it leads to lost business opportunities for American firms. In addition, reduced competition may result in foreign countries receiving poorer quality goods and services and paying higher prices. The other side stresses that many of the bribes in the end are paid by the taxpayers. They also argue that the act does not lead to American standards being imposed on the rest of the world.

Whether to engage in bluffing and deception is another moral dilemma facing business. On the one hand it is argued that these actions are nothing more than game strategy. The other side argues that it is lying which is morally wrong. They also argue that just because others do it does not make it right.

There are a variety of programs, policies, and actions which management can implement to help promote ethical behavior in a business organization. Promotion of ethical behavior should start with leadership from the top of the company. Realistic goal-setting and the establishment of an ethics audit are also ways to help promote ethical behavior.

The development and enforcement of a code of ethics, the establishment of an ethics committee, an ethics advocate, and a whistleblowing mechanism are other managerial tools available. In addition, ethics training may also help promote a better understanding of the ethical implications of a given action.

Questions

1. Suppose the male owner of a business continually makes sexually suggestive comments to an attractive female assistant.
   a. Analyze the ethics of the owner's behavior using each of the ethical concepts described in the chapter.
   b. Suppose you are the assistant. What would you do?

2. Several example cases of ethical dilemmas were presented in the chapter. Using the ethical tests, analyze the following:
   a. the conflict of interest experienced by the personnel director
   b. the choice regarding whistleblowing by the quality control manager
   c. extortion payments by the international consulting firm
   d. bluffing and deception used during labor contract negotiations

3. It is common practice by some retail stores to charge higher prices in low income areas than are charged for the same items in high income areas. From the point of view of the retailer, analyze the ethics of this practice.

4. In the early 1980's Johns Mansville Corporation filed for protection under Chapter 11 of the Bankruptcy Act. By doing this, the company hoped to minimize liability for lawsuits related to diseases resulting from the manufacture of asbestos. Analyze the ethics of this action.

5. Using a company where you or a member of your family works, analyze important ethical dilemmas in the present or near future.

Key Concepts

business ethics

relativism

egoism

utilitarianism

deontologism

categorical imperative

ethical tests

conflict of interest

internal whistleblowing

external whistleblowing

bribery

extortion

bluffing and deception

ethics audit

code of ethics

socialization process

Case Analysis: Polaroid In and Out of South Africa

American companies operating in South Africa have become increasingly sensitive to charges that their activities bolster a regime that practices apartheid—a legal system of racial segregation and oppression widely agreed to be immoral.

Apartheid is an ancient Afrikaan term, meaning "apartness," in this case racial apartness. This policy of white domination has been the cornerstone of social policy in South Africa since the beginning of the Union of South Africa in 1910. According to the classification scheme implementing this policy, South Africa's population is composed of 17 percent white, 70 percent African, 10 percent Coloured (mixed descent), and 3 percent Asian. Whites alone may be members of Parliament and the cabinet, and only whites may possess firearms or be arms-carrying members of the police and military forces. Organizations doctrinally opposed to apartheid are banned. There has also been a history of political involvement by indigenous industry aimed at promoting apartheid because industrialists have worked to keep labor both cheap and unorganized.

Despite these modes of enforced segregation, most nonwhites reside in white-owned urban territory or on white-owned farms whose economies depend upon their labor. Under this system, blacks are allowed to own only 13 percent of the land surface. These lands are designated "native reserves." Though whites constitute 17 percent of the population, they control 87 percent of the land. Whites also control all major business activities, and the system is constructed so that black workers are paid less than white workers for comparable work.

About 320 American companies currently have operations in South Africa. These include such major and respectable companies as General Motors, Exxon, Eli Lilly, Kodak, IBM, etc. South Africa is an attractive place for American investment, and a part of the attraction derives from the economic benefits of apartheid: Profits are very substantial, labor is remarkably cheap, capital is not threatened by the political insecurity created by unstable governments, the market is thriving and currency is hard and convertible, and South Africa is rich in natural resources, especially minerals. The United States is the second largest direct foreign investor in South Africa, a nation of 30 million people, 5 million of whom are whites. U.S. investments in South Africa were approximately $1.7 billion in 1976. American companies control 43% of South

Africa's petroleum market, 23% of auto sales, 70% of its computer business, and are easily the main suppliers of most major consumer products. Thus the American presence in South Africa is not an insignificant factor in the country's economic health[1].

American corporations began to trade in South Africa around 1880, when the white South African community alone was involved in commerce and employment. That is, whites at that time held all the available jobs, even in factories. There were no "black employees." Gradually, however, the South African economy was so spectacularly successful that there were not enough whites to fill available positions, and blacks began to move into factories and other low-paying jobs. Though salaries have always been extremely low, blacks have made enough money to purchase goods and become a factor in the South African economy. The more they interacted in the economy, the more repressive apartheid laws became, and this in turn bluntly presented dilemmas for American corporations about participation in the immoral activities of the South African government.

While American corporations have become increasingly sensitive to charges of immoral exploitation and opportunism in South Africa, very few have taken the initiative of complete withdrawal. Polaroid, however, has had a long history of sharply criticizing the South African government and — as we shall see in detail — has now withdrawn completely from all entanglement in South Africa. Not surprisingly, Polaroid was one of the first American firms to publicly condemn apartheid and to assume responsibility for the uses that government made of Polaroid technology. Polaroid views itself as a "corporation with a conscience" and has been a pacesetter in both race-relations policies and community-relations programs in the United States[2].

---

[1] See Richard DeGeorge, "U.S. Firms in South Africa," in his *Business Ethics*, pp. 253–55; and Dharmendra T. Verma, "Polaroid in South Africa" (Bentley College, 1978), distributed by Harvard Business School, HBS Case Services, p. 2.

[2] C. L. Suzman, "Polaroid Experiment in South Africa" (Johannesburg, South Africa: Graduate School of Business Administration, University of Witwatersrand, 1974, revised 1977), distributed by Harvard Business School, HBS Case Services, p. 2.

Nonetheless, in 1970 Polaroid too found itself embroiled in a controversy over its involvement in South Africa. The events in this controversy began in 1970 when a few of Polaroid's black American employees formed a group called Polaroid Revolutionary Workers Movement (PRWM). They were outraged in particular because they believed Polaroid products were being used in South Africa's repressive Pass Book system. The hated Pass laws were designed by the South African government to control the movement of blacks in urban areas. This practice has been described by Bishop Desmond Tutu, head of the South African Council of Churches, as "...among the most humiliating of the dehumanizing laws and regulations applied to this country"[3]. In brief summary form, these laws require: (1) that Africans citizens over 16 carry a Pass Book that enters details of where the person is permitted to be and other personal details such as the person's place of work and payment of taxes; (2) that Africans may not remain in an urban area longer than 72 hours without a permit unless special permission has been granted or the person has a long history of approved residence and work in the area[4].

PRWM employees at Polaroid in the United States distributed leaflets that charged in its title, "Polaroid Imprisons Black People in 60 Seconds." These leaflets were also placed on company bulletin boards. This campaign intensified and came to a point of confrontation in October 1970. The general charge by the employees was that Polaroid was (like other American companies) exploiting cheap black labor in South Africa, and (unlike other American corporations) was actually having its technology used to support the repressive aspects of the apartheid system[5]. The above-mentioned pamphlet and this last charge refer to the use of film and cameras involved in implementing the South

---

[3] Marjorie Chan and John Steiner, "Corporate America Confronts the Apartheid System," in George A. Steiner and John F. Steiner, *Casebook for Business, Government, and Society*, 2nd ed. (New York: Random House, Business Division, 1980), pp. 86f.

[4] See Muriel Horrel, *South Africa: Basic Facts and Figures* (South African Institute of Race Relations, 1973).

[5] David Vogel, *Lobbying the Corporation: Citizen Challenges to Business Authority* (New York: Basic Books, Inc., 1978), p. 173; Chan and Steiner, "Corporate America Confronts," pp. 86f; and Suzman, "Polaroid Experiment," p. 6.

African government's Pass Book system. At least one Polaroid executive (Tom Wyman, Vice-President of SALES) admitted an awareness that Polaroid products were being used at that time in the Pass Book identification program. The supply source was Frank and Hirsch Ltd., Polaroid's (independent) South African distributor[6].

On October 27, 1970 some large demonstrations organized by PRWM were held in Boston, and the more activist-minded members of PRWM called for a worldwide boycott of Polaroid products. In this same month Polaroid officials denied that the company's equipment was being used in the Pass law program. Polaroid's director of community relations was authorized to make the following statement in response to PRWM charges: "We have a responsibility for the ultimate use of our product ... In response to the charge we articulated a very strict policy of refusing to do business directly with the South African government ... We as a corporation will not sell our products in instances where its use constitutes a potential abridgement of human freedom"[7]. Mr. Edwin Land, owner and manager of the corporation, also reiterated his "personal ban" on the sale of Polaroid products to the South African government, a ban originally instituted in 1948, but less than diligently enforced in some years[8].

Instead of yielding to PRWM demands to have Polaroid put an end to all activities in South Africa, Polaroid management determined that it would rather investigate less radical alternatives. Management at Polaroid then formed a committee of fourteen employees, representing a cross section of the company's work force. This group was mandated to make a final withdraw-or-stay decision. This committee first recommended:

---

[6] See accounts in the *Boston Globe*, October 18, 1964, p. 64, and Suzman, "Polaroid Experiment," p. 7.

[7] As quoted in Vogel, p. 173.

[8] H. Landis Gabel, "Polaroid Experiment in South Africa" (Charlottesville, Va.: The Colgate Darden School of Business Administration, University of Virginia, 1981), distributed by Harvard Business School, HBS Case Services, p. 1; Suzman, "Polaroid Experiment," p. 7. See also *Business Week* (November 14, 1970), p. 32.

1. That a four member fact finding group be sent to South Africa to review the feeling of blacks in South Africa first hand. The four-man team was to report on the use of Polaroid products in South Africa, conditions of Frank and Hirsch, the use of Polaroid film in the Pass Book Program, and was to give recommendations on the engagement-disengagement decision.

2. That the committee would consult outside experts in economics, African history, politics, and other fields in order to assist them in making recommendations about Polaroid's future in South Africa and Polaroid's future business in "free Black Africa"[9].

This travel group had a reasonably free hand to assemble data and conduct interviews while in South Africa. Their final recommendation was that Polaroid should not pull out of South African operations, but instead should initiate a program that would come to be known as "The Polaroid Experiment." The program had four main points:

1. Sales to the South African government were to be discontinued, but the company would not disengage from the Republic and would set up an experimental program for one year.

2. Polaroid's local distributor and its suppliers were going to improve salaries and other benefits for black employees.

3. The company's South African associates were to be obligated to start a training program for blacks so as to enable them to take up important posts.

4. A proportion of Polaroid's South African profits was to be devoted to encouraging black education[10].

The South African government agreed to permit these employment practices by an American company, so long as no law was violated. The government specified, however, that any promotion of nonwhites into positions of authority over whites would not be permitted.

---

[9] Suzman, "Polaroid Experiment," p. 10.

[10] Suzman, "Polaroid Experiment," p. 12; see also Gabel, "Polaroid Experiment," p. 2.

One year later Polaroid evaluated the effects of this experiment and found that great improvements had been made in the salaries, advancement, and benefits of its nonwhite employees. The average monthly salary for blacks had increased 22% (including a "bonus" for black employees). The principle of the same pay for the same job had been accepted. Eight black employees were promoted to supervisory positions. Three programs were designed to improve the education of black employees' children, to establish a foundation to support black students and teachers, and to promote black leadership. Polaroid also contributed $75,000 in grants to black educational groups in South Africa[11].

This program continued successfully for six years. However, the actual measure of "success" can easily be disputed. Frank and Hirsch noted at the time, and Polaroid knew, that it would be extremely difficult to enforce a complete ban on the sale of all products to the South African government. It was easy to stop <u>direct</u> sales, but indirect sales through private photographers and retailers in other countries would be difficult to stop. Thus the effectiveness of the ban on the sale of Polaroid products during these years was questionable. Nonetheless, during these six years both Polaroid and Frank and Hirsch expressed virtually complete satisfaction with the program. The Managing Director of Frank and Hirsch noted that it was also a period when racial discrimination was attacked and virtually eliminated at Frank and Hirsch. Blacks and whites came to share the same offices and have the same working hours. Frank and Hirsch employees grew to be almost 50% black, and the company donated money to upgrade the education of black African children[12].

However, in November 1977 a dramatic new development occurred in Polaroid's "Experiment." On November 21 the *Boston Globe* ran a first-page story claiming that Frank and Hirsch had been clandestinely selling Polaroid products to the South African government in complete violation of its 1971 standing agreement not to permit such sales. This story emerged through the whistleblowing efforts of a former employee in the shipping department of Frank and Hirsch—a South African Indian named Indrus Naidoo. Mr. Naidoo had made photostatic copies of invoices documenting the delivery of Polaroid products to the Bantu

---

[11] Chan and Steiner, "Corporate America Confronts," p. 89.

[12] Suzman, "Polaroid Experiment," p. 14.

Reference Bureau on September 22, 1975. This is an agency that issues Pass Books for nonwhites. Mr. Naidoo passed on this photostatic copy and other information to Mr. Paul Irish, a staff member of the American Committee on Africa in New York. Irish then released the copy to the *Boston Globe* after a time when Naidoo was able to leave South Africa (as an exile, after discharge from his job). Naidoo's documentation showed that Frank and Hirsch had for years billed all its shipments to the South African government through a drugstore in Johannesburg. These shipments were packed in unmarked cartons containing both film and cameras. Deliveries had also been made to the military, including a large shipment of Polaroid sunglasses. Since all billing was done through the pharmacy, there was no record of direct sales[13]. Polaroid had been informed by the *Boston Globe* of these charges five days prior to the appearance of the story in their newspaper. The company immediately sent their Export Sales Manager to South Africa to investigate the charges. The Sales Manager was able to document several deliveries to the South African government, and to interview Mr. Hirsch (the owner of Frank and Hirsch), who expressed shock and complete ignorance of these sales. (Polaroid officials indicated at the time that they had long had suspicions about Frank and Hirsch, and had periodically attempted investigations.) Polaroid then immediately announced—on the same day the story appeared in the *Boston Globe*—that it was terminating its distributorship and all involvement in South Africa. Polaroid issued an official statement saying it "abhorred" the policy of apartheid, that it was largely the recommendations of Black Africans that had led to continued sales in 1971, that Polaroid's contributions to black African scholarships during this period amounted to approximately one-half million dollars, that there was considerable evidence that Polaroid had had a positive effect on black employees and foreign investors and that they would not establish a new distributorship in South Africa[14]. At this time Polaroid's

---

[13] George M. Houser, "Polaroid's Dramatic Withdrawal from South Africa," *The Christian Century* (April 12, 1978), pp. 392–93. Mr. Houser was then Executive Director of the American Committee on Africa, located in New York. See also Verma, p. 3; Vogel, p. 173; and Gabel, p. 1.

[14] Letter from the Polaroid Corporation, Monday, November 21, 1977.

South African annual sales were between three and four million dollars; the company's universal 1977 sales were over one billion dollars[15].

Source: Tom L. Beauchamp, *Case Studies in Business, Society, and Ethics*. Englewood Cliffs, NJ: Prentice-Hall, Inc., 1983, pp. 215–220. Reprinted with permission.

Case Questions

1. Many American companies did business in South Africa when apartheid was enforced. What were the <u>economic</u> reasons for their involvement? Evaluate the ethics of these actions.

2. Evaluate the apartheid system using the five concepts of ethics.

3. Was Polaroid responsible for the use of its products?

4. Was Polaroid's presence in South Africa a positive or negative influence for blacks?

5. What management actions resulted in the complete withdrawal of Polaroid from South Africa? Had you been in charge, what decision would you make and why?

6. Is it ethical to do business in countries that commit major human rights violations?

7. To what extent are corporations in general responsible for the use of their products?

8. The apartheid system in South Africa ended with the election of Nelson Mandella as president. What has happened to the economic plight of blacks now that they control the country?

---

[15] Verma, "Polaroid in South Africa," pp. 1–4, and Houser, "Polaroid's Dramatic Withdrawal," p. 392.

References

Alpern, K. D. "Moral Dimensions of the Foreign Corrupt Practices Act: Comments on Pastin and Hooker." A paper presented at the Conference on Business and Professional Ethics, University of Illinois at Chicago, May, 1981.

Beauchamp, T. L. and Bowie, N. E. *Ethical Theory and Business* (3rd edition). Englewood Cliffs, N. J.: Prentice-Hall, Inc., 1988.

Bok, S. "Whistleblowing and Professional Responsibility." *New York University Education Quarterly*, 1980, *2* (4), Vol. 4, 2–7.

Bowie, N. E. "Business Codes of Ethics: Window Dressing or Legitimate Alternative to Government Regulation," in W. M. Hoffman and J. M. Moore (Eds.), *Business Ethics*. New York: McGraw-Hill, Inc., 1990, 505–509.

Brenner, S. N. and Molander, E. A. "Is the Ethics of Business Changing?" *Harvard Business Review*, 1977, January–February, Vol. 55, 57–71.

Buchholz, R. A. *Business Environment and Public Policy* (4th edition). Englewood Cliffs, N.J.: Prentice-Hall, Inc., 1992.

Carr, A. Z. "Is Business Bluffing Ethical?" *Harvard Business Review*, 1968, January–February, Vol. 46, 143–153.

Carroll, A. B. "Management Ethics: A Post Watergate View." *Business Horizons*, 1975, April, 75–80.

Carroll, A. B. *Business & Society* (2nd edition). Cincinnati: South Western Publishing Co., 1993.

Chatov, R. "What Corporate Ethics Statement Say." *California Management Review*, 1980, *22* (4), 20–29.

Cressey, D. R. and Moore, C. A. "Managerial Values and Corporate Codes of Ethics." *California Management Review*, 1983, *25* (4), 53–77.

Frederick, W. C., Post, J. E., and Davis, K. *Business & Society: Corporate Strategy, Public Policy, Ethics* (7th edition). New York: McGraw-Hill, Inc., 1992.

Henderson, V. E. "The Ethical Side of Enterprise." *Sloan Management Review*, 1982, *23* (3), 37–47.

Hoffman, W. M. and Moore, J. *Business Ethics: Readings and Cases in Corporate Morality* (2nd edition). New York: McGraw-Hill, Inc., 1990.

James, G. G. "Whistle Blowing: Its Moral Justification," in W. M. Hoffman and J. M. Moore (Eds.) *Business Ethics: Readings and Cases in Corporate Morality*. New York: McGraw-Hill, Inc., 1990, 332–345.

Pastin, M. and Hooker, M. "Ethics and the Foreign Corrupt Practices Act." *Business Horizons*, 1980, *23*, 43–47.

Pattan, J. E. "The Business of Ethics and the Ethics of Business." *Journal of Business Ethics*, 1984, *3*, 1–19.

Purcell, T. V. "A Practical Guide to Ethics in Business." *Business and Society Review*, 1975, Spring, 47, Vol. 13, 43–50.

Ricklefs, R. "Executives and General Public Say Ethical Behavior Is Declining in U.S." *The Wall Street Journal*, October 31, 1983, pp. 23, 41.

Ricklefs, R. "On Many Ethical Issues, Executives Apply Stiffer Standard Than Public." *The Wall Street Journal*, November 1, 1983, pg. 33.

Ricklefs, R. "Public Gives Executives Low Marks for Honesty and Ethical Standards." *The Wall Street Journal*, November 2, 1983, pg. 33.

Ricklefs, R. "Executives Apply Stiffer Standards Than Public to Ethical Dilemmas." *The Wall Street Journal*, November 3, 1983, pp. 27, 30.

Weber, J. "Institutionalizing Ethics Into the Corporation." *MSU Business Topics*, 1981, Spring, pg. 47.

Wilson, G. T. "Solving Ethical Problems and Saving Your Career." *Business Horizons*, 1983, November/December, 16–20.

CHAPTER 6

GOVERNMENT REGULATION OF PRODUCTS, PRICES AND THE WORKPLACE

The model that was presented in Figure 2.1 depicting the impact of change in the external environment on business decision making illustrates possible public sector responses to societal element changes. The tools of government involvement include taxation, spending, direct provision of services, and regulation. When society feels that the market system has failed to meet the public's needs, then one or more of the public sector responses may be invoked. Often the response used is government regulation.

Regulation can be implemented using methods such as standard setting, prohibitions against certain practices or types of behavior, price setting, restrictions on entry and exit into and out of an industry, and grading and testing of products. Government regulation can be purely economic in nature or may have a variety of social goals such as product safety, protection of the environment, and non-hazardous workplace conditions. Government regulation is conducted primarily at the federal level, although state and local governments are also involved in these activities.

In Chapters 6 and 7, government regulation will be explored. This chapter concerns regulation of products, prices and the workplace. Chapter 7 deals with environmental and energy issues. These two chapters do not represent the entire story on government regulation, however. As seen in Figure 2.1, regulation permeates almost every facet of society and impacts managerial decision making at all levels. However, these two chapters represent a large segment of government regulatory activity that can be easily placed into distinct categories. In addition, regulation is the primary policy tool that government has used to address the social and economic issues discussed in these chapters. This is the rationale for discussing regulation separately. Other regulatory activities will be discussed in later chapters, where appropriate to the issue at hand.

The discussion of regulation of products, prices, and the workplace in this chapter will focus on traditional industry regulation, consumerism and the regulation of consumer products, and workplace safety and health regulation. In addition, the benefits and costs of regulation will be examined and possible alternatives to the regulatory activities of government will be explored. The chapter concludes with a case analysis of a firm's attempt to deal with lawsuits related to worker injury and death due to asbestos.

Scope of Government Regulation

The scope of government regulation and its impact on business and society in general can be gauged in a number of ways. One index of the extent of regulation by the federal government is the number of pages in the *Federal Register*. In this publication, federal regulatory agencies publish all rules and regulations which they promulgate. Between 1937, when the *Federal Register* was first published, and 1955, the number of pages grew to about 10,000 per year. From 1955 until 1975, the number of pages expanded to over 60,000 per year, with most of the growth occurring between 1970 and 1975. Gujarati (1984) reports that between 1955 and 1970, the number of pages grew at an annual rate of 5 percent. Between 1970 and 1975, the rate of growth in the number of pages in this publication increased to 25 percent per year. During the Reagan administration, the rate of growth slowed appreciably. However, in the beginning of the Clinton administration, the number of pages added to the Federal Register reached new highs (see Figure 6.1).

The expansion in federal regulatory activity is also illustrated by a history of some of the major laws enacted by Congress which expanded regulation. This is shown in Table 6.1. As can be seen in the table, since 1962, major thrusts in regulation have been in the areas of consumer product safety, the physical environment, energy and employment conditions.

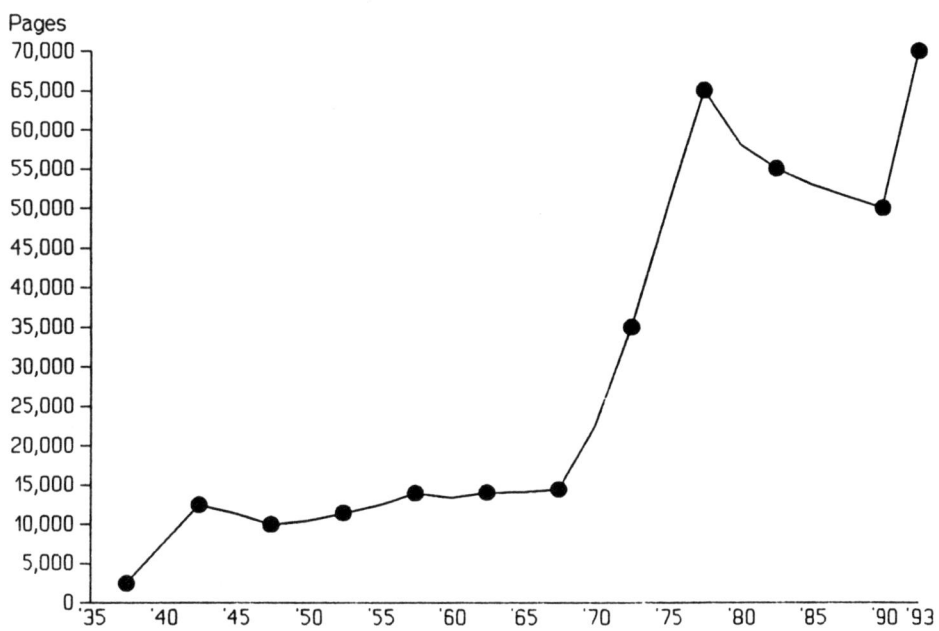

**Figure 6.1.
Number of Pages in the Federal Register
1936–1993**

Table 6.1. Growth of Government Regulation

Year	Name of Act or Amendment	Purpose and Function
1887	Act To Regulate Commerce	Established the ICC to regulate the railroads.
1933	Glass-Steagall	Created bank deposit insurance, prohibited interest on checking accounts, separated banking from underwriting, strengthened Federal Reserve's ability to stabilize the economy through open market operations
	National Industrial Recovery	First major attempt to plan and regulate the economy, first collective bargaining and wage and hour regulation (parts of the act declared unconstitutional)
1934	Communications	Centralized regulation of broadcasting telephone, and telegraph
	Securities Exchange	Extended full disclosure to all listed companies, provided for securities registration, regulated insider trading and stock exchange trading practices
1935	Motor Carrier Act	Extended ICC regulation to the trucking industry
	National Labor Relations (Wagner Act)	Promoted collective bargaining and prohibited unfair labor practices by employers
1936	Robinson-Patman	Anti-price discrimination law designed to protect small retailers from chain competition
1938	Food, Drug and Cosmetic	Established predistribution safety clearance of new drugs
	Fair Labor Standards	Provided for minimum wage, 40-hour week, overtime, and control of child labor
	Natural Gas	Regulated natural gas pipeline rates
	Wheeler-Lea	Banned false and deceptive advertising

Year	Act	Description
1939	Wool Products Labeling	Prohibited sale of mislabeled goods
1947	Taft-Hartley	Extended prohibition of unfair labor practices to union activities
	Outer Continental Shelf	Established jurisdiction over oil and gas exploration in federal offshore waters
1954	Atomic Energy	Opened nuclear technology, under regulation, to private industry
1956	Interstate and Defense Highway	Provided for interstate highway system
	Spence-Robertson	First comprehensive regulation of bank holding companies
1958	Federal Aviation	Centralized regulation of air safety
	Food Additives Amendment	Extended preclearance requirement to food as well as drugs
	Textile Fiber Products Identification	Controlled misbranding and false advertising
1962	All-Channel Receiver	Required all TV sets to be able to receive UHF channels
	Food and Drug Amendments	Required proof of effectiveness as well as safety before marketing of new drugs and labeling of drugs by generic names
1962	Air Pollution Control	Provides first modern ecology statute
1963	Equal Pay Act	First key anti-discrimination act; eliminated wage differentials based on sex alone
1964	Civil Rights	Banned discrimination in private employment on account of race, sex, or national origin; established the Equal Employment Opportunity Commission
1965	Water Quality Act	Extends environmental concerns to water

	Cigarette Labeling and Advertising Act	Requires labels on hazards of smoking
	Medicare	First major federal regulation of health care
	Motor Vehicle Air Pollution Act	First major environmental law to establish auto emissions standards
1966	Traffic Safety Act	Provides for a coordinated national safety program, including safety standards for motor vehicles
	Highway Safety	Set uniform safety standards for state highways
	Coal Mine Safety Amendments	Tightens controls on working conditions
	Fair Packaging and Labeling Act	Requires producers to state what a package contains, how much it contains, and who made the product
	Child Protection Act	Bans sale of hazardous toys and articles
1967	Flammable Fabrics Act	Broadens federal authority to set safety standards for inflammable fabrics, including clothing and household products
	Age Discrimination in Employment Act	Prohibits job discrimination against individuals aged 40 to 65
	Wholesome Meat Act	Federal assistance in interstate meat inspection system
1968	Consumer Credit Protection Act (Truth-in-Lending)	Requires full disclosure of terms and conditions of finance charges in credit transactions
	Interstate Land Sales Full Disclosure Act	Provides safeguards against unscrupulous practices in interstate land sales
1969	National Environmental Policy Act	Requires environmental impact statements for federal agencies and projects
1970	Clean Air Act	Provides for setting clean air quality standards

	Occupational Safety and Health Act (OSHA)	Establishes safety and health standards that must be met by employers
	Amendments to Federal Deposit Insurance Act	Prohibits issuance of unsolicited credit cards. Limits customer's liability in case of loss or theft to $50. Regulates credit bureaus and provides consumers access to files
	Securities Investor Protection Act	Provides greater protection for customers of brokers and dealers and members of national securities exchanges. Establishes a Securities Investor Protection Corporation, financed by fees on brokerage houses.
1970	Poison Prevention Packaging Act	Authorizes standards for child-resistant packaging of hazardous substances
1972	Consumer Product Safety Act	Establishes a commission to set safety standards for consumer products and bans products presenting undue risk of injury
	Federal Water Pollution Control Act	Established standards for federal regulation of water pollution
	Noise Pollution and Control Act	Regulated noise limits of products and transportation vehicles
	Equal Employment Opportunity Act	Gives EEOC the right to sue employers
1973	Highway Speed Limit Reduction	Limits vehicles to speeds of 55 miles an hour
	Vocational Rehabilitation Act	Requires federal contractors to take affirmative action on hiring the handicapped
	Safe Drinking Water Act	Requires EPA to set national drinking water regulations
	Emergency Petroleum Allocation	First price control and allocation for oil
1974	Campaign Finance Amendments	Restricts amounts of political contributions

	Employee Retirement Income Security Act	Set new federal standards for employee pension funds
	Motor Vehicle and School Bus Safety	Established auto recall and defect notification
	Commodity Futures Trading Commission	Extended federal control to all contracts on all exchanges
1974	Federal Energy Administration	Provided authority for mandatory conservation programs
	Hazardous Materials Transportation Act	Requires standards for the transportation of hazardous materials
	Magnuson-Moss Warranty Improvement Act	Establishes federal standards for written consumer product warranties
1975	Energy Policy and Conservation Act	Authorizes greater controls over domestic energy supplies and demands
	Federal Trade Commission Improvement	Funded public participation in rule making, added requirement for refunds and corrective advertising
	Securities Act Amendments	Ended fixed brokerage commissions and launched planning for national securities market
1976	Hart-Scott-Rodino Anti-trust Amendments	Provides for class action suits by state attorneys general; requires large companies to notify the Department of Justice of planned mergers and acquisitions
1977	Surface Mining Control and Reclamation	Provided for regulation of coal strip mining
1978	Airline Deregulation Act	Required all pricing, entry, and route regulation of domestic airlines ceased completely in 1985
	Natural Gas Pricing	Required elimination of all inter- and intrastate gas price controls by 1989
1980	Staggers Rail Act	Permitted railroads greater flexibility in pricing and in abandoning uneconomical rail routes

Year	Act	Description
1980	Motor Carrier Act	Permitted substantial freedom of pricing and new entry into the trucking industry
	Depository Institutions Deregulation and Monetary Control Act	Phased out interest rate ceilings, expanded services which could be offered by financial institutions, and raised FDIC insurance to $100,000
1982	Intercity Bus Deregulation Act	Allowed price and entry competition in passenger bus transportation
1986	Superfund Reauthorization	Requires companies that make or use chemicals to report inventories and emissions to the public
	Age Discrimination in Employment Act	Abolishes mandatory retirement. Extends protection against discriminatory employment practices to workers over 70
1988	Worker Adjustment and Retraining Notification Act (WARN)	Requires 60 days advance notice of layoffs or plant closings involving 50 or more employees
1990	Clean Air Act Amendments	Sets industry-by industry reductions standard for toxic pollutants, requires reformulated gasoline and employee trip reduction
	Americans With Disabilities Act	Requires employers to make "reasonable accommodations" for the disabled
	Nutritional Labeling and Education Act	Requires food manufacturers to list nutritional contents of food products in approved format
1992	Cable TV Regulation Act	Reinstitutes regulation of cable TV rates
1993	Family and Medical Leave Act	Gives employees a legal right to take a leave without pay for family or medical emergencies
1994	Trucking Industry Regulatory Reform Act	Reduced ICC regulation of the trucking industry
1995	ICC Elimination Act	Abolished the ICC and established the Surface Transporation Board to regulate transporation

Adapted and updated from Weidenbaum (1995, p. 48–52) and Gujarati (1984, p. 7–9).

Another way of measuring the growth in federal regulatory activities is through the growth in expenditures and personnel devoted to regulation. These are shown in Tables 6.2 and 6.3. Total expenditures grew from $1.4 billion in fiscal 1970 to an estimated $16.5 billion in fiscal year 1996. In 1987 dollars, total expenditures on regulatory activities were over three times as great in 1996 as in 1970. However, in the period 1970–1980, expenditures grew 447 percent. From 1980–1985, the growth rate slowed to 26 percent. Not only lower levels of inflation, but also the determination of the Reagan administration to reduce government regulations is evident from these figures.

Table 6.2 also documents the expansive growth in social regulation that occurred in the 1970's. Fiscal 1996 budget expenditures on social regulation are estimated to be almost 12 times as great as 1970 expenditures. Budgeted expenses on economic regulation also increased during this period with expenditures in 1996 estimated to be almost eleven times as great as those in 1970. These results are also shown in Figure 6.2.

Total personnel concerned with regulatory activities have grown from 69,946 in 1970 to 131,919 in 1996. During the Reagan years, total personnel actually went down. This is another indicator of the reduction in federal regulatory activities during the Reagan administration.

Budgeted expenditures and personnel whose jobs involve implementing regulations provide indicators of the scope of government regulation throughout the economy. However, these data ignore the costs that regulation imposes on business and other elements of society. These costs are in the form of reporting requirements, additional capital expenditures needed for compliance, and changes in work processes which have to be made. Nor can such measures be used to estimate the benefits of government regulatory efforts. What these data show is the expansion of federal government regulatory activities in the 1970's, the attempts in the 1980's to slow down and reverse that growth, and the acceleration of that growth during the Bush and Clinton years.

Table 6.2. Summary of Administrative Costs of Federal Regulatory Activities
(Fiscal Years, Millions of Dollars in "Obligations")

								(Estimated)		% Change
	1970	1975	1980	1985	1990	1994	1995	1996		1995-96
				Current Dollars						
Social Regulation										
Consumer Safety and Health	$710	$1,491	$2,349	$2,689	$3,796	$5,076	$5,228	$5,479		4.8%
Job Safety and Other Working Conditions	128	359	753	862	1,002	1,154	1,206	1,335		10.7%
Environment	214	841	1,651	2,495	4,164	5,232	5,360	5,920		10.4%
Energy	64	275	550	481	462	568	623	563		-9.6%
Total Social Regulation	$1,116	$2,966	$5,303	$6,527	$9,424	$12,030	$12,417	$13,297		7.1%
Economic Regulation										
Finance and Banking	$86	$151	$362	$624	$1,080	$1,290	$1,429	$1,384		-3.1%
Industry-Specific Regulation	91	160	279	289	320	454	473	497		5.1%
General Business	115	206	355	507	743	1,128	1,250	1,377		10.2%
Total Economic Regulation	$292	$517	$996	$1,420	$2,143	$2,872	$3,152	$3,258		3.4%
GRAND TOTAL	$1,408	$3,483	$6,299	$7,947	$11,567	$14,902	$15,569	$16,555		6.3%
Percentage Change		147.4%	80.8%	26.2%	45.6%	28.8%	4.5%	6.3%		
				Constant 1987 Dollars						
Social Regulation										
Consumer Safety and Health	$2,017	$3,030	$3,276	$2,849	$3,353	$4,022	$4,031	$4,104		1.8%
Job Safety and Other Working Conditions	364	730	1,050	913	885	914	930	1,000		7.5%
Environment	608	1,709	2,303	2,643	3,678	4,146	4,133	4,434		7.3%
Energy	182	559	767	510	408	450	480	422		-12.2%
Total Social Regulation	$3,170	$6,028	$7,396	$6,914	$8,325	$9,532	$9,574	$9,960		4.0%
Economic Regulation										
Finance and Banking	$244	$307	$505	$661	$954	$1,022	$1,102	$1,037		-5.9%
Industry-Specific Regulation	259	325	389	306	283	360	365	372		2.1%
General Business	327	419	495	537	656	894	964	1,031		7.0%
Total Economic Regulation	$830	$1,051	$1,389	$1,504	$1,893	$2,276	$2,430	$2,440		0.4%
GRAND TOTAL	$4,000	$7,079	$8,785	$8,418	$10,218	$11,808	$12,004	$12,401		3.3%
Percentage Change		77.0%	24.1%	-4.2%	21.4%	15.6%	1.7%	3.3%		

Note: Numbers may not add to totals due to rounding.

Source: Center for the Study of American Business, Washington University. Derived from the Budget of the United States Government and related documents, various fiscal years.

Table 6.3. Staffing Summary for the Federal Regulatory Agencies
(Fiscal Years, Full-time Equivalent Employment)

	1970	1975	1980	1985	1990	1994	(Estimated) 1995	1996	% Change 1995-96
Social Regulation									
Consumer Safety and Health	41,463	51,237	55,213	45,056	50,243	58,194	58,150	58,392	0.4%
Job Safety and Other Working Conditions	6,486	12,334	17,894	14,229	13,610	12,817	13,012	13,565	4.2%
Environment	4,525	11,907	16,993	16,054	20,057	22,817	24,306	24,233	-0.3%
Energy	219	5,045	5,433	3,954	3,441	3,481	3,411	3,374	-1.1%
Total Social Regulation	52,693	80,523	95,533	79,293	87,351	97,309	98,879	99,564	0.7%
Economic Regulation									
Finance and Banking	4,969	6,401	9,524	8,864	13,049	15,544	15,441	15,368	-0.5%
Industry-Specific Regulation	5,675	7,013	7,483	5,296	4,629	4,615	4,912	4,980	1.4%
General Business	6,609	8,306	9,251	8,739	9,611	11,098	11,697	12,007	2.6%
Total Economic Regulation	17,253	21,720	26,258	22,899	27,289	31,257	32,050	32,355	1.0%
GRAND TOTAL	69,946	102,243	121,791	102,192	114,640	128,566	130,929	131,919	0.8%
Percentage Change		46.2%	19.1%	-16.1%	12.2%	12.1%	1.8%	0.8%	

Source: Center for the Study of American Business, Washington University. Derived from the Budget of the United States Government and related documents, various fiscal years.

Figure 6.2. Federal Regulation: Spending and Staffing

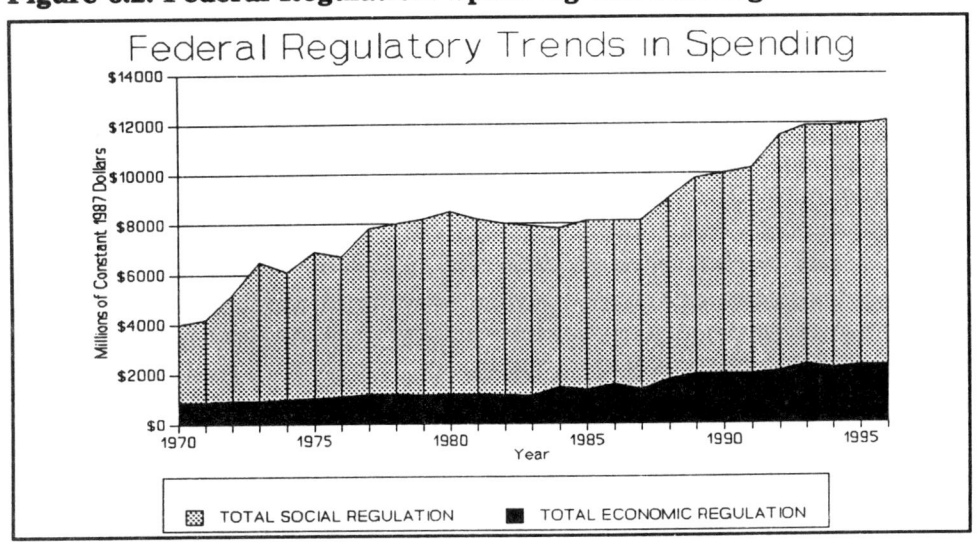

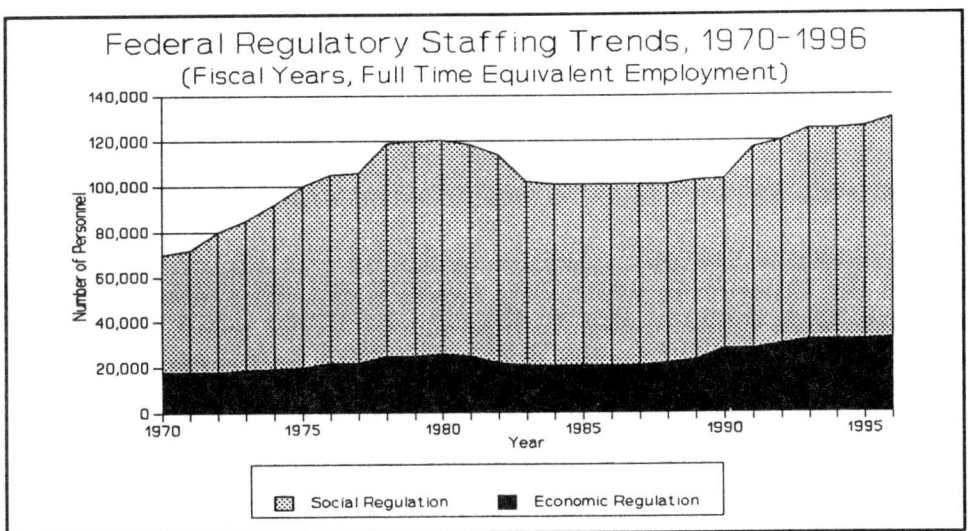

Source: Center for the Study of American Business, Washington University. Derived from the Budget of the United States Government and related documents, various fiscal years.

Reasons for Government Regulation: Public Interest Theory

In Chapter 3, reasons for government involvement in the free enterprise system were discussed. It was mentioned that while the free market system produces many desirable consequences, some undesirable results may also occur. The "public interest" theory of regulation states that government regulation exists to correct some of the shortfalls in the workings of the free enterprise system. Although the regulatory approach may be far from perfect and result in many distortions in economic decisions and cause many additional problems, proponents of the public interest theory argue that regulation primarily exists to foster the interests of the society as a whole.

Insure Competition

Government administers a wide range of laws and regulations in order to establish the "rules of the game." These include the definition of the legal status of business, the definition of private property and the legal status of contracts among individuals and businesses. One shortfall of the free enterprise system, which is addressed by regulation, is the tendency for some industries and markets to become concentrated so that only one or a few firms compete. The anti-trust laws and regulations are administered by government to deal with such tendencies.

Government also uses regulation in dealing with natural monopolies. This is the situation in which only one firm can efficiently exist in an industry. More than one firm in the industry would result in the costs of providing the good or service to increase. Thus, government regulates privately owned and operated utilities such as natural gas, electricity and cable TV. The regulation of the railroad industry was also justified on this basis.

Impact Externalities

Externalities, or third party effects, are costs or benefits of an activity which fall on groups or individuals not directly involved in the market transaction. Government regulation has been used extensively to attempt to reduce negative externalities and increase positive effects. Examples include pollution control regulations and regulation of the fuel economy of automobiles.

Provide Public Goods: Information

Another shortfall of the free enterprise system is that if left on its own, private business would either not produce public goods at all or produce them in less than optimal amounts. Public goods are those which we consume in common. They display the characteristics of non-exclusion in which individuals who do not pay for a public good cannot be excluded from consuming it, and joint supply which means that if the good or service is provided for one individual it is provided for everyone. The non-exclusion characteristic gives rise to the "free rider" problem.

Information about the safety, effectiveness and quality of the products and services provided by the market has the characteristics of a public good. Once information is provided about a product, it is difficult to exclude individuals from this knowledge. Thus, if the information is provided to one individual, it is effectively provided for everyone. Because of this, private firms would find it difficult (but not necessarily impossible) to make a profit in the testing and evaluation of products and services. Private provision of information concerning consumer products would not be provided at socially desirable levels.

In order to make intelligent decisions in choosing products, consumers need reliable information about the quality, effectiveness, and safety of products. However, such information is not easily obtained. Many products are so complex that most consumers would have great difficulty in evaluating them. How can consumers evaluate the safety of drugs, automobiles, computers, etc.? How does the consumer know if a simple pocket calculator is safe to use, or whether it will explode during operation?

In addition, many industrial workers may not be competent to judge the safety of their work environment. How does the worker know if the job may lead to exposure to hazardous chemicals or dangerous conditions? What might the long-term effects of working conditions be? Thus, one reason for regulation of workplace safety is to insure that the workers are aware of potential dangers to be found in their work environment.

Equalize Income

Another reason for government involvement in the free enterprise system, mentioned in Chapter 3, is to mitigate some of the inequality of income which results from the incentives provided by the marketplace. As an example, it was mentioned in that chapter that one of the results of minimum wage regulations is to redistribute income by keeping a floor under the incomes of people who work. One effect of these regulations, however, is to cause some jobs to be lost.

Posner (1971) argues that much regulation is a form of indirect taxation in which one group gains at the expense of another. For example, much industry level regulation was used for internal cross-subsidization purposes. This is the situation in which some markets are charged more for a good or service and the proceeds used to subsidize other markets. Rail line abandonment regulation forced the railroads to subsidize the carriage of goods to shippers located on unprofitable rail lines by charging higher rates for more profitable traffic. Airline regulation also had the same effect, requiring the airlines to fly to low density markets and make up losses from the proceeds derived from profitable flights.

Even minimum wage laws can be viewed as a form of taxation. These result in gains to those who work at a higher wage than their productivity would dictate and losses to those who are prohibited from working because employers cannot afford to pay this rate for unskilled labor. Which group experiences gains or losses may depend more on political power and the ability to influence the public policy process.

Stabilize the Economy

Government regulation has also been used to attempt to stabilize the cyclical fluctuations in the economy and as a means of promoting economic growth. Wage and price controls were attempted during the Nixon Administration in order to reduce the inflation rate which at that time was running at an unheard rate of four percent! National economic planning and industrial policy proposals are regulatory strategies for promotion of economic growth through government guidance of economic decisions.

Social Objectives

Government regulation has also been used to achieve a variety of social objectives. These include nondiscrimination in employment and housing and job safety. Some social objectives may involve using regulations to achieve a perception of fairness that the free market may not provide. For example, rather than rely on the marketplace to allocate some types of resources, government regulation is used instead. This includes allocation of broadcast rights and landing rights at overcrowded airports.

Reasons for Government Regulation: The Interest Group Theory of Regulation

A number of scholars have challenged the "public interest" view of government regulation. Stigler (1961), Lee (1980) and others have argued that regulation is government's response to the demands of groups who seek to advance their own self-interest. Industries seek out regulation in order to be able to legally engage in price fixing, establish restrictions on entry into the industry, and receive subsidies and other "benefits." This interest group theory implies that the public interest may be only an ancillary reason for some government regulation. In fact, the public interest may only be served by some regulation as long as it coincides with the interests of a particular group.

Why Regulation?

Regulation is only one of several policy tools available to the public sector. In some situations, other public sector responses such as taxation, subsidy or public provision may be viable alternatives to regulation. The question arises as to the reasons why regulation is chosen as the public sector response over other alternatives. Although each case of public involvement in the free enterprise system is unique, a number of justifications seem to permeate many policy decisions. These reasons seem to hold not only at the federal level, but also at the state and local levels as well.

First, regulation may simply be the best policy tool available. When the effectiveness of policy options are examined, regulation may be the most desirable alternative. For example, the requirement that manufacturers reveal the contents of processed food and provide nutrition information would be difficult to administer using other policy tools.

Second, regulatory proposals may stand a better chance of getting through the public policy process than other alternatives. The public policy process is extremely complex, and uncertain. Proposals must become part of the policy agenda, be examined, rewritten, debated, discussed, altered and compromised through the legislative process and finally implemented. In order to survive this process, policy options need to be understandable to many separate groups and clearly address the issue at hand.

The impact and implications of the use of other policy tools may not be clearly understood. Some alternatives to regulation might be very complex. Others might be designed to indirectly manipulate market incentives in such a manner that they are mistrusted by those who do not clearly understand the workings of the free market.

For example, one alternative to the regulatory approach of air pollution standards is to issue pollution licenses which could be traded in the marketplace. In the pollution license approach, the overall amount of pollution that can be emitted into the air is fixed, just as in a regulatory approach. However, pollution licenses result in a lower cost of reducing pollution than the regulatory approach. This is because those companies which can easily clean up their pollution will clean it up to a greater extent than those whose costs of clean up are more expensive. Trading pollution licenses in the marketplace allows this result.

The pollution license approach to pollution control was not adopted. Instead a regulatory approach mandated by the Clean Air Act of 1970 was taken. The advantages of a pollution license approach were so misunderstood that many individuals thought that more pollution would result from their adoption, rather than less.

Finally, policy options which entail the use of the price system rather than regulation may require a smaller force of bureaucrats to administer the program. Taxation and subsidy programs may result in little involvement on the part of the government bureaucracy. Regulatory strategies, on the other hand, not only require a massive government workforce, but also enhance the power and prestige of those bureaucrats already charged with regulatory activities. The result is a bias in government toward regulatory strategies rather than other policy options.

Methods of Government Regulation

Each government agency has at its disposal a variety of methods and techniques which can be used to enforce its regulation of business and the economy. These are shown in Table 6.4.

Table 6.4. Typical Methods of Enforcement of Government Regulation

Methods	Agencies Using this Method
Performance Standards	EPA, OSHA
Design Standards	OSHA, NHTSA, CPSC
Prohibitions	FDA, FTC
Licensing	ICC, FCC
Price Setting	ICC
Information Disclosure	FDA, SEC
Inspection, Grading and Testing	USDA, FDA, CPSC
Certification	USDA, FDA
Recalls and Product Seizures	FDA, NHTSA, CPSC

One common approach is to issue <u>performance standards.</u> These standards usually specify a level of performance with regard to the element being regulated. Those industries or individuals being regulated can determine how the performance is achieved. For example, the Environmental Protection Agency (EPA) may set standards regarding the amount of effluent that can be released into rivers and streams, or the maximum amount of pollutants that can be emitted into the atmosphere. The Occupational Safety and Health Administration (OSHA) may set standards for the volume of cotton dust which is allowed in the textile mills, and the National Highway Traffic Safety Administration (NHTSA) sets standards for the average fuel economy of the cars produced by a given manufacturer. In these cases, it is up to the business to decide how to achieve the prescribed level of performance.

While performance standard regulation concerns establishing objectives for the "end results," regulation through the use of <u>design standards</u> concerns government involvement in "how" to achieve those results. For example, OSHA sets detailed standards with regards to workplace safety. These include the type of mailings, the number of rungs in a ladder and even the design of toilet seats! NHTSA is actively involved in establishing safety standards for automobiles including the requirement that seat belts and air bags must be designed into each car. The Consumer Product Safety Commission (CPSC) sets standards for the distance between slats on baby cribs as well as enforcing voluntary standards set by trade associations representing manufacturers of many other products.

Government agencies also use outright <u>prohibition</u> as one regulatory technique. For example, the Food and Drug Administration (FDA) prohibits the use of certain food additives that have been demonstrated to be carcinogens. The anti-trust laws, which are enforced by the Justice Department and the Federal Trade Commission (FTC), prohibit anti-competitive practices such as price fixing and false advertising.

Another regulatory method is <u>licensing.</u> This approach is used not only by federal regulatory agencies, but also by state professional licensing boards. Agencies which control entry and exit into and out of an industry such as the ICC and the Federal Communications Commission (FCC) use this technique. This process also serves to allocate scarce resources such as broadcast channels and railroad routes.

At the heart of economic regulation is <u>price setting.</u> Many traditional industry regulatory agencies are involved in this type of regulation. The ICC and, formerly, the CAB both were heavily involved in setting prices in the transportation industry. While the CAB has been eliminated, the ICC continues to regulate prices of surface transportation, but within a much narrower scope.

Some government agencies require product <u>labeling and other information disclosure.</u> This type of regulation is wide ranging. The FDA requires proper labeling of foods and drugs. The Securities and Exchange Commission (SEC) requires publicly held companies to disclose certain financial information used by government regulatory agencies. Even the Federal Election Commission (FEC) requires disclosure of campaign contributors. Disclosure type of regulation, while neither altering a product or process, provides consumers, business, voters and others with increased knowledge and information upon which to base their decisions.

<u>Inspection, grading, testing and certification</u> are also methods used by government regulatory agencies. Both the USDA and FDA have extensive programs for grading and testing food and drugs. Drugs not certified by the FDA as safe and effective for their intended use cannot be marketed in interstate commerce in the United States. Foods which do not meet specific quality standards cannot be purchased by the U.S. government or receive certification of its grade when sold to the public.

Plant inspections are also conducted by the FDA, USDA, and CPSC to ensure production standards are met.

Finally, when products are found to be unsafe or are being marketed without certification, <u>recall</u> by the manufacturer may be suggested or ordered by the government agency involved. In some cases the products may be <u>seized</u> by the agency or <u>banned</u> from sale in the United States to make sure it does not reach the public. The FDA, NHTSA, and CPSC all use recalls and seizures to enforce the safety standards which have been set.

A Typology of Regulation

The first federal government regulatory agency was established in 1887. This is the Interstate Commerce Commission (ICC). The ICC typifies the traditional or industry specific approach to regulation that categorized most government regulation until the 1960's. Industry specific regulatory agencies, for the most part, are concerned with economic regulation. This type of regulation can involve setting prices, controlling entry and exit into and out of an industry, and requiring internal cross subsidy across markets and/or product lines.

Whether the traditional regulatory agency was established to address one facet of the public interest or to serve a special interest group, in time, this type of agency may be "captured" by the industry which it regulates. That is, rather than serving the public interest, the agency may serve the interests of the industry which it was designed to regulate.

This "capture theory" of regulation has gained prominence in the regulatory theory literature in recent years.[1] It is argued that members of the industry are chosen to serve on regulatory boards because of the unique expertise which they possess. Industry groups have greater incentive to testify before these boards and lobby for favorable decisions than do groups representing the general public. In addition, individuals who serve on regulatory commissions eventually are hired by the industry. This further strengthens the relationship between the industry

---

[1] See for example Gujarati (1984), Posner (1977), Kolko (1965), Weidenbaum (1995).

and the regulatory agency. Eventually, industry interests rather than the public interest is served by the agency.

A depiction of the variations in federal regulation is shown in Figure 6.3. In the figure, the traditional types of regulatory agencies are represented by the vertical lines. These include the Interstate Commerce Commission (ICC), the now defunct Civil Aeronautics Board (CAB), the Federal Communications Commission (FCC), and the Federal Energy Regulatory Commission (FERC). Weidenbaum (1995) notes that a large segment of the economy including manufacturing, trade and services is exempt from this traditional regulation.

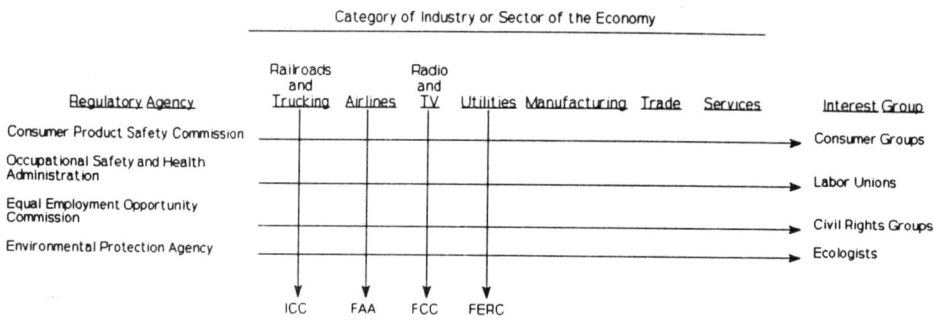

Figure 6.3. Variations in Federal Regulation of Business

Source: Weidenbaum, Murray L. *Business and Government in the Global Marketplace,* 1995. Reprinted with permission.

The horizontal lines in Figure 6.3 depict the "new wave" of regulation as Weidenbaum (1995) describes it. This type of regulation is primarily social in nature. That is, it is designed to achieve broad social goals such as protection of the consumer, protection of the environment and safety in the workplace. Rather than being directed at a particular industry, this type of regulation cuts across all industries.

In traditional regulation, the regulated industry has a very strong incentive to attempt to capture the regulatory agency since the profitability of the industry can be affected to a significant degree by many decisions of the agency. By contrast, the incentives to capture an agency engaged in social regulation are fewer. This is because the agency regulates all business, not just one industry. In addition, the same industry may be regulated by several social regulatory agencies. An individual industry gains only a relatively small amount by "capturing" one of these agencies. Then, who, if anyone, captures these organizations?

Weidenbaum (1995) argues that if there is any special interest that may dominate such an agency, it is the group which is preoccupied with the agency's tasks. That is, environmental groups may attempt to influence the decisions of the EPA, while labor would be concerned with occupational health and safety. The problem is that while the benefits of regulation are argued before the agencies, the costs do not receive as rigorous a hearing.

Traditional regulation focuses exclusively on one industry and thus the agencies are concerned about the overall performance and economic vitality of some if not most firms in that industry. By contrast, ". . . the new breed of regulators, and those public interest groups supporting their efforts, are usually oblivious to those economic factors. Many of them condemn as callous, or worse, any consideration of cost or other business aspects in deliberations on product, personnel, or environmental safety." (Weidenbaum, 1995, p. 43)

Thus, traditional regulatory agencies may be captured by the industry and focus on maximizing the returns to the industry which is regulated. Social issues may receive only a cursory examination. By contrast, social regulatory agencies may focus almost exclusively on the broad social goals which they were designed to achieve. The economic health of the regulated industries may receive only a cursory examination. Both types of regulatory agencies exemplify the problems created whenever public sector actions are taken.

It should be noted that not all government regulatory functions fit neatly into these two categories of agencies. Nothing about government is that simple! There are several agencies that are hybrids between the two categories. Examples include the Securities and Exchange Commission (SEC) and the Federal Trade Commission (FTC). The SEC regulates the securities industry, yet it impacts all firms which issue securities. The FTC has many social goals in mind such as protection of consumers against fraud and deception and investigation of discriminatory pricing. The FTC, however, also is involved in economic regulation since it is charged with enforcement of the anti-trust laws and thus the maintenance of competition in an industry. In addition, there is nothing "new" about the FTC which has been in existence since 1914.

Traditional Regulation: Interstate Commerce Commission

The best, and most enduring example of traditional industry regulation is the ICC. Established in 1887 by the Act to Regulate Commerce, the ICC is responsible for economic regulation of railroad, trucking and inland waterway transportation. In this section, we will examine the events leading up to the establishment of the ICC, the impact of the regulation on consumers and the industry and the subsequent deregulation of both the railroad and trucking industries. The ICC provides a good illustration of capture theory and the impact of both regulation and deregulation.

Events Prior to 1887

In the late 1800's, the only practical means of transportation in most situations was rail. The automobile had not been invented. The alternatives were water transportation which was limited to navigable waterways or horse-drawn wagon which was slow and undependable.

Railroad transportation is characterized by decreasing costs. This means that along any given route, per unit or average costs fall as the volume of traffic increases. This is because railroad transportation has high fixed costs and very low variable costs. Increased traffic along a given route results in spreading fixed costs over large volumes of output.

Decreasing costs are both beneficial and detrimental. They are beneficial because at large volumes, traffic can move at very low cost. They are detrimental since during a recession or periods of low demand for rail transportation, high fixed costs are still incurred. Railroads must try to attract large volumes of traffic in order to cover the fixed costs.

During the period following the Civil War, the railroads frequently were involved in cut-rate pricing in order to attract traffic from competitors. Rail profits suffered. In order to alleviate the problems of what some call "ruinous" competition, the railroads formed pricing pools. These were cartel arrangements in which competing railroads would meet secretly and fix prices. Frequently, some railroads would cheat on the cartel agreements and give secret rebates to selected customers. The railroads would also practice some forms of discrimination against shippers. Many shippers, especially farmers in the midwest, complained that short-haul rates were greater than the rates for the same traffic travelling greater distances.

The individual states had begun to regulate the pricing practices of the railroads. Led by Illinois, the "Granger Laws" prohibited a variety of pricing practices including long-haul/short-haul discrimination, secret rebates and free passes to public officials for railroad travel.

The right of state or federal legislatures to pass laws to regulate railroads and other public businesses was established by the case of *Munn* v. *Illinois*.[2] Munn ran a public warehouse in Illinois and did not meet the regulations for this business established by the state. Munn was indicted in the state courts for noncompliance and was found guilty. He appealed to the Supreme Court which ruled the state did have the right to regulate such public businesses.

There still remained a question of regulation of intrastate versus interstate commerce. Prior to 1887, states had laws which set rates across their borders by rulings pertaining to the portion of the trip within their jurisdiction. In 1886, however, the Supreme Court found in the case of the *Wabash Railway Co.* v. *Illinois*[3] that such state laws were improper since interstate commerce could only be regulated at the federal level. Since no federal legislation existed, there remained only a minimal level of railroad regulation. At this time there was a movement for federal action.

The Establishment of the ICC

A congressman from Texas (whose name incidentally was Reagan) introduced a regulatory bill in 1877 which did not pass. The Reagan bill was revised and reintroduced ten years later and in 1887 became the Act to Regulate Commerce.

The Act established the ICC as the regulator of transportation in the United States. This act and other subsequent legislation enacted in the early 1900's gave the ICC significant power over rail transportation. Rates were required to be "just and reasonable" without undue preference or prejudice. Short-haul rates were required to be less than long-haul rates. All rates were required to be published. "Collective rate-making" was allowed, but under the control of the ICC. Minimum rates

---

[2] *Munn* v. *Illinois*, 94 U.S. 113 (1877).

[3] *Wabash Railway Co.* v. *Illinois*, 118 U.S. 557 (1886).

were also regulated. The ICC was also given control over entry and exit into and out of the industry. Proposed rail abandonments were subject to hearings before the Commission before they could be accomplished.

Two Views of Regulation

There are two different views of why ICC regulation was enacted. One follows the "public interest" theory of regulation. This view argues that the railroads abused the monopoly power which they possessed. The establishment of the ICC was the result of a grass roots rebellion against the evils of monopoly.

The second view follows the special interest, capture theory. It is argued that the railroads were having trouble enforcing their cartel agreements. The cartel participants were cheating on the price-fixing arrangements by offering secret rebates to selected shippers. Since the railroad's enforcement of their agreements failed, they turned to the federal government for assistance. Who is better able to enforce price-fixing arrangements than the federal government? This view holds that the ICC was established, not over the opposition of the railroads, but rather because the railroads supported the legislation. The ICC became the policeman of their cartel agreements.

In addition, commissioners at the ICC were required to possess detailed knowledge of the intricacies of the railroad industry and rail-pricing practices. Such knowledge could only be obtained by working in the industry. Thus, individuals from the industry frequently occupied positions at the ICC. Individuals who worked at the ICC or served as a commissioner frequently found jobs in industry. The ICC was "captured" by the railroads, according to this view.

Motor Carriers

The Great Depression of the 1930's was disastrous for many industries, including the motor carriers. The trucking industry is characterized by low capital requirements, and thus easy entry. All that is needed is a truck and an individual is in business. Some individuals who lost jobs in other industries entered the motor carrier business out of desperation. The result was increased supply and reduced demand — both caused by the Depression. Rates fell significantly. The trucking industry was experiencing "ruinous" or "cut-throat" competition as some would describe it.

The rate cutting in the motor carrier industry also affected the railroads. Since trucks and railroads compete for some of the same traffic, the railroads were losing business to the trucking business. The stage was set for regulation of the motor carrier industry.

The trucking industry wanted regulation so as to control entry into the industry and increase rates. The railroads wanted the motor carriers to be regulated in order to reduce their competitive threat. In 1935, Congress added the trucking industry to the ICC's jurisdiction. Freight rates and entry and exit into and out of the industry became regulated by the ICC.

Impacts of ICC Regulation

The special interest capture theory of regulation would predict that the railroads would have prospered under regulation. This was not the case, especially after World War II. The railroad industry was characterized by low rates of return and frequent bankruptcies. The most visible example was the bankrupt Pennsylvania Railroad which was merged with the New York Central in order to save it. The resultant entity—the Penn Central subsequently went bankrupt itself and was replaced by CONRAIL.

In 1979, the year prior to the enactment of deregulation legislation, the average rate of return in the industry was 2.5 percent. This was at the time of double-digit inflation, resulting in a negative return in real terms.

Rate regulation resulted in double trouble for the railroads. On the shipment of bulk commodities such as grain and coal, it had a distinct competitive advantage over trucks. Rates on these large volume commodities were substantially lower by rail than by truck, so much so that many shippers felt that they were exclusively dependent on railroads to move their goods. The ICC exercised stringent maximum rate regulation on the traffic and did not permit the railroads to raise the rates on this traffic to a market determined price.

On the other hand, there are some types of traffic for which railroads compete head on with trucks. ICC regulation in many instances would not permit the railroads to lower their rates sufficiently to be a viable competitor. An example is the "Ingot Molds" case in which ingot molds were being shipped from Neville Island, Pennsylvania to Steelton, Kentucky.[4] Even though the molds could be shipped by rail for as low as $4.69 per ton (on a marginal cost basis), the ICC declared that the railroads could charge no less than $7.19 per ton (on an average cost basis). The result was that the molds were shipped by a truck-barge combination which was priced at $5.19 per ton.

In addition, ICC regulation made it very difficult for the railroads to abandon low-density, unprofitable lines. The railroads were forced to cross-subsidize these lines with earnings from profitable routes. The combination of rate regulation and abandonment regulation had a disastrous effect on the industry.

Another impact of regulation was the stifling of innovation. The introduction of new technology or innovative services often requires a change in rate structure. This is where many innovations were sidetracked—sometimes permanently. For example, in the early 1960's, the Southern Railway Co. decided to introduce a new aluminum grain car called the "Big John Hopper." This car had a larger capacity than other grain hopper cars. Reflecting the cost savings for large shipments experienced through this innovation, the Southern wanted to lower freight rates on grain hauls using these cars. The ICC refused to allow lower rates. The case ended up in the courts and only after four years was the railroad permitted to lower their rates.

Some capture theorists have argued that in the end, it was not the railroads that captured the ICC, it was the motor carriers. The trucking industry prospered under regulation. In order to haul commodities in interstate commerce, a certificate of public convenience and necessity must be obtained from the ICC. Such a certificate must be issued for each commodity carried and each destination served. Truckers who already haul a commodity for which a new certificate is requested could protest the issuance before the ICC. This resulted in very few new certificates being issued. This entry control was very effective in propping up the rates of existing carriers.

---

[4] *American Commercial Lines, Inc.* v. *Louisville & Nashville Railroad Co.*, 392 U.S. 571 (1968).

Circuitous route restrictions, in which a trucking company was not permitted to take the most direct route and gateway restrictions in which truckers were forced to pass through certain communities even though no freight was to be picked up or dropped off, resulted in substantial inefficiencies of vehicles and fuel utilization. Additional inefficiencies resulted from the large number of empty backhauls present in the industry. The empty backhauls were caused by truckers being unable to obtain certificates for backhaul movements.

The impact of regulation was to benefit existing trucking firms by keeping rates high and new entrants out. Shippers paid higher rates and inefficiencies were greater than would be the case in a freely competitive situation.

Deregulation

In 1980, Congress passed two major pieces of legislation which substantially affected the regulation of both railroads and motor carriers. The Staggers Rail Act and the Motor Carrier Act of 1980, although not totally deregulating either mode, made great changes in price, entry and exit regulations.

The Staggers Act had as its primary objective the revitalization of the railroad industry. It eliminates ICC regulation entirely on two-thirds of all freight rates. The remainder of rates could fluctuate within a zone of rate flexibility without ICC approval for changes. While still legal, "collective rate-making" was severely restricted. The Staggers Act also speeded up the process of rail line abandonment approval and made approval of rail mergers slightly easier.

The purpose of the Motor Carrier Act was to substitute competitive market forces for regulation. Congress believed this would result in lower costs of operation, increased energy efficiency and lower freight rates by truck. The Act eased entry restrictions by limiting the protestations that could occur when a certificate of public convenience and necessity was applied for. In addition, entry restrictions into a segment of the industry which is not subject to rate regulation was eased. These "contract carriers" also were allowed to carry a bigger variety of shipments. In order to increase energy efficiency, circuitous route limitations and gateway restrictions were eliminated. A zone of rate flexibility was also established in the motor carrier industry for those shipments still subject to rate regulation. The Act also severely limited "collective rate-making" in the trucking industry.

Both the Staggers Act and the Motor Carrier Act were designed to deal with many of the unintended effects of transportation regulation as administered by the ICC. This was accomplished by severely limiting the power and scope of responsibility of the Commission. Market forces, rather than government polices, were emphasized as the primary regulators of the railroad and motor carrier industries.

The Staggers Act and the Motor Carrier Act have been success stories for transportation. Rail rates of return have increased, and the wave of bankruptcies ended. Quality of service and innovation has improved in the railroad industry. As an example, double stack container trains began service three years after the concept was first developed, unlike the experience with the Big John Hopper. The trucking industry has undergone a major change with many large trucking firms going out of business, replaced by owner operators and smaller firms. Rates have been reduced and efficiency of operations improved. Many large corporations streamlined their transportation purchasing departments and now deal with only a few trucking companies, rather than the myriad of motor carriers required under regulation.

Building on the success of deregulation, Congress passed the Trucking Industry Regulatory Reform Act of 1994 (TIRRA). This act reduced the regulatory power of the ICC still further. Among other provisions, in order to obtain a license to haul freight from the ICC, a carrier need only provide proof of insurance and safety fitness. The filing of rates with the ICC was eliminated.

Because the workload of the ICC had continually shrunk under deregulation, serious questions were raised in 1995 by the Clinton Administration and the Republican Congress as to whether the ICC should continue to exist. Congress passed and the president signed the "ICC Elimination Act." The legislation abolished the ICC and in it place, established the Surface Transporation Board (or SurfBoard as it is known in Washington).

The STB has very reduced regulatory power and a reduced staff. However, rail mergers including the merger of the Union Pacific with the Southern Pacific, the Burlington Northern with the Sante Fe and a proposed merger of Conrail with CSX Corp. could reduce the number of major railroads to four. The CSX-Conrail proposal brought on calls for increased regulation of the railroad industry.

The Consumer Movement

Among the methods of regulation described above, several are targeted to product safety and consumer information. Inspection, grading, and certification provide a direct means for government to insure the quality and safety of products. Standard setting provides manufacturers, sellers, and consumers a yardstick against which to measure product safety while labeling requirements supply consumers information by which to judge products. In addition, truth-in-advertising laws provide information to consumers about the products they buy and the warranties they have should the product fail.

Over many years there has evolved a social movement known as "consumerism." This was defined by Philip Kotler (1972) as "a social movement seeking to augment the rights and powers of buyers in relation to sellers." Throughout the history of the consumer movement there has been an assumption that business had the upper hand in dealing with matters of product safety, liability, efficacy and information. In essence, consumerism seeks to shift the balance of power toward the consumer, providing a legal means to insure product safety and useful, correct information.

In the past, the consumer movement has gained strength from books and articles exposing abuses and dangers to the general public. Publication of *The Jungle* by Upton Sinclair in 1905 was followed by legislation dealing with food and drug labeling as well as the forming of the Federal Trade Commission in 1914.

In the 1930's, deceptive advertising practices were the subject of a book entitled *Your Money's Worth* by Stuart Chase and F. J. Schlink. These authors called for objective product information to allow the consumer to make informed judgments. In addition, drug safety became an issue when a number of people died from an Elixir Sulfanilamide (a liquid version of sulfanilamide). These areas were included in the 1938 Food, Drug and Cosmetic Act and the Wheeler-Lea Act (which expanded the power of the FTC).

During the 1960's, Ralph Nader gained recognition as a consumer advocate. His book on the Corvair, *Unsafe at Any Speed,* was followed by legislation regulating automobile safety. In 1972, the Consumer Product Safety Commission was established to insure the safety of all products not already covered by other agencies.

Thus, the key issues of interest to the consumer movement include: food safety, drug safety and efficacy, auto and other manufactured product safety, clear and correct product information, and product warranties. In addition, issues of deceptive advertising and unfair business practices which have a negative impact on consumers are of concern. In this chapter the regulation of product safety by the Food and Drug Administration (FDA), National Highway Traffic Safety Administration (NHTSA), and the Consumer Product Safety Commission (CPSC) will be described.

Food and Drug Administration

Since the 1890's, efforts of various interest groups have led to the initiation and later expansion of the activities of the Food and Drug Administration. In 1898, the National Pure Food and Drug Congress (formed by the Women's Christian Temperance Union and the National Temperance Society) supported legislation which would eliminate medical nostrums or patent medicines from the market. These were usually made with alcohol. In addition, pharmacies and physicians felt that these patent medicines were competing for their services and were both useless and dangerous to the public.

In 1906, the Food and Drug Act was passed which focused on the labeling of food and patent medicines. The FDA itself was not established until 1931 (formerly the FDA had been the Bureau of Chemistry in the Agriculture Department). Thus, the consumer was provided information regarding the contents of foods and patent medicines. However, the government did not insure the public that a medicine did what it was supposed to do or that it was safe. There was no testing or approval before products were sold.

In 1937, an Elixir Sulfanilamide was developed for individuals who could not take sulfanilamide tablets. Unfortunately, the elixir proved to be poisonous and 107 people died. This prompted the passage in 1938 of the Food, Drug and Cosmetic Act which extended the purview of the FDA to include cosmetics, increased control over advertising and labeling of the products under its jurisdiction, and required all new drugs to be approved for safety before being sold in interstate commerce. Government certification was beneficial to the drug industry since it assured the public of product safety and the law received their support.

In 1961–62, the public's awareness was again aroused by the Thalidomide tragedy in Europe where many women who had taken the drug while pregnant gave birth to deformed babies. The drug had been kept off the market by the FDA in the United States except for experimental purposes, so the tragedy did not strike here. In addition, Senator Estes Kefauver from Tennessee investigated the drug industry in 1961 and found there were many expensive but useless drugs on the market. These events led to the passage of the Drug Amendments of 1962 which added the requirement that a drug company demonstrate the efficacy of a product as well as its safety. In other words, a drug must do what it is supposed to do.

Several other amendments to the 1938 law have been added over the years which have clarified or extended the duties of the FDA. The Food Additives (or Delaney Amendment) was passed in 1953 and states that "no additive shall be deemed to be safe . . . if it is found, after tests which are appropriate for the evaluation of the safety of food additives, to induce cancer in man or animal." However, when the FDA proposed banning the artificial sweetener "saccharin" because it might be a carcinogen, there was considerable public outcry since no substitute was available. Saccharin was allowed to continue to be used as a food additive. In the early 1980's, the additive 'Nutrasweet' was introduced and was used in most artificially sweetened products, even though saccharin was not officially banned.

In addition, the Color Additive Amendments of 1960 and the Medical Devices Amendments of 1976 expanded the products regulated. The Radiation Control for Health and Safety Act of 1968 extended FDA control to this area as well.

Methods of Enforcement

The FDA requires premarket clearance of drugs and medical devices for both safety and efficacy. In general, the manufacturers provide the results of testing to the FDA for a new product to be certified. New food additives must be approved for safety before being sold while cosmetics do not require premarket approval.

In addition, the FDA tests thousands of samples of food, human and animal drugs, medical devices and cosmetics annually. Factory inspections are also a part of the duties of FDA personnel, requiring trained individuals to visit individual factories to determine if they are operating under the sanitary conditions required for food and drug production.

When products are found to be unsafe, the FDA can order a recall or directly seize the goods. Manufacturers will sometimes "voluntarily" recall a product when it is linked to a health hazard or otherwise found to be unacceptable. Finally, the FDA can bring companies to court and utilize the judicial system to enforce their standards and procedures.

Impact of FDA Regulation

Although the purpose of the FDA is to protect the public against impure and unsafe foods, drugs, and cosmetics, and to regulate hazards involved with medical devices and radiation, there have been a number of unintended effects. In recent years, the cost of bringing a new drug to market has escalated to the extent that only drugs which have the potential of high volume sales are developed. In addition, the testing requirements have resulted in long-time lapses before a drug can be brought to market. For example, a number of experimental drugs are being developed to treat Acquired Immune Deficiency Syndrome (AIDS). Since the disease is almost always fatal, many victims will die before the drugs are widely available in the United States and others will travel to other countries to obtain treatments or obtain drugs in the "underground" market.

The combined effect of FDA regulations is that drugs to cure rare diseases are not developed. Many people may die before drugs for more common diseases are approved. In addition, the relatively small number of new drugs introduced serves to protect from competition those companies with products already on the market. Are the costs greater than the benefits? Would the free market be a good substitute for government regulation of food, drugs, and cosmetics?

National Highway Traffic Safety Administration

In 1965, Ralph Nader published a book entitled *Unsafe at Any Speed* about the design of the popular Corvair, manufactured by General Motors. Not only was public attention drawn to the auto safety issue, but Congress responded to reports such as the following:

> The compelling need for the strong automobile safety legislation . . . lies embodied in these statistics: 1.6 million dead since the coming of the automobile; over 50,000 to die this year. And, unless the accelerating spiral of death is arrested, 100,000 Americans will die as a result of their cars in 1975 (Senate Report No. 1301, 89th Congress, Second Session (1966), pp. 1–2.)

Both the National Traffic and Motor Vehicle Safety Act and the Highway Safety Act (which set uniform safety standards for state highways) were passed in 1966. The National Highway Traffic Safety Agency (which became the National Highway Traffic Safety Administration in 1970) issued 29 specific automobile equipment standards between 1966-1970. After 1966, the automobile industry was required to design cars to meet these standards and to test new models for compliance.

The number of standards has gradually increased over the years, and can be classified into three major groups: pre-crash, crash, and post-crash standards. Pre-crash standards cover braking systems and tires, for example, while crash standards include head restraints, padded and collapsible steering systems, strong door latches, shatterproof glass, and restraints such as seat belts. Post-crash standards involve design of fuel tanks to minimize fire hazards and the use of flame resistant materials in auto interiors. In addition, retailers and manufacturers are required to keep records of purchasers should a recall be made.

In addition to regulating automobile safety directly, NHTSA enforces the 55/65 MPH speed limit, and (since 1975) sets and enforces mandatory average fuel economy standards for new motor vehicles. Both of these policies grew out of the energy "crisis" of the 1970's, when the Arab oil embargo, coupled with existing government policies regarding the pricing and distribution of gasoline, resulted in shortages throughout the United States. The goal was to reduce fuel consumption by forcing car owners to drive at a more "fuel efficient" speed and to require manufacturers to develop automobiles which meet ever-increasing fuel economy standards. Thus, regulation was chosen as a primary method to reach the objective of lower levels of fuel consumption in the United States.

Methods of Enforcement

NHTSA usually relies on the manufacturers to perform the testing needed to check on compliance with their standards. Certification is then given by the manufacturer for the product. In addition, a sample of automobiles are selected for testing by NHTSA directly.

In order to monitor the safety qualities of the cars which have been purchased, an Auto Safety Hotline is operated by the agency. It receives some 500-600 calls per day. In addition, reports of safety problems directly received by manufacturers are reported and when necessary a "defects investigation" is carried out.

When problems are found, recalls may be suggested or required and are carried out by the manufacturers. NHTSA may also levy fines against the guilty parties, although this method is not often utilized.

Impact of NHTSA Regulations

It appears there have been fewer deaths and injuries as a result of the changes in auto design, especially when compared to pre-1966 cars. However, the requirements have added several hundred dollars to the cost of each car manufactured and in some cases have required that heavier equipment be installed. The extra weight reduces the fuel efficiency of the automobile.

New cars do get better gas mileage than older models, although American manufacturers have achieved NHTSA fuel economy standards primarily through "down-sizing" the larger models and selling more subcompacts. However, by 1985, consumer tastes had changed and demand was for the larger, more profitable models rather than subcompacts which have a much smaller profit margin. General Motors and Ford went to NHTSA in early 1985 to try to have the fuel economy standards for 1986 relaxed.

The mix of large and small cars sold by these manufacturers did not achieve the 1986 standards. If the standards were not relaxed, both Ford and GM would either have to pay penalties or induce customers to buy more fuel-efficient cars. Chrysler argued to keep the standards, claiming they had invested in research to develop more efficient cars and therefore could meet the mileage requirement. Another reason for Chrysler's favorable position is the fact that only a small proportion of their sales come from larger models. Thus, Chrysler's fleet mix could achieve the 1986 standards. However, NHTSA agreed to relax the standards, resulting in a victory for Ford and GM.

Another impact of NHTSA regulation is that approximately 4500 lives are saved each year as a result of the 55/65 MPH speed limit. Thus, the goal of saving lives can be reached without any changes in automobile design. Other programs which have been suggested include more emphasis on driver education and enforcement of the drunk driving laws. Drunk drivers are involved in half of the two-car crashes and 80% of the one-car crashes. Stricter enforcement of existing laws and stiffer penalties for those arrested are proposed by interest groups such as Mothers Against Drunk Driving (MADD) and changes have occurred in several states.

Perhaps one of the most controversial proposals of NHTSA is the requirement of passive restraints on all new automobiles. As mentioned in earlier chapters, this issue began during the Carter administration with the recommendation that air bags be installed in all new vehicles. Such a move would add from $300 to $1,100 per vehicle and was opposed by manufacturers as well as by a number of citizens' groups. Opponents cited technical problems, inequity, since those already using seat belts were forced to pay for passive restraints, and infringement on individual freedom. When Ronald Reagan came into office, the requirement for passive restraints was dropped, although a compromise was introduced by Secretary of Transportation Elizabeth Dole in 1984.

The market changed, however, in the 1990's and consumers began to demand airbags. Introduced first in expensive, luxury cars, airbags became standard equipment in midsize and small cars. Many models also had passenger side airbags and some even had side impact airbags.

The airbag controversy was renewed in 1996. Although credited with saving over 1,600 lives, deploying airbags, studies indicated, killed over thirty small children. NHTSA held hearings and indicated they would allow motorists to have the passenger side airbag turned off. NHTSA viewed this as an interim step while safer airbags were being developed.

It is interesting that because of the threat of the Department of Transportation to require air bags in all new automobiles, several states passed laws requiring the use of car seats by children under two years old and the wearing of seat belts by all drivers and front seat passengers. These states have determined that some infringements on individual rights is worth a potential reduction in auto deaths and injuries, as well as reducing potential additional government regulation.

Consumer Product Safety Commission

In 1972, the CPSC was created to protect the consumer against unreasonable risks of injury or death associated with consumer products not covered by the FDA, NHTSA, or other agencies. This followed a study in 1967 by the National Commission on Product Safety which found exposure to hazards by consumers was "excessive by any standard of measurement." The recommendation of the Commission was that self-regulation by business would not be satisfactory and that a federal agency dealing with product safety was needed. As a result of this study, and related public awareness of product safety, CPSC was formed.

In order to identify products which may be causing injuries, CPSC uses data from 100 U.S. hospitals which is gathered by the National Electronic Injury Surveillance System. This allows trends to be identified and follow-up action to be taken regarding specific products. In addition, CPSC requires manufacturers to supply information on new products and, when necessary, conducts hearings or inquiries.

One of the primary activities of the CPSC is the setting of or overseeing of standards for the performance, design, construction and packaging of over 10,000 consumer products. Because of limited resources, CPSC relies to a large extent on the "voluntary" standards set by industry groups. The CPSC has final approval of such standards.

In addition, mandatory standards may be established by CPSC for products found to be unsafe. It has set standards for such diverse products as baby cribs, matchbooks, bicycles, fireworks and lawnmowers. Since the early 1980's, CPSC has used cost-benefit analysis to evaluate the results of its standard setting activities. Using this method, estimates are made of the additional cost to design and manufacture a product meeting CPSC standards versus the reduced cost of injuries and deaths from the unapproved product.

Methods of Enforcement

CPSC requires manufacturers to certify that their products meet government standards, in a process similar to that used by NHTSA. Specific testing procedures may also be set which must be used in the certification process.

Factory inspection and product testing are also done by CPSC directly. The results of these activities, plus information from the National Electronic Injury Surveillance System, a consumer Hotline, and reports from manufacturers are used to identify particularly hazardous products.

CPSC can use a number of methods to force manufacturers to meet their standards. Recalls of products found to be unsafe can be required, or, when necessary, seizure or bans on the sale of products can be enforced. If a company does not comply, both civil and criminal penalties can be used, ranging from fines up to $50,000 or one-year imprisonment. Private suits can also be brought against those not in compliance.

Impact of CPSC Regulation

The safety standards set by CPSC do not come without some cost to the manufacturer, and, ultimately, the consumer. If the price of manufacturing products meeting CPSC standards is too high, they will not be made and the consumer will not have the opportunity to purchase them. In addition, all consumers will be required to pay for the safety standards, even if not needed when a product is used according to manufacturer's directions. Finally, the material used to meet the standards may in itself be hazardous.

An example of the potential hazards of meeting CPSC standards occurred in the mid-1970's when manufacturers of children's sleepwear were required to meet new standards for flame resistance. The chemical used to achieve the required level of flame retardation was TRIS. Later TRIS was found to be a potent carcinogen and in April, 1977, the chemical was banned by CPSC for use in sleepwear. All products which contained it were recalled. The costs of this episode included: exposure of millions of children to a dangerous carcinogen, high costs to manufacturers, and a higher price for children's sleepwear (Friedman & Friedman, 1990).

When CPSC was formed in 1972, a "sunset" law was used which called for its reapproval in 1981 by Congress. At that time, the Reagan Administration, supported by a number of industry groups, recommended that the Commission be discontinued. However, consumer groups and, not surprisingly, CPSC officials, argued for its continuation. The CPSC was continued, but at a reduced funding level. Its long-term future depends in part on the political climate and public sentiment regarding such broad-based regulation of consumer products. It is still in existence today.

Occupational Safety and Health Regulation

Consumer protection regulations have as their primary goal the protection of the public at large from hazardous products sold in the marketplace. But, who protects the workers who produce these goods and services from unnecessary exposure to dangerous chemicals or other hazardous conditions? The regulation of worker safety and health has been a concern of unions, management, the general public, and government officials for many years. Prior to the passage of federal legislation regulating worker safety and health, each state administered workers' compensation laws which paid the worker or his/her family after an injury occurred. However, these laws were inconsistent from state to state regarding the level of compensation and enforcement. In addition, contracts negotiated by labor unions dealt with many safety issues, but again inconsistency across organizations was found and non-unionized workers were not formally protected at all.

During the late 1960's, the dangers of coal mining became evident as a result of accidents in which many workers were killed and a greater public awareness of "black lung" disease occurred. In 1969, the Federal Coal Mine Health and Safety Act was passed to attempt to reduce some of these problems. The situation in mining was found not to be unique when the 1970 results of a National Safety Council study found that 14,000 workers were killed and 2.2 million were disabled each year. In 1970, the Occupational Safety and Health Act was passed which established the Occupational Safety and Health Administration (OSHA), a research agency called the National Institute for Occupational Safety and Health (NIOSH) and a judicial arm known as the Occupational Safety and Health Commission (OSHRC). The primary goal of OSHA is:

> "to assure so far as possible every working man and woman in the Nation safe and healthy working conditions" (OSH Act, Public Law 91-596, Section 2(b)).

OSHA has both broad and specific standard setting capability. The agency got off to a bad start when it adopted existing voluntary standards without reviewing them for relevance and usefulness to the current workplace. The hodgepodge of standards was obsolete and focused on the design of equipment rather than its intended performance. For example, OSHA required firms to have U-shaped toilet seats in their restroom facilities. It was unclear why closed-end seats were not allowed. OSHA was also on the verge of requiring that restroom facilities be provided to cowboys when out on the range. Public awareness of the silliness of such a regulation seemed to have helped to stop the bureaucracy from implementing it. Over 900 of the standards originally adopted were purged in 1978 because of these problems.

Methods of Enforcement

Enforcement by OSHA centers on inspections and citations, followed by legal action if required. Inspections may be a part of a general program focusing on a sample of companies in high-hazard industries, or be triggered by the report of an accident resulting in death or injuries. In addition, an employee complaint or a follow-up to previous inspections may also result in an inspection. When violations are found, citations may be given and monetary penalties assigned. Appeals are heard through the OSHRC. If a problem is life-threatening, an "imminent danger" citation can be given, and if not corrected immediately, legal action can be taken.

OSHA also provides information and consultation to companies on how to improve the safety of the workplace, and has begun a program encouraging labor-management cooperation regarding safety issues. It is hoped that the level of voluntary compliance can be increased if the relationship between business and OSHA can be improved.

Impact of OSHA Regulation

The impact of OSHA regulation, in reducing the number of workplace injuries and deaths, is difficult to measure. Various studies indicate that the impact has been minimal, perhaps because the majority of injuries are the result of worker error rather than the design of equipment. The relationship of workplace conditions and employee health is especially difficult to determine. Many years may elapse before the symptoms of work-related illnesses develop and there are many environmental causes of these diseases in addition to exposure to substances found in the workplace.

OSHA regulations have had a severe impact on small business which frequently finds it difficult to comply with requirements. This was especially true when existing voluntary standards were first adopted. An example that was popularized by Ronald Reagan, when he first ran for President in 1980, concerns a small grocery store. The owner of the store was cited by OSHA inspectors for not having separate restroom facilities for men and women. However, the owner had only one employee—his wife.

While not nearly as onerous as when it began regulating the workplace, OSHA regulations have reduced competition in some industries by creating an additional barrier to entry. This is especially true of industries which are comprised primarily of small business.

In addition, OSHA horror stories continue to receive press coverage and interest from politicians. There was one story about ". . . the dry cleaner that was fined 'for not posting a piece of paper listing the number of employee injuries in the last 12 months,' even though there had been none . . . the Indiana construction company 'cited by OSHA for failing to fill out' a hazardous-materials form about a can of Lemon Pledge; the classification of children's teeth as a 'hazardous waste'" (Noah, 1995, p. A16). At least one dentist is known to have not given a small child back two extracted baby teeth so they could be placed under the pillow for the Tooth Fairy.

Alternatives to OSHA Regulation

Cost/benefit analysis such as that used by the CPSC is not used by OSHA. There must be some evidence that a particular level of exposure to a substance is harmful before standards can be set, but little regard is given to the costs of achieving the goal. The emphasis is on saving workers from death and injury, regardless of the cost to the employer. It has been suggested that OSHA place greater emphasis on cost-effectiveness and cost/benefit analysis (Greer, 1983).

An alternative to the current methods of OSHA inspections and citations is the use of an injury tax. This is similar to a pollution tax, in that each time a worker is injured, the company is subject to a tax. It is said that such a tax would be easier to administer than current methods since reporting requirements now used would provide the needed information. In addition, all injuries would be covered and companies would have the incentive to reduce worker-caused accidents as well as those caused by unsafe equipment. If injury taxes resulted in higher prices, consumers would also want safe workplaces. Finally, the elimination of standards would allow workers and employers to determine the most cost-effective way to reduce injuries and would encourage innovation in this area (Greer, 1983).

Injury taxes are not appropriate for work-related illnesses, however, since it may not be possible to trace which place of employment resulted in the illness. In addition, there is little political support for this idea since the incentives are indirect, relying on pressures from the marketplace. Neither the unions nor business support this approach to increasing workplace safety.

Another alternative to OSHA regulation that is sometimes mentioned is to require firms to carry insurance against worker injury or death. Higher insurance premiums, it is argued, would provide an incentive for firms to maintain a safe working environment. Mandatory insurance would work in a manner similar to injury taxes, except the marketplace would be relied on more heavily.

The Benefits and Costs of Government Regulation

Benefits

There is no doubt that government regulation has resulted in substantial benefits to society. Food and drug regulation has kept harmful and adulterated products off the market. Tragedies such as the birth defects caused by pregnant women taking thalidomide in Europe were avoided in the United States during the early 1960's.

The CPSC has kept many hazardous products off the market. The information that is provided consumers about the dangers of particular products no doubt has saved many lives and injuries. For example, Christmas time frequently brings recalls and consumer warnings about defective toys and dangerous ornaments.

OSHA has contributed to the safety of the workplace and the information provided as a result of these regulations have probably resulted in increased safety awareness among workers. The Federal Aviation Administration (FAA) regulates airline safety. Its regulations have helped to make air travel one of the safest of all modes of transportation.

Other government agencies such as the Equal Employment Opportunity Commission (EEOC), the Federal Trade Commission (FTC) and the Environmental Protection Agency (EPA) have made substantial contributions to ending discrimination in employment, providing accurate information to the consumer, and insuring a safe, clean environment.

The benefits of government regulation are many and substantial. One group of consumer advocates studied the EPA, NHTSA, FDA, and CPSC. The results of this research estimated that these agencies alone produce $80.6 billion in benefits (Green & Watzman, 1979). The issue is not whether government regulation is beneficial. The issue facing business, consumers and government is whether these benefits are worth the costs.

Costs

The costs of government regulation are as varied as the benefits. They are also quite substantial. Costs of government regulation include the administrative costs incurred by the government agencies and the compliance costs imposed on business. In addition, regulation produces a variety of unintended effects. These include inefficiency and waste, high prices, reduced innovation, exacerbation of problems, means rather than goal orientation of policies and programs, and overlapping regulations.

Administrative and Compliance Costs

Administrative and compliance costs are the actual expenditure of resources and money by the federal government in administrating the various regulatory programs and by business in complying with the regulations. Administrative costs are well-documented and are shown in Table 6.2 in the beginning of this chapter. In that table, expenditures by the federal government were estimated at $16.5 billion in fiscal year 1996.

Compliance costs, on the other hand, are not known with any degree of certainty. One estimate was developed by Weidenbaum (1979). He estimated that in 1979, compliance costs totaled $97.9 billion. Another type of estimate was developed by the federal government. The General Accounting Office estimated that during 1992, Americans spent nearly 6.6 billion hours filling out forms, answering survey questions, and compiling records for the federal government. "This is equivalent to employing more than 3 million people full-time every year solely to collect, maintain, and report information in response to federal requirements and requests." GAO (1993, p. 2).

The volume of paperwork that the government requires to be completed by business organizations each year is another measure of the cost of complying with government regulations. This was estimated at 12.6 million cubic feet.[5] Assuming each sheet of paper is 8.5 × 11 inches, then a file drawer 3,675 miles long would be required to hold all that paper. Such a file drawer would stretch from Washington, D.C. into the Pacific Ocean.

---

[5] Testimony of the Commission on Federal Paperwork, before the Senate Committee on Government Operations, May 3, 1976.

Unintended Effects

One unintended effect of government regulation that was mentioned in the discussion of the ICC is the promotion of inefficiency and waste. Trucking regulation resulted in empty backhauls and inefficient use of fuel through circuitous route limitations.

Government regulation has also resulted in higher prices for products and services. For example, restrictions on entry into the transportation industries resulted in higher prices for transportation services, and thus higher prices for final products (Friedlander, 1969). Drug regulation, by lengthening the approval process and increasing the cost of testing, has also resulted in increased prices of drugs.

Reduced innovation is also an unintended effect of government regulation. The example of the Big John Hopper is an illustration of the reduced innovation that resulted from regulation of the railroads. The reduced development and availability of drugs for rare diseases is another example of slowed innovation resulting from FDA regulation. OSHA standards which focus on specific machine design may lead to inefficient use of resources and fail to protect the worker.

Regulatory efforts sometimes exacerbate problems or create a different set of problems. The TRIS fiasco mentioned previously is an example in which children were needlessly exposed to a carcinogenic agent. Delays in approving drugs may result in needless deaths because treatment was not available in the United States.

Another problem with some regulatory efforts is that they begin to focus on the means rather than the goals which the regulations were designed to achieve. That is, the regulations themselves become the end product or goal rather than the larger social objectives which they were designed to achieve. A case in point is the air bag controversy involving NHTSA. During the Carter administration, air bags were pushed as "the" solution to the traffic safety problem. Regulations were issued requiring the installation of air bags in all new vehicles. Some observers felt that rather than focus on the goal of increased traffic safety, with the air bag as one means to achieve that goal, the air bag requirement became the goal.

Finally, many government regulations are overlapping and lead to tremendous confusion on the part of business. This occurs when one regulatory agency requires just the opposite behavior as another. For example, OSHA directed one sausage company to put protective guards on its meat-blending machine. The Department of Agriculture required that such guards not be installed since they made machine cleaning too difficult (Healy, 1979). Starling (1984) reports how OSHA required that special lounge facilities be provided in women's restrooms. However, the Equal Employment Opportunity Commission ruled that if such lounges were provided for women, they must also be provided for men.

Alternatives to Regulation

A variety of alternatives to existing regulatory processes have been either suggested or tried to some extent. The underlying concept behind most reforms is to attempt to preserve most of the benefits of regulation, while reducing or eliminating the costs.

Structural and Personnel Reforms

The concept behind this idea is to change the structure of regulatory agencies and hire only high quality, dedicated professionals to administer them. The notion is that structural changes, such as whether the agency should be independent or under a cabinet department, and good personnel will result in better regulations with fewer costs and more benefits to society.

To be sure, there is no substitute for dedicated public servants administering regulations in an agency that is responsive to the needs of society. However, there is no guarantee that such individuals will always be hired. In addition, even though dedicated, high quality people may be hired who have very good intentions, such intentions may not always result in good public policy. Thus, it is argued that such structural and personnel reforms will not lead to the high benefit, low cost regulations that those who espouse this position believe.

Friedman and Friedman (1990) argue that changing regulatory agencies so that only desirable regulations result is not possible. It is like trying to find a cat that barks. They argue that just as there are biological laws that specify the characteristics of cats and dogs, there are political laws which govern the behavior of government agencies.

"The error of supposing that the behavior of social organisms can be shaped at will is widespread. It is the fundamental error of most so-called reformers. It explains why they so often feel that the fault lies in the man, not the "system," that the way to solve problems is to "turn the rascals out" and put well-meaning people in charge. It explains why their reforms, when ostensibly achieved, so often go astray" (Friedman & Friedman, 1990, p. 209).

Deregulation

While structural and personnel reforms essentially keep the existing system of regulation intact, deregulation is at the opposite extreme. Deregulation involves reduction or complete elimination of regulations and regulatory agencies. The federal government has undertaken five major deregulation efforts. These are the 1978 Airline Deregulation Act, the Motor Carrier Act of 1980, the Staggers Rail Act of 1980, the Intercity Bus Regulatory Reform Act of 1982 and the Depository Institutions Deregulation and Monetary Control Act of 1980. Four of these deregulation efforts were in the transportation industry, with one dealing with financial services. The experience to date with these deregulation efforts can provide at least a partial understanding of how well deregulation might work for other forms of regulation.

Transportation Deregulation — The first major deregulation bill to pass Congress was the Airline Deregulation Act. Over a period of years, entry restrictions into the industry were gradually eliminated, fare regulation was abolished and the Civil Aeronautics Board (CAB), which was responsible for regulating the industry, went out of existence. This is the first major regulatory agency to be eliminated by the federal government. Airline safety regulation continues, however, through the Federal Aviation Administration (FAA).

The Motor Carrier Act, the Staggers Act and the Intercity Bus Deregulation Act did not accomplish the same degree of deregulation as in the airline industry. Nevertheless, these pieces of legislation substituted competitive market forces for government regulation to one degree or another.

The experience to date with transportation deregulation has been very good. The airline industry has seen increased service frequency to many areas. At the same time, fares for many travelers have fallen substantially. Super saver fares with prices 70 percent below regular fares have become commonplace. The "hub and spoke" system that the airlines implemented after deregulation resulted in substantial operating efficiencies and smaller markets having access to more frequent service than was possible before. At the same time, complaints from passengers concerning delays while changing planes at major hubs has increased.

Airline deregulation has resulted in massive changes in the industry and problems for carriers which existed prior to deregulation. Labor contracts were negotiated during the period of regulation. In these agreements, the financial benefits of regulation were shared with airline employees. Deregulation meant that lower cost, new operators could compete more effectively with existing carriers. Several major carriers experienced substantial losses which took many years to reverse. Part of the cost cutting involved trimming labor costs so as to be competitive with the more cost effective carriers. Wages for pilots, flight attendants and other personnel were reduced. Unprofitable lines were eliminated and growth concentrated in potentially profitable areas.

Many airlines could not adjust to the new competitive environment and either were merged into another airline or ended up on the scrap heap. Eastern, Republic, Piedmont, Pan Am, National, Western and Braniff are names that once were. There were many that came and went including Peoples Express, New York Air, Jet America, and Midway Airlines (although it could be argued that Midway was a casualty of the Gulf War).

However, these airlines have been replaced by a large group of newcomers including Tower Air, Kiwi Airlines, American Trans Air and a revived Midway Airlines. In addition, regional airlines such as Southwest Air have expanded to the status of major airlines, while offering low cost, convenient service.

The three surface transportation deregulatory efforts have resulted in lower freight rates, increased competition between truck and rail, and better service. Freight rates in the trucking industry have fallen, while the railroads have undertaken a variety of service improvements including piggyback truck trailer on rail car service, vegetable express trains and guaranteed delivery schedules. The increased competition in the intercity bus industry has resulted in lower fares over many routes.

The Motor Carrier Act, the Staggers Rail Act and the Intercity Bus Deregulatory Act have also resulted in costs and problems being imposed on some groups. Intercity truckers have suffered a net loss in income as wages in the trucking industry responded to competitive market forces. Several long distance, major trucking firms have gone bankrupt. Rail car manufacturers, such as Pullman Standard, which was discussed in Chapter 1, have seen their business decline precipitously. Some grain interests and utilities have complained that deregulation has resulted in less competition in the carriage of grain and coal than under the old system. These individuals argue for a return to regulation.

Thus, deregulation of transportation has resulted in both gainers and losers. The losers for the most part are those groups that gained from regulation. These include labor, existing carriers, and suppliers. The big gainer has been the consumer. Increased competition has resulted not only in lower air and bus fares, but also in lower costs of moving freight. Competitive market forces can result in these lower costs turning into a consumer gain as well.

Financial Deregulation -- During the 1970's and 1980's there has been a continuing trend to deregulate the financial industry. Regulations in this industry have traditionally determined what products could be offered and the interest paid by banks, brokerage firms, savings and loans and other financial intermediaries. In addition, there have been restrictions regarding the geographical areas served as well as various means to insure the stability of the institutions and the safety of deposits.

The financial industry dramatically changed, however, when during the inflation of the 1970's, brokerage firms began offering money market funds to customers which paid the market interest rates as high as 12% or more, rather than the fixed 5.25% offered for savings accounts at banks and savings and loans. The smaller saver was able to get the higher interest rates previously available only to the large depositor.

The result was termed "disintermediation" which is the movement of deposits out of banks and savings and loans into brokerage houses and money market mutual funds. In order to stem this loss of funds from the banking and savings and loan industries, Congress passed two deregulation acts. These are the Depository Institutions Deregulation and Monetary Control Act of 1980 and the Garn-St. Germain Depository Institutions Act of 1982. These laws phased out interest rate ceilings and allowed banks and savings and loans to offer a wide range of depository instruments at market competitive interest rates.

A problem that was not fully contemplated when the deregulation bills were debated is that savings and loan institutions had their assets tied up in long term fixed rate mortgages, at relatively low rates. By paying market interest rates for deposits, S&L's were borrowing short at high rates and loaning long at low interest rates. This was a prescription for disaster, which is exactly what occurred.

Seeing inevitable bankruptcy, many S&L executives tried to save their enterprises. Since the federal government insured S&L deposits up to $100,00, many were willing to engage in risky investments in order to stay solvent. If the risky investments turned out to go bad, depositors were protected. The federal government had inadvertently guaranteed a high stakes gamble. Many S&L's took the gamble and did not survive. Others did not gamble and also did not survive. The result was the largest government bailout in history, which the Congressional Budget Office estimates will cost over $181 billion. (Congressional Budget Office, 1993)

Was the S&L disaster the result of deregulation? Would these institutions have survived the loss of funds that resulted from government regulation of the rates they could charge? While we may never know the definitive answers to these questions, one point is clear. Even when it engages in deregulation, government can impose enormous costs on society and business. In the words of one observer, "They can't do anything right."

Other line-of-business and geographic restrictions have been relaxed in recent years. Banks and savings and loans now offer customers discount or "no frills" brokerage services, and in some cases have branch offices in various parts of the country which offer most of their services. Regional banking is also developing in some areas through the combination of institutions from adjoining states. Although the financial industry is not officially deregulated, by using the courts, state legislation, and mergers and acquisitions, several organizations have been able to achieve defacto deregulation. Coupled with modern telecommunications and ATM's, the customer has a wide choice of products and services throughout the United States. It has also resulted in increased competition for all institutions, a relatively large number of mergers and acquisitions, as well as a relatively large number of failures or near failures of both small and large banks and savings and loans. Thus, financial deregulation has forced changes throughout this industry with both costs and benefits to the institutions and to the consumer.

<u>Prospects for Deregulation</u> — If deregulation seems to be working, what are the prospects for eliminating vast amounts of government regulations in a similar manner? Could deregulation be successfully carried out on a massive scale?

While no definitive answer to this question can be made, a few issues can be raised. First of all, some argue that not all industries can be deregulated. The elimination of government regulation only works if sufficient competition exists or potentially could exist to assure that market forces will be strong enough to regulate the industry.

Secondly, it is argued that while deregulation is appropriate for traditional industry regulation, it would not work in the public interest if applied to social regulation. It is argued that there is no mechanism to assure that dangerous, shoddy products would not be on store shelves, or that unscrupulous manufacturers would not subject workers to hazardous conditions.

Friedman and Friedman (1990) argue that the marketplace is the mechanism for preventing this behavior. In the case of products, they suggest that several alternatives to regulation already exist. One is the middleman. Reputable retailers would not want to sell defective products. They will do the monitoring for the consumer. A second device is the brand name. They argue that it is in the interests of the manufacturer to maintain a reputation for producing dependable, reliable products. Finally, private testing organizations such as the Consumers Union provide valuable information to consumers on the condition of products.

Those supporting the other side of the issue would argue that yes, Friedman and Friedman may be correct. The marketplace has its own mechanisms for keeping shoddy products off the shelves. Labor unions and individual workers can also effectively monitor the safety of the workplace, as long as the business is not the sole purchaser of labor services. But, at what price do these market mechanisms work?

Take the case of airlines. There are very powerful incentives for all airlines to maintain a good safety record. If not because passengers will refuse to fly, but also to maintain the safety of the crew, and to minimize insurance costs. But, the one sure way that the marketplace would know if an airline is unsafe is if there were an accident. The marketplace works best after the fact, not before.

Thus, there is a role for government regulation in essentially providing a social insurance policy. To be sure, government regulation is not completely effective, and, it is quite costly. However, this point of view maintains that it provides an additional level of protection over and above that provided by the market.

Table 6.5. The Regulatory Spectrum

Form of Regulation	Examples	Degree of Government Involvement	Autonomy of Individual Firms
Unregulated industry	Publishing	Low	High
Pure self-regulation (no government intervention)	Motion picture rating and censorship	↑	↑
Self-regulation plus government provision of technical information	Voluntary product standards and the National Bureau of Standards		
Self-regulation plus government policing of deceptive practices	Securities industry self-regulation and the SEC		
Self-regulation plus an autonomous government agency with rule-making authority	Advertising self-regulation and the FTC		
Self-regulation embodied in federal or state statutes	Occupational licensing and certification		
Decentralized systems of public regulation	Effluent fees set by the EPA		
Federal or state standard setting	Air and water pollution control standards set by the EPA	↓	↓
Government price and output setting	Electrical utilities and state public utility commissions	High	Low

Source: Garvin, 1983, Reprinted with permission.

Self-Regulation

Another alternative to regulation is self-regulation defined as occurring "when industry members jointly pursue regulatory or standard-setting activities in the absence of explicit legal requirements" (Garvin, 1983). Table 6.5 illustrates a regulatory spectrum with government price and output setting on the one hand and a completely unregulated industry on the other. Several hybrid situations are described which combine self-regulation with various forms of government involvement.

But who gains and who loses from self-regulation? Certain industries may gain from self-regulation, especially when direct government regulation does not exist but is threatened. The standards themselves may be either more or less stringent than those which the government would develop.

If restrictions to entry are developed, as occurs with occupational licensing, then those already in the business will benefit. However, consumers may lose because of fewer services or products offered and possibly higher prices. If higher quality results, then the consumer benefits as well.

When the price and product uniformity are increased, the industry gains additional revenues, and the consumer loses. However, it is possible that less variation in products will result in more efficient production methods which will result in lower prices.

Some industry standards are set regarding deceptive practices. Examples exist in the accounting industry and the advertising business. Information from audits and that provided in advertisements should be more accurate, a benefit to both consumers and firms in the industry (Garvin, 1983).

Sunset Laws

Another approach to reforming the regulatory process involves sunset legislation. These laws would require that a regulatory agency go out of existence after a specified period of time unless Congress acts to continue it. Thus, the "sun" would be allowed to "set" on these agencies. The advantages of such an approach are 1) a periodic review of the activities of an agency would be required and 2) an agency could not continue solely because of inertia. In addition, 3) the agency would have a stronger incentive to regulate in the public interest, since termination could result if this is not done.

Although the concept is very appealing, several problems are associated with its implementation. One is that the automatic termination procedure may be too extreme. Gujarati (1984) notes that talk of eliminating some agencies such as the FTC or the FDA may be dismissed as nonsense. The threat of termination would lose much of its bite in these cases. Some have suggested a gradual termination process instead of an all or nothing approach as a means of mitigating this deficiency.

A second problem concerns the workload that would be created for Congress if sunset legislation were widespread. This may result in perfunctory reviews, with little or no impact on the regulatory agency.

Cost-Benefit Analysis of Regulations

The notion behind this alternative is to require that regulatory agencies conduct a cost-benefit analysis before adopting a proposed regulation. In the analysis, all the costs and benefits to society associated with the rule in question would be estimated. If the social benefits exceed the costs, then the regulation would be adopted. If the costs are estimated to be greater than the anticipated benefits, then the regulation would not be implemented.

While this proposal seems to be a very common sense approach to government regulation, many formidable obstacles need to be overcome before it can be used as a screening device for good and bad regulations.

Cost-benefit analysis requires that all the benefits and costs be quantified and then evaluated on the basis of some common denominator. This common denominator is usually money, so all benefits and costs must be valued in dollars. This process of quantification and valuation leads to the objective analysis that is the hallmark of the cost-benefit technique. It also leads to problems in applying the methodology.

Many of the costs and benefits defy quantification. How many lives would be saved if side impact air bags were required on all automobiles? What is compliance cost to business? How many injuries would be saved if a given OSHA standard were adopted? Similar types of questions would need to be answered in the process of quantifying costs and benefits.

Some benefits and costs may be quantified, but present problems of valuation. How much is a human life worth? What is the value of time saved for travelers or consumers? How should illness costs be estimated, when pain and suffering are included? The uncertainty associated with these estimates leads to uncertainty in the analysis of regulations.

Since there are so many problems in quantification and valuation in cost-benefit analysis, the technique can easily be abused. Regulatory agencies which are predisposed to adopting a particular regulation can probably find enough benefits to justify the rule if they look long enough and hard enough. Thus, the requirement of performing such an analysis may not be very effective as a screening device.

Regulatory Budget

One of the problems of the regulatory process is the lack of incentives on the part of regulatory agencies to take compliance costs into account in the decision process. Most often, industry groups and individuals must attempt to influence the political process early in order to have such costs considered.

The concept behind the regulatory budget is to force regulators to explicitly take compliance costs into account. In addition to providing the regulatory agency with a budget to be used for administration and enforcement, this proposal would require Congress to pass a limit on the costs that the agency could impose on the private sector. This maximum limit on compliance costs is the regulatory budget. Regulatory agencies would be required to not exceed this budget each year.

The regulatory budget concept has several advantages. It would require that regulatory agencies explicitly consider not only their own administrative costs, but also the costs imposed on society in the decision-making process. The agency would have an incentive to eliminate obsolete or low-priority items and find the least costly means of achieving the goals of regulation. In addition, Thompson and Jones (1981) note that the current system can result in a shifting of costs from the regulatory agency to the industry being regulated. This is because the agency has an incentive to keep its costs down, but not necessarily the costs imposed on business. The regulatory budget would help to reduce this cost shifting. Finally, the regulatory budget concept ". . . would provide a more accurate picture of the government's total impact on the economy, allowing Congress to determine how much of the nation's output will be directed by government and how much will be directed by the private sector" (Brown, 1980, p. 74).

The regulatory budget concept is not without its problems, however. First of all is the problem of actually measuring compliance costs. Thompson and Jones (1981) suggest that these costs be estimated by the private sector firms which incur these expenses. They suggest that government establish guidelines for costs to be included and that business estimate these costs within these guidelines.

One problem with this approach is that business has little incentive to estimate these costs correctly. Such incentives could be provided by allowing business to deduct a portion of the estimated cost from their income tax. Traditional auditing procedures used by the IRS could be used as a device to assure truthfulness in reporting.

A second problem involves ascertaining which costs should be counted. Should costs due to regulatory lag be considered, as in the Big John Hopper case mentioned previously? How about the cost of increased cancer risk caused by TRIS? Third, the regulatory budget approach focuses on costs, but ignores the benefits of regulation. It seems to be looking at only half the problem. Finally, because compliance costs are difficult to measure, there may be a tendency for regulators to attempt to rig the costs to make them seem less than they would be. Of course, this is a problem shared by cost-benefit analysis as well.

Managerial Implications

Both economic and social regulations have direct and indirect impacts on management. Most directly, if managers choose to ignore the law or its implications, and act in a manner which can be considered socially irresponsible or unethical, the chance for government litigation against them is increased and their long-term survival may be in jeopardy.

Indirectly, regulations can have a variety of impacts on the way business is conducted, including pricing, liability, relationships with employees, etc. Managers must be able to effectively adapt to a changing regulatory environment in order to assure competitive survival. In order to adapt to this changing regulatory environment, managers must evaluate the scope or extensiveness of government actions, the likelihood of future change (toward more or less regulation), and the potential costs and benefits to the firm. Once the regulatory environment has been scanned, the company must determine what changes may occur in the future and develop strategies for meeting new challenges.

Management must be able to adapt the functions of planning, organizing, controlling and staffing/rewarding to government regulatory efforts and to deregulation that may occur in the future. In some situations, a potential cost can turn into a net benefit to the firm.

Impacts of Regulation

From a strategic perspective, regulation often creates entrepreneurial opportunities. Mitnick (1981) has observed that these opportunities can be created in the areas of manufacturing of equipment to satisfy regulatory requirements and the marketing of expertise to solve regulation-induced dilemmas. For example, when the EPA introduced air and water quality regulations, some industries developed pollution control equipment for their own use. They quickly realized that this was a new, growing market and began producing and selling the equipment to other firms.

Regulation may also be technology forcing. That is, it may induce better managers to adopt new technology that can lead to profit opportunities. Mitnick (1981) cites the example of Dow Chemical who has been able to make a net profit from the recovery of wastes whose control was mandated by regulation. Eventually, recycling efforts may result in profitable businesses on their own.

There are a number of managerial responses to the threat of new or increased regulation which involve interaction with the political environment. First, the organization and its employees may become active in the political process. Testimony at hearings, supporting candidates sympathetic to the company's position, and lobbying to members of Congress can be effective. Legal action to postpone enforcement or clarify the laws may also be initiated by industry.

Another area of managerial action is involvement with trade associations or other organizations to form a united front for a particular position. If changes in regulation result in economic conditions which cannot support all existing firms, mergers between firms may occur. This took place in the savings and loan industry, especially after financial deregulation and the economic recession which occurred in the early 1980's.

Regulation also requires additional paperwork and specialists to interpret the law and implement the programs needed for compliance. It may be possible for several organizations to pool their resources to minimize these costs of compliance. For example, when Equal Employment Opportunity (EEO) regulations were first introduced there were only a few individuals knowledgeable in the specifics of EEO reporting, selection and validation techniques, etc. Initially consultants were hired, but as time passed and the need for EEO specialists continued, courses were offered by trade associations and professional groups. Companies were able to develop in-house EEO specialists and today this area is a normal part of the human resource function.

As the regulatory environment changes, firms may also find it useful to communicate with other companies. When it does not violate anti-trust laws, joint planning and research efforts may help all firms successfully adapt. In addition, shared services and facilities may be cost-effective over the long run. For example, small- or medium-sized air carriers often contract with larger airlines for maintenance and baggage handling services, especially in small cities. In this way, they only pay for the services they need rather than paying employees who only work a few hours a day.

Impacts of Deregulation

The prospect of deregulation may result in a variety of competitive threats to existing companies. Bleeke (1983) argues that deregulation often results in new, low-cost producers entering the market, a proliferation of new products or services, and rapid introduction of new technology. Firms bound by high-cost labor contracts or those which are unable to effectively utilize new technology to increase productivity will operate at a disadvantage.

Bleeke (1983) analyzed five industries following deregulation. These are brokerage, airlines, trucking, railroads and business terminal equipment. He categorizes four strategies which seem to be successful in repositioning a firm in a deregulated environment. These are shown in Figure 6.4.

Type 1 firms serve a broad range of customers who buy a full line of products. Successful firms in this category integrated their operations nationwide, built strong marketing capabilities and upgraded their reporting and production systems. Bleeke (1983) concludes that Type 2—low-cost producers utilize a variety of tactics including taking sales from established firms by streamlining the distribution system, and offering a narrow range of products at deeply discounted prices.

The specialty firms which characterize Type 3 shift to new product and customer segments, and tend to grow through competition rather than acquisition. Finally, Bleeke (1983) argues that Type 4 firms which provide a broad line of products to a customer base in small, protected markets can follow a number of successful tactics. These include pricing selectively, increasing productivity and cutting costs, expanding into other, small markets and emphasizing personal relationships with customers.

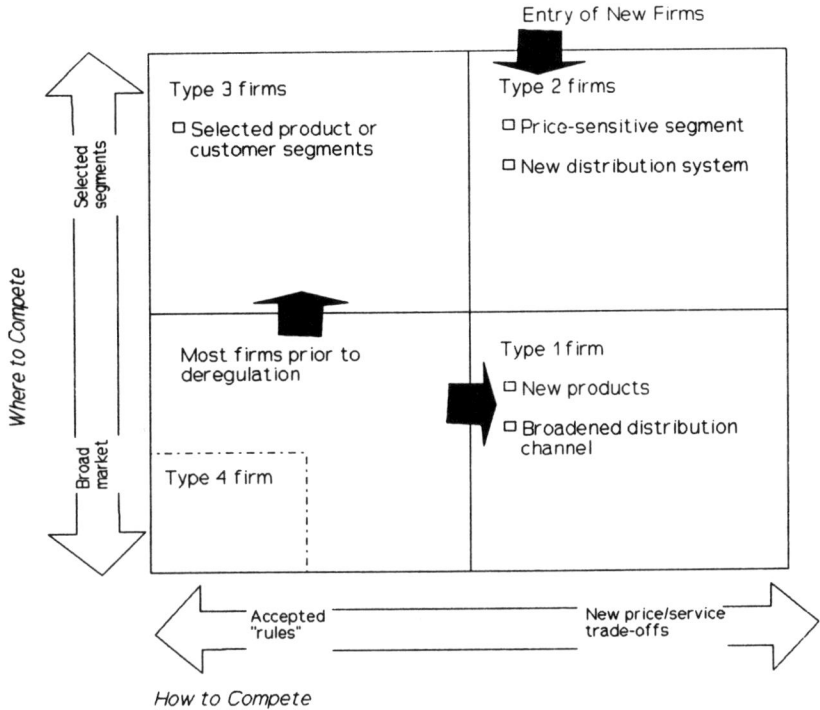

Figure 6.4. Competitive Repositioning Following Deregulation

Source: Bleeke (1983). Reprinted with permission.

Deregulation also involves changes in organizing, controlling, and staffing/rewarding. The skills of some employees will become irrelevant or less important. For example, legal and accounting skills will be less important while Bleeke (1983) argues that marketing and operational skills will become more critical. Some jobs such as freight rate clerks will all but disappear. He argues that reward policies may need to be changed to reflect free-market realities. Regulated industries often pay wages and provide benefits above the market rate, leaving them in an uncompetitive position after deregulation. Finally, the corporate culture may need to be altered. Frequently, firms in heavily regulated industries display a lack of innovation, are bureaucratic and often are not cost efficient. A culture of innovation, customer service orientation, and high productivity may need to be cultivated for a firm to be successful.

Summary

Government regulation and its impact on business can be gauged in a number of ways. These include the number of pages in the *Federal Register,* the history of the major laws enacted by Congress, and the number of personnel and expenditures devoted to regulation. By all of these measures, government regulation has increased dramatically over the years.

The "public interest" theory of regulation states that government regulation exists to correct some of the shortfalls in the workings of the free enterprise system. The "interest group" theory of regulation argues that these laws, instead, are government's response to the demands of groups seeking to advance their own self-interest.

Each government agency has at its disposal a variety of methods and techniques which can be used to enforce its regulation of business and the economy. These include: setting performance standards, establishing design standards, outright prohibitions, licensing, price setting, information disclosure, inspection, grading and testing, certification, and recalls and product seizures.

Government regulation can be categorized as industry-specific economic regulation or social regulation. The "capture theory" argues that members of the industry are chosen to serve on regulatory boards because of the unique expertise which they possess. In this way the industry "captures" the boards since such individuals will tend to be biased in their favor. An example is the Interstate Commerce Commission.

The consumer movement seeks to shift the balance of power toward the consumer, providing a legal means to insure product safety and useful, correct information. Key issues include: food safety, drug safety and efficacy, auto and other manufactured product safety, clear and correct product information, deceptive advertising, product warranties, and unfair business practices. Agencies dealing with these matters include the FDA, CPSC and NHTSA.

The health and safety of working men and women is the primary concern of OSHA. This agency sets standards and enforces them through review of company accident records and on-site inspections. It also provides information and consultation to companies to help improve the safety of the working conditions they provide.

The benefits of regulation are many and varied. Harmful products have been kept off the market, workplace safety has improved, and many injuries avoided. However, the costs of government regulation are substantial. These include: administrative and compliance costs, increased inefficiency and waste, higher prices for products and services produced, reduced innovation, and general confusion for businesses trying to comply with often overlapping regulations.

A number of alternatives have been suggested or tried. These include: structural and personnel reforms, deregulation, self-regulation, sunset laws, benefit-cost analysis, and the regulatory budget.

The changing regulatory environment requires management to adapt to both the current situation and plan for future changes. The political and judicial process may be used to influence government regulatory activities. If the environment changes, firms may choose to merge, new products may be developed, new technology may be utilized, and resources may be combined to increase efficiencies.

Key Concepts

internal cross-subsidy

"public interest" theory

"interest group" theory

traditional regulation

social regulation

"capture" theory

deregulation

consumerism

self-regulation

sunset laws

regulatory budget

Questions

1. What factors will affect the prospects of federal government regulation in the future?

2. How can the actions of the FDA, CPSC, NHTSA and OSHA be explained using the "public interest" and "interest group" theories?

3. Choose a regulatory agency not described in this chapter. Describe the methods and techniques used to enforce its regulations. Why were these methods chosen?

4. The American Trucking Associations opposed deregulation of the trucking industry. Why?

5. What methods are available to business to influence social regulation?

6. FDA regulation works as long as you don't need a drug for a rare disease. Comment.

7. How have the fuel economy standards impacted the choice of automobiles available?

8. What impact has CPSC had on product safety? What alternative approaches are available to protect the consumer?

9. Comment on the effectiveness of OSHA regulations. How effective would an injury tax be as an alternative?

10. Select an example of a regulatory area. Analyze this area with respect to costs and benefits, including administrative and compliance costs and unintended effects.

11. If you were the President, what alternative approaches to regulation would you take? Who would be for and against each of these approaches?

12. Choose an industry which is likely to be affected by increased regulation. What alternatives are available to management to impact the regulatory process and to meet the challenges of any changes which may occur?

13. Choose an industry which may be a candidate for deregulation in the future. If you were a manager of a firm in this industry, how would you adapt your enterprise to the changing regulatory environment?

Case Analysis: Manville Corporation
Worker Safety and the Use of Bankruptcy Laws

"Nobody is going to tell us what a lung is worth."
— Robert J. Rosenberg
Lawyer for Manville Workers

On August 26, 1982, Manville sought legal shelter from over 50,000 pending and prospective asbestos-related lawsuits under Chapter 11 of the federal bankruptcy laws. This was a bold maneuver for a company with a positive cash flow and a net worth of $1.1 billion.

Asbestos is a grayish mineral fiber hailed for its flame retardant abilities, and previously used in hair dryers, ironing board covers, artificial logs, roofing, textured paints, floor tiles, and insulation in schools, naval ships and space ships. Even brief exposure to asbestos can cause significant harm. For example, women have contracted mesothelioma, a painful, lethal cancer of the linings of the chest or abdominal cavities, even though their only exposure to asbestos came from shaking out their husbands' work clothes.[1] Mesothelioma and other less rare forms of lung cancer can occur 20–40 years after exposure to asbestos. Men who have worked in shipyards, even for periods as short as a few weeks, appear to have an increased risk of developing lung cancer. The risk is high even for people whose jobs did not require them to directly handle the asbestos insulation used in ships.

Breathing asbestos dust can also cause asbestosis, a nonmalignant scarring of lung tissue that eventually overtaxes the pulmonary system. Fibers inhaled into the lungs cause the tissue around them to become hard. As a result, these tissues cannot transfer oxygen to the blood, breathing becomes difficult, and the pulmonary system breaks down under the strain. This type of damage usually shows up 20 or more years after a person is first exposed. Because such small amounts of asbestos have been demonstrated to cause disease, experts have been unable to agree on an acceptable level of exposure to this material.

Asbestos was the substance Henry Ward Johns built his business on in 1858. It also could be what caused a chronic lung condition that led to his death 40 years later.[2] The H. W. Johns Company merged in 1901 with Manville Covering Company, and was renamed Johns-Manville. It is now a subsidiary of Manville Corporation, a holding company formed in 1981. The merged company became known as the free world's largest producer of asbestos.[3] Asbestos accounts for little of the company's business today, which consists mainly of construction and forest products. Manville has sold off its asbestos operations since filing in bankruptcy court. How long Manville, the other asbestos companies that are its codefendants, and the government knew about the hazards of asbestos before warning workers is still in contention. Doctors first diagnosed asbestosis in the late 1920's, and published related studies beginning in 1930. By 1935, asbestos fibers were linked to lung cancer, and later with mesothelioma. Manville acknowledges that evidence, and says it acted on the dangers of working with raw asbestos in the 1930's.

But, as for finished products, the company maintains it wasn't aware of dangers until 1964, when Dr. Selikoff reported that even brief exposure to asbestos fibers breaking free from finished products could lead to lung disease. At that time, he estimated that 8,000 to 10,000 deaths a year were caused by asbestos-related diseases. However, medical reports linking asbestosis to handling finished asbestos products such as insulation were common in the 1950's, and the disease itself was diagnosed in insulation workers as early as 1932.

However, statements of Kenneth W. Smith, Manville's medical director from 1952 to 1966, indicate he informed company lawyers and executives in 1952 that he believed insulation workers "were exposed to the same potential hazards" as those working directly with asbestos and that warning labels were called for. Manville's workers' compensation records show settlements were made in the 1950's with employees claiming they developed asbestos-related diseases while installing insulation at Manville construction sites in the 1930's.[4]

Manville executives have said all along they were not aware of health risks from asbestos products until the 1960's, when Dr. Irving Selikoff's landmark report linked lung disease to even brief exposure to free asbestos fibers breaking out of finished products. Direct exposure through mining, milling, and factory work with the raw fiber was implicated in lung disease as early as the 1930's in medical and scientific literature.

Surprisingly, Manville had only 120 health-related lawsuits pending against it in 1976. By 1979, the number had grown to 1,500 and a "FORTUNE" article said that "Asbestos litigation is almost a separate business" at Johns-Manville—a prophetic statement in light of the November 1983 reorganization plan the company filed seeking to separate its non-asbestos businesses into a separate company.[6] Publicity about the initial cases may have in part caused the flood of lawsuits that followed, but since asbestos-related diseases show up 20–40 years after exposure, some workers exposed during World War II have only recently discovered that they are afflicted.

By August 1982, lawsuits were increasing against Manville Corporation — 16,500 were pending and another 35,500 to 100,000 were expected. Although settlement costs were expected to average $40,000 per case, for a projected total of $2 billion, Manville's Chairman, John A. McKinney, still opposed taking the company into bankruptcy until an outside accounting firm said that the company would need to bank $1.9 billion reserve against possible settlements.[7] Punitive damages, which had already been awarded in eleven asbestos-related cases involving Manville, could easily multiply the company's legal costs. Those eleven cases, decided in 1981 and 1982, cost Manville an average of $666,000[8] each. The day after filing for reorganization, McKinney stated in newspaper advertisements that "To avoid Chapter 11, we would have had to strangle the company slowly. . . . We would have had to cannibalize our good businesses just to keep going."

Chapter 11

Under Chapter 11, which was made more flexible in a 1972 revision of bankruptcy laws, a company receives court protection from creditors while it works out a reorganization plan. Many see its chief virtue the fact that it favors saving companies by protecting them from creditors whenever a breathing period, even an extended one, will allow an opportunity to regroup. Others, however, criticize the revision for making the law too loose. Some point out that Chapter 11 does not actually require a filing for bankruptcy to be made in good faith.

The ambiguity of the law has led to a wide variance in expert opinion ranging from speculation that this unprecedented move could lead to the company's demise; or that Manville could emerge from bankruptcy court stronger and leaner, with its liability for asbestos-related diseases limited and its creditors cheering it.

While Manville was the first healthy company to use Chapter 11 to try and dilute potentially overwhelming liabilities, other companies have not waited for Manville's case to be settled before trying the same route.

Continental Airlines, Wilson Foods, and Bildisco broke their existing labor contracts and negotiated new ones while under Chapter 11 proceedings. Chapter 11 seems to be "a marvelous escape hatch" for companies with pending labor or legal problems, an October 1983 "FORTUNE" article says, adding that filing under it "has become an effective management strategy."

The plaintiffs in the Manville asbestos case are appealing Judge Lifland's January 1984 ruling that Manville, though solvent, was proper before the bankruptcy court. When the bankruptcy code was rewritten in 1978, the requirement that a company had to be insolvent was left out. Washington lawyer Daniel Lewis quotes drafters of the 1978 reform as saying they didn't think the phrase was needed—"they couldn't conceive that a company would file for reorganization if it wasn't insolvent."[9]

Corporate Maneuvers

Manville's use of Chapter 11 on August 26, 1982 drew the attention of the entire financial community as well as the anger of those seeking damages—many of whom were irreversibly headed for painful deaths because they were exposed to Manville asbestos products. At first, the company's move produced an air of cooperation from most of its commercial and trade creditors, whom it owed $600 million. As the first solvent company to file under Chapter 11, Manville was able to conduct "business as usual," as one Manville executive said, while putting both creditors and plaintiffs on hold.

According to McKinney, if the company had not filed for reorganization of its debt, potential legal fees and settlements with people who developed asbestosis, lung cancer, or mesothelioma after exposure to Manville products would probably have swallowed the corporation. However, the company's solution to its dilemma means that people harmed by asbestos exposure, or their families, will not be able to receive any settlement until the company comes out of bankruptcy. In addition to this, many plaintiffs will probably have to accept smaller settlements than would have been awarded if the company had not opted for Chapter 11.

In November 1982, three months after filing for bankruptcy, Manville started a positive advertising campaign. The advertisements were part of Manville's aggressive, upbeat approach, designed to ally its commercial and trade creditors' concerns. But the company's self-promotion at such expense ($500,000) so infuriated the plaintiffs' lawyers that Manville agreed to consult with a creditors' committee, including the lawyers, on future ads. Despite negotiations, the rift between Manville and the plaintiffs only broadened with time.

In July 1983, Manville tried to recover $1 million in settlements it already had paid by suing the federal government. Manville charged that the Navy and other government agencies were aware of asbestos hazards and did not protect persons exposed to it while they worked in naval shipyards during World War II. The company filed a similar suit in April 1984, seeking $97,000 from the government. Though Manville's assertion that the government should pay some of the asbestos-related claims is nothing new, it could not legally sue the government until a 1983 Supreme Court ruling in a Lockheed case opened that door.[10]

A major area of contention in the reorganization plan is Manville's proposal for a panel of medical experts to evaluate claims and judge whether plaintiffs deserve more or less than standard settlements of $50,000 for mesothelioma, $45,000 for lung cancer, $40,000 for asbestosis, and $1,000 for pleural thickening. Lawyers for the claimants protested that much larger awards have already been made to their clients in similar lawsuits against other asbestos companies.

After ten extensions and several negotiating sessions with plaintiffs' lawyers, Manville's long-awaited reorganization plan once filed with the bankruptcy court was immediately rejected by the plaintiffs' lawyers. They asked bankruptcy court Judge Burton R. Lifland to rule against it. The plan calls for a benefits schedule—something litigants' attorneys have repudiated all along—and outlines Manville's intent to fully repay its commercial and trade creditors. By January 1984, with disagreement between Manville and the plaintiffs' lawyers growing, it seemed more and more likely that creditors would join forces with the plaintiffs.[11] Growing impatient for their $600 million, the creditors were pleased by a report that said the company was worth as much liquidated as operating.

Outlook

... For Manville

Manville stockholders may benefit if the company comes out of bankruptcy court as an operating concern. A week before the Chapter 11 filing, Manville's stock was at $7 to $8 a share, falling to $4.25 a share August 17, the day after filing took place. It had rebounded to $9.50 a share by December 1982. One analyst projects the company's stock at $20 a share by 1986.[12]

Regardless of projections, the company was well enough in December 1982 that a "NEW YORK" article was headlined "Manville's Robust Bankruptcy." The article noted the company's upbeat advertising campaign and that third-quarter earnings were nearly double those for the same period in 1981.[13] But a financial analyst commented that most of Manville's 1982 third-quarter earnings were due to the company's not having to pay interest in its long-term debt.

Because of Manville's unorthodox use of Chapter 11, its competitors in the asbestos business were hurting. Smaller asbestos companies were not being protected from consumer lawsuits or their creditors. In the asbestos-related court cases, these companies generally are Manville's codefendants, but since Manville is legally protected from financial claims against it, the smaller companies are bearing the brunt of pending lawsuits. With Manville's chunk of money missing, fewer plaintiffs are willing to settle out of court with the smaller companies. An attorney for one of the companies said it is "obscene" for the smaller concerns to take a beating while Manville is not being touched because of being in bankruptcy.[14]

... For Public Policy

Standards used for deciding punitive damages in product liability cases vary with laws in individual states. In some instances, companies are held liable from the time the products are sold or used even if no evidence of potential or proven health hazards existed when marketing began. On the federal level, Senator Robert Kasten of Wisconsin sponsored a bill in the spring of 1984 that set nationwide product liability standards. Under the proposed law, consumers charging that an item was poorly designed or inadequately tested for possible hazards must prove that the company had not acted reasonably. Kasten's bill also limited punitive damage awards to the amount of compensatory damages.

Government agencies such as the Consumer Product Safety Commission and the Occupational Safety and Health Administration have generally done little to see that workers are protected from asbestos, taking a particularly laissez-faire attitude under the Reagan administration.[15] The Labor Department, though, is considering lowering the limit on asbestos exposure in the workplace to 500,000 fibers per cubic meter of air, down from the current standard of 2 million set in 1972.

Even broader than the question of occupational exposure is that of environmental exposure. Some school districts are billing Manville for the cost of clearing asbestos out of school buildings.[16] The Environmental Protection Agency has started cleaning up areas such as Hudson, N.H., where landowners let Manville dump asbestos waste on their property. EPA officials plan to go after Manville when the company emerges from bankruptcy for reimbursement of its superfund monies used in the Hudson clean-up.[17] Some residents, though, do not want the EPA on their land despite the health threat, and are afraid that agency officials will end up bringing the clean-up bill to them.

Notes

1. *Fortune*, May 7, 1979.

2. *Fortune*, May 7, 1979.

3. *New York Times*, October 13, 1983.

4. *Fortune*, May 7, 1979.

5. *Washington Monthly*, December 1977.

6. *Wall Street Journal*, November 22, 1983.

7. *Wall Street Journal*, January 31, 1984.

8. Manville Corporation, 1982 Annual Report, p. 48.

9. *Wall Street Journal*, February 24, 1984.

10. *Los Angeles Times*, May 1, 1984.

11. *Wall Street Journal*, January 31, 1984.

12. *Forbes*, March 26, 1984.

13. *New York Times*, December 10, 1982.

14. *New York Times*, January 10, 1984.

15. *New York Times*, September 5, 1983.

16. Manville Corporation, 1982 Annual Report, p. 51.

17. *Wall Street Journal* (September 13, 1983.

Adapted from Starling, Grover and Baskin, Otis, *Issues in Business and Society: Capitalism and Public Purpose,* Kent Publishing Co., Boston, Mass., 1985, pp. 255–262.

Case Questions

1. How would you characterize the level of social responsibility of the Johns Manville Corporation?

2. Was Manville's action of filing for bankruptcy ethical?

3. Should Manville be held responsible for damages caused to employees or consumers by their products?

4. What alternative courses of action might Manville take?

5. How would this situation change had OSHA and CPSC existed?

6. What is the current status of Manville and the asbestos-related lawsuits?

References

Bleeke, Joel. "Deregulation: Riding the Rapids," *Business Horizons,* 1983, (May–June), 15–25.

Brown, Clarence J. "Legislating a Regulatory Budget Limit." In T. B. Clark, M. H. Kostes, and J. C. Miller (eds.) *Reforming Regulation.* (Washington, D.C.: American Enterprise Institute for Public Policy Research, 1980).

Congressional Budget Office, *Resolving the Thrift Crisis.* Washington, D.C.: U.S. Government Printing Office, 1993.

Friedlander, Ann. *The Dilemma of Freight Transport Regulation.* (Washington, D.C.: The Brockings Institution, 1969).

Friedman, Milton and Friedman, Rose. *Free to Choose: A Personal Statement.* (New York: Harcourt, Brace, Jovanovich, 1990).

General Accounting Office, *Paperwork Reduction: Reported Burden Hour Increases Reflect New Estimates, Not Actual Changes.* GAO/PEMD-94-3. Washington, D.C., December, 1993.

Garvin, David A. "Can Industry Self-Regulation Work?" *California Management Review,* 1983, *25* (4), 37–52.

Green, Mark and Watzman, Norman. *Business War on the Law: An Analysis of the Benefits of Federal Health/Safety Enforcement.* (Washington, D.C.: Corporate Accountability Research Group, 1979).

Greer, Douglas F. *Business, Government and Society.* (New York: MacMillan Publishing Co., Inc., 1983).

Gujarati, Damodar. *Government and Business.* (New York: McGraw-Hill Book Co., 1984).

Healy, Robert E. (ed.). *Federal Regulatory Directory 1979–1980.* (Washington, D.C.: Congressional Quarterly, Inc., 1979).

Hilton, George. *The Transportation Act of 1958: A Decade of Experience.* (Bloomington, Indiana: Indiana University Press, 1969).

Kolko, Gabriel. *Railroads and Regulation, 1877–1916*. (Princeton, N.J.: Princeton University Press, 1965).

Kotler, Philip. "What Consumerism Means for Marketers," *Harvard Business Review*, 1972, *50* (3), 48–57.

Lee, L. W. "A Just Theory of Regulation," *Economic Review*, 1980 (December), 848–862.

Mitnick, Barry M. "The Strategic Uses of Regulation and Deregulation," *Business Horizons*, 1981, *24* (2), 71–83.

Noah, Timothy, "GOP's Rep. DeLay Working in Every Corner To Exterminate Regulations That Bug Business," *The Wall Street Journal*, March 6, 1995, p. A16.

Posner, Richard A. "Taxation by Regulation," *Bell Journal of Economics and Management Science*, 1971, *2* (1), 22–50.

Senate Study on Federal Regulation, *Framework for Regulation*, Vol. VI. (Washington, D.C.: U.S. Government Printing Office, 1977).

Starling, Grover. *The Changing Environment of Business (2nd ed.)*. (Boston, Mass.: Kent Publishing Co., 1984).

Stigler, George J. "The Theory of Economic Regulation," *Bell Journal of Economics and Management Science*, 1971, *2* (Spring).

Thompson, Fred and Jones, L. R. "SMR Forum: Reforming Regulatory Decision-Making—The Regulatory Budget," *Sloan Management Review*, 1981 (Winter), 53–61.

Warren, Melinda and Jones, Barry. *Reinventing the Regulatory System: No Downsizing in Administration Plan*. Center for the Study of American Business, Occasional Paper 155, Washington University, June, 1995.

Weidenbaum, Murray L. *Business and Government in the Global Marketplace (5th ed.)*. (Englewood Cliffs: Prentice-Hall, Inc., 1995).

Weidenbaum, Murray L. *The Future of Business Regulation*. (New York: AMACOM, 1979).

CHAPTER 7
ENERGY AND THE PHYSICAL ENVIRONMENT

Since the 1973 oil embargo by Arab members of the Organization of Petroleum Exporting Countries (OPEC), oil prices and energy costs in general became major factors in business and consumer decisions. The "energy crisis" elevated petroleum, natural gas, and other energy sources to a position of importance in management decision making unequaled since the Industrial Revolution.

Closely linked to energy matters are concerns over the physical environment. This linkage includes the use of some sources of energy which result in greater amounts of environmental pollution than others. It also includes the production of electricity through nuclear power which raises a variety of environmental issues. In addition, different production techniques have different energy requirements and environmental implications. Finally, in some cases, energy efficiency is obtained only through increased pollution, while in other situations, such a tradeoff may not exist.

Both directly and indirectly, business can have an impact on environmental quality. The types of pollution control devices which are utilized at the plant, the way in which goods are produced, and the types and quality of raw materials used all can have a direct and visible effect on the physical environment. Indirectly, the goods produced by business can contribute to pollution when they are used by consumers.

Energy-related issues and concern for the physical environment have become important areas for public policy action. Government regulatory activities, taxation, and spending programs expanded greatly during the 1970's. From 1970 to 1980, federal administrative expenditures for environment ant energy regulation increased 692 percent. Staffing of regulatory agencies concerned with energy and environmental goals increased by 298 percent (Tramontozzi, 1984). Even during the 1980's with concern over budget deficits, regulatory expenditures increased by an estimated 47 percent from 1980 to 1986. Thus, energy and the physical environment continue to be high on the list of national priorities and thus important issues for business.

This chapter begins with a discussion of the energy crisis and energy-related issues. Government regulatory activity in the wake of the Arab oil embargo of 1973 provides an interesting illustration of how the public sector response to a change in the external environment builds on itself and creates a variety of unintended effects. In this section, a number of federal energy-related programs will be discussed such as the Windfall Profits Tax and the Entitlements program. Prospects for oil prices and energy costs in the future will also be examined. A number of issues related to the physical environment will be discussed. These include alternative concepts of environmental regulation, alternatives to regulation, the acid rain controversy, and toxic wastes. The chapter concludes with a case study of the Union Carbide disaster in Bhopal, India.

Government Policy and the Energy Crisis

The 1970's was a period of rising energy prices, shortages of petroleum and the other fuels, gasoline lines, and skyrocketing inflation. The federal government's response to the events of the 1970's provides a useful illustration of how public sector actions to deal with a perceived problem can lead to a variety of unintended effects requiring further government action.

Government actions with respect to energy date back to the 1930's. From that time until the early 1970's the concern of public policy was to keep domestic oil prices high and to prevent a flood of cheap foreign imports from "destroying" U.S. producers. Through production allocation schemes among domestic producers and restrictions on importation of foreign oil, U.S. oil prices were kept substantially above world prices. For example, in 1960 domestic crude oil sold for $5.55 per barrel, while Saudi Arabian oil was priced at $2.95 per barrel (Gugarati, 1984). Even as late as 1970, domestic oil prices were 65 percent higher than world levels (Cabinet Task Force, 1970).

Government regulation of the oil industry began to change in 1971. Concern over inflation prompted President Nixon to establish a 90-day general wage and price freeze, followed by limitations on future increases. (At that time inflation was running at an unprecedented rate of four percent per year) Oil prices were included in the general price freeze and the subsequent price rise limitations. Public policy had made a complete reversal, from attempting to keep domestic prices high, to limiting price increases. However, public policy changed even more drastically after the Arab oil embargo of 1973.

In response to political events in the Middle East, the Arab members of OPEC decided in 1973 to place an embargo on the export of oil products to the United States. In addition, OPEC almost quadrupled the price of oil, increasing the price from $2.95 to $10.95 per barrel (Strickland, 1980). Spot shortages of oil began to appear in the United States.

The "oil crisis" that began with the Arab oil embargo produced a variety of concerns and dire predictions, in addition to price increases and shortages. Some said that OPEC was taking advantage of natural phenomena. That is, it was argued that the real cause of the oil crisis was not OPEC action, but rather the eminent running out of energy resources. These individuals believed that the world was beginning to scrape the bottom of the barrel of oil reserves, and that the last of the economically feasible production was at hand. Others believed that by the year 2000, oil would be selling for $100 per barrel and gasoline would cost $3 to $5 per gallon. The gasoline lines, allocation schemes and continued upward movement in all energy costs convinced many that energy resources would soon run out. The earth it was argued could not sustain the large population and high standard of living that it once did.

Initial Public Sector Response

Because of the problem of inflation and the public fear of running out of oil, the federal government promulgated a series of regulations to deal with the energy crisis. The primary objective of these regulations was to keep domestic oil prices from rising to the world level. From this standpoint, government regulation was quite successful. In 1974, OPEC oil was price around $12 per barrel, while domestic crude averaged $8 per barrel (Gugarati, 1984). However, these regulations also had several unintended and undesirable effects.

The effect of price controls on the domestic market for oil is depicted in Figure 7.1. Public policy determined the maximum domestic price while international oil prices were determined by OPEC and market forces. In the figure, D-D represents the domestic demand for oil products and S-S represents the domestic supply curve. Although this

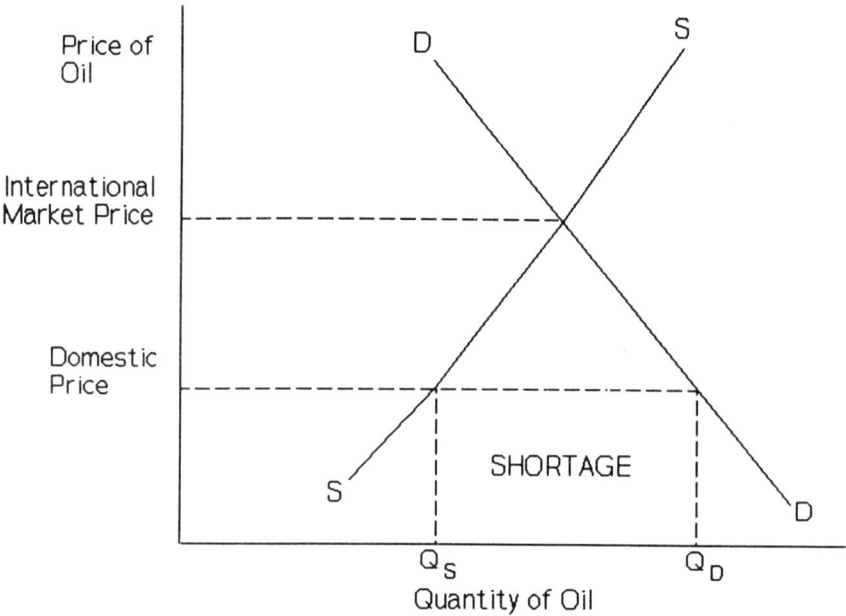

Figure 7.1. Effect of Price Controls on the Market for Oil Products

figure simplifies the oil market at that time, it provides a good indication of the forces at work in the marketplace.

In Chapter 2, the role of prices in a free enterprise system was discussed. Prices were said to have four functions: transmitting information to buyers and sellers, providing incentives, allocating resources and determining the distribution of income. Public policy with respect to petroleum affected all of these functions.

Price controls for domestically-produced oil products interfered with the information transmission mechanism and the incentives created by the price system. Both consumers and producers were given the wrong information. By not allowing domestic prices to rise to world prices, consumers received the information that it was not necessary to conserve energy. Fewer incentives were provided to buy smaller cars, use public transportation, insulate homes and reduce energy consumption in general. Business similarly was not provided as many incentives to reduce oil consumption, use alternative energy sources and conserve on energy use in general. Domestic producers were not provided the incentives to explore for new oil, increase production from existing wells and develop alternative energy sources that an increase in prices to the world level would have produced.

In addition, resources were not allocated to the best use. That is, additional resources should have been allocated to oil production, exploration and distribution. More resources should also have been allocated to production of energy from alternative sources. Instead, producers, explorers and energy consumers allocated resources to these activities as if few energy problems existed in this country.

The result of price controls interfering with the information transmission mechanism, incentives and the resource allocation functions was a shortage. This shortage is represented by the difference between domestic demand Q_d and domestic supply Q_s in Figure 7.1. Spot shortages for all oil products appeared but the most visible was the shortage of gasoline.

Gasoline Lines

One of the most irritating and peculiar phenomena of the "energy crisis" was gasoline lines at automobile service stations. The lines were most unusual because they did not appear in all areas. Some states never had a single gasoline line. In addition, the lines would suddenly appear in one city or region, be present for a while, and just as suddenly they would vanish. The lines would then reappear in another close by community or in another state or area of the country.

At the time, many theories were suggested to explain why gasoline lines occurred, and why they acted in such an unusual fashion. OPEC and the oil companies were blamed for conspiring to cause an artificial shortage in order to force prices higher. Some suggested that gas lines were a natural turn of events as oil resources began to be depleted. Most theories however, were well off the mark. Gasoline lines were a result of public policy.

The federal government realized that a gasoline shortage was created by its price control policy. This shortage of gasoline and oil products needed to be "allocated" across the country in some manner so that everyone would share equally in the pain. Federal regulators devised a complicated system that essentially reduced shipments of oil products to all states by an equal percentage amount. The previous year's consumption of gasoline and oil products was used as a base.

There was, however, one problem with this procedure. Demand for gasoline was not the same as the previous year's demand in all parts of the country. In some states, demand increased. In others, gasoline demand actually fell. For example, during the winter months, fears of gasoline shortages persuaded many individuals not to make their normal automobile trips to Florida and other southern states. Instead, these people remained in the Northeast and Midwest. Gasoline demand increased in their home states while it was reduced in the South. The allocation scheme failed to take these changes in demand into account.

Another factor which helped to produce gasoline lines was consumer fear of running out of gas. Since most people needed their cars to get to work, many were afraid that if gasoline shortages appeared, they would be unable to drive to their jobs. Once the news that a gasoline station in their neighborhood had run out of gas spread, panic struck.

Immediately, many individuals drove to a gasoline station to fill up their tanks. Some went merely to top off a nearly full tank. The lines would get longer as more stations would run out of their month's allocation, and more and more people became more and more anxious.

Once a motorist had a full tank of gas, he or she would not be in the gasoline lines. The lines began to shrink as motorists filled up. The lines would finally disappear when all individuals who wanted a full tank got it. The lines would then reappear elsewhere.

Gasoline lines, then, were the product of several events and forces. First, there was the Arab oil embargo and the increasing price of world oil. Second, and most importantly, was government's reaction to increasing oil prices. Price controls and faulty allocation schemes set the stage for gasoline lines. Consumer fear of running out of gasoline was the final ingredient needed to create these lines.

Gasoline lines were not the product of a conspiracy between greedy oil companies and OPEC. They were not caused by the imminent end of oil resources in the ground. Although several factors explain gasolines lines, the main cause was public policy. Without government regulatory actions, gasoline lines would not have occurred. Gasoline lines were not made in Saudi Arabia or the board rooms of the major oil companies. Gasoline lines were made in Washington, D.C.

Entitlements Program

The government's price control policy for domestic crude oil created a distributional problem. While domestic oil prices were controlled, world oil prices were not. However, imported oil was not consumed at the same rate across the United States. Some regions of the country, such as the Northeast, were heavier users of imported oil than other areas. These regions would lose under price controls and other parts of the country would gain at their expense. A redistribution of income and jobs from the high cost area to the low cost area would occur.

In order to reduce this redistributional impact of price controls, the federal government devised the "Entitlements Program." The goal of this program was to equalize oil prices across regions of the country (Thurow, 1980). The way this was done was to tax domestically-produced oil and then subsidize imported oil with the proceeds of the tax. The result was that everyone paid the same price for oil, regardless of its source. A simplified example shown in Table 7.1 illustrates how the entitlements program worked.

Table 7.1. How the Entitlements Program Worked

	Initial Price of Oil	Final Cost to Oil Consumer	
		Company A	Company B
Domestic	$4	$4 + $3 tax = $7	
Imported	$10		$10 − $3 subsidy = $7

As shown in the table, assume the domestic oil price is $4 per barrel and the imported oil price is $10. Company A buys domestic oil exclusively and company B buys imported oil only. Without the entitlements program, company A would be at a competitive advantage to company B, since it would pay $4 versus $10 per barrel for oil. The entitlements program involved levying a tax on the production of domestic oil. In this example, it is assumed to be $3 per barrel. Company

A under the program pays $7 for each barrel of oil. The $3 tax is then used to subsidize company B's purchase of imported oil. Both companies pay the same net cost for oil, regardless of its source.

The entitlements program, however, created its own set of unintended effects. By placing a tax on domestic production, incentives to explore and produce oil within the United States were further reduced beyond the effects of price controls. In addition, the subsidy on imported oil encouraged the use of foreign oil. At that time, it was the stated policy of the U.S. government to encourage domestic oil production and reduce reliance on foreign oil. "Project Independence" was the name of this policy. The entitlements program had just the opposite effect.

In Chapter 2, it was mentioned that society has two primary economic goals. One is to increase incomes and living standards in general. The second is fairness and equity in income distribution. In that chapter it was stated that there is a conflict between those two goals. Public policies aimed at stimulating incentives inevitably result in an unequal income distribution. Policies which attempt to achieve the second goal conflict with the first. The entitlements program is a good example of a public policy aimed at one goal which adversely impacts the other. This program evened out the impact of price controls across regions. In the process, however, incentives to explore and produce crude oil domestically were substantially reduced and foreign oil dependence was exacerbated.

Other Regulatory Programs

Recognizing the adverse impact that federal programs were having on domestic exploration efforts, the government devised several additional regulatory approaches. The objective of these policies was to counteract the negative effects of the programs described so far.

Utilizing a distinction that was first developed under President Nixon's wage and price freeze, a two-tier pricing system was established for domestically produced crude oil. In this system, a distinction was made between "old" oil and "new" oil. Old oil was defined as oil which was produced from oil wells prior to 1972. New oil was defined as production from wells which were placed in operation after 1972 as well as additional production from old wells above their 1972 levels (Gujarati, 1984). New crude oil was free of price controls, while old oil was subject to federal price regulation. The idea behind this system was to partially counteract the reduced incentives to explore and produce crude oil created by the price control system.

One problem with this approach was that old oil became scarcer and new oil became more abundant. At times it seemed that old oil was almost magically transformed into new oil. The incentives that were created by the two-tier pricing system encouraged producers to manipulate records and production to achieve this transformation.

To encourage conservation and counteract the negative impact caused by price controls, several other programs were implemented. First, the federal government established a national 55 MPH speed limit on the highway system since it was known that motor vehicles operate more efficiently at lower speeds. Second, fuel economy regulations were established for automobiles produced in the United States. Third, the Congress passed legislation establishing tax credits for individuals and businesses installing solar energy devices, energy saving mechanisms, storm windows and additional insulation.

Finally, one of the most ludicrous and potentially intrusive regulations was implemented. The federal government established maximum and minimum temperature regulations for public buildings. Although never enforced, these regulations would have required a bureaucracy on a massive scale to mandate compliance. To borrow from an old saw, "What a tangled web we create when we first begin to regulate."

Further Developments

Several other energy-related policies and programs emanated from Washington, D.C. One was an organizational change. In 1977, President Carter established the cabinet level Department of Energy (DOE) to house a variety of energy programs that had been scattered throughout the government. Proponents of this organizational change argued that it was necessary in order to emphasize the importance of energy related problems. In addition, they argued that this consolidation could result in the reduction or elimination of overlapping and sometimes conflicting programs.

Opponents of the new DOE saw it as just one additional bureaucratic maneuver to deal with energy problems. Further, they felt that the DOE would be used as a permanent lobbying mechanism for energy programs whether needed or not. One of the opponents of DOE was Ronald Reagan. In 1980, one of his campaign promises was to abolish the Department of Energy. To that end, he appointed James B. Edwards as Secretary of the Department. Dr. Edwards is an oral surgeon, and some argued that he was appointed to extract the Department from the government. Attempts to eliminate the Department were unsuccessful, however.

The Carter Administration took three additional steps to deal with oil related matters. The process of deregulation of domestic oil prices began during that administration. Subsequently, the Reagan Administration sped up the process of deregulation and eliminated all price controls on crude oil in 1981.

Fearing that large profits would accrue to oil companies as oil prices were decontrolled, a Windfall Profits Tax was established. The Windfall Profits Tax is somewhat of a misnomer, however, since it was in fact an excise tax on domestic oil production. The amount of the tax was based on the difference between the world oil price and the previous regulated price of domestically produced oil products.

The third step taken by the Carter Administration was to establish the Synthetic Fuel Corporation. Part of the proceeds of the Windfall Profits Tax was used to fund projects which involved developing processes to extract oil from shale and coal tar. Other, more exotic approaches were examined as well.

Many questions were raised about the efficiency of producing oil from these sources. It was argued by many in Washington that synthetic fuels were not economically justified since they could not be produced at a cost which was even remotely close to the price of oil. It was argued that if synthetic fuels were economically viable, then these would be produced by the free enterprise system without government subsidy.

On the other side, it was argued that as part of Project Independence, synthetic fuels were necessary to prevent the United States from being captive of the whims of foreign powers. In the case of a national emergency, synthetic fuels would become strategically important. Further, it was argued that the size of these projects was so large, that a government program was needed. Private enterprise would not want to incur the risks associated with these projects. However, by 1986, the synthetic fuels program was all but eliminated.

The Future of Oil Prices

The course of oil prices since the Arab oil embargo of 1973–1974 has been tumultuous. In 1972, crude oil prices were around $2.50 per barrel. In 1974, prices had risen to over $10 per barrel. By 1981, crude oil was selling above $30 per barrel with some spot prices as high as $40. Since that time, prices headed steadily downward. A major price break occurred at the beginning of 1986. Prices fell to around $16 per barrel from a high of $30.25 in December, 1985 (*Wall Street Journal*, January 22, 1986, p.1). Spot prices dipped below $12 per barrel. Prices increased during the Gulf War, but then continued their downward trend. These price movements are shown in Figure 7.2.

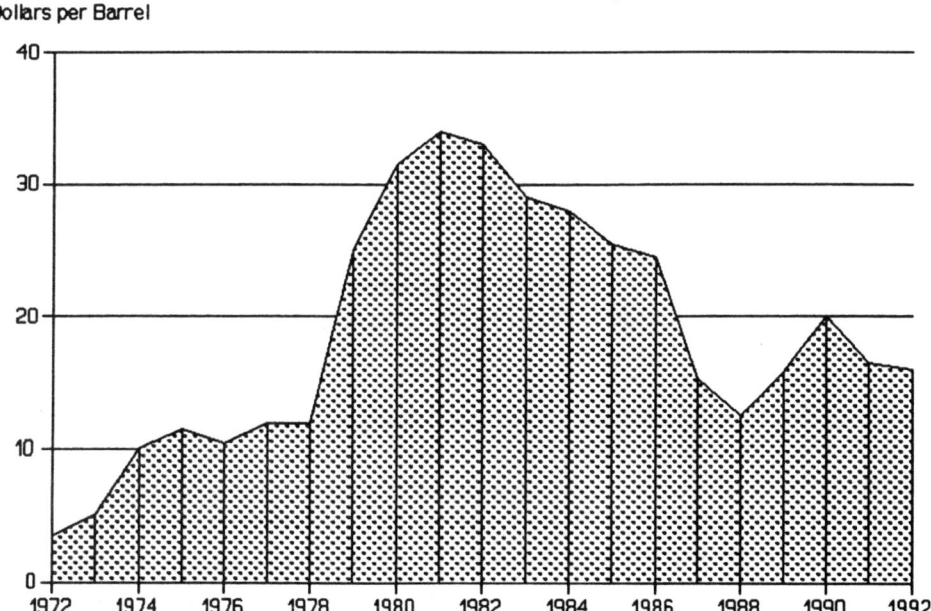

Source: *Wall Street Journal*, March 6, 1985, p.1 and *Statistical Abstract of the United States*, 1994.

Figure 7.2. Mideast Light Crude Oil Prices

What is the future course of oil prices and energy costs in general? Are previous price movements indicative of what will happen in the future? Are lower oil prices permanent? What lies ahead: abundant oil and gasoline of 39 cents per gallon as in the 1960's, or a return to the upward oil price spiral that some forecasters predicted would result in $100 per barrel of oil by the next century?

New Production

Those who believe that oil prices over the long term will not rise to previous high levels put forth a number of arguments. They argue that high oil prices have brought forth new production from all over the world. Alaskan north slope oil, British and Norwegian oil from the North Sea, Mexican production and additional output within the United States have all developed since the Arab oil embargo of 1973-74. Oil from the Middle East, it is argued, is far less important to the world economy that it once was. For example, the biggest suppliers of oil to the United States in the first half of 1985 were Mexico, Canada, Venezuela, the United Kingdom and Nigeria (Ibrahim, 1985).

Another factor to consider is the production of alternative fuels. Increased oil prices have encouraged production of natural gas, coal, and non-fossil fuels such as solar and geothermal energy. Methanol from corn has become an important gasoline additive. The research, development, exploration and investment in production facilities for these energy sources has created additional competition for petroleum-based fuels.

In addition, public policy has shifted from inadvertent discouragement of the production of alternative fuels to either a neutral or positive role. For example, natural gas prices were heavily regulated during the 1970's, creating shortages of this energy source. The Natural Gas Policy Act of 1978 made significant headways in eliminating the disincentive effects of price controls. A two-tier pricing policy was established and prices were gradually increased according to a set formula. All federal price controls on natural gas expired in 1989.

Conservation

The high price of oil has encouraged conservation efforts all over the world, not just in the United States. Oil consumption in the industrialized countries fell from a high of 42 million barrels per day in 1978–79 to an estimated 35 million in 1982. U.S. consumption fell from 18.8 to 15.8 million barrels per day over that same period (Singer, 1982). Since then, U.S. consumption has increased at a fairly constant rate. However, by 1992, U.S. consumption stood at 17.03 million, which was still less than the amount of 1978–79.[1]

High oil prices have resulted in a variety of conservation efforts. Additional insulation has been installed in homes. Home heating has shifted away from oil. Other heating sources, including wood stoves have gained at the expense of oil. Automobiles have become much more fuel efficient. Gasoline consumption in the United States fell to 8.5 billion gallons in 1985 compared with 20 billion gallons in the early 1980's (Petzinger, 1986). Automobiles averaged 13.52 miles per gallon in 1970. By 1992, the typical automobile driven in the United States averaged 21.6 miles per gallon of gasoline.[2]

High energy costs have increased consumers' awareness of the energy component of machines, household appliances and automobiles. Prior to the events in the 1970's, most consumers ignored the cost of operating consumer appliances and cars. Energy costs were so low that the only relevant cost to consider in most purchases was the initial cost. Increased energy awareness has resulted in consumers giving consideration to operating costs as well.

Business has decreased its use of oil and has switched from oil to gas or coal. Many industrial processes are easily converted from oil to these other fuels. The fuel that is used is the one with the lowest price. Business is also much more cognizant of energy costs and has taken actions to curtail energy use. These actions include energy efficient production techniques, new equipment and construction, and fuel efficient vehicles.

---

[1] Source: U.S. Energy Information Administration, *Annual Energy Review* and *Monthly Energy Review*.

[2] Source: U.S. Federal Highway Administration, *Highway Statistics*, Annual.

The adjustments to higher oil prices have taken a considerable period of time. The national automobile stock, for example, is not suddenly replaced, but rather becomes more fuel efficient as older vehicles wear out. Fuel efficiency is incorporated into industrial processes on a gradual, not a sudden basis.

Over the long term, oil prices should remain low for another reason. The conservation changes that have been made are permanent changes. It is unlikely that consumers and business will decide to squander oil as prices fall. Individuals are not going to rip the insulation out of their houses and begin to drive gas guzzlers again. Maybe they will drive bigger cars, but these will get far better gas mileage than those of the 1960's and early 70's.

Role of OPEC

It is the prospect of these permanent changes in the demand for oil products that has concerned a variety of OPEC producers. The countries which comprise OPEC are not monolithic with regard to pricing goals in the short and the long term. Some OPEC members, like Algeria, have small oil reserves. These countries are interested in keeping oil prices as high as possible to maximize short-term profits. Other producing countries, like Saudi Arabia and Kuwait, have massive reserves. These countries are interested in perpetuating a long-term, stable demand for oil and oil products. High prices, which permanently curtail demand, reduce the long term stream of profits which will accrue to these countries (Singer, 1982). Thus, OPEC itself is interested in keeping prices at a low enough level so that demand for oil products will not drop off.

Proponents of the view that oil prices should stay low in the future also argue that as prices fall, demand for oil should not increase to a very great extent. The demand for oil is very <u>inelastic</u>. This means that demand is not very responsive to price changes—at least in the short term. A large change in price will result in a very small change in quantity demanded.

Inelastic demand means that the massive price increases of 1973-74 and 1979-81 did not result in corresponding immediate reductions in oil demand. Inelastic demand helped OPEC as prices were driven up. On the down side, inelastic demand can destroy a cartel. As prices go down, the quantity demanded will not go up appreciably, creating surpluses and further reductions in price. In the short term, at least, prices should stay low according to this view.

Cartel Behavior

Those who believe that oil prices will remain low also base their analyses on prior experience with cartels in other industries. Cartels seem to go through a certain cycle. Usually, a cartel is formed in an industry because low prices and "cutthroat" competition result in heavy losses for most or all organizations producing the product or service. Members of the industry realize that it is to their mutual advantage to collude and fix prices. The cartel is then formed and price fixing results in higher prices and profits for most if not all member organizations.

Higher prices usually mean that not all the output that was produced prior to the formation of the cartel will be sold. Production cutbacks are required to maintain the agreed upon price levels. In most cartels, an allocation system is devised so that all members share in the reduction in output.

In the case of OPEC, the swing producer was Saudi Arabia. Rather than all OPEC members cutting back production, Saudi Arabia cut back its production from a high of 10 million barrels per day to 2 million barrels per day or lower. However, around 1984–85, Saudi Arabia asked other OPEC members to share in the production cutbacks. Saudi Arabia felt that it could no longer keep oil production at such low levels and continue its health economy.

With production cutbacks, most members of any cartel experience excess production capacity. Usually, the marginal cost of additional production is very low, so that increased output above the level mandated by the cartel can result in greatly increased profits. Cartel members thus have an incentive to cheat on the agreement. Usually, this takes the form of secret rebates and other under the table deals to just slightly undercut the cartel price.

Soon the cheating spreads. Those cartel members not secretly price cutting have difficulty selling their production at the fixed price. The cartel agreement collapses, prices fall, cutthroat competition and heavy losses for cartel members ensue. This cycle has occurred several times since the oil embargo of 1972–73.

A Reassurance of OPEC?

It is this cycle that most cartels experience which forms the basis for the arguments that oil prices will increase in future years. Analysts holding this view believe that it will be in the interest of OPEC members to collude once again as low prices cause heavy losses for member countries. Indeed, low oil prices hurt producing countries not associated with OPEC such as Mexico, Norway and Great Britain. Seeing their trade deficits mount and unable to generate sufficient foreign exchange to pay for their international debts, it is argued that many non OPEC producers will eventually agree to deal directly with the cartel. The OPEC cartel will expand and incorporate a larger share of world oil production, it is believed.

In addition, it is argued that low prices will discourage exploration and new drilling activities. In the long run, this will result in a shortage of oil supplies as existing reserves are depleted. This should strengthen OPEC's hand in the future. Allirio Parra, managing director of Petroleos de Venezuela in London sums up this point of view, "sooner or later the world goes around again" (Ibrahim, 1985, p. 16).

It is the fear of a resurgence of OPEC that assures its demise, according to those who feel that oil prices will remain low. Singer best sums up this view, "As long as these fears exist, consuming nations will continue with investments to back out of oil and diversify their sources of supply by finding more oil. But these actions are making more certain the demise of OPEC as a world power" (Singer, 1982, p. 30).

The political instability in the Middle East deserves consideration as well as economic issues. The prospect of a lasting peace has been enhanced through the Arab-Israeli peace process that has begun. This should have a soothing effect on oil prices. Political problems in both Iran and Iraq continue to make this part of the world an unsettling place, however. The possibility of a replay of the Gulf War will have a chilling effect on declines in oil prices for some time to come.

The Physical Environment

The second major theme of this chapter concerns the physical environment. Public awareness of environmental problems and public policy with regard to the environment have changed significantly over the years. This can be illustrated by the environmental history of Pittsburgh, Pennsylvania.

Pittsburgh in the 1930's epitomized the environmental problems that were present in the United States. Pittsburgh at that time was enveloped in a perpetual shroud of black, dirty smoke. Plumes of fire and smoke would bellow from the landscape which was dotted by steel mills, foundries and other steel related industries.

Frequently, the city would become so engulfed in black smoke that noon would appear as dark as midnight. Cars, buses and trolleys would keep their headlights on and street lights would be lit at midday.

The buildings of Pittsburgh were blackened by the soot and dirt. Many structures today still wear a black coat acquired 50 years ago. Men who ventured out of doors in the morning wearing a white shirt would have to change in the afternoon. The shirt would be covered with black dirt from the air.

Pollution in Pittsburgh was not confined to the air. The Ohio River originates there where the Allegheny and Monogohela Rivers join. The Ohio would appear in various shades of brown, sometimes even with a layer of red or green film floating on its surface. The foul appearance of the rivers was matched only by their stench.

The "Point" where the three rivers join is a place of historical significance. This was the site of Fort Duquesne when the French occupied the area and Fort Pitt when the region was taken by the British during the French and Indian War. In the 1930's this entire area was devoted to railroad yards whose ugly appearance was hidden only by the blackened air.

Pittsburgh has changed a great deal since then. Environmental concerns led the city to enact stringent pollution standards. The area has undergone a "Renaissance" with new office construction and rejuvenation of the central city. The Pittsburgh skyline today looks much like New York, Chicago, or Washington, D.C. Gone are the freight yards. Gone are the bellowing fire and smoke, helped in part by the decline of the steel industry. Gone are the days that looked like night and the blackened buildings. Even the rivers have improved with fishing and boating becoming important recreational activities in the region. The quality of life has improved to such an extent that in 1985, Pittsburgh was named the best city in which to live in the United States.

The history of pollution in Pittsburgh in many ways parallels the course of environmental concerns in the United States. At first, little or no public interest was expressed over the air, water, noise and visual pollution which affected the industrial cities. Gradually, however, concerns over the physical environment grew. Public policy, especially government regulation was used as the mechanism to enforce a cleaner environment.

Public policy must answer two broad areas of questions in its attempts at dealing with pollution problems. One is to decide what is the optimal level of cleanliness of the physical environment. Once this is determined, the public sector must decide how best to achieve this environmental goal. Most of the public policy decisions concerning pollution can be placed within these two questions: how much cleanliness is desired and how should it be achieved?

A Model of Environmental Goals

Chapter 3 mentioned that one of the roles of government in a free enterprise system is to adjust for externalities. An externality was defined as a cost or benefit of an activity which falls on others. It was stated that the free enterprise system, if left on its own, will not create the proper incentives for business and individuals to take externalities into account in their production and consumption decisions. There is a role for government in correcting this shortfall. The classic example of an externality is pollution. Thus, there is an important role for government in adjusting private sector outcomes with regard to the quantity and types of pollutants released into the physical environment.

But, what is the optimum level of cleanliness of the physical environment that public policy should be designed to achieve? Is it a perfect, pristine environment as may have been present before the industrial revolution? Or, is unbridled pollution associated with rapid economic growth the most desirable objective? Should public policy be aimed to achieve an objective between these two extremes? If so, what should it be?

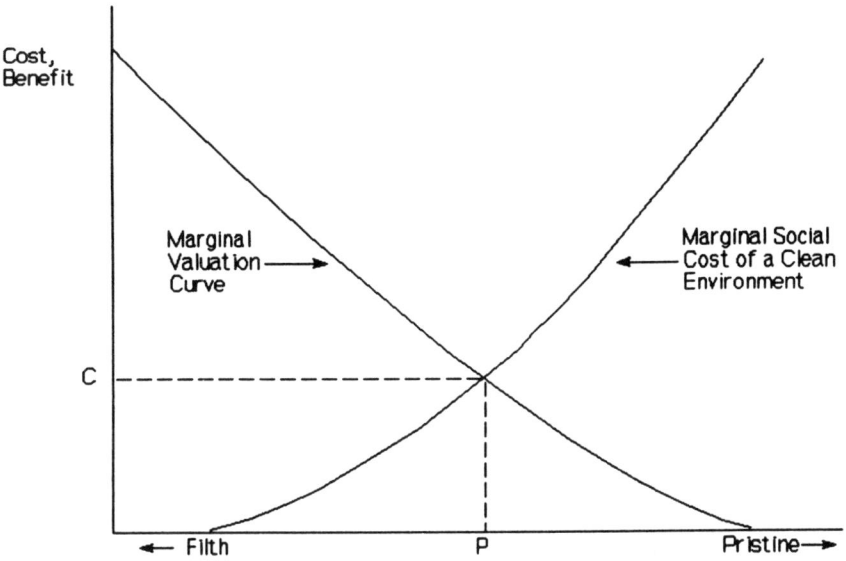

Figure 7.3. Optimum Degree of Cleanliness of the Physical Environment

In Figure 7.3, an approach to conceptualizing this public policy question is shown. The figure shows costs and benefits on one axis and the degree of cleanliness of the physical environment on the other. At one end is the filth of unbridled pollution. At the other extreme is the pristine environment that results from the elimination of all pollutants. The achievement of a certain degree of cleanliness results in benefits to society and an associated cost as shown on the vertical axis.

The downward sloping curve in the figure is the <u>marginal valuation curve</u>. It indicates how much society benefits from one additional unit of a clean environment. It is downward sloping reflecting the concept that as the physical environment becomes progressively cleaner, additional increments in cleanliness are valued to a lesser degree. In Chapter 2, it was stated that the demand curve measures how much consumers as whole value one additional unit of a product or service.

317

This marginal valuation curve is essentially society's demand curve for a cleaner physical environment.

The upward sloping curve in the figure is society's <u>marginal social cost</u> of cleaning up the physical environment. The curve is upward sloping, reflecting the concept that as the environment becomes progressively cleaner, it is more and more costly to extract additional increments of pollution. For example, Gujarati (1984) reports that the cost of eliminating 90 to 95 percent of the water pollution in the United States is estimated at $119 billion, while the cost of eliminating the last 5 to 10 percent is $319 billion. The curve is society's supply curve for a cleaner physical environment.

Optimum Degree of Cleanliness

Figure 7.3 illustrates that it may not be in society's best interest to have a 100 percent clean environment. The costs of achieving such a goal would far exceed the benefits. On the other hand, it may not be in society's best interest to have unchecked pollution either. As long as the marginal social cost of cleaning up the physical environment are less than the marginal social benefits to be obtained, environmental cleanup should proceed. At point P in the figure, the marginal costs of additional cleanup are exactly equal to the additional benefits to be derived. Beyond P, the costs exceed the benefits. Thus, the optimal degree of cleanliness of the environment is neither filth not pristine, but somewhere in between. The public policy debate concerns how to determine point P. This requires knowledge of society's benefits and costs of a cleaner physical environment.

But what constitutes society's benefits and costs of a clean environment? Benefits include health effects such as reduced cancer and emphysema rates, recreational benefits, beauty, and a variety of other intangibles. Social costs include the economic costs of installing, maintaining and operating pollution control devices, enforcement, administration, and all other costs associated with cleaning up the environment.

In order to isolate the socially desirable degree of cleanliness of the environment (point P), both the marginal social cost and the marginal valuation curves must be estimated. That is, both costs and benefits of environmental cleanup must be known. But many problems exist in estimating these.

Benefit Estimation

Benefit estimation is by far the most difficult. What must be done is to establish a relationship between pollution and health, beauty, crop yields, etc. and then value the increments in these intangibles which result from reduced despoiling of the physical environment. Two almost insurmountable problems must be overcome in order to estimate the benefits of pollution controls: problems of <u>quantification</u> and problems of <u>valuation</u>. These were mentioned in Chapter 6 concerning the benefit—cost analysis of government regulation.

Take the case of the health benefits resulting from a cleaner physical environment. A relationship between disease rates and levels and types of pollution must be established. It must be known to what extent an incremental reduction in pollution will result in reduced incidence of disease. The relationship between health and pollution must be <u>quantified</u>. Medical and engineering data are required to establish such relationships. However, these relationships are imprecisely known at best. Many other factors affect the incidence of disease, in addition to the levels and types of pollution.

But, suppose the problems of quantifying the relationship between the quality of the physical environment and health effects can be overcome. Death and illness rate reductions then need to be expressed on the same basis as the costs of pollution reduction, so the two can be compared. Usually, both costs and benefits are expressed in dollars. Thus, the next problem to be dealt with is that of <u>valuing</u> the health effects of pollution reduction. But, this involves placing a monetary value on human life, illness, and suffering. How much is a human life worth? How much is it worth to reduce the incidence of emphysema, cancer, asthma, or even the common cold? Problems of valuation of the benefits of pollution reduction are not easily overcome.

Cost Estimation

Estimating the marginal social costs of pollution reduction are not nearly as difficult as measuring the benefits. However, a variety of problems still must be dealt with. Control costs differ for different industries, for different plants within the same industry, and for different regions of the country. In addition, estimates of the costs of achieving current standards are not sufficient. What is needed to estimate marginal social costs are estimates of the future costs of achieving a hypothetical reduction. Costing pollution abatement is imprecise at best.

What this all means is that there is tremendous uncertainty associated with estimating the shape and location of the two curves shown in Figure 7.3. There is, thus, little certainty as to what the optimal degree of cleanliness of the environment should be.

The Public Policy Debate

The public policy debate concerning the degree of pollution control desirable can be conceptualized through the use of Figure 7.4. Because of the uncertainty concerning the shape and location of the two curves, and thus the costs and benefits associated with increases in the cleanliness of the environment, agreement is difficult to reach on the most desirable level of pollution control.

Environmentalists would tend to believe that the marginal valuation curve lies considerably to the right as drawn in the figure. They feel that the benefits of pollution reduction are very great. On the other hand, those who do not favor as clean an environment (these might be called industrialists) would feel that the marginal valuation curve lies considerably to the left of the environmentalists' concept. Industrialists would believe that the benefits of a cleaner environment are considerably less than the other side states.

Both sides also would tend to believe that the costs of cleaning up the environment are somewhat different. Environmentalists would argue that the cost curve is relatively flat. Industrialists would state that the costs increase rapidly.

Both points of view are illustrated in Figure 7.4 P^I and P^E represent the degree of cleanliness that would be advocated by the industrialists and environmentalists, respectively. Neither side can be proven right or wrong, because in order to do so, benefits and costs must be known. Instead, a stalemate seems to have developed, with the debate over how

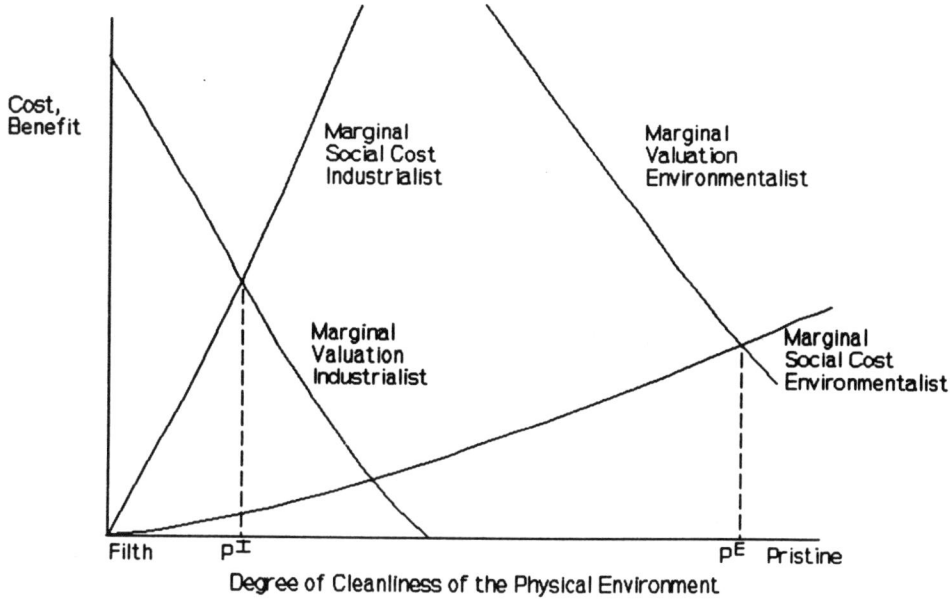

Figure 7.4. Optimum Cleanliness of the Physical Environment: Environmentalists and Industrialist Points of View

to achieve environmental goals replacing the argument over how much pollution reduction is desirable.

Federal Environmental Policy

Although state and local governments exercise some control over environmental matters, the primary focus of government regulation of the physical environment is at the federal level. The Environmental Protection Agency (EPA) is the principal federal agency responsible for enforcing the environmental laws.

The EPA was established in 1970 and consolidated into one agency the environmental enforcement efforts which were spread over 15 separate departments and agencies. It is an independent regulatory agency. Beginning with under 4,000 employees in 1970, EPA staff increased to over 18,000 by 1992. EPA enforces the environmental laws primarily by establishing performance and design standards and through outright prohibitions.

The agency is responsible for regulating a variety of sources of environmental pollution. Air pollution controls are one responsibility. The EPA regulates both stationary source air pollution from industrial and utility discharges, and mobile source air pollution which primarily results from automobile use. Water pollution discharge regulation and the licensing of pesticides are also under EPA's purview. Other responsibilities include toxic substance and hazardous waste disposal regulation, setting standards for drinking water, controlling noise pollution and regulation of radiation sources. In 1984, the EPA spent almost $1.7 billion in its enforcement efforts. Its expenditures increased to $6.539 billion by 1994.

The two most pervasive areas of EPA responsibility are air pollution regulation and water pollution discharge rules. These are discussed in the next two sections. Hazardous waste disposal regulation has gained in importance over the years as public awareness of the potential adverse impacts has grown. This is discussed later in the chapter.

Air Pollution Policy

Federal involvement in setting air pollution policy began in 1963 with the enactment of the Clean Air Act. This law, however, provided for only a very weak federal role in air pollution policy. The government was empowered to convene hearings and conferences on state air pollution problems (Crandall, 1983). The Air Quality Act of 1967 required the establishment of air quality control regions (AQCR) throughout the country. However, the federal government still had no enforcement power included in this law.

The role of the federal government in developing policies and regulations with respect to air pollution was increased dramatically with the passage of the 1970 Clean Air Act Amendments. The goal of the legislation was to "protect and enhance the nation's air resources." To achieve this goal, the amendments required the federal government to set air quality standards and to require the states to develop plans to achieve them. The amendments empowered the government to set standards for automobile pollution and to regulate industries and utilities. In 1977, Congress passed further amendments which lengthened the timetables which were originally specified to achieve the air quality goals.

In 1990, additional amendments to the Clean Air Act were enacted by Congress. This was by far the most sweeping revision of the Clean Air Act to date. Among others, the elimination of ozone-depleting gases, requirements for reformulated gasoline to reduce emissions in urban areas, and some additional flexibility regarding emissions trading were written into the law.

Many provisions of the 1990 Amendments were very controversial. For example, states whose urban areas were classified as non-attainment areas were required to develop employee trip reduction laws or face losses of federal highway funds. These laws would require employers of 100 or more employees in urban areas to develop programs to reduce employee trips to work in single occupancy vehicles. Car-pooling, van-pooling, public transit, telecommuting and a compressed work week were some of the options that could be used by businesses to reduce employee auto trips to work.

In typical bureaucratic fashion, the employee trip reduction program was later dubbed employee commute options (ECO) to make it sound positive. States were required to develop an implementation plan, and enforce the provisions of the law. Businesses were required to submit detailed plans to the state and periodically survey their employees to ascertain how they travelled to work.

Business interests reacted very negatively to the ECO requirements. A great deal of political pressure was exercised in each of the ten affected states to not enforce the ECO provisions, even though a loss of federal highway money could result. With the Republican takeover of Congress in 1994, it was evident to EPA and many political analysts that the ECO requirements would not stand.

By June of 1995, seven of the ten states that were required to enforce the ECO provisions decided to suspend their programs. Many turned their mandatory programs into voluntary ones. Faced with increased Congressional pressure, EPA began to show a great deal of flexibility and did not take action against the states, as bills moved through Congress to eliminate the employee trip reduction provisions.

Air Quality Standards

The various air pollution acts and amendments required the federal government, through the EPA, to administer a variety of policies, programs and regulations. Air quality standards were set for seven known pollutants[3]. These are:

1. Particulates — These are solid particles or minute drops of a liquid suspended in the air. Particulates include dust, soot and smoke, as well as other toxic substances.

2. Carbon Monoxide — (CO) is a poisonous gas which is colorless and odorless. The EPA has estimated that over 75 percent of carbon monoxide is emitted by motor vehicles.

3. Sulfur Oxides — These are gases which result from burning fuels containing sulfur. These are primarily coal (especially high sulfur content coal) and oil. Certain industrial processes also emit sulfur oxides. The effects on health are accentuated when other pollutants are also present. Ninety-five percent of this class of pollutant is sulfur dioxide (SO_2).

4. Nitrogen Dioxides — (NO_2) results when any fuel is burned at a high temperature. It is a brownish-colored gas which reacts with water to form nitric acid which is highly corrosive.

5. Hydrocarbons — This is a whole category of pollutants. Hydrocarbons are unburned gaseous or vaporized fuels. Evaporation of gasoline is a major source of hydrocarbons.

6. Oxidants — The most well-known oxidant is ozone which is a poisonous form of oxygen. Pure oxygen has two atoms (O_2), while ozone has three (O_3). It is formed when sunlight reacts with hydrocarbons and nitrogen dioxide. It is also called photochemical smog.

7. Lead — This is a metal that was widely used as an anti-knock compound in gasoline. It is absorbed in the body and may be fatal, especially to young children.

---

[3] Much of the material in this section was derived from *Air Pollution and Your Health*, Environmental Protection Agency, Washington, D.C., 1979.

Two sets of standards were developed for these seven pollutants. A primary standard was implemented which ". . . must protect the health of the most sensitive groups in the population with an adequate margin of safety" (Crandall, 1983, p. 8). A more rigorous secondary standard is aimed at protecting the public welfare, including economic effects on crops, animals and plants. The main concept behind these standards is that there exists a <u>threshold</u> of pollutants above which human health or public welfare is threatened.

The EPA has designated 247 Air Quality Control Regions (AQCR) in the United States. Each state must develop a state implementation plan (SIP). This plan details the strategy the state will utilize to bring each AQCR into compliance with the air quality standards set by the EPA. If an AQCR is found to be in nonattainment, the EPA can force compliance only indirectly, such as withholding federal grant money. In addition, if an AQCR does not meet the primary standards for oxidants and carbon monoxide, the federal government can require a state to implement a mandatory vehicle inspection system in which pollution control devices are checked.

Through the SIPs, individual states are responsible for controlling air pollution from existing sources. The EPA, however, has the authority to regulate emissions from new sources. Generally, new source regulation is considerably tougher than restrictions imposed by the states on existing sources. New sources of pollution are permitted in nonattainment regions, provided the polluters purchase <u>offsets</u> from existing sources in the area. Offsets are guarantees from other polluters that they will reduce their emissions of the same pollutant by a greater extent than the new source.

The federal government, through the court system, can impose penalties on violators of the air pollution law and regulations implemented by the EPA. Fines of up to $25,000 per day and one year in prison can be levied. Additional violations can result in a doubling of both the fine and the jail term. There are also severe penalties for the sale of automobiles which are not certified by the EPA or in which emission control devices have been disconnected.

Water Pollution Policy

Although the federal government has been involved in water pollution control to some extent since 1899, the major focus of modern federal regulation is the Water Pollution Control Act of 1972. With additional amendments, this law is now known as the Clean Water Act. The act states two major water pollution goals: (1) wherever possible, to achieve a level of cleanliness that allows swimming, other recreational activities and protection of fish, (2) no more discharges of pollution into the waters of the United States.

The Clean Water Act uses the same general approach to water pollution regulation as the government's efforts for air pollution. A set of standards were developed and specific deadlines stated to achieve the water pollution goals. Standards were specifically stated for point sources of pollution. <u>Point</u> sources of water pollution are specific, definable locations from which pollutants are emitted. Examples are sewage pipes and plant discharges. <u>Nonpoint</u> sources are broad areas of land in which seepage or runoff occurs.

Existing point source emissions regulation required that pollutants initially achieve a level of discharge that was obtained with the Best Practical Technology (BPT). This is the level of emission from the best plants in the industry. More rigorous, Best Available Technology (BAT) is required at a later date. Where BAT technology is shown to be uneconomical, Best Conventional Pollution Control Technology (BCPCT) can be used. Separate New Source Performance Standards (NSPS) were established for new point sources. Nonpoint sources are required to use Best Management Practices (BMP) in dealing with water pollution discharges.

Penalties for violation of the standards are fines of up to $10,000 per day. Willful or negligent violations can incur a $25,000 per day fine and up to one year in prison. Penalties can be doubled for additional violations.

Benefits and Costs of Federal Environmental Policy

Benefits

One measure of the benefits of federal policy is its effectiveness in achieving environmental goals. Progress in reducing air pollution is shown in Figure 7.5. As can be seen in the figure, significant progress has been made in cleaning up the atmosphere. Since 1970 particulate emissions have been reduced by 59%, sulfur oxides by 25%, and carbon monoxide by 41%. Only nitrogen oxides have increased, by 6%. However, these data are far from conclusive. Drawn from as few as 84 sites across the country, the changes in pollution levels in the figure could actually reflect a reduction of industrial activity, rather than absolute increases in air quality.

Information needed to evaluate the effectiveness of the Clean Water Act is also very poor and uncertain. However, the general conclusion seems to be ". . . the data that do exist seem to indicated that while certain bodies of water have improved significantly during the time the act has been in place, the general trend in overall water quality has been more or less constant" (Fredrick, 1982, p. 235).

Thus, both air and water pollution benefits, as measured by reduced emissions and higher air and water quality, have been difficult to assess. Crandall (1985, p. 20) states:

> ". . . there is precious little evidence that federal environmental policy has made the nations's air and water appreciably cleaner. The truth of the matter is that we don't know whether our environmental policies have worked at all despite the expenditure of at least $50 billion a year on pollution abatement."

In addition to not being able to document whether federal environmental policy has worked, a variety of problems exist with the programs administered by the EPA. One is that dangers to life and health do not result solely from the few pollutants identified by the government. Orloff (1985) notes that the problem of air pollution is much more complex. Scientists have found that as many as 100 different pollutants may adversely affect health. These include asbestos, benezene, formaldehyde and radon gas. These other pollutants, while emitted in much smaller quantities, are far more toxic than the original list. The EPA has found that 2,000 cases of cancer each year result from these other pollutants, in addition to the 5,000 to 20,000 cases resulting from radon gas (Orloff, 1985).

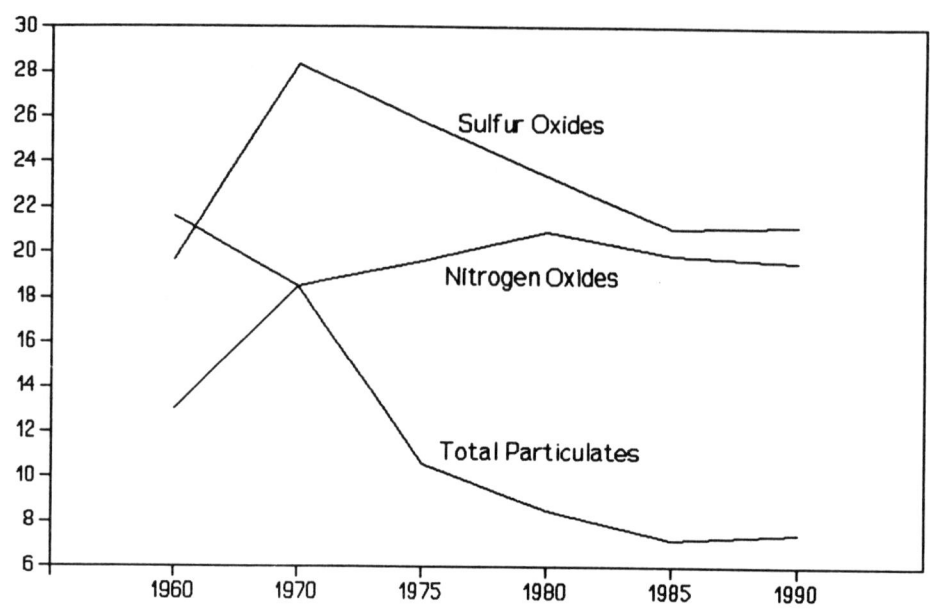

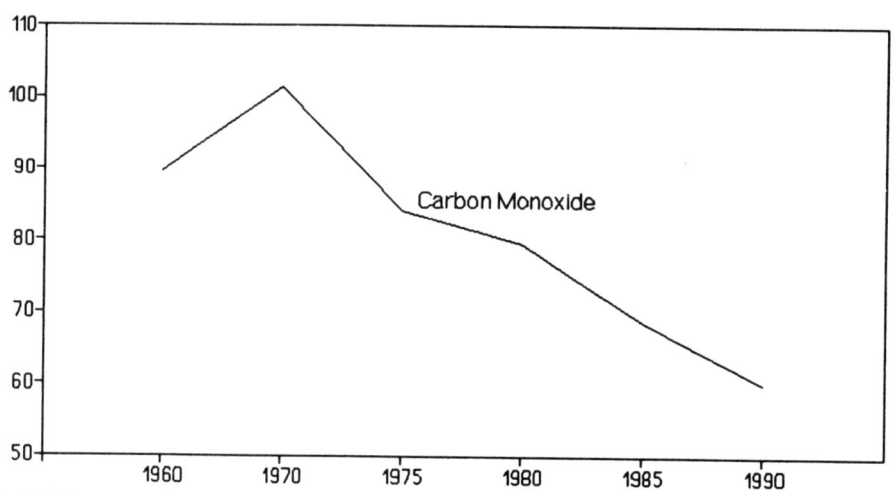

Pollutants measured in Teragrams/Year   1 Teragram = 500 Metric Tons
Graphic developed from information in U.S. Environmental Protection Agency, *National Air Pollutant Emission Estimates 1940-1990*, Nov. 1991.

Figure 7.5. Trends in Air Quality, 1960–1990

Growing scientific evidence also indicates that the concept of a threshold concentration of pollutants above which human health is threatened is erroneous. There is no line which separates harmful concentrations from those which are not. Rather, Orloff (1985) notes that a broad continuum exists in which increased exposure causes more and more severe health impacts. Crandall (1983) states that in order to maximize the health of the community, elimination of all harmful pollutants from the physical environment is necessary.

Costs

The total cost of pollution control by business, consumers and the government has been estimated at $91.456 billion in 1991. Expenditures on air pollution control alone accounted for $28.060 billion.[4] These aggregate cost estimates, however, mask the considerable variation in costs across different industries. Crandall (1983) has synthesized the results of two studies of the air pollution control costs of various industries. One study was performed by Battel Laboratories and the other was done by the EPA. Both studies estimated the cost of removing three different pollutants from existing and new sources. The pollutants are particulates, hydrocarbons, and sulfur dioxide. The results are shown in Table 7.2.

As can be seen in the table, pollution control costs vary widely across industries. For example, the cost of removing particulates for existing utilities varies between $36 to $680 per ton, while secondary aluminum removal costs are $1,010 to $3,030. Particulates removed from a coke oven cost $30,800 per ton.

The air quality standard approach to pollution control, however, makes no distinction between clean-up costs among different industries. The total pollution control bill for the nation could be reduced by providing incentives for those industries which have lower clean-up costs to reduce emissions by a greater extent than those industries whose costs are more. The standard approach to pollution regulation does not recognize this potential cost savings. Thus, pollution control costs are greater than they otherwise could be.

---

[4] Source: U.S. Department of Commerce, *Statistical Abstract of the United States*, 1994.

Table 7.2. Costs of Pollution Control for Different Industries
Dollars per metric ton removed

INDUSTRY AND POLLUTANT	Existing sources		New sources	
	Battel study (1979 dollars)	EPA case (1980 dollars)	Battel study (1979 dollars)	EPA case (1980 dollars)
PARTICULATES				
Electric utilities				
Eastern coal	36–680	252	—	2,577
Western coal	80	—	10	66
Coal cleaning	10	—	—	29
Petroleum refining	753	1	479	1
Chemicals				
Phosphate fertilizer	10–96	9–123	—	—
Phosphorus	22–45	—	—	—
Deflourinated phosphate	18–30	—	—	—
Dicalcium phosphate	1,200–2,600	—	—	—
Iron and steel				
Raw materials	823–7,359	982	194–126,243	1,759–2,872
Sintering	246–1,683	260–670	442–8,306	470–21,459
Coke ovens	16–17,759	179–6,285	1,360–38,734	1,356–27,387
Blast furnaces	990–7,542	308–10,429	1,170–297,570	2,130–16,600
Basic oxygen furnaces	87–3,735	353–3,110	1,380–101,000	2,461
Electric arc furnaces	254–8,165	1,291–2,448	4,020–160,654	15,589
Autosatic scarfing	12,080–23,472	25,473	—	—
Continuous casting	—	—	6,300–23,646	—
Secondary aluminum	1,010–3,030	—	810	—
Secondary brass and bronze	100–23,900	24–569	—	602–1,259
Farroalloys	400–760	—	—	—
Secondary lead	40–70	34–124	—	—
Asphalt and concrete	—	22	60–1,790	343–1,030
Lime	10–80	27–132	—	—
Feed mills	340–630	1,745	370	1,525
Grain handling	90–210	96–20,397	160	176
Pulp and paper	0–160	0[a]	120–2,440	92–7,206[a]
HYDROCARBONS				
Petrochemicals	40–621	34–260	—	—
Structural clay products	1,001	4,143	—	—
Paint	1,250	998	—	—
Dry cleaning	163–2,070	—	—	105–6,905
Motor vehicles	186–2,720	20–154	—	—
Wood furniture	5,460	—	73–127	—
Coil coating	—	—	—	145

Table 7.2. *(continued)*
Costs of Pollution Control for Different Industries
Dollars per metric ton removed

INDUSTRY AND POLLUTANT	Existing sources		New sources	
	Battel study (1979 dollars)	EPA case (1980 dollars)	Battel study (1979 dollars)	EPA case (1980 dollars)
SULFUR DIOXIDE				
Electric utilities				
Eastern coal	60–230	412	150–370	265–298
Western coal	—	—	1,090	1,167–1,414
Natural gas processing	118–372	340–824	—	0[b]
Petroleum refining	217	409	164	—
Iron and steel coking	295–473	513	560–700	184–579
Sulfuric acid	170–290	210	54	—
Primary copper	380–700	24–28	1,750	22
Primary lead	150	64–346	—	315
Primary zinc	780	38	—	222
Structural clay products	530–650	530–841	—	—
Paper (total reduced sulfur)	80	0–324[b]	—	92–12,437[b]

Source: Robert W. Crandall, Controlling Industrial Pollution, Brookings Institute, Washington, D.C., 1983, pp. 36–37.

[a] Existing plants are said to have negative control costs; new plants remove particulates and sulfur as joint products.
[b] Some estimates are negative; others are joint with particulate removal.

Table 7.2 also shows that the costs of removing pollutants from new industrial sources is more expensive than from existing ones. This is because of the tougher standards imposed on new sources by the EPA. This has two unintended effects. One is that it can be counterproductive. Firms have an incentive to postpone replacement of older facilities with more modern ones. The modernized facilities not only may be more productive, but also may result in less pollution than existing plant and equipment. Secondly, as argued by Crandall (1985) and others, such regulations bear most oppressively on new, growing industries and less on older, dying ones. Thus, the rate of industrial development can be slowed by these regulations.

It has been argued that these additional pollution control costs imposed on new sources result in a bias against new emerging growth areas, especially the sun belt. Thus, the effect of this regulatory system is to favor rust belt areas in the midwest and northeast and to stem the growth of southern and western industry.

Federal environmental regulations have also reduced competition in some industries by indirectly reducing the number of smaller plants in high pollution industries. Pashigian (1983) has found that federal environmental rules have reduced the number of plants in high pollution industries and have made it more difficult for small plants to compete with larger ones. As with the OSHA regulations discussed in Chapter 6, small business seems to bear an unusually heavy burden in complying with federal standards.

Alternative Approaches to Pollution Reduction

Given the variety of problems created by the standards approach to regulating the physical environment, several alternatives have been suggested to achieve environmental goals at lower social cost. Three of these alternatives will be discussed in this section. These are better enforcement, effluent charges and marketable pollution rights. The EPA has implemented a number of reforms of the standards approach. These fall into the categories of offsets, banking, bubbles and netting and are discussed at the end of this section.

Better Enforcement

Data on air and water pollution levels, mentioned earlier, indicate only small gains that have been achieved in cleaning up the physical environment. One suggestion is to increase the enforcement of existing pollution standards as a method to increase the quality of the environment. Crandall (1983) notes that the EPA certifies compliance with air pollution standards using three methods. These are stack monitoring, on site inspection of equipment and voluntary certification by the polluter. Stack tests are used 5 percent of the time, on site inspections 38 percent, and voluntary compliance is used to enforce the pollution laws 57 percent of the time.

Data on compliance with air pollution standards indicate that this system is not working. One study found 22 percent of the sources exceeded maximum emissions, while another study found that 70 percent of the sources studied had documented incidents of violations of emissions standards (Crandall, 1983).

Effluent Charges

In Table 7.2, it was shown how pollution control costs vary across industries and are higher for new pollution sources. The standard approach to pollution regulation results in control costs being higher than they otherwise could be since incentives are not provided for low-cost clean-up industries to reduce emissions to a greater extent than high-cost ones. Effluent charges are a way of providing these incentives.

EPA requires polluters to use the Best Available Technology (BAT) or Best Conventional Pollution Control Technology (BCPCT). But, what is best? Crandall (1983) argues that there is no logical definition of the best technology. Any technology can be improved with the additional expenditure of money. In addition, choosing the best technology for each firm in each industry can become an "administrative nightmare." He suggests that polluters should choose their own best technology. The effluent charge, if properly implemented, would do just that.

The way an effluent charge would work is that the EPA would establish a tax or fee for each pound of pollutant emitted into the environment. Tax rates may differ for each type of pollutant. Individual firms can clean up their pollution, pay the fine, or do some combination of both. Most polluters would combine partial clean-up with paying a fine for the remaining pollution. Each firm would evaluate the cost of clean-up versus the cost incurred in paying a fine. Clean-up would proceed so long as it is less expensive than simply paying the fine.

An industry in which clean-up costs are great would pay more fines and clean up less. On the other hand, industries in which clean-up costs are low would control their pollution to a greater extent and pay fewer fines. Thus, effluent charges should result in a lower overall total cost of achieving pollution control goals. In addition, the individual polluters and not the EPA decide which technology is "best."

The EPA would be free to set the effluent charge so that the same degree of cleanliness of the environment is achieved as if the pollution standards approach were being used. In Figure 7.3 (p. 317), such a charge is shown as the horizontal line C. The effluent charge can be raised or lowered until the desired level of clean-up is obtained. In addition, effluent charges would generate revenues which can be used for research and development into better methods of pollution control and for environmental clean-up.

One argument against the use of an effluent charge is that it would increase enforcement costs. With an effluent charge, emissions would have to be monitored rather than the EPA observing if the proper equipment is in place. Those in favor of effluent charges believe that this is not a major problem. Enforcement could proceed similar to the manner in which the IRS collects taxes. That is, largely voluntary compliance with random sampling of polluters would be relied on. Besides, it is argued, the level of compliance with the standards system could be improved, so that enforcement costs may go up under a standards approach anyway.

A second and more fundamental problem with effluent charges is distributional. Under a standards approach, polluters pay for clean-up and no more. Under an effluent charge, polluters pay twice: for the control devices, and the effluent charge on the remaining pollution. Crandall (1983) argues that pollution standards are essentially licenses to pollute at a zero price up to the standard and then prohibitions on pollution levels exceeding the standard. Polluters would not willingly give up this right to pollute. Thus, it would be very difficult politically to have effluent charges implemented. Business would generally oppose such a system.

Marketable Pollution Rights

An alternative to effluent charges which substitutes market forces for regulation standards is marketable pollution rights. This concept allows firms to emit pollution up to a certain amount or control emissions and sell the right to pollute. A market for pollution rights would develop in which businesses would be free to purchase or sell rights. Trading of rights would be restricted to occur within the same region of the country, such as Air Quality Control Regions (ACQR) for the case of air pollution. The right to emit one type of pollution could not be traded for the right to emit another.

Firms in industries in which clean-up costs are low would sell their rights and clean up their emissions. Polluters which are from high clean-up cost industries would purchase pollution rights in the marketplace and control pollution to a lesser extent.

By concentrating pollution reductions on low clean-up cost industries, marketable rights result in a lower total pollution control cost than the regulatory standards approach. No distinction is made between old and new pollution sources. In addition, the rights approach allows polluters to choose the technology rather than the regulators. Thus, marketable rights have the same advantages as emissions charges.

Marketable pollution rights also eliminate the primary objection that many businesses have regarding emission charges. Business is not taxed by the government and also required to pay for pollution control under this system.

An Example of Pollution Rights

An example of how the marketable pollution rights approach would work is shown in Table 7.3. In the table, it is assumed that there are two firms in a particular region. These are a steel mill and a dry cleaning plant. The upper portion of the table calculates pollution control costs under a regulatory standards approach.

Table 7.3. Marketable Rights vs. the Standards Approach to Pollution Control

Standards Approach

	Initial Pollution Level (Hydrocarbons)	Pollution Standard	Required Clean-up	Clean-up Cost $/lb.	Total Clean-up Cost
Steel Mill	30,000 lbs.	10,000 lbs.	20,000 lbs.	$1.00	$20,000
Dry Cleaning Plant	20,000 lbs.	10,000 lbs.	10,000 lbs.	$0.10	$ 1,000
TOTAL	50,000 lbs.	20,000 lbs.	30,000 lbs.		$21,000

Marketable Rights Approach

	Initial Pollution Level (Hydrocarbons)	Marketable Rights	Pollution Level After Rights Trade	Reduction	Clean-up Cost $/lb.	Total Clean-up Cost	Marketable Rights Cost $.50
Steel Mill	30,000 lbs.	10,000 lbs.	20,000 lbs.	10,000 lbs.	$1.00	$10,000	$ 5,000
Dry Cleaning Plant	20,000 lbs.	10,000 lbs.	0 lbs.	20,000 lbs.	$0.10	$ 2,000	$ –5,000
TOTAL	50,000 lbs.	20,000 lbs.	20,000 lbs.	30,000 lbs.		$12,000	$ -0-

Initially, the steel mill emits 30,000 pounds of hydrocarbons and the dry cleaning plant emits 20,000 pounds. The control standards require each firm to emit only 10,000 pounds. The steel mill must clean up 20,000 pounds of hydrocarbons, while the dry cleaning plant must clean up 10,000 pounds. Clean-up costs are $1 per pound and $.10 per pound for the steel mill and dry cleaner respectively. Total clean-up costs under the standards approach amount to $21,000.

In the lower part of the table, the pollution rights approach is illustrated for the same two firms. Instead of setting a standard, the EPA would issue each firm a set of marketable rights for a total allowable emission of 10,000 pounds each. The allowable emissions are the same under this system as the standards approach. However, unlike the previous situation, the rights to pollute can be traded by the two firms.

The two firms might negotiate and decide to trade rights at a cost of $.50 per pound. The exact price depends on the supply and demand for rights, and the relative clean-up costs of the firms. Since the steel mill's control costs are $1 per pound, it is cheaper for the firm to purchase rights at $.30 per pound than to clean up. For every right purchased, the firm saves $.50 per pound. The dry cleaning plant would sell its rights at $.50 each and control its emissions at a cost of $.10 per pound. For every pound of emission controlled, the dry cleaner makes $.40.

After the rights trade, the steel mill would emit 20,000 pounds of hydrocarbons into the atmosphere. The dry cleaning plant would emit none. The total allowable emissions and the total reductions are the same as the regulatory standards approach. However, clean-up costs are substantially lower. Total clean-up costs are $12,000, consisting of $10,000 for the steel mill and $2,000 for the dry cleaning plant. The same emission control objective as the standards approach is achieved at lower total clean-up cost.

There is one cost element that is not present under the standards approach. This is the cost of the marketable rights. This cost of $5,000 for the steel mill is directly offset by a negative cost (or gain) of $5,000 for the dry cleaning plant. Thus, the marketable rights cost of one firm is in turn a revenue source for another. Marketable rights costs are not resource costs of cleaning up pollution. These remain at $12,000. Marketable rights costs are merely transfers of income from one firm to the other.

Problems with Pollution Rights

Two problems with marketable rights have been raised by those that oppose this approach. One is that the EPA enforcement programs would be greatly complicated by such a system. It is argued that both buyer and seller would have to be monitored. However, enforcement of this system may not be more difficult than enforcement of standards.

Secondly, it is argued that this system will not work in rural areas where there are few buyers and sellers. If only one firm in a region emits a certain type of pollution, who would it sell rights to? This situation, it is argued by supporters of the rights approach, is not a problem. The marketable rights would merely become a pollution standard.

Offsets, Banking, Bubbles and Netting

The curious set of words offsets, banking, bubbles and netting are the incentive-based reforms that have actually been implemented by the EPA. The agency recognized that a standards approach alone was not sufficient to achieve cost-effective pollution reductions. However, rather than adopting an emissions tax or marketable rights program, the EPA implemented four different but interrelated policies.

Offsets

The offset policy was designed to be implemented in AQCR's which were nonattainment areas. No new industrial development is possible in these areas under the standards approach. Rather than eliminate all development, the offset policy was established. New industry can locate in these areas provided it meets the new source standards and guarantees are obtained from other polluters in the region to reduce their emissions to a greater extent than the pollution generated by the new source. The total amount of pollution in the area is reduced and industrial development can occur.

This policy has created a market for offsets in various AQCR's. Occasionally, advertisements will appear in trade publications and *The Wall Street Journal* for these offsets.

Banking

If a firm achieves a level of pollution below the EPA standards, it can bank its right to pollute up to the standard either for future use or to sell as offsets to future industrial development. Without this banking policy, firms may want to continue operating plants which emit high pollution levels in order to preserve their right to pollute in the future. Crandall (1983, p. 86) notes, "It is obviously bad environmental policy to induce firms to continue to operate old, polluting facilities in order to avoid sacrificing their valuable pollution rights."

Levin (1985) describes a case that occurred in 1981 in Louisville, Kentucky. General Electric wanted to expand its plant, but could not without a substantial expenditure for emissions control. Instead, it paid $60,000 to lease emissions reductions from International Harvester. GE saved $1.5 million in capital expenses and $300,000 in operating costs.

Bubbles

The "bubble" policy was implemented by EPA in 1979. Under this policy, the agency treats a plant as being enclosed in an imaginary bubble with a single hole at the top. Rather than regulating the emissions of each smokestack or pollution source, only the total amount of pollution which emanates from the hole is regulated. Plant managers can comply with pollution control regulations by controlling emissions to a greater extent from those sources within the plant that are less expensive to clean up. Sources which are more costly to control can emit pollutants above that permitted by the regulatory standards, so long as the entire plant is in compliance.

The bubble policy was implemented in order to reduce pollution control costs. It has been quite successful. Levin (1985) notes that as of the fall of 1984, this policy has saved industry almost $800 million.

The bubble policy, however, has raised a variety of issues. The policy was designed only to be implemented in air quality attainment areas. However, in 1986, the EPA moved to extend the policy to nonattainment areas as well (Taylor, 1986, p. 4). Some critics believe that the policy allows credit for emission reductions that would have taken place anyway. Those in favor of the bubble concept argue that it should be extended so that trades can occur between different plants in the same area.

Netting

This concept applies to situations in which a plant is being modernized or substantially updated. Should the updated facility be required to comply with the new source pollution standards, or the less rigorous existing source standards? The EPA designed netting policy to require that if a modification of a plant resulted in increased pollution, new source standards would not apply so long as offsetting reductions in emissions occurred elsewhere in the plant. Thus, pollution increases and decreases are netted to ascertain the appropriate standards to be used. This policy only applies to attainment areas, however. The courts struck down the application of this concept in nonattainment regions.

Acid Rain

One issue that has gained recent scientific and governmental interest is acid rain. This is the situation in which sulfur dioxide and nitrogen oxides are released in the air and then return to the ground in rain or snow or as dry deposits. A substantial scientific controversy exists on the causes of acid rain and its impact on the physical environment.

The most widely held theory is that the sulfur dioxide and nitrogen oxides emitted by industry and electric utilities are the main causes of acid rain. Automobile exhaust also contributes to nitrogen oxide emissions. The acidity of precipitation in the United States is concentrated in the Northeast and Upper Midwest. A map of the acidity of precipitation is shown in Figure 7.6.

It is argued that acid rain results in damage to forests, streams and lakes. It is believed that acid rain results in destruction of populations of fish, and killing of trees and plants in forests. Damage caused by acid rain has so far been confined to upper New York State and Canada. Acid rain damage has also occurred in Sweden, Norway and West Germany.

Proposals to deal with acid rain involve severe limitations on industrial and power plant emissions. It has been suggested that over 75 percent reduction in emissions may be necessary to reduce acid rain effects. However, it is unclear that even if such reductions occur that acid rain damage will be reduced.

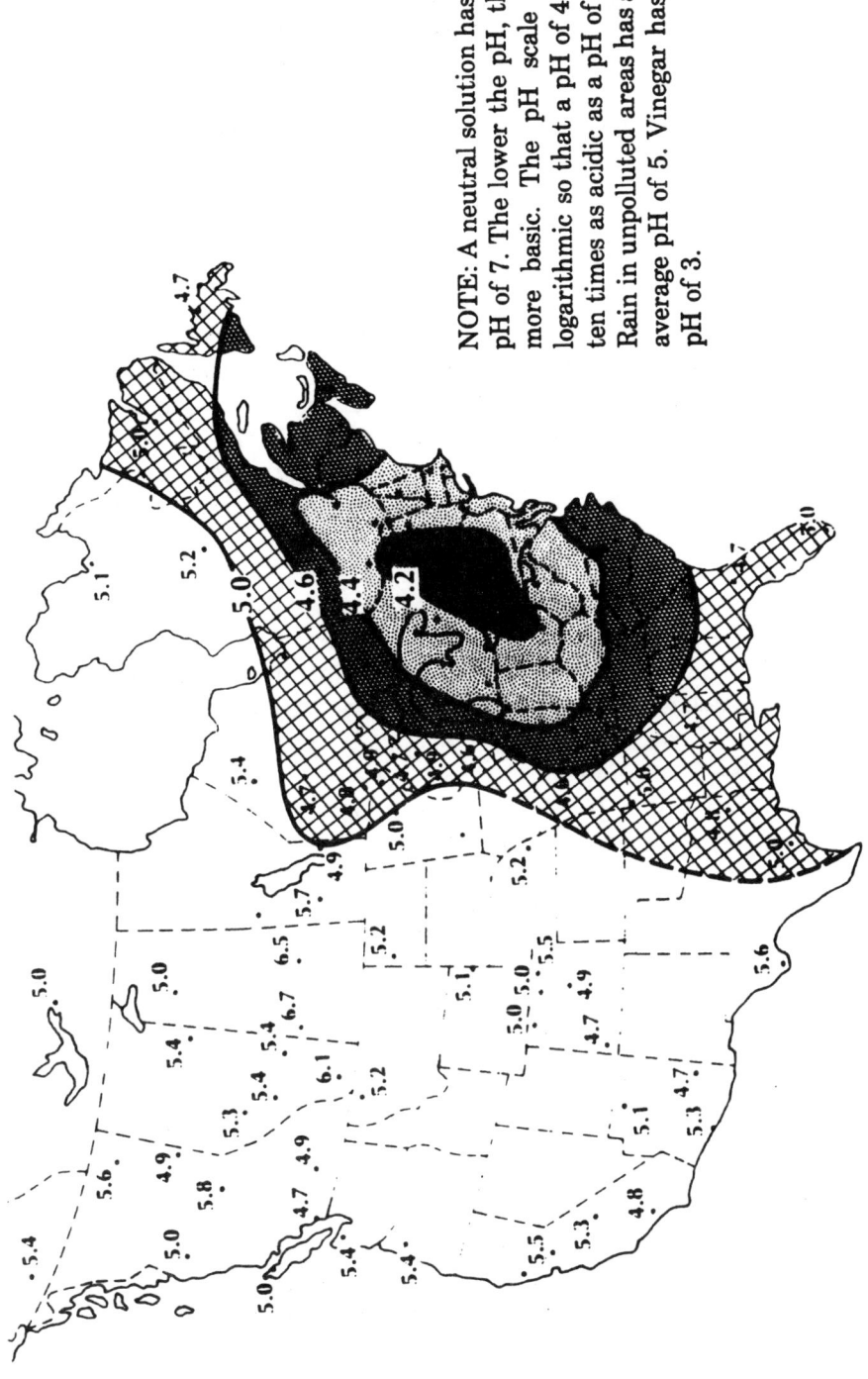

Figure 7.6. Acidity of Precipitation on North America, 1982

NOTE: A neutral solution has a pH of 7. The lower the pH, the more basic. The pH scale is logarithmic so that a pH of 4 is ten times as acidic as a pH of 5. Rain in unpolluted areas has an average pH of 5. Vinegar has a pH of 3.

Source: Comptroller General's Report to The Congress, An Analysis of Issues Concerning Acid Rain, Government Printing Office, Washington, D.C., 1984, p. 185.

If and when the federal government moves to reduce the effects of acid rain, severe impacts on northeastern and midwestern industry may result as air pollution controls become more stringent. The use of low sulfur coal may also be stimulated over concern for acid rain. The long-term implications of not dealing with acid rain are still unclear. So are the implications of alternative policies designed to deal with it.

Hazardous Wastes

Hazardous wastes are discarded substances from industrial processes. The chemical, primary metals and petroleum refining industries are the primary sources of hazardous wastes. Not all industrial wastes are toxic. Some are quite mundane such as wood and paper products, metals and food products. Others, however, can be severely hazardous to humans. Death, genetic damage and severe illness can result from exposure to some of these substances.

In the past, industry would dispose of these wastes by burying them at dump sites throughout the country. Often, residential or commercial developments would occur at or near these sites. National awareness of the health effects created by these sites heightened in the late 1970's over the experience at Love Canal.

Located in Niagara Falls, New York, Love Canal was used by the Hooker Chemical Company as dump site for its chemical wastes. The canal was considered an ideal dumping site in the 1940's since it was not very populated and consisted of a clay which would hold wastes without seepage. The chemicals were buried in sealed containers.

During the 1950's, a school, shopping center and homes were built near or at the dump site. In the 1970's, heavy rains and snows resulted in the buried chemicals leaching to the surface. Residents of the area experienced a higher than normal incidence of cancer, birth defects, liver damage and miscarriages.

By 1980, almost 1,000 Love Canal area families were forced to abandon their homes. President Carter, in 1980, signed emergency legislation providing relocation assistance to the affected people. The Love Canal area stands as an abandoned monument to toxic wastes.

Unfortunately, Love Canal is not the only hazardous waste dump site in the country. No one knows the full extent of the problem. Estimates of dump sites range from 10,000 to over 100,000. As many as 2,200 may pose significant risks to human health.

In order to combat the hazardous waste problem, Congress in 1980 created the Superfund clean-up trust fund. This is a program funded by a special tax on producers of petrochemicals, toxic organic chemicals and oil importers. The Superfund money is used to clean up toxic waste dumps. The fund is administered by EPA. Through 1992, EPA committed $10.6 billion for clean-ups (Acton, 1993). The Superfund is only the beginning of a massive clean-up effort. It has been estimated that a complete clean-up may require over $100 billion in funding and take 20 to 50 years (Taylor, 1985, p. 1).

The EPA's Superfund programs does involve some controversy. The basic problem is what to do with the wastes once removed from the dump sites. Frequently, the substances are moved to another location. Some critics charge that this is nothing more than an elaborate shell game. John Hackler, chief of EPA clean-ups in New England argues, "We were creating a hole in Massachusetts and a hill in New York" (Taylor, 1985, p. 16). Some environmentalists believe that incineration, solidification, and neutralization of toxic wastes are the best approaches. However, these methods may cost eight to ten times as much as land disposal.

Managerial Implications

Issues related to energy and the physical environment will affect managerial decision-making for a long time to come. Management must know how to effectively adjust planning, organizing, controlling, and staffing/rewarding activities for future changes in these two areas.

Energy

The most important aspect of energy concerns its price in the near and the long term. Because of businesses' ability to substitute different types of fuels, movements in petroleum prices should eventually affect prices of all other fuels and energy sources. However, there is a great deal of uncertainty associated with oil prices.

Environmental scanning efforts are critical in detecting short- and long-term movements in this potentially volatile price. Political events in the Middle East, OPEC's ability to reach a price fixing agreement with its members, consumer behavior, scientific discoveries and possible public sector actions are some of the factors that need careful scrutiny.

Energy considerations should be factored into capital investment decisions which are part of business planning. As a hedge against uncertainty, it may be wise to install equipment that is easily convertible to alternative fuels whenever possible.

It may also be useful to incorporate an energy price sensitivity analysis into the capital investment decision process. Sensitivity analysis involves changing the values of key variables to see how the ultimate results may change. Alternative possible energy prices over the life of the asset should be factored into the analysis to see under what price range the investment is viable. Management can then decide the likelihood of alternative price levels occurring.

The Physical Environment

The physical environment involves much more complex consideration. Since government regulation is the primary mechanism through which environmental control costs are imposed on business, managers must remain keenly aware of changes in regulation. Environmental scanning efforts need to be directed at EPA, including changes in personnel and administrations which may change the course of regulatory efforts. State level agencies should also be monitored.

The issues of acid rain and hazardous waste disposal may be the most intractable environmental problems, lasting well into the next century. Public policy efforts with regard to these two areas need to be carefully scrutinized. Regulations can affect the desirability of certain types of investments, the economic potential of certain regions of the country and the profitability of some industries. Investment decisions need to be made with an eye on current and possible future regulations.

The managerial implications of issues related to the physical environment go beyond anticipating and reacting to public policy outcomes. Managers have a great deal of leeway in managing environmental resources. With the advent of the bubble policy, business can comply with regulation in the least costly manner. Potential savings in environmental control costs can be substantial.

Bodily and Gabel (1982) suggest several ways in which managers can achieve compliance with environmental standards at reduced costs. These involve changes in production planning and alterations in investment choices. They suggest the following options:

1. Varying the output rate or product mix

2. Varying the types of raw materials used

3. Changing production processes

4. Using different types of pollution control devices

5. Purchasing, selling, or banking offsets

6. Closing down a production facility

In addition to the planning function, environmental considerations can enter the staffing/rewarding activities as well. Environmental control specialists can be hired. Such specialists should be used to provide expert advice as to the least cost manner of achieving environmental objectives. Plant managers can be rewarded for achieving compliance with governmental regulations in the most efficient manner.

Finally, business can sometimes utilize the necessity to comply with environmental regulations for profitable advantage. For example, research and development costs into control technologies may lead to the development and selling of control equipment to other firms in an industry. Some firms have found how to utilize formerly discarded wastes for productive purposes. Industrial wastes products and emissions can sometimes be recycled and even sold as raw materials to other manufacturers. Effective managers may be able to turn a cost item into a profit generating asset.

Summary

Government action with regard to the oil crisis was aimed primarily at keeping domestic prices low. Price controls, however, interfered with the free market functions of information transmission, providing incentives and allocating resources. Gasoline lines were one of many unintended effects of public policy. The entitlements program, the two-tier pricing system, speed limits, automobile fuel economy regulations and temperature regulations of public buildings were some of the policies designed to remedy the unintended effects of the price control system. The future course of energy prices depends on a number of factors including new production, conservation, cartel behavior and whether OPEC will experience a resurgence.

The public policy debate with regard to the physical environment concerns the level of cleanliness of the environment and the means to achieve that goal. Federal environmental policy is administered by the EPA. Air pollution regulation increased dramatically with the passage of the 1970 Clean Air Act amendments. Air quality standards were set for seven known pollutants. The main concept behind these standards is that there exists a threshold of pollutants above which human health or public welfare is threatened. The major focus of federal water pollution regulation is the Clean Water Act. Both point and nonpoint sources are regulated.

The benefits of federal policy to date have been inconclusive. In addition, the threshold concept itself may be erroneous. Several alternatives have been suggested to reduce the costs of compliance with environmental regulations. These include effluent charges and marketable pollution rights. Both concepts substitute market forces for regulation. Recent changes in federal environmental policy involve the implementation of offsets, banking, bubbles, and netting. Each method moves federal regulation a step closer to using the marketplace to achieve environmental objectives.

Acid rain and hazardous waste disposal are expected to be the two most intractable environmental problems of the future. Proposals to deal with acid rain may adversely affect industry in the Northeast and Midwest. The Superfund is the first program that the federal government implemented to attempt to clean up hazardous waste sites.

Managers need to be aware of future developments in energy prices and to factor energy considerations into capital investment decisions. Managers can achieve compliance with environmental standards at reduced costs. In addition, compliance costs can sometimes be turned into profit-generating assets.

Questions

1. Analyze current proposals of the federal government for dealing with energy supplies and prices. What would be the unintended effects of the implementation of these policies?

2. What are the unintended effects of the 55 MPH speed limit and the fuel economy regulations? What have been the benefits and costs for the producer and/or the consumer?

3. What has been the impact of high energy prices during the 1970's and 1980's? Which of these changes is likely to remain if prices drop permanently?

4. What is the current status of the OPEC cartel? What are the future prospects for this cartel?

5. What is the current price of crude oil and oil products? What does the future hold for the price of these products?

6. Suppose you are a manager of a firm which values social responsibility very highly. How would you interpret Figure 7.3? What costs and benefits would you consider when you are evaluating possible investment in pollution control equipment?

7. What have been the primary strategies of the EPA in achieving its goals? How effective has this agency been in achieving its objectives? What changes in strategies used by the EPA might be desirable?

8. As a manager, what strategies are available in addition to installing pollution control equipment in an existing plant to reduce pollution?

9. Describe the various alternative approaches to pollution reduction. What are the costs and benefits of each one from the point of view of business and of society in general?

10. How would firms following each of the levels of social responsibility deal with pollution?

11. Discuss the ethics of polluting the environment. Are there situations in which it is ethical to pollute above the legal limit?

12. What changes in the environmental laws are desirable from the point of view of business? What can managers do to impact public policy in this area?

Key Concepts

OPEC Cartel

Entitlements Program

two-tier pricing system

Windfall Profits Tax

Synthetic Fuels Corporation

marginal valuation curve

marginal social cost

AQCR

offsets

point and nonpoint sources

effluent charges

marketable pollution rights

banking

bubbles

netting

threshold concept

Case Analysis: Union Carbide and the Disaster at Bhopal

On December 3, 1984, an underground storage tank in a pesticide plant which was located in Bhopal, India, leaked deadly methyl isocyanate (MIC) gas into the air. The plant was owned and operated by Union Carbide Corporation. The poisonous gas leaked into the city of Bhopal for forty minutes. A factory siren that was to alert local residents of a leak did not sound until two hours after the leak began. Rescue workers did not arrive until four hours later. By then, the gas had permeated a 25 square mile area. Over four hundred people died immediately with initial injury estimates placed at 10,000. The final death and injury toll was never known with certainty. The best estimates placed it at 1,750 dead, and over 200,000 injured. The incident at Bhopal was the worst industrial accident in history.

Bhopal is located 370 miles south of New Delhi. It is the capital of the Indian state of Madhya Pradesh. Approximately 630,000 people reside in the city. Most of the residents are illiterate manual laborers who were attracted to the jobs at the Union Carbide pesticide plant. Poverty was rampant in Bhopal. Income from market wages averaged $127 per year.

Union Carbide Corporation was a 110-year-old organization headquartered in Danbury, Connecticut. It ranked third worldwide in the chemical business with 1983 sales of $9 billion. Peak sales of $10.17 billion were achieved in 1981. Assets in 1983 totaled $10.8 billion and net worth was $5 billion. The chemical giant employed 99,000 people worldwide. At the time of the accident, it operated 700 factories, mills and laboratories in 35 countries. Although the bulk of its sales were to industry, Carbide produced a variety of well-known consumer products including Prestone antifreeze, Glad bags and Eveready batteries. Sales from different business segments were:

Business Segment	Percent of Sales
Chemicals	29%
Industrial gases	15%
Metals and Carbon products	11%
Consumer products	21%
Technology, Services & Specialty Products	24%

Sales per employee were $90,000. This compared to $201,000 for industry leader, Dow Chemical Company.

Union Carbide had been considered a major world leader in promoting environmental goals. *The Wall Street Journal* reported: "Carbide is credited by some environmentalists as the leading chemical company in pushing for safer use of pesticides in the third world" (Meyer & Winslow, 1984, p. 1).

Methyl Isocyanate is a chemical used to make agricultural pesticides. Carbide produced MIC at the Bhopal plant and at a second plant in the United States. This plant was located in Institute, West Virginia near Charleston. In addition, a plant in Woodbine, Georgia processed MIC produced at Institute to manufacture pesticides.

MIC is an insidious gas that attacks the mucous membranes, eyes, nose and throat. Victims have asthma like symptoms of constricted breathing, shortness of breath, wheezing, coughing and chest pains.

The Bhopal plant began MIC production seven years before the accident. The plant was 51 percent owned by Union Carbide and 49 percent owned by the Indian government. Indian law required that the plant be designed, built, operated and maintained with local labor. At the time of the accident, the plant was totally managed by Indian nationals. Carbide stated that Union Carbide, India Ltd. was operated as a separate company. Safety procedures were the responsibility of the Indian management team.

Carbide seemed to have adopted a hands off attitude in its relationship with the Indian subsidiary. They acknowledged that there was "no direct authority link" between U.S. headquarters and India. One set of analysts observed ". . . Carbide headquarters had little substantive knowledge of what was really going on in India. No detailed knowledge of the safety standards, safety systems or evacuation plans in existence at the Bhopal plant, or blueprints of the facility, could apparently be found at Carbide headquarters" (Gladwin & Walter, 1985, p. 20).

Even before the December third incident, the Bhopal plant did not operate accident-free. At least 5 other accidents occurred there since 1977. In that year, six people died after exposure to phosene gas. Over the years, one additional person was killed and a minimum of 30 injuries occurred as a result of incidents at the plant.

Although Carbide produced MIC both at Bhopal and at Institute, West Virginia, safety precautions at the two plants were not the same. The Institute plant was equipped with a computerized early warning system to detect a buildup of temperature or pressure in tanks that can lead to gas leakage.

The system in place in the Bhopal plant was a "fail safe" series of devices that were to activate in case of a leak. The system consisted of a chemical scrubber system and a flare tower that incinerated gas escaping the scrubber. A water curtain, refrigeration system and spare tank were used as additional safety precautions.

A company spokesman stated that the system in Bhopal was just as effective as the computer-driven system in use at the Institute plant. The spokesman said, "What we can tell you is that everything that could have been installed . . . was installed" (*Wall Street Journal*, December 5, 1984, p. 4).

A report on the accident published in India, however, stated that at least five fail safe systems were either shut down for maintenance or failed to operate effectively when the leakage occurred. The Indian government felt that poor safety measures were responsible for the accident. They arrested six plant managers soon after the disaster. All were Indian nationals.

Previous problems with the plant prompted Union Carbide in May of 1982 to send a safety team to evaluate the effectiveness of the system in place. The 1982 report raised a number of issues with regard to safety procedures at the plant. The safety team found both personnel and equipment problems in Bhopal. They found that plant personnel received insufficient training in safe operating procedures. Training was frequently done by rote memorization without a basic understanding of the reasons behind the procedures. The safety team also found instances of maintenance personnel signing permits that they could not read.

The 1982 report raised questions "about the adequacy of the tank relief valve to relieve a runaway reaction." The report also expressed a concern about the lack of backup equipment to prevent overfilling of the tanks.

Finally, the safety team expressed concern about the high turnover rate of personnel working at the plant. They felt that people were working without gaining sufficient understanding of safe operating procedures. However, no safety experts from Carbide headquarters ever returned to the Bhopal plant to make sure that the 1982 recommendations were implemented (Gladwin & Walter, 1985).

As the death toll mounted, Carbide's reaction to the Bhopal tragedy was multi-faceted. Executives at the Danbury, Connecticut headquarters had learned from the experience of General Public Utilities Corporation, owner of the Three Mile Island nuclear generating station, and Johnson & Johnson, whose Tylenol capsules were sabotaged. They were determined not to make the mistakes made during the Three Mile Island crisis, and to react quickly as was done in the Tylenol case. A "crisis management" strategy was drawn up and implemented immediately.

First, Union Carbide chairman Warren M. Anderson decided that he and five other company officials would fly to Bhopal to direct an investigation into the disaster and to give aid to the victims. Anderson was quoted as saying, "I'm head of this company and I can't sit here and learn things second hand" (Winslow, 1984, p. 27).

He envisioned cutting through government and corporate bureaucracies to provide aid to the victims in Bhopal. Hospitals, orphanages and vocational schools would be built. "The battlegrounds of yesterday are the monuments of today" was his inspiration.

Once Anderson arrived in Bhopal, Indian officials arrested him and charged him with criminal negligence. They urged that he be deported for his own safety. He left India in less than a week.

The second action taken by Carbide management was to halt production of MIC at the Institute, West Virginia plant until an investigation determined the cause of the Bhopal disaster. Company spokespersons also stated that the Bhopal plant would not reopen if this is what Indian officials desired.

Alec Flam, president and chief operating officer, communicated over closed circuit TV, video tape, mail, telex and computer to all Union Carbide employees worldwide. He assured the employees that the company was still financially sound and it was doing everything possible to address the needs of the victims. A letter to company shareholders was also written. The letter expressed confidence that the financial structure of the company was not threatened by the incident.

Another crisis management action was a press tour of the Institute plant to explain the manufacturing process of MIC. The tour seemed to be designed to assure local residents of the safety of the plant. However, the tour raised many questions and put the company on the defensive concerning the disaster in Bhopal.

Another action taken was to assemble a small army of company communications specialists. These people were used to handle inquiries about the incident. Questions poured in from around the world, from the press, individuals, customers, and stockholders. Even with the designated communications specialists, long waits were required to get answers from the corporation.

The company also established a fund to aid victims and to start an orphanage. Carbide began with an $800,000 aid package. This emergency aid, however, was turned down by the Indian government. Indian officials called the aid "insulting." Aid from foreign governments was also rejected.

Carbide chairman Warren Anderson was not the only person to travel to Bhopal in the wake of the tragedy there. In what was described as the greatest ambulance chase in history, personal injury lawyers from across the United States descended on the hapless city. Some critics of the attorneys, including other lawyers, disapproved, calling it "unseemly." However, the lawyers who went to Bhopal said they went there at the invitation of Indian attorneys who represented victims.

Among the personal injury lawyers was the well-known attorney Melvin Belli from San Francisco. Belli held a reception for prominent citizens of Bhopal in a colonnaded courtyard at a local hotel. An Indian video crew was hired and recorded Belli's address to the crowd. He told the group, "You can't punch back at death. The only thing you can do is sue the bastards. If you want to join us, you can. If you don't, you can sue here, but you won't get nearly as much money" (Newman, 1984, p. 16).

Within a few weeks of the accident, lawsuits were filed in the United States seeking between $15–$50 billion in damages. Lawsuits were filed on behalf of the victims, families of victims, the City of Bhopal, and Union Carbide shareholders. The largest was a $50 billion class action suit charging the company with gross negligence. At the time of the accident, Union Carbide had insurance that would cover $200 million in damages.

Legal claims could be filed either in India or the United States. Both court systems use potential lifetime earnings of the victims to determine wrongful death compensation. Due to the poverty in the Bhopal area, such compensation would not be as great as if the incident had occurred in the United States. For example, the Rand Corporation conducted a study of wrongful death awards in Chicago and found an American life to be worth $500,000.

One difference between the two court systems was that punitive damages could be awarded in United States courts. Indian law did not recognize such damages. Due to the low earning potential of the victims, punitive damages could conceivably exceed compensation for loss of future earnings by a considerable amount. In addition, the Indian court system may not be equipped to handle cases of this magnitude. Accordingly, most lawsuits were consolidated into one class action suit which was filed in Federal District Court in New York. The government of India, however, sued Union Carbide separately for $1 billion.

Initially, it was feared that some surviving victims would experience permanent blindness. This seemed not to have occurred. Some had reported vision problems, but not blindness. The main problems were associated with the respiratory system, including shortness of breath, coughing and wheezing. Typical comments from victims include those of M.L. Khanna who was not able to work at his civil service job after the gas leak. "After 15 minutes of reading, I feel a tightness in my chest and head and then some sort of shivering nervousness" (Kramer, 1985, p. 18). A cart puller, Kistan Lal, had chest pains and blurred vision. "I become breathless, so I have not been able to do the same work" (Kramer, 1985, p. 18).

The death and injury toll was not known with certainty. While the official death toll inched towards 2,000, other private estimates ranged from 3,000 to 10,000. Injuries were estimated at 200,000. Since most of the victims were illiterate people living in extreme poverty, many were not aware that a death certificate needed to be filed for a victim. Instead, many victims were simply taken to a funeral pyre to be cremated. Many of those injured may simply have left the area. Since there are few if any records of these people to begin with, it is doubtful that the full extent of the disaster will ever be known.

The state of Madhya Pradesh promised a 10,000 rupee ($850) payment to survivors of each person killed and 1,000 rupees ($85) to each individual who was injured. However, by April, 1985, less than half of those who applied for survivors' benefits had been paid and only a few thousand injury payments were made. Injury payments were stopped after only a few days. Some individuals complained that most of the payments had been skimmed off by corrupt Indian officials.

The Indian national government developed a relief effort that included feeding 700,000 people, more than 75 percent of the Bhopal population. Clinics and mobile hospitals were manned by government and volunteer doctors from across India. This effort was mounted without help from foreign governments or Union Carbide.

In New York, Federal District Judge John F. Keenan, who was hearing the consolidated lawsuit, chastised Union Carbide for not providing immediate aid to the victims. He urged an interim relief package of $5 to $10 million as a matter of "fundamental human decency" (Meyer & Stewart, 1985, p. 22). Carbide responded with a $5 million relief effort.

On August 11, 1985, another problem befell Union Carbide. A chemical leaked from its Institute, West Virginia plant, injuring 135 people. Fortunately no one was killed. Another toxic chemical, aldicarb oxime, leaked into the atmosphere rather than the MIC that poisoned the air in Bhopal. OSHA conducted an investigation of the plant soon after the incident occurred.

The impending lawsuits spawned another problem for Union Carbide. Its stock price was depressed because of the potential damages that could be awarded. The price fell 28 percent, from around $48 per share to near $33 per share in a few days. It lost a total of $960.6 million in market value. This loss in share price meant that the company was vulnerable to a takeover attempt. In January of 1985, the Bass brothers of Texas acquired 5.4 percent of Carbide stock. Late in July of that same year, GAF Corporation began buying stock as well.

In an attempt to combat a takeover, Carbide instituted a number of cost savings, including elimination of 10 percent of its white collar jobs and selling several unprofitable businesses. By November, 1985, its stock price had risen to $61.25. However, by that time, GAF had increased its stake in the company to 9.9 percent.

On December 9, 1985, GAF made a $68 per share all-cash offer for Union Carbide Corporation. Carbide's assets were estimated to be worth $85 per share as an operating company and $100 per share if the company were liquidated.

Top management at Union Carbide resolved to fight the proposed takeover. They decided to buy back 55 percent of the stock outstanding. Shareholders were offered $85 per share in cash and debt securities. In addition, Carbide managers decided to sell its consumer products division. Part of the proceeds of the sale would go to the remaining shareholders in the form of a one-time dividend. GAF subsequently raised its bid to $78 per share for a total of $5.06 billion. However, this could not compete with the Carbide plan. Beaten by Union Carbide, GAF soon gave up its bid.

Over time, company executives turned skeptical with regard to both the Institute leakage and the Bhopal disaster. They felt there was a public overreaction to both events which was promoted by the media. With regard to the Institute, West Virginia leak, Chairman Anderson felt that most of the alleged victims are hypochondriacs. He was quoted as saying, "I think that if we had a release of Arpege (at the plant), 135 would go to the hospital" (Meyer & Stewart, 1985, p. 22). He felt that accounts of suffering in Bhopal were exaggerated. "By our information, there are absolutely no cases of blindness. There are probably half-dozen cornea transplant requirements" (Meyer & Stewart, 1985, p. 22).

The corporation first accepted "moral responsibility" for the gas leak in Bhopal. Their perception of the cause of the leak also changed over time. They felt that the disaster was an act of sabotage, suggesting that radical Sikhs may have been the perpetrators. However, there was not any direct evidence to support that theory.

Negotiations with attorneys representing the plaintiffs who had consolidated their cases in Federal District Court continued. In March, 1986, an agreement was reached between Union Carbide and the attorneys. The company agreed to pay $350 million to the victims. This would produce a total fund of $500-$600 million when interest payments are included. The money would be paid to victims and their families over a period of 8 to 10 years. The settlement was subject to the approval of Union Carbide directors, and U.S. District Judge John F. Keenan.

The Indian government reacted to the tentative $350 million settlement by announcing its opposition. The government said that it would contest the standing of the plaintiff's lawyers who agreed to the plan. There was speculation that the Indian government would prefer that the case be tried in India. If such a change occurred, U.S. lawyers would not receive fees since they took cases on a contingency fee basis. Indian law does not permit such a fee plan.

Soon after the announcement of the proposed settlement, OSHA announced it had completed its investigation of the Institute plant. In their report, OSHA inspectors listed 221 alleged health and safety violations at the plant. The agency proposed a $1.4 million fine against the corporation, the largest in history.

The government of India indicated that it might move against Carbide to prevent distribution of the proceeds of the sale of its consumer products businesses to stockholders. Both Indian government and private U.S. attorneys felt that such a distribution would deplete funds available to victims in Bhopal.

In May of 1986, Judge Keenan ruled that India was a more appropriate place for the cases than the United States. The legal scene shifted to India.

The Indian government sued Union Carbide in Bhopal district court in September. The government sought $3 billion in compensation for the victims of the disaster. Union Carbide argued that the disaster was caused by sabotage and that there was a conspiracy between Carbide India employees and the government to conceal evidence of the sabotage. Further, they argued that the plant was run by Union Carbide, India, Ltd. and that no US citizen had worked there for over two years before the disaster. Thus, Carbide argued that they were not liable for the damages that resulted.

As the courtroom theatrics and behind the scenes negotiations dragged on into late 1987, the case had not yet gone to trial. Bhopal District Judge M.W. Deo decided that something needed to be done to compensate the victims of the tragedy. He ordered that Carbide pay the victims $270 million in interim relief before the trial.

Judge Deo's relief order was upheld by Indian High Court Judge S.K. Seth, who reduced the amount to $190 million. This was considered one of the most extraordinary developments in the field of mass-disaster law. "In essence, the judge ruled that a defendant in a personal-injury suit can be required to pay damages to accident victims even before the defendant has been found liable at a trial." (Adler, 1988)

In his ruling, Judge Seth argued that a company that engages in a hazardous activity is "absolutely liable" for damages from an accident. The judge stated that this would be true even if the company had not been negligent in its running of the plant. Further, his ruling stated that Union Carbide had sufficient control of Carbide of India that the parent company is responsible for the accident. Thus the judge argued that the victims should get some of the money now, instead of waiting for the trial and appeals to run their course.

As Carbide lawyers continued to argue against paying interim damages, a settlement was reached. On February 14, 1989, Union Carbide directors agreed to a "full and final settlement of all claims rights, and liabilities related to and arising out of the Bhopal gas disaster." Carbide agreed to pay a settlement of $470 million.

The settlement was far less than many analysts anticipated. Assuming 200,000 is a reasonable estimate for the total number of victims in the Bhopal disaster, the agreement amounts to $2,350 per death or injury.

Case Questions

1. Should Union Carbide, as a multinational, adhere to the safety standards and environmental regulations of the U.S. or the foreign country in which the plant is located?

2. Did Union Carbide exercise enough managerial control over the plant in Bhopal? With whom did responsibility for plant safety lie?

3. Did Union Carbide act in a socially responsible way in their efforts to help the victims in Bhopal? What level of social responsibility did they attain?

4. Apply the ethical tests to Union Carbide's behavior. From your analysis, did Carbide behave in an ethical way?

5. Is the standard of lifetime earnings a desirable method of estimating the value of human life?

6. What is your opinion of Judge Seth's ruling that Union Carbide had to pay interim damages to the victims?

7. If the trail had been held in the United States, would the settlement have been different?

8. Was the agreement that was reached a fair compensation for the damages incurred?

Case References

Adler, Stephen J. "Bhopal Ruling Tests Novel Legal Theory." *The Wall Street Journal*, May 18, 1988, p. 33.

"Carbide to Settle Bhopal Claims for $350 Million," *The Wall Street Journal*, March 24, 1986, p. 3.

"Death Toll Rises From Lethal Gas at Carbide Plant," *The Wall Street Journal*, December 6, 1984, p. 2.

Gladwin, Thomas M. & Walter, Ingo. "Bhopal and the Multinationals," *The Wall Street Journal*, January 16, 1985, p. 20.

Kramer, Barry. "For Bhopal Survivors, Recovery Is Agonizing, Illnesses Are Insidious," *The Wall Street Journal*, April 1, 1985, p. 1, 18.

Lepkowski, W. "Bhopal Settlement: Carbide to Pay India $470 Million." *Chemical & Engineering News*, February 20, 1989, p. 4–5.

Meier, Barry & Winslow, Ron. "Union Carbide Faces a Difficult Challenge Without Bhopal," *The Wall Street Journal*, December 27, 1984, p. 1, 7.

Meier, Barry & Stewart, James B. "A Year After Bhopal, Union Carbide Faces a Slew of Problems," *The Wall Street Journal*, November 26, 1985, p. 1, 22.

Newman, Barry. "Death In Bhopal: Compensation Seem Not Quite the Point," *The Wall Street Journal*, December 19, 1984, p. 1, 16.

Stewart, James B. & Hertzberg, Daniel. "Outstanding Directors Led the Carbide Defense that Fended Off GAF," *The Wall Street Journal*, January 13, 1986, p. 1, 14.

Prost, Cathy. "OSHA Plans to Fine Carbide $1.4 Million, Alleges Violations at West Virginia Plant," *The Wall Street Journal*, April 2, 1986, p. 2, 16.

"Union Carbide Starts Inspecting Two U.S. Plants," *The Wall Street Journal*, December 5, 1984, p. 4.

Winslow, Ron. "Union Carbide Mobilizes Resources to Control Damage from Gas Leak," *The Wall Street Journal*, December 10, 1984, p. 27.

Winslow, Ron. "Union Carbide Confirms that Problems with Tanks in India Were Found in '82," *The Wall Street Journal*, December 11, 1984, p. 3, 16.

References

Acton, J.P., Testimony before the Committee on Energy and Commerce, U.S. House of Representatives, Washington D.C., April 21, 1993.

Bodily, Samuel E. & Gabel, H. Landis. "A New Job for Businessmen: Managing the Companies Environmental Resources." *Sloan Management Review*, Vol. 23, No. 4 (Summer), 1982, pp. 3–18.

Cabinet Task Force on Oil Import Control. *The Oil Import Question*, U.S. Government Printing Office, Washington, D.C., 1970.

Crandall, Robert W. *Controlling Industrial Pollution*, The Brookings Institution, Washington, D.C., 1983.

Crandall, Robert W. "Environmental Ignorance Is Not Bliss," *The Wall Street Journal*, April 22, 1985, p. 20.

Environmental Protection Agency. *National Air Pollutant Emission Estimates 1940–1990*. Washington, D.C., November, 1991.

Environmental Protection Agency. *Air Pollution and Your Health*, U.S. Government Printing Office, Washington, D.C., 1979.

Frederick, Kenneth D. "Water Supply," in Portney, Paul R. & Haas, Ruth B. (eds.), *Current Issues in Natural Resource Policy*, Resources for the Future, Inc., Washington, D.C., 1982.

Gujarati, Damodar. *Government and Business*, McGraw-Hill Book Company, New York, 1984.

Ibrahim, Youssef M. "A New Era in Energy May Be Commencing as OPEC Flounders," *The Wall Street Journal*, December 16, 1985, p. 1, 16.

Levin, Michael H. "Building a Better Bubble at EPA," *Regulation*, March–April, 1995, pp. 33–42.

Orloff, Neil. "Climbing the Pollution Learning Curve," *The Wall Street Journal*, November 5, 1985, p. 30.

Pashigian, B. Peter. "How Large and Small Plants Fare Under Environmental Regulation," *Regulation*, September–October, 1983, pp. 19–23.

Petzinger, Thomas, Jr. "Prices at the Gas Pump Won't Fall Soon, But Some See Sharp Declines in Late '86," *The Wall Street Journal*, January 22, 1986, p. 22.

"Plunge in Oil Prices Will Bring Benefits But Spur Trouble Too," *The Wall Street Journal*, January 22, 1986, p. 1, 22.

Singer, S. Fred. "What Is Happening to World Oil?" *The Wall Street Journal*, March 10, 1982, p. 30.

Strickland, Allyn Douglas. *Government Regulation and Business*, Houghton-Mifflin Company, Boston, 1980.

Taylor, Robert E. "Toxic-Waste Cleanup Is Expensive and Slow and Tough to Achieve," *The Wall Street Journal*, May 16, 1985, p. 1, 16.

Taylor, Robert E. "EPA's Chief Is Said to Have Endorsed Expanding Air-Pollution 'Bubble' Policy," *The Wall Street Journal*, March 7, 1985, p. 4.

Thurow, Lester C. *The Zero-Sum Society*, Penguin Books, Inc., New York, 1981.

Tramontozzi, Paul N. *Regulatory Cutbacks Resume: Reagan's 1986 Plan for the Regulatory Agencies*, Center for the Study of American Business, Washington University, St. Louis, Mo., April, 1984.

Weidenbaum, Murray L. *Business and Government in the Global Marketplace*, 5th Edition, Prentice-Hall, Inc., Englewood Cliffs, N.J., 1995.

CHAPTER 8

REGULATION OF MARKETS AND COMPETITION

In Chapter 2, the nature of free, competitive markets was discussed. It was shown how the marketplace allocates resources to the production of goods and services so that consumer preferences and valuations are exactly met. The price that is determined in a free, competitive market reflects consumers' value of a product and the cost of producing it.

But what happens if markets are not free? What happens if small amounts of market power become very large? What are the distortions that are introduced? What should be the role of government in attempting to assure that markets are competitive (or at least act like it)? What has government done to regulate markets and competition? How well have these attempts to correct for the distortions in these markets actually worked? How are the antitrust laws and regulations enforced?

Regulation of markets and competition is the subject of this chapter. The characteristics of markets which are structured with few competitors are discussed. These include monopoly, oligopoly, and contestable markets. Various anti-competitive behaviors that may occur in such markets are examined including cartels, price fixing, price leadership and predatory pricing.

The chapter then discusses the government's response to such market structures. This response has been almost exclusively through the use of government regulation. Key provisions of the federal anti-trust laws and their enforcement are presented. Three anti-trust laws serve as the basis for the federal government's response. These are the Sherman Act, the Clayton Act and the Federal Trade Commission Act. Each will be discussed in turn.

The globalization of industry places new demands on anti-trust enforcement and provides opportunities for new entry into markets with few competitors. In addition, many of the provisions of the antitrust laws are felt to be outdated and in need of reform. This is the subject of the last part of this chapter.

Monopoly

A monopoly is a single seller of a good or service. Unlike a competitor in a free market, monopolists have control over both price and output. A profit-maximizing monopolist will not charge any price, however. There is a specific price-quantity combination that optimizes the monopolist's profit potential. However, price will be higher than if the good or service were provided by a free, competitive market and the quantity of output will be less.

A model of a monopoly market is shown in Figure 8.1. In a competitive marketplace, price and quantity are determined by the forces of supply and demand. If the good or service in question were produced in such a competitive market, the quantity Q_c would be produced and sold at a price of P_c. The monopolist, however, does not equate supply and demand as in a competitive market to determine price and quantity. Instead, the monopolist equates marginal revenue to marginal cost.

Marginal revenue can be defined as:

The additional revenue to be derived by selling one more unit of the good or service.

In a purely competitive marketplace, price is determined by the forces of supply and demand. Each supplier's decisions to produce more or less do not perceptively affect the market price. A monopolist's decisions to sell more or less, however, do affect the market price. Rather than accept price as given, the monopolist faces the downward sloping demand curve labeled D in the figure. Each additional unit of output must be sold at a correspondingly lower price. The monopolist must assess the additional revenue to be derived from selling one more unit of the product.

The line labeled *MR* is the monopolist's marginal revenue curve. It shows the additional revenue that the monopolist would derive from selling one more unit of the good or service. When a monopolist sells more of a good or service, it must be sold at a lower price, in order to clear the market. Further, unless the monopolist practices price discrimination in which different units are sold at different prices, all units of the good or service must be sold at that lower price. The marginal revenue curve shows the additional revenue to be obtained, given that all units must be sold at the lower price.

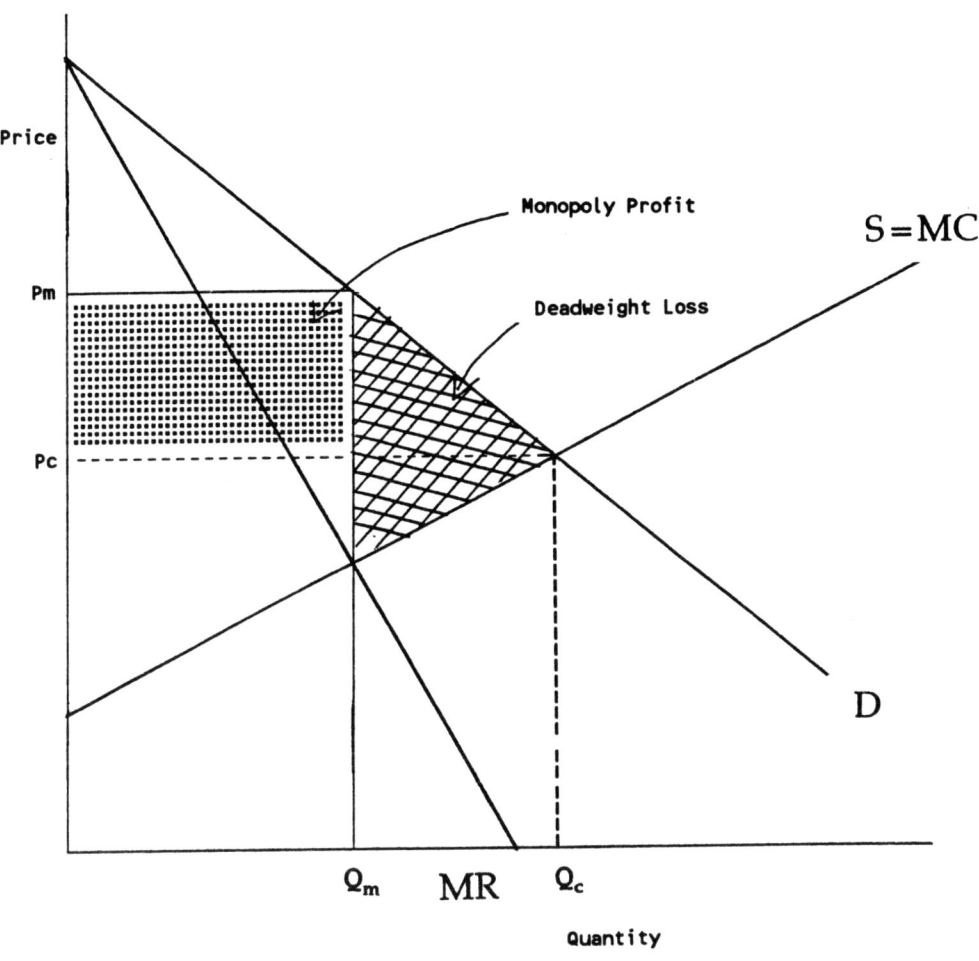

Figure 8.1. The Social Waste of Monopoly

Marginal revenue can be negative. In that case, additional units can only be sold at such a reduction in price that total revenues will actually fall, since all units must be sold at the lower price.

In order to maximize profits, the monopolist equates marginal cost to marginal revenue and produces a quantity of Q_m. Marginal cost is the additional or extra cost incurred in producing one more unit of the good or service. If the marginal revenue to be derived from producing one more unit is greater than the marginal costs incurred, then profits will increase through increased production. On the other hand, if the marginal or additional costs incurred are greater than the marginal or additional revenues obtained, then profits will fall if that extra unit is produced. Only where marginal revenue is exactly equal to marginal cost will profits be maximized.

The monopolist, however, does not charge the competitive, market clearing price P_c. Instead, the monopolist uses knowledge of demand to determine the price to charge. This is P_m in the figure. Two results are readily apparent from this analysis. One is that monopoly output is less than what a competitive market would produce (Q_m versus Q_c). Second, monopoly prices are higher than if the good or service were produced in a competitive marketplace (P_m versus P_c).

Higher prices and lower output are not the entire story, however. There are also redistribution and efficiency effects. By being able to charge a higher price for the product, the monopolist reaps a certain amount of monopoly profit. This is represented by the shaded area in Figure 8.1. It is the difference in price, P_c -P_m times the quantity of output produced Q_m. If a competitive market would have produced the good or service in question, this amount would not be paid by consumers. Instead, it is transferred from consumers to the monopolist. It is a *redistributional* effect of monopoly power.

The *efficiency* effect concerns a loss to both consumers and producers that is not transferred from one group to another. To understand this effect, it is necessary to introduce the concept of the *consumers' surplus*. The demand curve shows the different quantities of a good or service which consumers are willing and able to purchase at each and every possible price. Consumers do not have to purchase each separate unit of a good or service at a different price. Consumers pay one price, the market price. The difference between the set of prices consumers are willing and able to pay and what is actually paid is the Consumers' Surplus. In a competitive market, the Consumers' Surplus is the area under the demand curve whose lower bound is the competitive price P_c in Figure 8.1.

The monopolist is able to extract part of the Consumers' Surplus in the form of monopoly profit. This is the shaded area in the figure. However, part of the surplus is not transferred to the monopolist and is not kept by the consumer. This loss in Consumers' Surplus is part of the efficiency loss of monopoly. This loss is represented by the cross-hatched area above the price line P_c in the figure.

There is also an efficiency loss to producers. Since the monopolist produces less output than what would be produced in a competitive market, the profits to be derived from greater production are lost. This loss in *producers' surplus* is represented by the cross-hatched area below the price line P_c in the figure.

The efficiency loss caused by monopoly is the combination of the loss in consumers' surplus and the loss in producers' surplus. This is called the *deadweight loss* of monopoly. The deadweight loss is the net value of lost production because of monopoly. In Figure 8.1, it is depicted as all of the cross-hatched area.

In summary, the social waste of monopoly consists of the following:

1. Monopoly prices tend to be higher than goods and services produced in a competitive marketplace.

2. Monopolies produce less output than would be produced in a competitive industry.

3. A transfer of income occurs from consumers to the monopolist in the form of monopoly profits.

4. A social efficiency loss occurs, which is called the deadweight loss. This is a combination of the loss in consumers' surplus and loss in producers' surplus. It is the value of lost production.

Social Waste in Practice

What has the experience been with respect to monopoly power? Have the different elements of social waste of monopoly been observed in practice? One important piece of information can be obtained from industries in which a great deal of monopoly power was present and the firms were first regulated then deregulated.

A good example is the airline industry. Since deregulation, and with the advent of competition on many routes, fares have fallen an average of 11 to 30 percent. However, in cities where one airline exercises a great deal of monopoly power, such as the case of Pittsburgh with USAir, fares are substantially higher. For example, in the summer of 1996, a round trip fare to Pittsburgh from Chicago with a stay over Saturday night was $586, while the cost of the same round trip to Cleveland from Chicago was $145. (Pittsburgh is about 100 miles from Cleveland).

The breakup of ATT&T was followed by a massive influx of new technologies and new services, which were unavailable when ATT&T held the monopoly in telecommunications in the US. This includes wireless communications, data transmission, teleconferencing, etc. Would such technologies be available if an AT&T monopoly were allowed to continue? Possibly, but the incentives for new companies to experiment, innovate and invent would not be there.

A monopoly AT&T whose hands were tied by government regulation may have been able to implement such technological change, but at a much slower pace. Today, we are a long way from the single black rotary dial phone which was the standard for the industry prior to the divestiture of ATT&T. The Telecommunications Reform Act of 1996 which allows competition among cable, telephone, wireless and satellite is poised to have an even more startling impact on this industry.

But how about profits? Many studies of industries in which there is a great deal of market concentration reveal that there is no general pattern of high profits and high rates of return. Is the theory of monopoly wrong on this account? There are several reasons to expect that this is not the case.

One is that monopolists must frequently employ resources to erect barriers to entry to keep competitors out of the industry. This may involve pricing, or coercive activities. In addition, where barriers are created through government franchise, the monopolist must spend considerable time, effort and money in lobbying the government to maintain this exclusive arrangement. For example, when it was heavily regulated by the Interstate Commerce Commission, the trucking industry spent considerable effort to influence the ICC to not grant licenses to other trucking firms to allow them to carry goods in competition with the existing firms in the industry.

Second, monopoly profits may be spent on purchase of an exclusive government franchise. For example, in many cities, the number of taxicab medallions, which are licenses to operate one cab, are fixed by government regulation. Fixing the number of medallions in turn fixes the number of cabs that can operate. These medallions are then traded in the marketplace. In Chicago in 1996, such a medallion had a market value of $35,000. The cost in New York was over $150,000!

Third, some of the profits may be paid to those who work for companies having monopoly power. Professional sports is a classic example. The system in professional sports is for the league to grant a franchise to a person or group of people to operate a sports team in a given city. Larger cities may have more than one franchise. The franchise grants the team a monopoly in that city. No independent group can operate a new franchise in that city without the approval of the owners of the existing league franchises.

The enormous revenues generated by sports teams through ticket sales, TV, concessions and team related goods do not all go to increasing the profits of the owners. Much of the revenues become part of the escalating wages paid to baseball, basketball and football players. No doubt, some players, such as Michael Jordan, possess talents that could justify the high salaries. However, there are many .230 hitters in baseball making multi-million dollar salaries. A strong dose of market competition would fragment the revenue base and no doubt lead to lower salaries and in the end lower prices paid by fans.

Finally, monopolists can spend some or all of their monopoly profits seeking the good life. It takes much effort to keep costs down, increase productivity, and adopt new technologies. Instead, the monopolist can relax, take it easy and not expend the emotional effort and trauma that it takes to make a business a well-oiled machine. Part of the monopoly profits can be spent in seeking the good life of relaxation, low stress and inefficient production.

Government Monopolies

Although much has been written in various textbooks about private monopolies, there is a sparse literature concerning the behavior of monopolies operated by the public sector. Yet, many public services including public transit, the post office and public education operate in markets sheltered from competition to one degree or another. In Chapter 3, a number of problems of government involvement in the economy were enumerated. These include the unintended effects of government action, the tendency for programs to serve special interests at the expense of the public interest, the incentive to implement benefits first-costs later programs, and the paucity of incentives for government programs to be implemented in an efficient manner.

With government run monopolies, we have the problems of government action coupled with the social waste of private monopoly. The lack of incentives for government programs to be implemented efficiently along with the tendency for monopolists to seek the good life almost assures inefficient production and lack of customer service orientation. In essence, such an arrangement is the worst of all possible worlds. It is no wonder that those industries consistently in trouble tend to be government run monopolies.

Oligopoly

An oligopoly is an industry in which there are only a few firms. Businesses are large enough so that decisions to expand or contract output will affect the market price. Such an industry may be dominated by a few firms, with many smaller followers, or the entire industry may be comprised of only a few large companies. The U.S. automobile industry in the 1950's and 60's is a classic example of an oligopoly. General Motors accounted for over 50 percent of domestic production, with the remainder of the industry consisting of Ford, Chrysler, and the now defunct American Motors. Other examples are the steel and aluminum industries.

An oligopolistic industry is characterized by mutual interdependence of decision making. That is, firms cannot act on their own, but must take their rival's response into account. Decisions to produce more or less, to improve products or services, or to alter price must all take into account what the other firms in the industry will do in response.

As an example, suppose a firm in an oligopolistic industry is considering lowering prices in order to gain market share. What will be the reaction of the other firms in the industry? If the other firms lower their prices also, then everyone sells the product at a lower price. Market shares will stay the same. Profits for the entire industry may fall.

On the other hand, if rivals in the industry don't follow and keep their prices high, then the firm that lowered its prices will gain market share at the expense of the others. Its profits may increase.

Suppose, instead, that a firm in the industry is considering increasing prices. If the industry participants follow, then everyone will experience an increase in profits, and market shares will stay the same. On the other hand, if the rest of the industry does not increase its prices, the company that increased prices loses market share to others. The oligopolist's dilemma is shown in Table 8.1.

The ultimate impact of a firm's actions to raise or lower price is dependent on what other firms do in response. There are dangers involved in unilateral action in an oligopolistic industry. The firm can lose market share, and lose profits. A price war may also ensue, if price decreases are matched by competitors. Thus, there is little to gain and much to lose for the individual oligopolist to raise or lower prices.

Table 8.1 The Oligopolist's Dilemma

		A Typical Oligopoly Firm	
		Decrease Price	Increase Price
Rest of the Industry	Follow	o Market Share Same o Profits Fall	o Market Share Same o Profits Rise
	Don't Follow	o Gain Market Share o Profits Rise	o Lose Market Share o Profits Fall

For these reasons, oligopolistic markets tend to exhibit fairly rigid prices. Many oligopolists follow "don't upset the apple cart policies" and do nothing. This does not mean that prices and output decisions are completely inflexible. Prices, for example, may change when significant and mutually applicable cost changes occur across the industry. For example, in automobiles, if wages increase across the industry, all firms may raise price simultaneously. As another example, in the spring and summer of 1996, oil prices increased substantially. This was caused by a variety of factors including an exceptionally cold winter that depleted heating oil supplies. Gasoline prices were increased by all firms in the industry, almost in lock-step.

Price Leadership

Because of the potential rigidity of prices in oligopolistic industries, a variety of industry responses have developed. One industry response is *price leadership*. This is a situation in which one firm serves as the leader for the industry. If the price leader raises prices, industry participants follow. If the price leader lowers prices, others follow. There is no collusion involved, just a follow-the-leader attitude that evolves. The steel industry is a classic example. During the 1950's through the 1970's US Steel was the price leader. Whenever it raised or lowered prices, the rest of the industry followed. Such price leadership also seems to be the case in the automobile industry today, but it is not clear that any one firm serves as the leader. Rather, leadership responsibility seems to be shared.

Cartels

Another response to rigidity of prices in oligopolistic industries is for firms to get together and fix prices. When industry participants agree to fix prices and share the market, they have formed a *cartel*. Cartels are illegal in the United States. The best known cartel is the Organization of Petroleum Exporting Countries (OPEC), the oil cartel. In its heyday, OPEC was able to exert a great deal of leverage over the price of oil, although primarily through production cut-backs on the part of Saudi Arabia. Since cartels cannot enforce their agreements, unless government regulation is present, cheating frequently occurs. This results in the cartel agreement collapsing and in many cases price wars ensuing. This may lead to the reestablishment of the cartel agreement.

One of the more notorious cartel agreements occurred in the electric power switching industry in the 1950's. Part of the agreement concerned price fixing in sealed bid competitions for government contracts. Each bidder was assigned a predetermined share of the market based on their previous market share. For example, General Electric was assigned a 40.3 percent share, while Allis-Chalmers was assigned 8.8 percent (Scherer, 1980). The agreement allowed a particular firm to be low bidder on their percent share of the business. The problem for the cartel members was to design a bidding system, so that low bidders would seemingly "win" bids in an apparently random fashion.

Justice Department investigators felt that there might be illegal price fixing occurring, but they were initially unable to determine how the low bidder was designated. On the surface, the pattern of low bids for power switching equipment seemed to be random. The big breakthrough in the case was the discovery of how low bids were determined. The conspirators had used the phases of the moon to assign low bid status. Once this "phases of the moon" system was discovered, the pattern of low bids became readily apparent.

It is not necessary for firms to meet secretly to fix prices. In fact, no tacit agreement or secret meeting in smoke filled rooms is necessary, as the price fixing among big airlines in the 1990's demonstrates. The airlines were accused of using computerized fare information systems to send each other signals of impending fare changes and whether the change would be matched by competitors. Anne Bingaman, assistant attorney general for antitrust stated that the airlines used the ". . . fare dissemination system to carry on conversations just as direct and detailed as those traditionally conducted by conspirators over the telephone or in hotel rooms. Although their method was novel, their conduct amounted to price fixing, plain and simple" (Davidson, 1994, p. A2).

A former Bush administration antitrust official, J. Mark Gidley noted that the case took antitrust into the high tech era, with price fixing made with computers (Davidson, 1994, p. A2). After settling with the Justice Department, however, the airlines still were able to signal price increases. Instead of high tech electronic signals, they raised fares during slow periods such as on weekends. If everyone went along, the price increase would stick. If not, the price hike would be rescinded on Monday. "The process may not be as smooth as electronic signals, but the effect is the same" (Davidson, 1994, p. A2).

Contestable Markets

Contestable markets are those in which potential competitors can easily enter. This potential competition may be enough to keep prices low, even if there are few actual producers in the industry or market. Industries that would appear to be highly concentrated may actually be quite competitive because of this threat of potential entry. It is argued that in some industries, capital and other inputs to the production process is quite mobile. Potential entrants can engage in "hit and run" entry if prices are abnormally high. This keeps a lid on prices since firms currently in the market would not want to raise prices and invite new entry.

One example of a contestable market is the airline industry. Aircraft can be easily moved to different locations depending upon the possible profits to be made. In addition, the costs of starting up a new airline are low since aircraft, maintenance and other services can be leased. This keeps prices low because of fear of entry. However, Wilson (1993) argues that potential barriers to entry may exist at some airports because of gate and landing restrictions. Thus, some markets may not truly be contestable as the example of Pittsburgh mentioned earlier in the chapter illustrates.

Another example of a contestable market is the private bus industry. The private transit industry probably comes closest to a "contestable" market than most any other industry. This is especially the case when competitive contracting with public sector agencies is implemented in a metropolitan area. With mobile capital, competitors can easily move equipment from one metropolitan area to another. The Olympics held in Atlanta in 1996 relied heavily on private buses and drivers from all over the country. Public transit agencies contracting with private operators are able to switch easily among competitors. Thus, prices tend to be low in this industry because of the threat of potential competition.

Sources of Market Power

There are a variety of reasons why firms may have a certain degree of market power. These sources of market power can occur because of the nature of the production process, through government action or through actions of a particular organization. Such power can vary from a minimal sheltering from competition to pure monopoly. Each involves the creation of some type of barrier to entry from potential competitors.

Almost every firm has to some extent a portion of the market that is sheltered from competition. Indeed, the essence of strategic planning is to create a competitive advantage over other firms that may involve development of a partially sheltered market. However, such competitive advantage is fleeting unless one or more of the sources of market power are present.

Natural Monopoly

A natural monopoly is a situation in which the nature of the production process results in only one firm being able to provide the good or service in an efficient manner. More than one firm in the market would involve higher costs of production. If more than one firm provides the good or service, market forces will result in the eventual elimination of all but one competitor. Classic examples of natural monopolies include public utilities such as electricity, natural gas, water and sewage.

In the case of public utilities, if two water companies or gas companies existed, for example, then parallel gas and water lines would have to be built. This would involve duplication of service and higher costs. Natural gas or water utilities must incur substantial fixed costs to build a distribution network. These fixed costs can be spread over larger numbers of users if only one firm exists in the industry. This need to spread large fixed costs over greater numbers of users leads to mergers, price wars, etc., to capture as much of the competition's customers as possible, until only one firm is left.

The production process can change with changes in technology. This is the case in the telecommunications industry where cable TV and local telephone service were thought to be natural monopolies. Technological change has resulted in this industry becoming potentially much more competitive with wireless services competing with phone and cable services. This potential competition was recognized by Congress when it passed the Telecommunications Reform Act of 1996 that allows competition among these previously thought to be natural monopolies.

Patents and Copyrights

A patent gives an inventor an exclusive right to control the product for 17 years. A copyright usually deals with written materials, movies, and other electronic communications. The copyright gives the holder an exclusive right to reproduce the work. Patents and copyrights have been the building blocks of many companies such as DuPont in chemicals, Intel in computer chips, and Disney in entertainment.

Ownership of Scarce Resources

If one firm owns practically all the raw materials used to produce a good or service, then no other company can enter the industry. During the early 1900's, ALCOA owned almost all the bauxite reserves in the world. Its holdings were estimated to constitute 90 percent of the known reserves at the time. Bauxite is the raw material used to produce aluminum. Through its reserves, and other means, ALCOA was able to sell 90 percent of the virgin aluminum consumed in the United States (Lanzillotti, 1965a).

Government Regulation

If market forces cannot create barriers to entry for competitors, the government can be used to create them. This was the approach taken by the trucking industry when it was regulated by the ICC. A certificate of public convenience and necessity was required in order to haul goods for hire in interstate commerce. This certificate could only be obtained from the ICC through a very difficult, time consuming and costly process.

The post office was concerned about competition from the free enterprise pony express system. So the express statutes were passed by Congress in the 1880's making it illegal for anyone except the post office to deliver the mail. The post office's monopoly on mail service continues to this day.

Mergers and Acquisitions

Another approach to develop market power is to acquire it through mergers and acquisitions of competitors. This was the approach taken in the early 1900's with the formation of General Motors. General Motors was developed through a series of acquisitions of smaller automobile and accessory companies. These included Buick, Cadillac, Oldsmobile, and the Chevrolet Motor Company. It even tried to buy Ford, but was unsuccessful. By 1931, GM controlled 43 percent of the U.S. automobile market. Its share had grown to over 50 percent of the market by 1956. In that year, the Big Three of GM, Ford and Chrysler accounted for 94.7 percent of new car sales in the United States (Lanzillotti, 1965b).

Evidence at the time concerning optimum plant size in the automobile industry indicated that General Motors was five to ten times the size needed for optimum efficiency. Yet the Justice Department did not attempt to break up GM into a number of smaller companies.

No doubt GM and the other members of the Big Three spent some of their market power in seeking the good life mentioned earlier. Models began to look more and more alike. The industry was accused of shoddy workmanship by consumers and the media. Ralph Nader's book *Unsafe At Any Speed* documented the safety problems of the Corvair. GM was discovered to have used Chevrolet engines in some Oldsmobiles, without informing the buyers. The entire industry was accused of a lack of innovation, high prices and poor quality.

Market power does not last, however, unless substantial barriers to entry are present. This was not the case in the automobile industry. The problems in the industry created opportunities for Japanese and other foreign manufacturers to enter the U.S. market. Today, not only do the Big Three survive, but have been joined by Toyota, Mitsubishi, Honda, Subaru, Nissan, Volkswagen, etc. One of the most popular models in the mid 1990's was the Accord, made by Honda Motors. Although it took many years, market forces have done to the automobile industry what a Justice Department suit could have done years ago.

Collusion Among Firms

Market power can also be enhanced through collusion among firms. This is, of course, illegal in the United States. Price fixing and market sharing agreements among firms do not last, however. There are incentives for firms to cheat on these agreements. Cheating eventually becomes widespread. Unless enforced through government regulation, market forces eventually cause these agreements to collapse. A good example was the railroad industry of the late 1800's which was discussed in Chapter 6. The railroads attempted to fix prices through pricing pools. These agreements frequently broke down as secret rebates and other forms of cheating became widespread.

Predatory Pricing

Predatory pricing is the notion that a firm which seeks monopoly power can do so by eliminating competitors through very low prices. It is pricing the product so low that competitors cannot match the price without sustaining losses. Eventually, the predatory pricing drives these less capital rich competitors out of business, leaving only one firm in the industry who is free to raise prices and extract monopoly profits.

The problem with the notion of predatory pricing is that any firm which attempted to eliminate current competitors must also eliminate future competitors as well. If there are few barriers to entry to an industry, predatory pricing, if tried, will only lead to low prices for consumers.

This is not to say that firms have not tried to eliminate their competitors through pricing. Such tactics, however, tend to be self defeating in the absence of entry barriers. Of course, there are many instances of companies practicing low pricing in attempts to gain market share or enter new markets. Many of these attempts tend to be futile, as market shares return to previous levels when prices return to normal.

Geography

Market power is also bestowed on firms because of their location. The single gas station or country store in an isolated area has a great deal of market power over the few people who are its customers, because the nearest competitor may be many miles away. Thus, geography plays a role in sheltering markets from competition. While an industry may look very competitive on a national basis, closer examination at the regional or local level may reveal this not to be the case. Within certain regions, there may be few competitors, even though the industry as a whole is comprised of many firms.

Measures of Industrial Concentration

How concentrated is industry in the United States? Are most industries highly concentrated with a great deal of market power exercised by a few firms, or does American industry come closer to the purely competitive model discussed in Chapter 2?

In order to shed some light on this question, two measures of market power are shown for a variety of industries in the US. These measures are used by the Justice Department to examine potential market concentration.

Table 8.2 Measures of Market Concentration for Major Manufacturing Industry Groups

SIC code	Major group[1]	Companies[2] (number)	Total (million dollars)	Value of shipments[3] Percent accounted for by[4]— 4 largest companies	8 largest companies	20 largest companies	50 largest companies	Herfindahl-Hirschman Index for 50 largest companies[5]
	All Industries	310 341	2 475 901.0	9	12	18	27	36
20	Food and kindred products	15 692	329 725.4	11	18	32	47	68
21	Tobacco products	98	20 757.1	82	94	99	99+	2 345
22	Textile mill products	4 982	62 786.4	15	25	38	52	113
23	Apparel and other textile products	21 301	64 242.6	10	14	20	29	36
24	Lumber and wood products	32 014	69 746.7	11	16	23	31	45
25	Furniture and fixtures	10 775	37 461	10	15	25	36	47
26	Paper and allied products	4 215	106 968.7	18	30	52	68	172
27	Printing and publishing	57 376	136 195.6	7	13	23	34	34
28	Chemicals and allied products	8 313	229 546.1	14	21	34	53	97
29	Petroleum and coal products	1 320	130 414.0	30	49	72	89	375
30	Rubber and miscellaneous plastics products	12 149	86 634.3	9	13	21	31	46
31	Leather and leather products	1 965	9 082.4	13	21	38	55	95
32	Stone, clay, and glass products	12 682	61 476.6	11	18	30	41	62
33	Primary metal industries	5 400	120 249.2	17	26	41	55	121
34	Fabricated metal products	32 470	147 306.1	9	13	18	26	33
35	Industrial machinery and equipment	48 900	217 669.9	13	17	26	37	70
36	Electronic and other electric equipment	13 523	171 266.4	19	27	39	52	129
37	Transportation equipment	9 158	332 935.7	52	64	76	85	1 044
38	Instruments and related products	8 962	107 324.8	19	28	44	60	150
39	Miscellaneous manufacturing industries	16 082	32 012.0	6	10	16	25	19

Source: US Department of Commerce, Bureau of the Census, 1987 Census of Manufacturers: Concentration Ratios in Manufacturing. Washington, D.C., pp. 6–4 to 6–42

Concentration Ratios

One measure of the market power in an industry is the *concentration ratio*. This is a measure of the percent of sales or other measure of output accounted for by the 4 largest, 8 largest, 20 largest, and 50 largest companies in the industry. If only a few firms sell a very large proportion of an industry's output, then the industry is deemed to be highly concentrated. Conversely, if the largest firms produce only a small part of the industry's output, then the industry is considered not to be highly concentrated and market power is thought to be low.

Concentration ratios for major manufacturing industry groups in the United States are shown in Table 8.2. Manufacturing industries are classified by *SIC Code*. This is the *Standard Industrial Classification Code* which was developed by the U.S. Department of Commerce. It is a method of classifying firms based on the major products produced.

As can be seen in Table 8.2, for all manufacturing, the four largest companies shipped nine percent of total shipments, while the eight largest shipped 12 percent. However, concentration ratios for major industry groups vary widely. Heavily concentrated industries include tobacco products, petroleum and coal products, and transportation equipment. The industries with low concentration ratios include food and kindred products, printing and publishing, rubber and miscellaneous plastics products, and fabricated metal products.

One problem with the concentration ratios shown in Table 8.2 is that the major industry groups are so broad that many firms which may not compete with each other are included in the same group. For example, the Sic Code 23-Apparel and other textile products seems to be quite unconcentrated. But this industry includes producers of men's and boys suits and coats where the 4 largest firms produce 34 percent of the output, and men's and boy's underwear and nightwear where the four largest firms produce 58 percent of the total shipments. Thus, the degree of concentration of American industry may be underestimated when major industry groups are examined.

The major industry groupings shown in Table 8.2 are at the two digit SIC code. The code is designed so that more specific industries are coded at the three digit and four digit level. Thus, apparel and other

Table 8.3 Measures of Market Concentration for Four Digit SIC Industry Groups

SIC Code	Industry	Companies (Number)	Total Value of Shipments (Millions of $)	Percent of Shipments Accounted for by			
				4 Largest Companies	8 Largest Companies	20 Largest Companies	50 Largest Companies
2011	Meat Packing Plants	1328	5266.9	32	50	66	80
2022	Cheese	508	12971	43	55	68	82
2211	Broadwoven Fabric Mills, Cotton	246	5508.3	42	59	81	96
2231	Broadwoven Fabric Mills, Wool	106	1050.7	55	68	87	97
2311	Men's and Boy's Suits and Coats	285	2863.3	34	47	64	82
2322	Men's and Boy's Underwear	71	1045.4	58	73	92	99
2451	Mobile Homes	207	4102.4	30	44	65	84
2512	Upholstered Household Furniture	1030	5263.1	24	35	51	66
2621	Paper Mills	122	28918	33	50	78	94
2841	Soap and Other Detergents	683	11558.5	65	76	84	89
3523	Farm Machinery and Equipment	1576	6879.9	45	52	60	69
3524	Lawn and Garden Equipmnet	149	4594.4	52	71	92	98
3632	Refrigerators and Freezers	40	3518.9	85	98	99	100
3635	Household Vacuum Cleaners	28	1324.2	69	90	99	100
3641	Electric Lamp Bulbs and Tubes	93	3096.7	91	94	98	99
3651	Audio and Video Equipment	360	5911.2	39	59	81	92
3711	Motor Vehicles and Car Bodies	352	133345.6	90	95	99	99
3713	Truck and Bus Bodies	657	4588.7	29	37	51	68
3743	Railroad Equipment	150	2470.9	52	71	88	96
3861	Photo Equipment and Supplies	717	19240.5	77	84	90	94
3873	Watches, Clocks and Parts	213	1220.9	45	60	80	94
3911	Jewelry, Precious Metal	2294	4078.1	12	18	30	45

Source: US Department of Commerce, Bureau of the Census,
1987 Census of Manufacturers: Concentration Ratios in Manufacturing.
Washington, D.C., pp. 6–4 to 6–42

textile products are classified at the two digit level - SIC code 23, while men's and boys suits and coats are assigned SIC code 2311, and men's and boy's underwear and nightwear are assigned the four digit code 2322.

Concentration ratios for a selection of industries classified at the four digit SIC code level are shown in Table 8.3. As can be seen from the table, concentration ratios are much higher for industries classified at the more specific, four digit SIC code. The percent of shipments for the four largest companies varies from 12 percent for SIC 3911 - Jewelry, Precious Metal to 90 percent for SIC 3711 - Motor Vehicles and Car Bodies.

The Herfindahl-Hirschman Index (HHI)

Another measure used by the Justice Department to gauge the market concentration of an industry is the Herfindahl-Hirschman Index or HHI. Changes in this index are used to determine whether a proposed merger will result in excessive market concentration in an industry. The greater the value of the index, the more concentrated an industry is thought to be. The index sums the square of the market share of each firm in an industry. The index is defined as:

$$HHI = \sum S_i^2$$

where S_i is the market share of firm i in the industry under consideration.

For example, suppose there are five firms in an industry as shown in Table 8.4. The largest firm has a 30 percent market share, while the smallest has a 10 percent share. The table shows how the HHI is calculated by squaring, then summing the market shares. HHI is 2250 in this case.

Table 8.4 Calculation of HHI

Firm	Market Share % S_i	Mkt Share Squared S_i^2	Firms 4,5 Merge-Mkt Share% S_i	New Mkt Share Sq. S_i^2
1	30	900	30	900
2	25	625	25	625
3	20	400	20	400
4	15	225	25	625
5	10	100	--	
HHI		2250		2550

Suppose firms 4 and 5 merge. Then their combined market share is 25 percent. HHI is recalculated in the last column and is 2550. The index rose by 300 points through the merger.

The U.S. Justice Department uses the index as one means of deciding whether to oppose a proposed merger in court. Generally, it is felt that if the value of HHI is 1,000 or less, then the market is unconcentrated. This is indicative of having at least 10 equal sized firms in the industry. Moderately concentrated markets are considered those with values between 1,000 and 1,800. Highly concentrated industries have index values over 1,800. Mergers will be challenged if more than 100 points are added to the index. The merger probably will not be challenged if less than 50 points are added to the index (Corley, Reed and Shedd, 1990). The last column of Table 8.2 shows the HHI calculated for the 50 largest companies in major industry groups in the United States.

Federal Antitrust Policy

As the industrial revolution spread in the latter half of the nineteenth century, problems arose regarding the concentration of economic activity. One of the problems of the time was the creation of the great trusts such as the Standard Oil Trust founded by John D. Rockfeller in 1882. In its heyday, the Trust controlled approximately 90 percent of the U.S. petroleum industry.

The steel industry was also heavily concentrated with U.S. Steel Corporation controlling 65 percent of the steel capacity of the country. The president of U.S. Steel was Judge Elbert H. Gary. Judge Gary conducted periodic dinners known as the "Gary Dinners" where his guests were representatives of 90 percent of the steel industry. Judge Gary urged the guests to follow the price leadership of U.S. Steel. "He exhorted them like a Methodist preacher at a camp meeting to follow the price leadership of U.S. Steel" (Adams, 1965, p. 146). Adams notes that the Gary dinners were a singular success and ". . . presented but another vivid illustration of Adam Smith's observation that 'people of the same trade seldom meet together, even for merriment and diversion but the conversation ends in a conspiracy against the public or in some contrivance to raise prices'" (Adams, 1956, p. 146).

The monopolies, price fixing, and conspiracies of the time prompted several states to enact antitrust laws. These were largely ineffective, due to the difficulty of enforcement across state lines. In 1890, Congress enacted the Sherman Antitrust Act, which was the first Federal statute in this field. The Sherman Act followed by three years the Act to Regulate Commerce which established the ICC and federal regulation of transportation in 1887. Since then, Congress has enacted several antitrust laws, including the Clayton Act, the Federal Trade Commission Act and the Robinson-Patman Amendments to the Clayton Act. These laws prohibit certain industry structures and behaviors that lead to anti-competitive practices or concentrations of economic power.

The Sherman Act

The Sherman Act attempts to preserve competition by prohibiting contracts, combinations, and conspiracies in restraint of trade, and monopolies and attempts to monopolize. The Act subjects the offender to fine or imprisonment, or both. As amended by the 1990 Antitrust Amendment, the Act subjects individual offenders to imprisonment and fines of up to $350,000 and corporate offenders to fines of up to $10,000,000 per violation. The Act gives the Federal district courts the power to issue injunctions restraining violations, and anyone injured by a violation is entitled to recover *triple damages*. In addition, states' attorneys general may bring suit for triple damages. The United States Justice Department and the Federal Trade Commission are responsible for enforcement.

In 1992, the Justice Department expanded enforcement of the Sherman Act to cover conduct by foreign companies. The department is concentrating on boycotts and cartels that harm U.S. exports. The department is examining conduct to determine whether it would violate the law if it occurred within the borders of the United States.

Restraint of Trade

Section 1 of the Sherman Act concerns what one author calls the Three C's of restraint of trade. These are contracts, combinations and conspiracies (Warner, 1995). Judicial interpretation has played a significant role in establishing what constitutes a violation, because the language of the section is so broad. The courts have interpreted this section to invalidate only *unreasonable* restraints of trade. The courts have used the *rule of reason test*, to determine a company's unreasonable or reasonable behavior on a case-by-case basis. Unreasonableness can be based on the nature of the contract or the surrounding circumstances that infer a restraint of trade.

Per Se Violations - The courts have ruled that certain types of restraints of trade are unreasonable by their nature, that is, *illegal per se*. The rule of reason test is not required in these cases. Unreasonableness of such restraints can be proved just by their existence. For example, the existence of a price fixing agreement among competitors is illegal per se.

Horizontal and Vertical Restraints - There are two types of restraints: horizontal and vertical. A *horizontal restraint* involves collusion among competitors at the same level in the chain of distribution. For example, an agreement among manufacturers, among wholesalers, or among retailers would be horizontal.

A *vertical restraint* involves some sort of supplier, customer relationship in the manufacturing/distribution chain. Thus, an agreement between a manufacturer and a retailer is vertical. This is sometimes called *retail price maintenance.*

Concerted Action - One person or business by itself cannot violate Section 1. An organization has the "right to deal or refuse to deal, with whomever it likes, as long as it does so independently." The concerted action requires the agreement between two or more separate firms. However, no written agreement is required to prove a conspiracy.

Price Fixing - Price fixing agreements can be horizontal or vertical. *Horizontal price fixing* is characterized by an agreement among competitors, while *vertical price fixing* arises between buyers and sellers, usually between manufacturers and retailers.

Market Allocations - *Market allocation* is a type of agreement where competitors agree not to compete in particular markets. These markets could be specific geographic areas, customers or products. All *horizontal* agreements to allocate markets are *illegal per se*. On the other hand, *vertical* restrictions can be subject to the rule of reason and in some cases they can be legitimate. For example, a manufacturer may deal with specific firms within a market area and provide exclusive franchising for its products. Examples of vertical restrictions which are legal include McDonald's, Burger King, and Boston Market.

Boycotts - The Sherman Act prohibits group boycotts where two or more firms agree not to deal with a third party. Some boycotts are illegal *per se* while others are subject to the rule of reason. Group boycotts are illegal *per se* if the group has market power.

Tying Arrangements - A tying arrangement is where the seller of a product requires the buyer to purchase a second product as a condition of the sale of the first. For example, assume that a manufacturer of computers were to require that all purchasers of its computers also buy from them all of the floppy disks to be used with the computers. The manufacturer would tie the sale of its computer to the sale of the floppy disks. Such tie in arrangements are illegal if the seller has a great deal of economic power in the marketplace, coercion is involved, and a "not insubstantial" amount of interstate commerce is involved (Corley, Reed and Shedd, 1990, p. 756). Such arrangements may violate both Section 1 of the Sherman Act and Section 3 of the Clayton Act.

Monopolization

Section 2 of the Sherman Act prohibits monopolization and attempts or conspiracies to monopolize. A firm must have either attained the monopoly power unfairly or abused that power, once attained to be in violation of Section 2. Possession of monopoly power is not considered a violation of Section 2 because a firm may have obtained such power through its competitive skills.

Section 2 prohibits both attempts to monopolize and conspiracies to monopolize. The differences between attempts to monopolize and conspiracies to monopolize are not always clear. At least two elements must exist to classify the attempt to monopolization to be a crime: there must be an attempt to create a monopoly and second, there must be a "dangerous probability" that it will succeed. There are also two aspects to conspiring to monopolize: there must be planned collective action intended to create a monopoly and the conspirators must have committed at least one overt action.

Clayton Act

The Clayton Act, was designed in 1914 "to supplement existing laws against unlawful restraints and monopolies." It was felt that the Sherman Act was inadequate and that supplementary legislation was needed. The Clayton Act was intended to stop certain trade practices before they become violations of the Sherman Act. Another purpose of the Clayton Act was to exempt labor unions and nonprofit agricultural organizations from the antitrust laws. (The Supreme Court had ruled that the Sherman Act applied to labor unions.) Only a civil action is possible under the Clayton Act. The Act deals with price discrimination, predatory pricing, tying contracts, exclusive dealing, mergers and acquisitions, and interlocking directorates.

Price Discrimination

Price discrimination is practiced when a good or service is sold at different prices to different individuals or in different markets. Differences in price cannot be explained by differences in the cost of providing service. Price discrimination is widely practiced in transportation. For example, airline fares which require Saturday night stays or advance purchase to obtain a lower fare are ways of segmenting the market and charging different prices for business versus pleasure travel.

In 1936, Congress passed a change in the Clayton Act called the Robinson-Patman amendment. The purpose of the amendment was to strengthen provisions in the Clayton Act regarding price discrimination and predatory pricing. The amendment forbids price discrimination when goods are for resale. It does not apply to sales to final customers by retailers.

The amendment was called the Chain Store Act at the time, since it was designed to prevent local grocery stores from being put out of business by big grocery chains. The chains were thought to have an unfair advantage in that they could extract large quantity discounts from suppliers, which were not available to the little stores. For example, one shopkeeper observed that the A&P sold bread at a lower price than what the small store could purchase at wholesale. Today, these same arguments are made when Wal-mart, HomeDepot, Builders' Square or another "Category Killer" moves into a community.

The Robinson-Patman amendment does not make price discrimination illegal *per se*. Rather, price differences that adversely affect competition are prohibited. The law applies to both buyers and sellers. It is illegal, according to the amendment, to receive the benefits of price discrimination as well as to practice it (Corley, Reed and Shedd, 1990).

Predatory Pricing

As was mentioned earlier, predatory pricing is the notion that firms seeking a monopoly can eliminate competitors through very low prices. The Robinson-Patman amendment made it illegal to engage in such practices. Aside from the futility of predatory pricing as a means to eliminate competition in industries in which there are few entry barriers, the courts grappled with what constitutes predatory pricing. Is it pricing below average total costs, marginal costs, fully distributed costs, or what? Today, proof of predatory pricing can be made by establishing that price is below average variable costs. However there are exceptions such as sales of perishable merchandise, liquidations, etc.

The Robinson-Patman amendment has been called the "Typhoid Mary of anti-trust" (Warner, 1995, p. 493). Its rationale has been criticized. Many economists argue that it has resulted in higher prices, encourages inefficiency and restricts new entry into markets. All of this, while offering little protection to small business. The Federal Trade Commission, which is charged with enforcing the provisions of the amendment, brings up very few cases under the act. However, the amendment still influences the pricing decisions of many corporations.

Tying Contracts and Exclusive Dealing

Section 3 of the Clayton Act prohibits tying arrangements and exclusive dealing when the effect may be to substantially lessen competition or tend to create a monopoly. This section is intended to stop anti-competitive practices before they violate the Sherman Act.

Tying arrangements, which were already discussed, have been labeled by the Supreme Court as serving "hardly any purpose beyond the suppression of competition."

Exclusive dealing arrangements are agreements by which the seller prohibits the buyer from dealing with competitors. The most common exclusive dealing arrangement is where a manufacturer prohibits a retailer from carrying the products of competitors.

Mergers

A *merger* is the acquisition of one company by another. This can be accomplished through asset purchase, stock swaps, or one firm purchasing a controlling interest in the other. The acquired company may retain its name and identity, continue to exist as a subsidiary, or cease to exist as a separate entity. Section 7 of the Clayton Act prohibits mergers that either substantially lessen competition or create a monopoly.

Mergers are usually classified as horizontal, vertical, or conglomerate, depending upon the relationship between the acquirer and the acquired company.

Horizontal mergers involve the joining of companies in the same industry. The companies may or may not be competitors. For example, the wave of mergers in the telecommunications industry involved horizontal mergers. Pacific Telesis Group (Pac-Tel) in 1996 announced a merger with SBC Communications, Inc. Pac-Tel and SBC are two of the *Baby Bells* which came into existence after the breakup of ATT&T. Pac-Tel serves California and the west, while SBC serves the southwestern United States. Two other Baby Bells also announced a merger in 1996. Nynex which serves New York and New England announced its intention to merge with Bell Atlantic which serves the eastern seaboard. In the defense industry, the merger of Lockheed with Martin-Marietta to create Lockheed-Martin is another example of a horizontal merger. In this case, the two companies were direct competitors for defense and aerospace contracts.

A *vertical merger* is where one company is the supplier of another. In the movie industry, there has been a tendency for mergers to occur in which production studios are merged with movie houses, television and other forms of distribution. For example, the merger of Time Warner, Inc. with Turner Broadcasting System, Inc. created a company capable of producing movies and TV shows and then televising them on their own cable TV channels. Disney's acquisition of the ABC television network has the same effect.

The third type of merger, the *conglomerate merger*, involves the merger of firms in different industries or firms which produce different products. Conglomerate mergers were at one time very fashionable in business. For example, in the 1970's, LTV industries acquired the Jones and Laughlin Steel Company. LTV was not a steel maker, but produced a diversified line of goods and services. General Motors purchased Electronic Data Systems (EDS), a computer firm founded by Ross Perot. The 1960's and 1970's was a period when conglomerate mania had swept American business.

The trend in business in the 1990's however, swung in exactly the opposite direction from conglomerate mergers. Managers were concerned with defining and maintaining their core business, and selling off those parts of the business not directly related to the core. Thus, General Motors spun off EDS as a separate entity. ATT&T also decided to divest itself from production of switches and other technology (Western Electric) and research (Bell Labs, now Lucent Technologies) to focus on long distance, wireless and other technologies.

Interlocking Directorates

Section 8 of the Clayton Act prohibits interlocking directorates. This is a situation in which members of the board of directors and officers of one corporation serve on the board of a competitor. Some exceptions are made if firms are capitalized at less than 10 million dollars and for certain financial institutions, among others.

Federal Trade Commission Act

The Federal Trade Commission was created by Congress in 1914 as a companion to the Clayton Act. The FTC was established as an addition to the courts for anti-trust enforcement. The FTC also enforces Section 5 of the Federal Trade Commission Act. This provision makes *Unfair Methods of Competition* illegal. An amendment to the FTC Act in 1938 also made *Unfair or Deceptive Acts or Practices in Commerce* illegal. However, the legislation did not provide a definition of unfair methods of competition and unfair or deceptive acts or practices. Thus, the FTC was left with broad powers to define these activities. Practices such as false adverting, misleading labeling, and the use of false testimonials have been declared violations by the FTC.

A summary of the behaviors and market structures covered by the US anti-trust laws is shown in Table 8.5.

The Future of Antitrust Regulations

The antitrust regulations and enforcement are not without controversy. Many provisions are outdated, unenforceable, not grounded in economic theory, or subject to very broad interpretation. For example, the Robinson-Patman amendment has been seen by many analysts as resulting in higher prices and little or no protection for small business. What is meant by unfair methods of competition, unfair or deceptive acts or practices, unreasonable restraints of trade, per se violations, etc? Many provisions are so broad and so subject to judicial and regulatory interpretation as to provide little guidance for business as to whether a specific action is a violation or not.

Table 8.5 Behaviors and Market Structures Covered by U.S. Antitrust Laws

Restraints of Trade
- Unreasonable Restraints of Trade
- Per Se Violations
- Horizontal and Vertical Restraints
- Concerted Action
- Price Fixing
- Market Allocations
- Boycotts
- Tying Arrangements

Monopolization

Price Discrimination

Predatory Pricing

Exclusive Dealing

Mergers

Interlocking Directorates

Unfair Methods of Competition

Deceptive Acts or Practices in Commerce

The globalization of industry has made many of the concepts of market concentration outdated. What is the relevant market? Is it the U.S., North America or the whole world? Industries which seem very concentrated when viewed from the standpoint of U.S. industry, seem very competitive on a world-wide basis. The automobile industry is a good example.

Many economists feel that the anti-trust laws are in dire need of overhaul. Business and industry has changed radically since the 1890's and early 1900's when the Sherman and Clayton Acts were passed. Recognition of the problems inherent in anti-trust enforcement has led the Federal Trade Commission to issue new merger guidelines.

The FTC has proposed that greater weight be placed on cost savings as a reason for mergers than previously. (The Supreme Court has been reluctant to even listen to arguments that mergers can create lower costs of production.) In addition, from the standpoint of global industry, some mergers may result in a stronger U.S. industry competing with other firms throughout the world. The FTC argues that some mergers may actually strengthen competition rather than weaken it. The FTC recommendations would:

o Give more weight to evidence of potential cost savings and how merger-related efficiencies could increase competition in an industry

o Pay more attention to competitive conduct in industries employing networks and standards such as the computer industry

o Develop guidelines that clarify and simplify antitrust policy as it relates to joint ventures (Gruley, 1996, p. A3).

Managerial Implications

Anti-trust regulations have implications throughout the business enterprise, but no managerial function is influenced to a greater extent than planning. Primarily affected is corporate level planning in which new products and markets are planned and mergers and acquisitions of other enterprises are conceived, evaluated and possibly implemented.

When a company is planning to enter a new business area, examination of the number of current and potential future competitors is necessary. Will your firm's entry result in price reductions which impact all competitors' market share? What is the current HHI for the area you are considering?

Likewise, when a firm considers a merger or acquisition, the HHI will be affected. Because of the vagueness and interpretation attached to the implementation of the anti-trust laws, a great deal of uncertainty exists as to whether a proposed merger will pass muster with the courts, the FTC and the Justice Department. As a first step, a good legal team is an essential ingredient for any proposed merger. But managers should not stop there. Meeting with regulators to discuss issues and concerns about a proposed merger can many times lead to a restructuring that will avert an anti-trust challenge.

Not only is the entire market restructured when two organizations merge or one acquires another, but each entity is reorganized. Will one company be brought into the other, losing its original identity and having its staff functions taken over by the other company, sales forces merged, etc? Or will each company retain its identity and key functions, perhaps with one centralized corporate office providing financial services for all companies? The final organization structure determines what jobs are needed in the new entity and how much change will be required to get there.

The staffing and rewarding function will be the key area to implement the change. Even before a merger takes place, the company being purchased may negotiate a benefit package for employees who lose their jobs as a result of the merger. This could include outplacement services, severance packages, programs to facilitate movement to other jobs in the new organization, and early retirement options. When a poorly performing company is acquired and downsized, although some people do lose their jobs, the others who remain have a job with a healthier organization.

Even with the best of plans, however, a variety of ethical and social responsibility issues must be dealt with. Many mergers are justified on the basis of the cost savings that may occur as duplicate systems are eliminated. However, such savings are realized through the elimination of jobs. How will this be handled? Will employees be terminated quickly, to achieve the maximum cost reductions, or will disruption of individuals' personal lives also be considered? Is a strategy in which the merger is implemented through attrition and job retraining a viable option?

Sometimes a merger results in plant, office and store closures. What will be the impact on the local community? To what extent should these effects be taken into account, both from ethical and social responsibility perspectives? Managers should use the ethics tests developed in chapter 5 and the concepts of social responsibility of chapter 4 to evaluate alternative courses of action.

The reward structure in the organization is also an important ingredient. Price fixing schemes and market allocations can result from undue pressure placed on managers to achieve unrealistic profitability objectives. The result can be short run profit maximization, but long run anti-trust problems. A rigorously enforced code of ethics that includes dealings with competitors can be helpful in providing guidance for managers in how far to go in discussing pricing and other business related issues.

The controlling function also may change after organizations are combined. Budgeting, productivity measurement, and performance appraisal systems may need to be modified to reflect the new entity. Completely new systems may be needed and personnel may need to be trained in using the new procedures. In order to reap the benefits of the merger or acquisition, it is important to implement these changes as smoothly and efficiently as possible.

Summary

A monopoly is a single seller of a good or service. Unlike a competitor in a free market, monopolists have control over both price and output. The social waste of monopoly consists of the following: Monopoly prices tend to be higher than goods and services produced in a competitive marketplace. Monopolies produce less output than would be produced in a competitive industry. A transfer of income occurs from consumers to the monopolist in the form of monopoly profits. A social efficiency loss occurs, which is called the deadweight loss. This is a combination of the loss in consumers' surplus and loss in producers' surplus.

An oligopoly is an industry in which there are only a few firms. Businesses are large enough so that decisions to expand or contract output will affect the market price. An oligopolistic industry is characterized by mutual interdependence of decision making. That is, firms cannot act on their own, but must take their rival's response into account. Because of the potential rigidity of prices in oligopolistic industries, a variety of industry responses have developed. One industry response is Price Leadership. Another response to rigidity of prices in oligopolistic industries is for firms to get together and fix prices. When industry participants agree to fix prices and share the market, they have formed a cartel. Cartels are illegal in the United States.

Contestable markets are those in which potential competitors can easily enter. This potential competition may be enough to keep prices low, even if there are few actual producers in the industry or market. Industries that would appear to be highly concentrated may actually be quite competitive because of this threat of potential entry.

There are a variety of reasons why firms may have a certain degree of market power. These sources of market power can occur because of the nature of the production process, through government action or through actions of a particular organization. Such power can vary from a minimal sheltering from competition to pure monopoly. Each involves the creation of some type of barrier to entry from potential competitors.

One measure of the market power in an industry is the Concentration Ratio. This is a measure of the percent of sales or other measure of output accounted for by the 4 largest, 8 largest, 20 largest, and 50 largest companies in the industry. Another measure used by the Justice Department to gauge the market concentration of an industry is the Herfindahl-Hirschman Index or HHI.

The Sherman Act attempts to preserve competition by prohibiting contracts, combinations, and conspiracies in restraint of trade, and monopolies and attempts to monopolize. The Clayton Act, was designed in 1914 "to supplement existing laws against unlawful restraints and monopolies." The Clayton Act was intended to stop certain trade practices before they become violations of the Sherman Act. The Act deals with price discrimination, predatory pricing, tying contracts, exclusive dealing, mergers and acquisitions, and interlocking directorates.

Questions

1. What are the social losses resulting from monopoly provision of goods and services?

2. Suppose professional football were opened up to competition so that individuals meeting certain financial criteria could start an NFL team. What would be the impact on ticket prices, salaries and team profits? Would this lead to a more socially desirable result?

3. Suppose the express statutes were repealed so that the post office would no longer have a monopoly on provision of first class mail. What impacts would this have on mail delivery?

4. One characteristic of oligopolistic industries is the tendency for price wars to occur. Explain how this could happen.

5. Price fixing is illegal in the United States. Is it unethical? Is it unethical to be involved in international price fixing agreements?

6. Choose an industry in your area. Calculate the concentration ratio and HHI for that industry. Would you classify the industry as concentrated or competitive?

7. With the globalization of industry, Federal anti-trust policy is outdated. Comment.

Key Concepts

marginal revenue

consumers' surplus

producers' surplus

deadweight loss

social waste of monopoly

price leadership

cartel

natural monopoly

predatory pricing

contestable markets

concentration ratio

SIC code

HHI

restraint of trade

monopolization

price discrimination

tying contracts and exclusive dealing

mergers

interlocking directorates

Case Analysis: The Union Pacific - Southern Pacific Railroad Merger

by Gary S. Wilson, Ph.D.
The Logistics and Transportation Management Program
Elmhurst College

Railroad Industry: An Economic Policy Overview

The railroad industry is best characterized as a "natural monopoly" since initial start-up and operations of a company require a significant investment in terminals, equipment and trackage. Because there is a high degree of fixed costs in comparison to total costs, entry into the railroad industry is more difficult than other modes of freight transportation such as the motor carrier or the airline industries.

If high fixed cost industries, like the railroads, are not economically regulated, direct head to head competition can have an opposite effect on price and service levels than would be expected. Excessive competition between railroads can cause destructive short run rate making practices and in the long run force the companies into bankruptcy. Since railroads are vital to the North American economy, the outcome of such competition might result in considerable amounts of government aid and promotion to keep the nation's railroad network viable. This occurrence is evidenced by the numerous times that direct subsidies and loans have been provided to the railroad industry during the last one hundred years. As a result of the market structure, it could be argued that the fewer railroads competing in a geographic region, the more efficient the entire industry becomes. The public benefits since individual companies are allowed to take advantage of the inherent large scale economies.

The Current Railroad Market Structure

The number of railroads declined significantly since the 1930's to the point where there were only seven major railroads operating in the United States by 1993; the Burlington Northern, CSX Transportation, Norfolk Southern, Atchison, Topeka and Santa Fe, Southern Pacific and Union Pacific railroads. These major railroads controlled well over 80% of the total traffic, trackage and employees in the industry.

The consolidation of the railroad industry continued through the 1990's as a result of a series of mergers and acquisitions. One of the most significant events occurred when the former Interstate Commerce Commission (ICC) approved the merger application of the Burlington Northern and Santa Fe Railroad (BNSF) in 1995. The merger left the Union Pacific (UPRR) and Southern Pacific (SPRR) Railroads to compete with the new BNSF Corporation and effectively reduced the number of railroads competing in the west from four to three.

The BNSF merger created one of North America's largest railroads with 31,000 miles of track, service in 27 states and two Canadian Provinces, and 44,000 employees. This new rail network covered the western two-thirds of the United States from the major ports in California and the Pacific Northwest to the Midwest, Southeast and Southwest and from the Gulf of Mexico to Canada.

The Union Pacific Railroad had operating revenues in excess $6.2 billion in 1995 and employed more than 35,000 workers. The UPRR operated more than 22,600 miles of track in 23 states ranging from the Midwest to the West Coast, Southeast and Southwest. Major cities served by the UPRR included Chicago, Minneapolis, Duluth, St. Louis and Omaha in the Midwest; Oakland, Los Angeles and Seattle on the West Coast; and Dallas, Houston and New Orleans in the Southeast and Southwest.

The other remaining competitor in the Western United States, Southern Pacific, posted operating revenues of more than $3.2 billion in 1995 with over 18,000 employees. The SPRR network was similar to the UPRR in that most of the 14,500 miles of track ran from Chicago to points in Texas, Arizona and California. Cities served included Dallas, Houston, New Orleans, El Paso, Nogales, Los Angeles, Oakland and Portland. In many of these instances, the rail routes from certain cities were not direct connections which resulted in slower transit times for the shippers and often added expense to the railroad's operation. Unlike the other major railroads in the West, the SPRR faced some hard financial times. The SPRR had a negative operating cash flow in many years since the early 1980's. Most of the SPRR's capital programs were focused on merely maintaining the current railroad network rather than upgrading the system to meet competition from the other major Western railroads. In several instances, the railroad was forced to rely on the sale of its non-rail assets to offset the negative cash flow situation.

The BNSF merger forced the two remaining railroads into a difficult competitive position. If some drastic actions were not taken, industry experts believed the SPRR would probably collapse from the financial strain of losing millions of dollars per week. According to one SP official, "We are not going bankrupt, but we are going backwards." This would leave the UPRR to try and effectively compete with the larger, more dominate BNSF in numerous markets.

A Competitive Strategy

Both the UPRR and SPRR were forced to evaluate many different alternatives and opportunities as a result of changes in the railroad industry. One such business strategy explored by the UP and SP Railroads was the possible merger of their two operations.

The merger would create one financially strong, efficient railroad to compete with the new BNSF. A proposed merger would create the nation's largest rail carrier in North America operating 31,000 miles of tracks, 53,000 employees with more than 2,000 trains serving 24 states in the Western two-thirds of the United States. If approved, the merger strategy would develop new opportunities for the two railroads, their employees, the shipping public, states, ports and many cities west of the Mississippi. According to various company studies, the UPSP merger would greatly improve operating efficiencies by reducing transit times and increase the percentage of direct routes throughout the Western part of the United States. Specifically, the benefits of the merger included:

(1) More direct routes thus reducing many hundreds of miles from current methods of operation.
(2) Faster transit times which would cut hours and days from many routes.
(3) Specialized use of parallel tracks in which traffic would flow in one direction on the UP track and in the opposite direction on the SP track.
(4) Many customers' freight would bypass terminals, eliminating congestion and frequent interchanges.
(5) Alternative mainline routes which would allow planned and unplanned traffic diversion with little or no loss in transit time.
(6) Improved and more efficient use of train crews
(7) More efficient utilization of locomotives and freight car equipment.

A detailed benefit/cost analysis was performed by the Union Pacific to determine what types of savings could be anticipated as a result of the proposed merger. The study revealed there were more than $750 million in annual benefits for both railroads and the shipping public. Projected savings included more than $580 million in operational efficiency gains and $90 million in savings for shippers. However, the plan would cause the elimination of about 3,500 jobs and the abandonment of duplicate and surplus track miles.

UP Corporation Chairman, Drew Lewis summed up the competitive position of the two remaining railroads. He commented that without the UPSP merger there would be no other way for the two companies to achieve the capacity enhancements, services improvements and cost reductions that the BNSF already achieved with their merger in 1995.

After much research and deliberations, the strategic decision was made by the two railroads to seek permission from the three member Surface Transportation Board (STB) of the Department of Transportation to merge operations. The STB is the successor to the Interstate Commerce Commission which rendered railroad merger decisions for the last one hundred years before being disbanded by Congress in 1996.

Reactions to Proposed Union Pacific and Southern Pacific Merger

Reactions to the initial proposal to merge operations were mixed. Evidence presented by the UP and SP Railroads convinced many people that the merger was overwhelmingly in the public interest, pro-competitive and provided remarkable benefits to customers. Those supporting the merger included more than 1250 shippers, 20 states, 13 port authorities, many short-line railroads, seven of the strongest unions in the railroad industry and even the BNSF.

Those in opposition suggested that the end result of the merger could be that the western two-thirds of the United States would be left with two giant railroads--UPSP and BNSF to dominate the market. The cost and market structure make it likely that the two remaining railroads would find it in their best interests not to directly compete and could raise rates to the shipping public. Those opposed to the merger included many industry organizations such as the National Industrial Traffic League and Western Fuels Association, companies such as Dow Chemical and Proctor and Gamble as well as some railroads like the Kansas City Southern and Conrail. Four states, including Louisiana, Arkansas, Nevada and Texas, strongly opposed the consolidation of the two networks. One of the major reasons that these states were against the initial merger proposal was that it would leave shippers with a choice of one railroad -- the combined UP/SP operation. For example, many utilities expressed concern that any contracts for hauling coal which would expire in the near future could contain rate escalations as a result of the lack of competition.

In order to provide solutions to these expressed concerns, the UP and SP Railroads offered either the outright sale of portions of the new combined network or trackage rights to the BNSF. With trackage rights, the BNSF would be allowed to operate their trains over specified portions of the UPSP system. The compromise included 3800 miles of trackage rights from Memphis, TN to Little Rock, AR to Shreveport, LA and onto Houston, Brownsville and San Antonio, TX. Another portion of the proposed rights ran from Denver, CO to Salt Lake City, UT to Reno, NV and onto Oakland, CA.

An additional provision called for haulage rights in those geographic areas where the number of rail carriers dropped from two to one as a result of the merger and the BNSF could not efficiently establish operations. With haulage rights, UPSP would handle BNSF traffic and be paid accordingly. For instance, if a city had been served by both the UPRR and SPRR and the merger effectively eliminated any competition, the BNSF had a chance to establish competitive rates without actually providing the physical service. The service would be provided by the combined UP/SP operation.

The goal of these proposals was to grant access by the BNSF to shippers that would lose competitive rail service because of the merger. This effectively allowed BNSF, the UPSP's major competitor, access to more than a billion dollars worth of business.

One of the major opponents of the proposed merger was the Department of Justice's Antitrust Division. Since the DOJ does not hold decision making power in railroad mergers, its role is restricted to submitting views to the STB. The DOJ's position was a combination of three major arguments surrounding the competitive outcome of the merger.

First, the DOJ felt that the projected savings to the two railroads and shipping public were overstated by $246 million to as high as $768 million. Instead of the $750 million per year benefits suggested by the railroads' studies, the Antitrust Division expected annual savings to be between $56 million and $506 million. According to the DOJ, several of the public benefits claimed were actually private benefits and many of the monetary savings cited would come from a continuation of the industry trends rather than the approval of the merger.

Second, the DOJ contended that the 3800 miles of trackage rights given to the BNSF would not create enough competition to keep the rate levels down. According to the DOJ, the BNSF would not be an effective competitor in those affected markets as a result of excessive compensation to be paid to UPSP for trackage rights as well as inadequate guarantees to ensure BNSF quality of service on the impacted lines. The DOJ's rough estimate was that the total harm to shippers and consumers would be in excess of $800 million. This would be a result of an increase in rates where the BNSF agreement was not able to correct for the lack of competition created by the merger and in instances where a third railroad was eliminated by the merger.

Lastly, the DOJ believed that the SPRR was financially viable, capable of raising the capital necessary to continue its role as a major competitor in the Western United States market. The DOJ explained much of the shipper support for the merger resulted over the fear that many companies would be without service if the SPRR were to declare bankruptcy or down size to profitability.

The UP-SP Oral Argument Before Surface Transportation Board

The Surface Transportation Board scheduled the time and date to hear final arguments on both sides of the UPSP merger controversy. The major purpose of the hearings is not to restate the written findings and arguments but rather to summarize and emphasize the key points of each party's position and to provide the STB with a chance to ask questions.

Case Questions

1. How could it be argued that it is in the "public interest" that the merger be approved by the STB?

2. As the lead attorney for the combined UP/SP organization, what final points, in support of the merger, would you make to the STB and against the anticompetitive allegations of the DOJ?

3. Were the UPRR and SPRR acting in an ethical manner?

4. Comment on the social responsibility of railroad mergers.

Case References

BNSF Company Profile and History, BNSF Corporate Communications, Burlington Northern-Santa Fe Internet Web Site, November 1996.

Burke, Jack, "UP: Some Tweaking May Be Needed In Merger-Related BNSF Trackage Deal," *Traffic World*, April 22, 1996, 36-37.

Merger Update: National Summary. Union Pacific and Southern Pacific Railroads, April 1996, Omaha, NE, 1-22.

Merger Update: Pacific Northwest Ports Support UP/SP Merger, Union Pacific Railroad Corporate Communication, March 11, 1996, Omaha, NE.

Sparkman, David, "Justice, States Call UP-SP Union Anticompetitive," *Transport Topics.* October, 1996. Website, http://WWW.ttnews.com/weekly.archive/04.22.tw5.html

The Transportation News Digest, Walter Weart, July 1, 1996, Number 125, WLG Publications, Inc. Arvada, CO (pp. 1).

The Transportation News Digest, Walter Weart, August 1, 1996, Number 126, WLG Publications Inc., Arvada, CO (pp. 1).

Union Pacific Overview, Fast Facts In The USA, Union Pacific Corporate Communications, Union Pacific Internet Web Site, http://WWW.uprr.com/UPRROVER.htm, October, 1996.

Union Pacific Railroad Chronology, Union Pacific Railroad Corporate Communications Union Pacific Internet Web Site, http://WWW.uprr.UPRRCHRON.htm, October 1996.

"UP- SP Oral Argument Set" *The National Industrial League Notice,* June 21, 1996 Volume 60, The National Industrial League, Washington, DC, 11-18.

References

Adams, Walter, (ed) *The Structure of American Industry, 3rd Edition*. Macmillan Company, New York, NY, 1965.

Corley, Robert N, Reed, O. Lee, and Shedd, Peter J., *The Legal Environment of Business*. McGraw-Hill, New York, NY, 1990.

Davidson, Joe, "Six Big Airlines Settle U.S. Suit on Price Fixing." *The Wall Street Journal*, March 18, 1994, p. A2.

Gruley, Bryan, "FTC's Proposed Shift in Merger Reviews Helps Drug, Defense, High-Tech Firms." *The Wall Street Journal*, June 4, 1996, p. A3.

Gruley, Bryan, "FTC to Weigh Cost Savings In Mergers." *The Wall Street Journal*, June 3, 1996, p. A3.

Lanzillotti, Robert F., "The Aluminum Industry." In Adams, Walter, (ed) *The Structure of American Industry, 3rd Edition*. Macmillan Company, New York, 1965 (a), pp. 185-232.

Lanzillotti, Robert F., "The Automobile Industry." In Adams, Walter, (ed) *The Structure of American Industry, 3rd Edition*. Macmillan Company, New York, 1965 (b), pp. 311-356.

Scherer, F.M., *Industrial Market Structure and Economic Performance*. Rand McNally, Chicago, IL, 1980.

Warner, Daniel M., *The Legal Environment of Business*. The Dryden Press, Orlando, FL, 1995.

Wilson, Gary S., *Airport Dominance: A Case Study Approach to Competition, Concentration and Policy*. Unpublished Ph.D. Dissertation, University of Illinois at Chicago, Chicago, IL, 1993.

CHAPTER 9

FACTORS AFFECTING THE EMPLOYER OF THE FUTURE

As we move into the 21st century, successful businesses will be those which are able to adapt to external environmental change affecting human resources and to government regulation of employment practices. This chapter will describe the major factors affecting employers of the future. The managerial responses to these factors will then be reviewed with suggestions for possible strategies to successfully adapt to the business environment of the future.

A good way of understanding the relationship between external factors and the role of business as employer is through the model of the impact of change in the external environment on business decision making shown in Figure 2.1. In this model, underlying forces such as demographics, social norms, cultures and beliefs serve as the underpinnings of the changes that occur. The model is one of change and interaction showing how changes in societal elements may result in public sector and marketplace responses through the political and market systems. A business response may affect the societal elements through the marketplace, the political system or directly through business social involvement. This model will serve as the basis for understanding the impacts and relationships discussed in this chapter.

Underlying forces which impact external change are demographic changes including shifts in the age distribution of the population and increasing cultural diversity. Immigration also is a force underlying other changes. Societal element changes which result from these underlying forces include an older workforce, continued influence of working women, and changes in labor unions. Public sector issues which impact employers include affirmative action, social security, and medicare. Employee practices regulated by the government are sexual harassment policies, the treatment of disabled employees, workers' compensation, and unemployment insurance, among others. Managerial responses include health care and life insurance, corporate wellness programs, child care support, alternative work arrangements, and managing employee behavior.

Underlying Forces

In 1987 a report was issued by the Hudson Institute entitled *Workforce 2000*. It was predicted that an aging population will impact the workforce with a simultaneous shortage of younger workers. The report concludes that the workforce will become more diverse and the participation of women in the workforce will continue to grow.

Age Distribution

National population projections until the year 2050 have been made by the US Census Bureau. It is projected that the median age of the population will increase from 34.0 years in 1994 to a high of 39.1 years in 2035 and decrease slightly to 39.0 by 2050. Although the total population of the US is expected to increase to 392 million by 2050, the growth rate (average annual percentage change) is expected to slow from 1.10 percent per year between 1990 and 1995 to .54 percent per year between 2040 and 2050. These projections both reflect the aging of the baby boomers born between 1946 and 1964 and lower birth rates.

Diversity

Diversity in society and in the workforce presents many challenges. Broadly defined, diversity includes not only racial differences, but variations in religion, gender, urban vs. rural backgrounds, and educational experiences. The national population projections indicate that the US population is becoming more diverse by race and Hispanic origin. Figure 9.1 shows each major ethnic group's percent of the population in 1990 and projected for 2000, 2025, and 2050.

In 1990, over three-fourths of the population was White, 12% was Black, 9% Hispanic, and the remainder Asian & Pacific Islander or American Indian. The proportion of Whites in the population is expected to drop to 72% in 2000, with increases in both the Hispanic and Asian populations. The Black population is projected to increase less

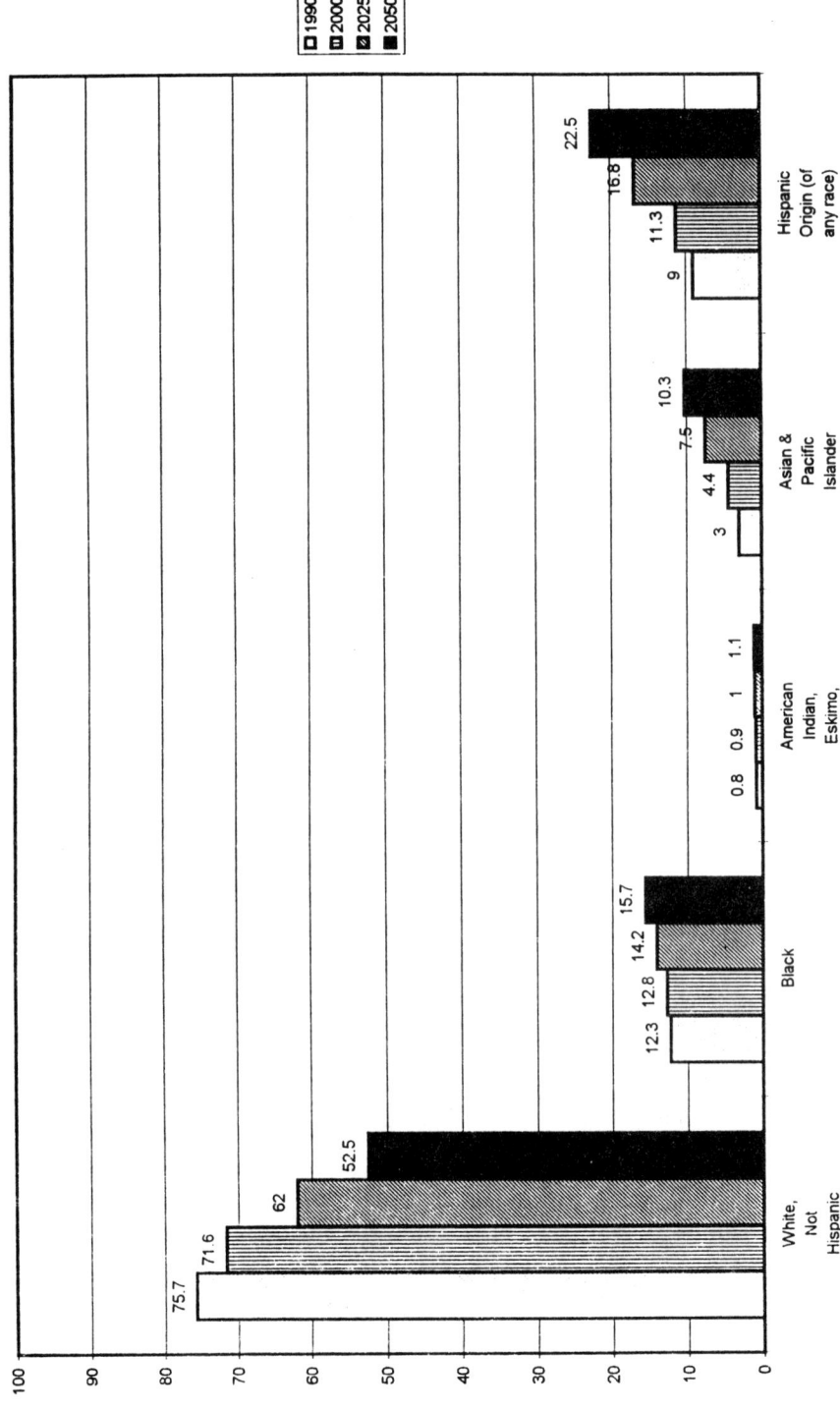

Figure 9.1: Percent of the Population by Race and Hispanic Origin: 1990, 2000, 2025, 2050

Source: Day, 1996

than 3% between 2000 and 2050, to a high of 15.7%. By 2025, Whites are expected to have dropped to 62% while Asian & Pacific Islanders will have doubled to 7.5%. Hispanics will have increased from 9% in 1990 to 16.8% of the population in 2025.

The percentage of the workforce that is White will only be 52% in 2050, with Asian & Pacific Islanders increasing to 10.3% and Hispanics increasing to 22.5%. These projected shifts reflect expected birth and death rates of the current population and assume a continuation of immigrants from these areas.

As the population becomes more diverse, so will the workforce. Businesses will need to maximize the talents brought to their organizations from these various groups. Differences among these groups also will lead to increased demand for goods and services which cater to the tastes and lifestyles of the members of each group. Also, awareness of these products may also increase the demand of the general population. For example, an increased interest in ethnic foods and music may result.

Businesses face several challenges as the workforce and customer base becomes more diversified. Employees from diverse backgrounds must learn to work together, regardless of differences. Training which emphasizes strategies to maximize the contributions of employees from diverse groups is offered by many companies. US WEST had provided a 3-day program entitled "Managing a Diverse Workforce" to all managers and union stewards and a one-day session called "The Value of Human Diversity" for all 65,000 employees by 1993. These efforts began in the 1980's and have led to diversity at all levels in the organization. (Caudron, 1992)

Diversity of customers, especially in service industries, is also a challenge. Employees who are bilingual may become more valuable because of their ability to effectively communicate with the growing number of non-English speaking customers.

However, some firms have found the English-language skills of some of their bilingual employees need to be improved. AVCO Financial Services in Irvine, California has introduced an employee based program that provides English as a second language (ESL) tutoring. The program called "Each One, Teach One" is run by the South Coast Literacy Council. AVCO employees are trained to provide ESL tutoring and meet with other employees who have volunteered for the training. This is an example of a program that benefits the employees involved as well as the organization as a whole. (Stuart, 1994)

Another example is healthcare providers that are offering language courses to employees who serve multilingual customer groups. Alternatively, they are making arrangements with organizations to provide translation services for the patients who require it. The diversity of both employees and customers offers new opportunities to businesses with the foresight to develop innovative solutions.

Immigration

Another factor impacting the number and type of workers available is immigration. In 1986, the Immigration Reform and Control Act was passed requiring all employers to screen employees systematically for proper documentation to work in the US. Discrimination on the basis of national origin continues to be illegal, however.

The U.S. Immigration and Naturalization Service reported the characteristics of legal immigrants who arrived during 1995. Two out of three immigrants intended to reside in California, New York, Florida, Texas, New Jersey, or Illinois. The largest share of immigrants was from Asia (37.2%) followed by 32.1% from North America. Mexico was the leading source country with 89,932 legal immigrants or 12.5% of the total. The average age of immigrants was 28 years and 54% were female. Over 46% of those between 16 and 64 years old reported having an occupation at the time of entry. Based on this profile, it appears that the impact of immigration may be felt by employers in the key destination states or with jobs frequently taken by members of these groups (U.S. Immigration and Naturalization Service, 1996).

The overall increase in the number of immigrants and the shift in proportions of different ethnic groups may lead to increased competition among these groups. Areas of conflict include: job competition, public benefits, and differentiation within each minority community. (Schuck, 1994).

Immigrants compete with established minority groups for jobs, especially in the garment manufacturing, hospitality, and agricultural industries. It is argued by those in favor of immigration that these are jobs that Americans won't take because welfare payments and benefits result in a higher income. Also, the number of jobs is not fixed since the money that immigrants spend creates new jobs. In addition, there are a number of high tech jobs which cannot be filled by Americans alone.

Those opposed to further immigration point out that immigrants tend to take low skilled jobs which results in fewer entry level jobs for Americans. In addition, many professional jobs may go to foreigners rather than Americans. In part, this may be because many immigrants are classified as minority group members for affirmative action plan reporting, while many Americans are not. In some circumstances this may lead to a tendency to hire immigrants over Americans.

It is felt that some immigrants come to the United States to collect welfare benefits. The Welfare Reform Act of 1996 excludes legal immigrants from collecting welfare benefits. The assumption is that legal immigrants must be sponsored by a family which meets certain income requirements and takes responsibility for the immigrants' economic needs. Another provision of the Welfare Reform Act limits the time welfare can be received by American citizens and requires work of able-bodied adults. As decisions concerning welfare are shifted to the state and local levels, competition for jobs between traditional American minorities and immigrants is likely to increase.

Immigration has been a continuing source of new ideas, entrepreneurship and capable and determined workers. Legal immigrants have long been an important source of labor and small business development. One hallmark of US society is the creativity and new ideas brought by immigrants. In addition, many high tech, medical and other professionals have came from immigrant ranks. It is argued that immigration is a source of strength of this country rather than its weakness. Those in favor of easy immigration policies view restrictions as a negative hurting not only those who wish to come to the US, but the country as a whole.

Illegal Immigration

In the 1990's, the political climate changed to more severely restrict illegal immigration. Local, state, and the federal government's support of illegals were reduced. Laws were passed or were being considered which would no longer require government subsidized non-emergency medical care, public schools, legal services, or other welfare payments to be provided to illegal immigrants.

It was felt that in addition to the social cost of illegal immigrants and their children, businesses who hire illegals are at an unfair competitive advantage. First, companies that hire illegal immigrants for lower wages have a cost advantage over those who don't. Second, companies who follow the law by hiring documented workers and paying minimum wages and associated taxes are operating at a competitive disadvantage and are indirectly supporting the social service needs of illegal immigrants and thus their competitors who hire them. Third it is argued that illegal immigrants take jobs that may be available for US citizens.

Societal Element Changes

Older Workforce

Because of the demographic trends of an aging population and lower birth rates, there will be a shortage of traditional entry level workers between the ages of 16-24 as we move into the 21st century. At the same time, corporate downsizing, early retirement programs, and the overall aging of the population will result in additional older workers being available. Simultaneously, service industries will be growing and looking to older workers and retirees to fill their open positions.

As can be seen in Figure 9.2, the percentage of the workforce between 16-24 in 1993 was only 16%, slightly less than in 1991. Between 1991 and 1993, the percentage of workers between 35-44 increased to 27% and the percentage of workers between 45-54 was up to 18%. These trends are expected to continue in the future.

In a study of the productivity of older workers in a Days Inn reservation center in Atlanta in the late 1980's, it was found that older workers "remained on the job much longer than younger workers, received higher wages, but only because of seniority, and although they spent more time talking to callers, they were more successful in booking reservations." (McNaught & Barth, 1992) In fact, the authors conclude that older workers were better salespersons than younger workers. With appropriate placement and retraining, older workers may provide an excellent labor pool in the future.

A number of companies have successfully recruited and trained older workers. McDonald's ReHIREment Program began in the 1980's to meet the employment needs of its restaurants. Home Shopping Network established the Prime Timers program in 1990 to fill its many part-time openings for individuals to answer phones and take orders. Turnover has been 30% less than for other workers. (Solomon, 1995)

Working Women

Women have always worked — on the farm, in the home, and in the paid workforce. As shown in Figure 9.3, the labor market participation rate of women has increased from 34% in the 1950's to 46% in 1993. There are many reasons for this shift including: the high inflation rate of the early 1980's and high taxes resulting in the need for the two income family, increased opportunities for women due to the overall expansion of jobs, and increased numbers of women completing college and entering professional and graduate schools. Other reasons include the impact of the 1960's & 1970's civil rights laws prohibiting discrimination against women in compensation and employment, the Pregnancy Discrimination Act of 1978 and the Family and Medical Leave Act of 1993.

The Pregnancy Discrimination Act of 1978 requires employers to cover pregnancy, childbirth, and related medical conditions in the same manner that other conditions are covered, if health or disability plans are offered to employees. This coverage must be available to both female employees and wives of male employees. Women cannot be forced to stop working before their baby is born, if they can perform their job. The length of their leave cannot be dictated by the employer. (Corley, et.al., 1996).

The Family and Medical Leave Act of 1993 applies to both male and female employees. It gives a legal right to take a leave without pay for family or medical emergencies. This leave can be up to 3 months in length and the individual is guaranteed their job back upon return to work. Although most frequently referring to maternity leave taken by female employees, fathers may also take unpaid leave to care for a newborn. The law also covers leaves to care for adopted children and sick family members.

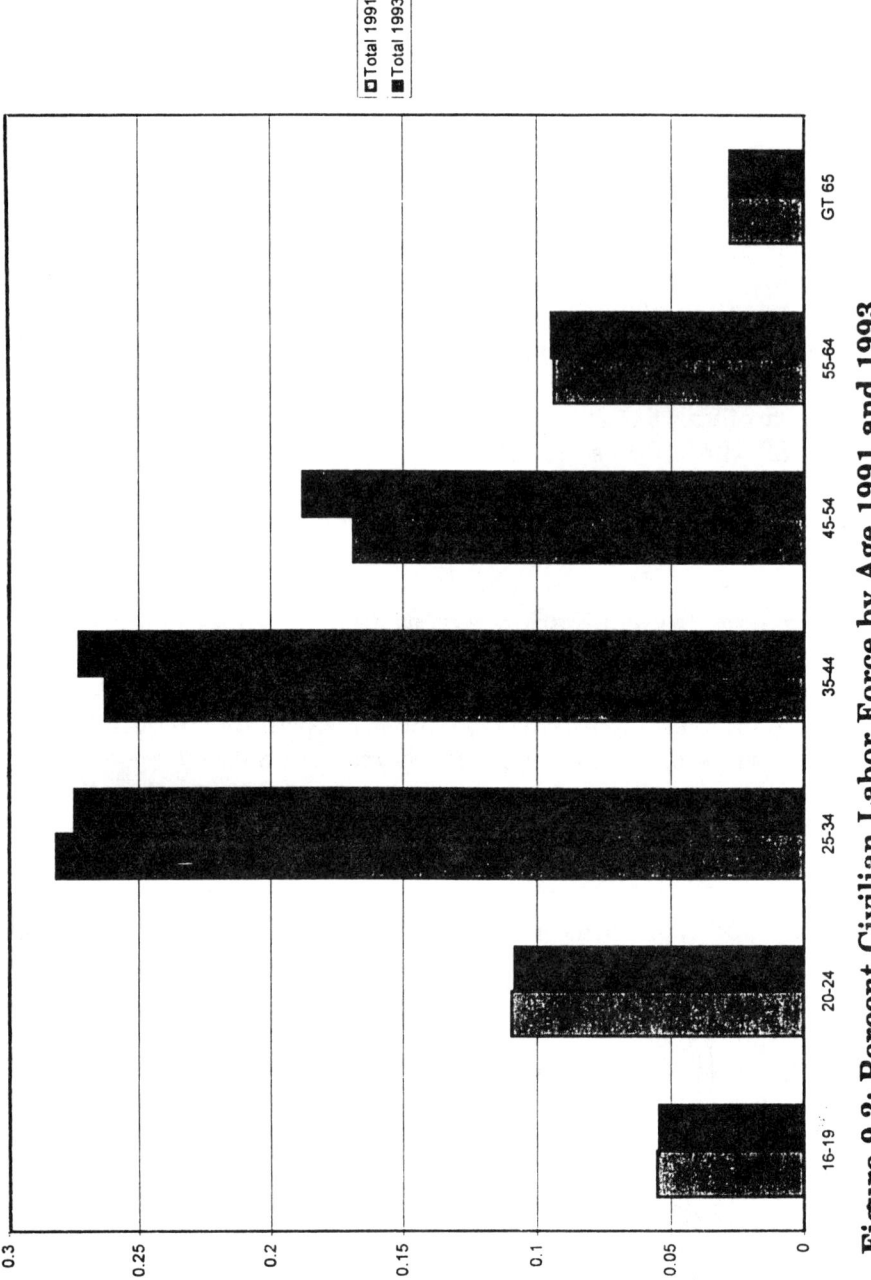

Figure 9.2: Percent Civilian Labor Force by Age 1991 and 1993
Source: Statistical Abstract of the United States, 1994

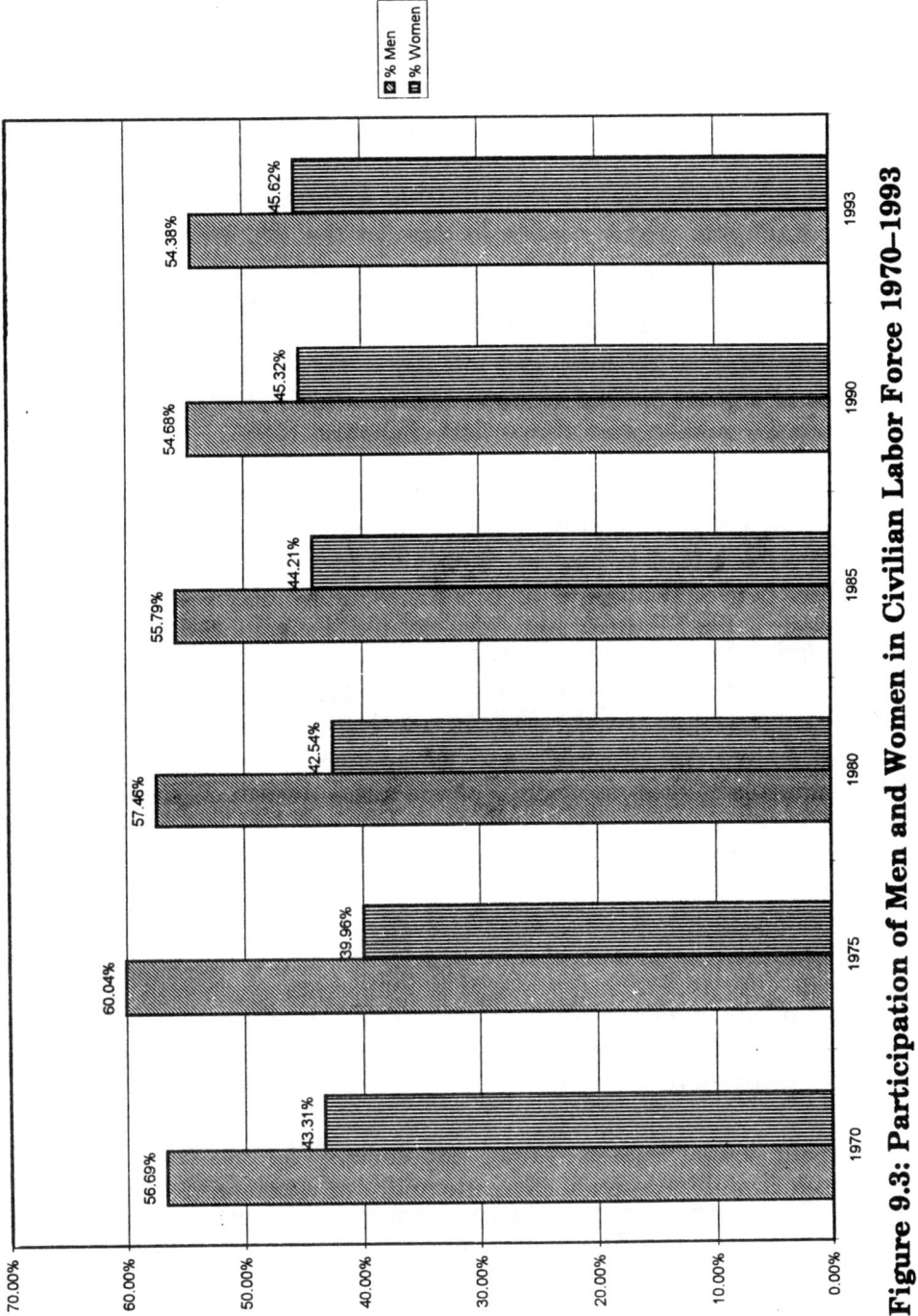

Figure 9.3: Participation of Men and Women in Civilian Labor Force 1970–1993

Although their labor force participation rates have increased substantially, women still are paid significantly less than men overall. The median weekly earnings for women as a percent of men's median weekly earnings rose from 64% in 1980 to 77% in 1993. Figure 9.4 shows that women earn less than men at every educational level, indicating that education alone does not eliminate this earnings differential.

A number of reasons are given for this difference. First, women tend to have staff jobs which results in gaps in the experience needed for promotion to relatively higher paying line positions. Second, many women move in and out of the labor force or work part-time as a result of childcare and other family responsibilities. This results in less overall experience relative to men and consequently lower pay. Third, the existence of a *glass ceiling* in some organizations presents a barrier to promotion for women and minorities. (Snavely, 1993).

The Glass Ceiling Commission is a 21-member body appointed by the President and Congressional leaders and chaired by the Secretary of Labor. It was created as part of the Civil Rights Act of 1991. It focuses on barriers to promotion and opportunities for women and minorities in three areas: 1) the filling of management and decision making positions; 2) developmental and skill enhancing activities; and 3) compensation and reward systems. These objectives are addressed through three activities of the Commission: 1) The Frances Perkins-Elizabeth Hanford Dole National Award for Diversity and Excellence in American Executive Management which is an annual presidential award; 2) studies of the advancement of minorities and women, and 3) public education activities. (Glass Ceiling Commission, U.S. Department of Labor, 1996).

Labor Unions

You load sixteen tons and what do you get? Another day older and you're deeper in debt. St. Peter don't you call me cause I can't go. I owe my soul to the company store.

The old song "Sixteen Tons", popularized by the country singer Tennessee Ernie Ford, made clear the plight of workers in the early part of the Twentieth Century. Many workers were exploited by their companies. They were forced to endure long hours, hazardous working

Males

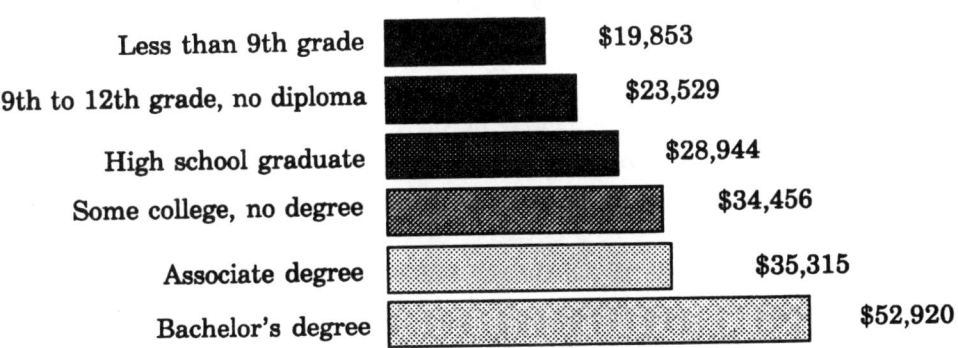

Females

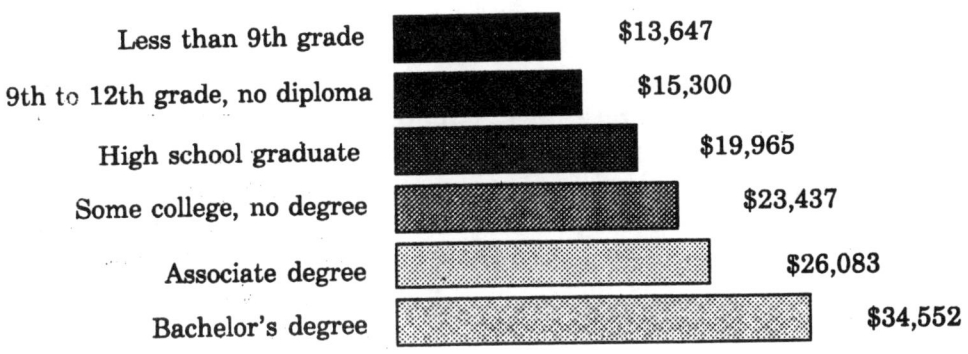

Figure 9.4 Average Earnings of Year-Round Full-Time Workers in 1992

conditions, low pay and abuse. The sweat shops, child labor, and misuse of immigrant labor brings to mind conditions found in third world countries today.

Many books were written and movies produced about the plight of workers during the industrial revolution. One book, entitled *Black Fury* by Michael A. Musmanno, later was made into a movie. It is the story of immigrant miners in Western Pennsylvania. The men worked 10 to 12 hour days, six days a week. They lived in company towns around the mines and were paid in script which they exchanged for food and necessities at the company store at inflated prices. Speaking little English, and unable to leave because of the lack of transportation, the immigrant workers were easy prey for unscrupulous bosses.

Unions were established during this period to give workers the opportunity to bargain collectively and so improve wages and working conditions. Management resistance to unions grew as the union movement expanded. Labor violence was a frequent occurrence. One of the most famous incidents was the 1886 Haymarket riot in Chicago where workers were killed as they struck and demonstrated for an eight hour work day.

Today, many of the reforms sought by unions have been enacted into law. Forty hour work weeks, prohibitions against child labor, workplace safety, minimum wage legislation, unemployment compensation, etc. are all part of federal and state laws. Union workers benefit from much higher wages. In addition, exploitation of the workforce is much more difficult due to increased worker mobility as the result of the proliferation of the automobile. Workers not satisfied with working conditions or wages can now get in their automobiles and find another job. The automobile has increased the job opportunities available to individuals by an exponential amount.

For all of these reasons, many argue that unions have outlived their usefulness. It is argued that unions are an anachronism that a post industrial society no longer needs. It is argued that unions should organize workers in developing countries who are exploited and forced to accept low wages, rather than in the United States where high income workers are the rule rather than the exception.

On the other hand, labor union advocates argue that unions still are needed and play an important role in the workplace. They state that even industries that are not unionized benefit by the union movement. In many instances, it is argued, the threat of unionization is enough to insure that workers are treated fairly. There are also still vestiges of worker exploitation that require unions. For example, migrant workers and immigrant workers many times can be easily taken advantage of. These advocates point to dangers that are still present in the workplace. Brown lung disease, caused by inhaling textile fibers is one example. Another is the southern chicken processing plant in the early 1990's which caught fire, but had emergency exits locked causing the loss of workers' lives. It is argued that unions are the only way for workers to assure that they get their fair share. In the age of corporate downsizing, the union advocates argue that unions are necessary to protect workers from job loss and outsourcing to low wage countries.

Trends in Unionization

In the mid-1950's, 35% of the nonagricultural workforce was in labor unions. This had dropped to 23% by 1980, and in 1994 it was less than 15%. In private nonagricultural industries, 10.4% of the 9.4 million workers were unionized. By contrast, 37.8% of the 6.9 million government workers at the federal, state, and local levels were union members. Most growth in union membership recently has been in the public sector. This pattern is shown in Figure 9.5 below. Craver (1993) suggests that for future union organizing efforts to be successful, campaigns need to target previously unorganized groups including women, minorities, white collar and service personnel and move into areas of the country not traditionally covered.

Labor Laws

Over the years, a number of laws have been passed regulating various aspects of labor union formation, operation, and the activities of employers and employees. The most important laws are the *National Labor Relations Act*, also called the *Wagner Act* of 1935 and the *Labor-Management Relations Act*, passed in 1947 which is also known as the *Taft-Hartley Act*. The Wagner Act gives workers the right to organize and established the National Labor Relations Board (NLRB) to settle unfair labor practice suits. The Taft-Hartley Act places a variety of restrictions on union activities. This includes requiring a written agreement to deduct dues from paychecks, allowing employers to file charges against unions if they are not bargaining in good faith, and permitting employees to initiate union decertification

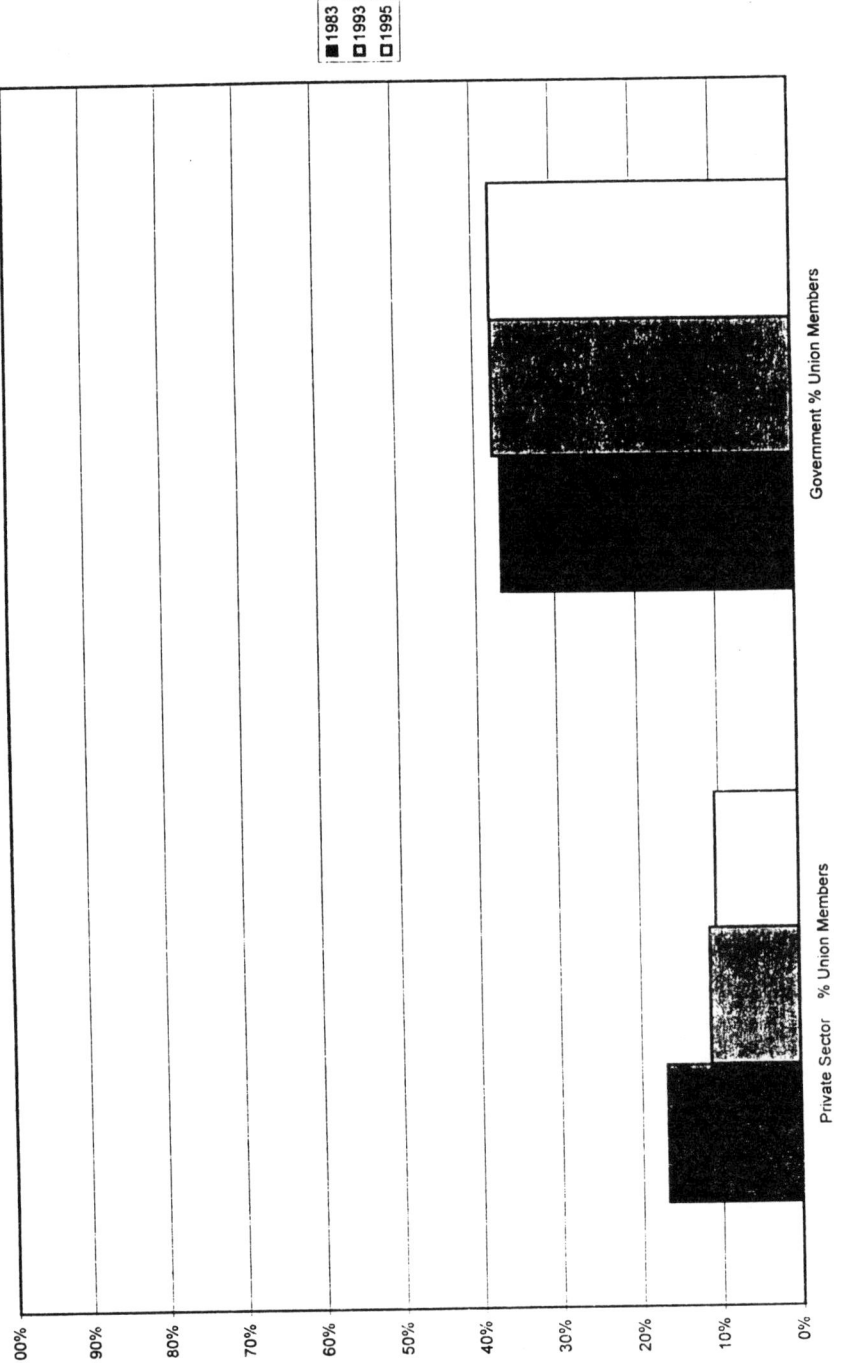

Figure 9.5: Percentage Union Membership - Private Sector and Government

elections. States also were given the power to enact *right-to work laws*. In states which passed these laws, the closed union shop is outlawed. A closed shop is a situation where only union members can be hired. The Taft-Hartley Act also provides for an 80 day cooling off period which the President can invoke in cases where a strike imperils the national health or safety.

Most workers are covered by the provisions of the Wagner and Taft-Hartley Acts. However, workers in the railroad and airline industries are covered by a different set of labor provisions which are contained in the *Railway Labor Act* of 1926. The act created the National Mediation Board to mediate differences between unions and employers. The act established a procedure for mediation of disputes if a settlement is not reached at the bargaining table. The procedure may require an act of Congress, which has occurred periodically in the railroad industry.

Public Sector Response

There are a variety of issues affecting individuals and their employment which are on the national agenda. These issues are both controversial and important to both employees and business. Three of these issues are dealt with in this chapter. These are equal employment opportunity, social security and medicare.

Equal Job Opportunity

The modern civil rights movement can be traced to immediately after the Civil War. At that time, civil rights was concerned with providing equal opportunity for all Americans. In 1866, Congress passed the Civil Rights Act, and the 13th, 14th and 15th Amendments to the Constitution. All of this legislation greatly expanded the concept of equal protection of the law. However, in the 1870's, Jim Crow laws were passed and in 1896 the Supreme Court decision in *Plessy vs. Ferguson* upheld the doctrine of separate but equal.

In 1909, the National Association for the Advancement of Colored People (NAACP) was formed and had as its focus to bring about changes through political action. The organization was concerned with attainment of equal voting rights for minority Americans, equal educational opportunity, equal access to public services and equal employment opportunities, among other objectives.

Segregated schools were found illegal by the Supreme Court in the *Brown vs. Board of Education* ruling of 1954. In 1964, the Civil Rights Act was passed forbidding job discrimination based on race, color, religion, and national origin. The Equal Employment Opportunity Commission (EEOC) was created at this time to enforce the provisions of the Act. Later, executive orders, laws, and amendments required affirmative action plans by government contractors and brought other groups under the jurisdiction of the EEOC and the Office of Federal Contract Compliance Programs (OFCCP). These protected groups included persons over 40 years of age, women, and the physically and mentally disabled.

Beginning in the 1960's, there were a series of laws which protected various groups from discrimination in the workplace. The public interest theory of regulation (see Chapter 6) includes two of the reasons behind these laws. The first is equalization of opportunity by allowing access to employment to all individuals, regardless of race, sex, religion, or national origin. The second is to accomplish the social objective of nondiscrimination.

A third reason is found in the interest group theory of regulation. The focus since the 1960's has been on "making up" for past discrimination of particular "protected groups." These groups include women, minorities, persons over 40 years of age, and disabled persons as defined by the law. Members of these groups achieved this protected status through the political process. Recently, gay men and lesbians have tried to gain protected status through these laws.

The Affirmative Action Controversy

The concept of *affirmative action* is that organizations should take actions to remedy situations where there is an under-representation of certain minority employees. Organizations should develop procedures, analyses, and policies that would result in improvements in the hiring, training and promotion of minorities and females in all parts of an organization. This is especially true of government contractors who have been required to provide affirmative action plans with goals, timetables and statistical analyses for their geographic areas.

The American Civil Liberties Union supports the concept of affirmative action:

"The ACLU believes that even though no single measure can eradicate discrimination, affirmative action remains a moral imperative and an indispensable strategy for giving those disadvantaged by discrimination a temporary leg up. In addition, the unique diversity of its human resource pool gives our nation enormous potential for developing solutions to all the problems it confronts—in education, criminal justice, childcare and affordable housing, to name a few. The key to maximizing that potential is an end to discrimination and fulfillment of the Constitution's promise of freedom and equality, so that all Americans can have a chance to live productively and contribute to society."

Source: (ACLU Briefing Paper Number 17, p. 3)

Affirmative action, however, has been very controversial. It has been argued that it is merely a quota system for minorities. It substitutes *reverse discrimination* against white males for discrimination against minorities. Those opposing it further argue that affirmative action results in the unqualified getting preference over the qualified. In addition, minorities hired under such circumstances are always suspected of being unqualified, even if their qualifications are outstanding.

There are also problems with minority set asides which are portions of government contracts reserved for minorities. One abuse is where white men set up a company that is 51% owned by their wives, thus qualifying as a woman owned business. Second, many of the government contracts seem to go to well established minority businesses that could easily compete with non-minority establishments. This tends to shut the door on the small, start-up minority companies that could use a set aside.

Once the appropriate diversity of a student body or employee base is reached, others ask if the special treatment of protected groups should continue? Also, many programs give preference to women and minority owned businesses. Once a business becomes established, should it be required to compete in the marketplace without receiving special treatment?

In a report to President Clinton written in 1995, a review of the affirmative action programs of the federal government was done.

Continuous review of these programs was recommended so steps would be taken to eliminate or reform any program that:

- creates a quota
- creates preferences for unqualified individuals
- creates reverse discrimination
- continues even after its equal opportunity purposes have been achieved.

On November 5, 1996, an initiative was passed in California aimed at ending government mandated racial preferences in that state. Depending on a final ruling by the courts, affirmative action in California may no longer be practiced by public sector organizations in that state. Since California seems to be the "bellwether" state on many issues, it is likely that the California initiative may be replicated in other parts of the US. The initiative states:

> "The state shall not discriminate against, or grant preferential treatment to, any individual or group on the basis of race, sex, color, ethnicity or national origin in the operation of public employment, public education or public contracting."

Source: (California Proposition 209)

However, racial and other forms of discrimination are still present in American society and business. In 1996, Texaco settled a class action lawsuit in the amount of $115 million. The lawsuit charged the company with racial discrimination in hiring and promotions. Other companies charged with racial discrimination in the 1990's include Denny's restaurant chain and publisher RR Donnelly, located in Chicago. If affirmative action is eliminated, there would still be a need to deal with problems of inequality and discrimination in employment and promotions.

Several concepts have been suggested as alternatives to affirmative action. One concept is to replace affirmative action based on race and gender with affirmative action based on income. In this approach, any low income person could qualify for affirmative action regardless of race, sex or national origin.

A second approach is to recognize that African-Americans and Native Americans as a whole have not advanced sufficiently in American society because of past discrimination, slavery, and other abuses early in the history of the country. Other groups who where only recent immigrants to the US have not endured such abuse. Women as a group, while discriminated against in employment, never endured the institutionalized abuses experienced by Blacks and Native Americans. This approach would continue affirmative action, but only for African Americans and Native Americans to redress past abuses.

Social Security

The Social Security system was founded in 1935 as a means of dealing with poverty of the elderly through a national retirement program. It was originally sold as a trust fund, similar to a private pension system. Individual and employer contributions would be invested in government bonds and the proceeds then used to fund retirement.

Social security has never lived up to what was envisioned when it was created. It consists of part retirement program and part welfare program. Retirees in the 1990's can expect to get back all of their social security contributions and their employers' with interest within a few years. After that, social security ceases to act like a pension plan and more like welfare. Social security is basically a pay-as-you-go system with taxes from current workers being transferred to retirees. Any surplus of taxes over payments is used to purchase government bonds.

Surpluses used to buy government bonds are used to fund federal government expenditures. Essentially, social security taxes are just another tax, except that before being spent, a government bond is purchased. So, the Viet Nam war, welfare programs, tobacco subsidies, foreign aid etc. were funded in part through social security taxes.

The system works as long as there is a large base of workers whose taxes are used to fund a small group of retirees. When the system first began, there were 25 workers for each retiree. In the 1990's, this had fallen to 3.2 workers per retiree. And herein lies the rub.

The massive population of baby boomers will begin to retire around the year 2010. As more and more baby boomers swell the retirement ranks, there will be fewer and fewer workers per retiree. Its been estimated that the ratio of workers to retirees will fall to 2 to 1.

Existing social security tax rates cannot support the large retiree population.

But, how about the trust fund? Can't the Social Security Administration draw from it? Yes they can. But, this trust fund consists of nothing but government bonds. The Social Security Administration could cash in its bonds, but where will the government get the funds to pay off the bonds?

Two sources come to mind. One is to run up the federal deficit. The other is to increase taxes on those in the workforce. Either solution is not very appealing. For example, the Clinton Administration in 1995 estimated that in order to fund social security and existing government programs, average tax rates would have to rise to 80 percent. Its been estimated that by 2030, workers would have to pay close to 40 percent of their incomes for Social Security taxes alone. (Genetski, 1993).

Social Security is a classic example of a benefits first, cost later program. It is essentially a massive Ponzi or pyramid scheme that works as long as the base is large and growing and the payees are few. Like a chain letter that collapses, Social Security is headed to impoverish either the generation of baby boomer retirees, or their children and grandchildren. It is the ticking time bomb of the 21st century.

Proposals For Reform

The Social Security Board of Trustees has estimated that income from taxes and interest should be able to pay benefits until 2019. The system is estimated to be bankrupt by 2029. Because of the strong political influence of the elderly population and interest groups such as the American Association for Retired People, it has been very difficult make significant changes in these programs. However, change is essential. Several proposals have been suggested.

1. *Raise Social Security Taxes* - This would help to keep the system solvent, but would result in extremely high tax rates on the working population. Tax rates would be so high that there would be few incentives to save, invest and work hard.

2. *Change Eligibility Requirements* - The number of recipients can be reduced if the age at which one can receive benefits is raised or the number of years of payments into the system is increased.

The retirement age is in the process of being raised to 67 to receive full social security benefits. The retirement age would have to be increased further. Since this approach involves reducing benefits for some individuals, this approach may be politically difficult to implement.

3. *Means Testing of Benefits* - To be eligible for social security benefits, all one has to do is meet the age requirements and retire. There is no means test to see if the retiree needs the benefits. This proposal would gradually reduce benefits as retiree incomes increase from other sources and then eliminate benefits at high incomes. There are many retired multi-millionaires who collect Social Security benefits. Their benefits are being paid by middle income working age individuals, most with much lower incomes. Means testing would reduce this transfer of income from lower to upper income individuals. By means testing Social Security, the system would become more like an insurance program to keep the elderly out of poverty.

Means testing has been opposed in the past because it is argued that it would destroy the aura of the Social Security system as a national retirement system available to all. It is feared that this may reduce the political support for the system.

4. *Encourage the Birth Rate* - Since the problem with Social Security stems from too few workers and too many retirees, this approach would encourage families to have more children through tax incentives. For example, increasing the personal deduction and tax credits for children could be implemented to reduce the economic disincentives to have children.

5. *Increase Immigration* - This approach would use immigration to increase the working age population. Immigrants of certain age groups would be given a higher priority, especially if they have marketable skills in the United States.

6. *Diversify Trust Fund Investments* - Rather than using all of the excess of revenues over expenditures to purchase government bonds, this approach would allow Social Security to invest a portion of the funds in stocks in order to obtain a higher rate of return. By investing in the private sector, trust fund surpluses would be used to expand the productive capacity of the economy.

If we are more productive, the burden of providing for the elderly population would be spread over a larger base. A problem with this approach is the tremendous power that the Social Security system would have over individual companies. The vast resources at command could be a potential source of corruption, or government influence of business decisions.

7. *Privatization* - In this approach, payments into a retirement system would still be mandatory. However, workers would have the option to invest some portion of their money in the private investments of their choosing. The concept here is to empower workers to make prudent investments with their contributions. It is anticipated that a higher rate of return would result. Privatization has been tried in several countries, most notably Chile. The experience in Chile is that economic growth has accelerated and the savings rate has skyrocketed. By owning a part of the economy, Chile's workers have economic power they could have only dreamed of before privatization.

The solution to the problems with the US Social Security System probably lies in a combination of several of these approaches. If nothing is done, then Kevorkian type solutions will surely come about in the not too distant future.

Medicare

Medicare provides health insurance for retirees. It was one of the Great Society programs instituted in the 1960's. It pays most of the medical expenses of individuals over 65, although many people have supplemental insurance as well. Medicare suffers from the same demographic problems as Social Security. In addition, the medical inflation rate has far exceeded the general rate of inflation, further adding to its problems. Benefits are paid from a fund which is financed through payroll taxes on current workers. Predictions of the bankruptcy of Medicare were frequent during the 1990's. Possible consequences of the financial problems with Medicare may include:

o   Healthcare services may be rationed, which may involve excluding or limiting services. Recipients may be moved into Health Maintenance Organizations (HMO's) and other managed care settings. In this way, the payers (Medicare and the insurance companies) select the providers on the basis of fixed fee contracts for specific procedures and services.

o Reduced revenues for the healthcare industry providers serving the Medicare population. If hospitals, outpatient clinics, health professionals, and skilled care facilities cannot meet their expenses, they will go out of business or stop providing services for this patient population.

o The healthcare system may become more efficient. Threatened by reduced earnings, the trend to form hospital networks and alliances through mergers, acquisitions, and contractual arrangements may accelerate. These groups often include primary care services, inpatient hospitals, outpatient facilities, home care agencies, and other services such as physical and occupational therapy. The entire continuum of care is included in one organization. This allows for efficiencies in purchasing and support services and increases competition for managed care contracts involving "one stop shopping."

Several alternatives to dealing with a possible crisis in Medicare financing have been suggested. These include:

1. *Self Pay and Tax Law Changes* - This approach would increase the amount individuals pay for their Medicare coverage. Simultaneously, the amount of medical expenses that can be deducted from taxable income would be increased. The idea is to allow individuals to take a more proactive stance toward purchasing health care.

2. *Socialized Medicine or Government Controlled Healthcare* - This approach would be similar to the socialized medicine of the Canadian plan where the government would be the single payer for all healthcare expenses in the US. This approach would include all Americans, not just Medicare recipients. The Clinton healthcare proposal which was not enacted in 1992 had elements of this approach.

3. *Medicare Privatization* - The federal bureaucracy governing healthcare would end. In its place, Medicare recipients would receive a stipend to purchase healthcare insurance from the private market, along with an additional amount to pay for

deductibles. The elderly could keep any money left over after the end of the year, after paying for mandatory insurance and the deductible. This approach would add a dimension of consumer choice to the healthcare purchase decision.

Government Regulation of Employment Practices

Virtually every aspect of employment practice is regulated to some extent. These include the selection process, compensation and benefits, training, and employee behavior on the job. If the actions and policies of a company do not support the laws in these areas, the government may bring suit, levy fines, and require compliance with the law. The laws associated with each of these areas are summarized in Table 9.1.

Several regulatory areas are discussed below. These are sexual harassment, disabilities, workers' compensation and unemployment insurance. Sexual harassment has been illegal since 1980 and the Americans with Disabilities Act (ADA) was signed into law in 1990. Employers are also required to provide Workers' Compensation and Unemployment Insurance to all employees.

Sexual Harassment

In 1980, an Amendment to the 1964 Civil Rights Act was passed which prohibits sexual harassment in the workplace. Guidelines were issued and enforced by the EEOC. Behavior constitutes sexual harassment when:

1. Submission to such conduct is made either explicitly or implicitly a term or condition of an individual's employment;

Table 9.1 Federal Regulation of Employment Practices

Year	Law	Key Provisions
1963	Equal Pay Act	First anti-discrimination act; eliminates wage differentials based on sex alone
1964	Civil Rights Act	Bans discrimination in private employment on account of race, sex, or national origin; established the Equal Employment Opportunity Commission (EEOC)
1967	Age Discrimination in Employment Act (and Amendments in 1986)	Prohibits job discrimination against individuals based on age, prohibits mandatory retirement
1972	Equal Employment Opportunity Act	Gives EEOC the right to sue employers
1973	Vocational Rehabilitation Act	Requires federal contractors to take affirmative action on hiring the handicapped
1978	Pregnancy Discrimination Act	Requires employers to cover pregnancy, childbirth and related conditions in the same manner as other conditions
1980	Amendment to 1964 Civil Rights Act	Prohibits sexual harassment in the workplace and establishes guidelines on discrimination on the basis of sex
1988	Worker Adjustment and Retraining Notification Act (WARN)	Requires 60 days advance notice of layoffs or plant closing involving 50 or more employees
1990	Americans with Disabilities Act	Requires employers to make "reasonable accommodations" for the disabled
1991	Civil Rights Act	Makes it easier for employees to sue employers over discrimination based on race, religion, color, sex, national origin or disability
1993	Family and Medical Leave Act	Gives employees a legal right to take a leave without pay for family or medical emergencies

2. Submission to or rejection of such conduct by an individual is used as the basis for employment decisions affecting such individual; or

3. Such conduct has the purpose or effect of unreasonably interfering with an individual's work performance or creating an intimidating, hostile, or offensive working environment.

Source: "Guidelines on Discrimination on the Basis of Sex," Equal Employment Opportunity Commission (Washington, D.C.: November 10, 1980).

Unwelcome advances and abuse of power of a superior over a subordinate are subject to litigation. Over time, the situations which are covered under these guidelines have been broadened to include a harassing environment. Employers should control the workplace so employees are not forced to tolerate abusive conditions to earn a living. In addition, harassment can occur even if no job benefit is involved. For example, coworkers can be abusers. The employer is liable if they knew about the situation and the behavior occurs frequently. Employees may bring suit against their employers for emotional damages and suffering. (Dworkin, 1993).

In order to prevent sexual harassment in the workplace, businesses need to proactively address the issue through training programs for all employees. These might include role playing a harasser, and targeting and analyzing the types of responses which can occur. Visible top management support is essential. Specific company policies which guarantee confidentiality of a complaint, prompt and tactful investigation, and a written guarantee there will be no retaliation for filing a complaint are needed. Disciplinary action should be taken against proven harassers and managers or supervisors who retaliate against those who file complaints. (Thacker, 1994).

The Americans with Disabilities Act

The Americans with Disabilities Act (ADA) was signed into law on July 26, 1990 as a bipartisan effort. The ADA was passed to extend protections against discrimination to the 15 million workers with disabilities in the public and private sectors. It covers employers with 15 or more employees. It is illegal to discriminate against a disabled individual who is otherwise qualified to perform the essential functions of the job with or without reasonable accommodation. It requires business and government to pay the cost of accommodation. Complaints are filed with the EEOC.

> **Title I** requires reasonable accommodation for employees that can perform the essential functions of the job.
>
> **Title II** prohibits discrimination by state and local governments in the delivery of programs and services, including public transportation.
>
> **Title III** bans discrimination in access to hotels, restaurants, theaters, food stores, and other retail facilities. When remodeling, up to 20% of costs should be for access.
>
> **Title IV** mandates special telecommunications and closed-caption services for the hearing-impaired.

A disability is very generally defined and may include individuals who are visually impaired, hearing impaired, physically or mentally handicapped. This definition may include

"A.   a physical or mental impairment that substantially limits one or more of the major life activities of an individual

B.   a record of such impairment or

C.   being regarded as having an impairment" (Kohl & Greenlaw, 1992).

Reasonable accommodation may include changes in the workplace equipment needed to do the job, or changes in the production process. It may also require flexible schedules.

As a result of the ADA, we have seen a number of technological changes which benefit all individuals with disabilities. New elevators have both visual and voice cues, new models of televisions have written captions benefiting the hearing impaired, and recent breakthroughs in computer voice recognition allow anyone with limited movement of their hands to use computers. New buses are brought into service, which are lower and have lifts to accommodate wheelchairs. The lower design makes entering and exiting the vehicle easier for everyone and the lift can be used for individuals who can walk but have difficulty climbing stairs. Also, some of the technology developed to meet the requirements of the ADA may be beneficial in other areas.

However, a number of problems have been identified with this law. It is a classic case of good intentions being overwhelmed by a one-size-fits-all approach that results when policy is set for an entire country from Washington D.C. For example, a strip club in Bellevue Washington was threatened with a $4,500 fine for not having a wheelchair lift attached to the stage for performers. The company that hires the strippers argued: "It's just asinine. If you can't dance, why should you even be on stage?" (Bovard, 1995, p. A14).

Empty handicapped spaces abound at Builders' Square and Home Depot. But how many handicapped people are involved in home improvement projects? At the University of Illinois at Chicago, a 226 seat lecture hall was modified for wheelchair access. Twenty six seats were eliminated to make room for a virtual army of wheelchairs. One or two spots would have done just fine.

ADA has been the basis for numerous suits. Bovard (1995) reports on a 410 pound Bronx subway cleaner who sued the New York Transit Authority for not promoting him to subway train operator. But, a train operator must be able to climb under a stalled train to make adjustments. His 60 inch waistline created doubts that he would be able to fit.

A Tufts University student used the ADA to claim that the university was obliged to accommodate her aversion to taking tests. A Madison, Wisconsin telephone operator sued because her employer did not accommodate her narcolepsy which resulted in her being constantly late for work.

Finally, the EEOC expanded the definition of mental disability, to include problems in "thinking, concentrating and interacting with other people" (Bovard, 1995). Wait until creative college students learn about that one!

Workers' Compensation and Unemployment Insurance

Workers' compensation insurance is covered by state laws. Premiums are paid by the employer. Employees who are injured at work or suffer job related illnesses are eligible for disability income, medical expenses, rehabilitation, and lump-sum amounts for certain injuries. Since the premiums are determined by past history of injury and the risk level of jobs, it is important that workers' compensation claims are carefully monitored and that all claims are legitimate.

Unemployment insurance is part of the Social Security Act and provides a subsistence payment for individuals who have worked to some minimum level, have been laid off or dismissed by their employer, and are willing and able to accept a similar job. These plans are operated by the state and the specific eligibility requirements and benefits vary.

Managerial Responses

Companies have taken a variety of approaches to deal with the variety of forces and factors affecting employers today and in the future. Some of these programs are fairly standard practice. But, other, cutting edge concepts are breaking new ground in dealing with government regulation of employment practices and the challenge of recruiting and retaining competent workers.

Medical and Life Insurance

Insurance programs include medical and life insurance. In order to compete effectively for the best employees, most firms find it necessary to offer some type of medical benefits. However, part-time employees often do not qualify for this benefit and many small businesses cannot afford to offer it. Contract employees and self-employed individuals often find it difficult to obtain affordable medical insurance. Medical insurance is offered as a number of options including Health Maintenance Organizations (HMO), Preferred Provider Organizations (PPO), and traditional fee-for-service plans. The cost to the employee varies with each of these plans. HMOs cover all health care needs for a fixed fee, but the services that are provided are determined by the HMO. The individual has the maximum choice of providers with a traditional plan. PPOs allow choice among participating physicians and providers. The percentage of individuals covered by traditional fee-for-service plans has continued to decrease throughout the 1990's.

Life insurance is often provided as a multiple of an individual's salary. Some companies also offer the option to purchase additional insurance at group rates.

Corporate wellness programs are strategies to reduce the cost of medical care by avoiding injuries and illness. Programs include onsite fitness centers or reduced fees for local health clubs, information on improving lifestyle, good nutrition, etc., newsletters, and special events. Coors Beer found the following elements necessary for program success:

- Obtaining critical CEO support and direction which is included in the company values statement
- Making wellness a family affair
- Making the program available to all employees and their families
- Asking for employee input
- Conducting periodic needs assessments
- Ensuring programs meet objectives
- Communicating internally
- Keeping close tabs on related issues
- Becoming involved with the community
- Hiring qualified specialists
- Establishing a separate internal budget

(Stead, 1994)

The number of sick days, outpatient costs, and hospitalization costs were reduced as a result of participation in wellness programs at several companies. Table 9.2 shows the benefit to cost ratio of wellness programs at these companies. (Stead, 1994).

Table 9.2 Benefit/Cost Analysis of Corporate Wellness Programs

Company	Benefit/Cost Ratio
Travelers Insurance Co.	$3.40
Kennecott Copper	5.78
Metropolitan Life Smoke Cessation	3.15
Equitable Life	5.52
Blue Cross/Blue Shield of Indiana	2.51
Mesa Petroleum	2.16
Prudential	1.91
Motorola	3.00
New York Telephone	1.90

Women in the Workplace

Child Care Support - A number of factors have resulted in increased need for child care support. Baby boomers are now having their own families, often when they are in their thirties and hold management and professional positions. It is often necessary for both parents to work to meet the needs of the family. Child care makes it possible to return to work full-time rather than resign or work part time. New parents have to be offered the option of a 3-month unpaid leave of absence according to the Family and Medical Leave Act. Once that is over, many employees find high quality, affordable child care is unavailable in their area. Firms have found it is to their advantage to provide vouchers or child care facilities for their employees.

Bank One in Milwaukee piloted a parenting skills program developed at Marquette University's Parenting Center. The lunch time program was entitled STAR (Stop, Think, Ask, Respond) and parents attended voluntarily for 5 weeks. The goals of the program included:

o Learning to appreciate their own strengths and weaknesses as parents
o Developing reasonable expectations for their children
o Practicing effective nurturing techniques
o Using positive discipline strategies when dealing with young children using the STAR strategy
(Platz, 1995)

Evaluation of the program indicated that participants felt they had lowered their stress levels, improved relationships with their children, and strengthened their confidence levels (Platz, 1994). To the extent that stressful situations at home impact on an employee's productivity at work, this type of support benefits the individual employee and the organization.

Alternative work arrangements include flextime, four-day work week, and telecommuting. These arrangements provide alternative ways to balance work and family life for both full-time and part-time employees. According to the Bureau of Labor Statistics, 12.3% of the workforce in 1985 and 15% in 1991 worked on flexible schedules. (US BLS, 1992).

Flextime was offered by 14% of a sample of private firms and is defined as work schedules that permit flexible starting and quitting times within limits set by management (Keish & Stroh, 1994). The purpose of flextime is to improve motivation and morale, the ability to better balance work and family, to increase production capability, to help recruit a wider group of applicants, and to decrease commuting problems. Potential problems include: lack of coverage of the department, difficulty in monitoring attendance, and possible abuse. Flextime allows an organization to extend its hours without paying overtime or hiring new staff and meet the needs of the changing workforce.

The *four-day work week* is a schedule where employees work four ten-hour days. Usually they have Friday or Monday off, giving them a three day weekend. Benefits are fewer days of commuting each week, it appeals to single people and married people without small children, and it can be used to provide extended service hours. Potential problems are fatigue in some jobs after working for ten hours; resistance by management for some employees, especially supervisors, to work only four days per week; and the difficulty for some employees, mainly those with young children, to stay extended hours.

Telecommuting is defined as the substitution of communications technology for travel to a central work location (Ford & McLaughlin, 1995). Although it is frequently discussed, it has not been widely implemented. Benefits of telecommuting are that it reduces commuting time and saves office space. It is particularly appropriate for sales personnel, consultants, and contract workers who work at various customer locations as well as for computer programmers and others who work at off shifts.

There are a number of reasons telecommuting is not more frequently implemented. Managers do not feel comfortable when they cannot see employees, there is a lack of opportunity to communicate on a face to face basis, some jobs do not lend themselves to this setting, and equipment and space may have to be made available in employees' homes. Telecommuting requires a reduction of hierarchical control. Management must trust that employees are working. Power and control remain with the employer, however, who continues to set deadlines and work assignments (McQuarrie, 1994).

Some companies have experimented with a telecommuting center located close to employee residences. This allows for group interaction and some supervision, but reduces the commuting time to employees' homes and possibly to customers as well. Employers should not use telecommuting to avoid making changes required by the Americans for Disabilities Act, to try to reduce demand for child care benefits, and to shift office costs to employees. There is also a potential negative impact on businesses whose customers are commuters since there will be fewer trips made to the office. (McQuarrie, 1994).

A survey of 1,827 HR managers indicated that 15% had some type of telecommuting program. The 126 managers who had programs were surveyed. Three fourths indicated they were satisfied and 50% saw an increase in quality and volume of work. The programs were limited to relatively few employees in sales, computing, and independent contractors. To be successful, it was important to have top management support, be willing to risk an innovative program, and to select jobs with measurable output that can be monitored. Half of the jobs required a minimum time at the workplace, separate space at home, and had a written policy on telecommuting. Communication with supervisors and proper selection of employees who can organize their time effectively are extremely important. It was felt that telecommuting expands the labor pool to include the disabled, remotely located, and parents with children. (Ford & McLaughlin, 1995).

Another benefit offered by many firms is subsidized or free parking and special carpooling programs. Some organizations facilitate the use of public transportation by selling transit passes and tokens, providing low cost shuttle service to and from nearby train stations, and furnishing information about routes and schedules. A low cost strategy to increase the number of employees taking public transit or carpools is to provide a guaranteed ride home program. This program assures that employees who have to leave in an emergency will be reimbursed for taxi fares or provided a ride when it is needed.

Managing Employee Behavior

Companies must deal with issues of employee behavior, especially when it may endanger customers or other employees. Abuse of drugs or alcohol and smoking in the workplace are two examples of areas which must be dealt with fairly and effectively.

Abuse of drugs and alcohol has increased in society in general and in the workplace. Pre-employment drug testing is required in certain jobs such as railroad engineers, school bus drivers, airline pilots, nuclear power plant employees, and fire fighters (Hodgetts and Kroeck, 1992). It is now done in many other areas as well. Employee privacy and the accuracy of tests must be considered in the design of drug testing programs. Consideration also must be made of the costs and benefits of random drug testing programs. Employee assistance programs are often available to employees who have a substance abuse problem.

In the November, 1996 elections a proposition to legalize marijuana for medical use was passed in California. Some groups support the complete legalization of all drugs, assuming this would eliminate the crime associated with the sale of illegal substances. However, this also may lead to increased use and abuse of these substances in the states where these laws are in effect.

Smoking in the workplace is becoming more uncommon. Numerous external environmental forces have resulted in a significant decrease in the number of organizations which allow their employees to smoke on the job. These include: a change in culture to recognize the impact of second hand smoke, the FDA wanting to regulate tobacco as a drug, numerous anti-smoking laws and policies which ban smoking in public places, office buildings, hospitals, restaurants, etc., and enforcement of the law prohibiting the sale of cigarettes to minors.

Because smokers are susceptible to a variety of diseases to a greater extent than nonsmokers, there is a cross-subsidy from nonsmokers to smokers and extra costs imposed on business. It has been found that smokers have higher absentee rates, lose more time on-the-job for smoking breaks, use more medical care, have more accidents, and have a higher mortality rate (Cascio, 1982). To help their employees quit smoking, businesses may provide quit smoking programs as part of the wellness programs or charge additional insurance premiums to smokers.

Summary

An aging population will impact the workforce and begin to be felt with a simultaneous shortage of younger workers. The workforce will become more diverse and the participation of women in the workforce will continue to grow. Diversity in society and in the workforce presents many challenges. Broadly defined, diversity includes not only racial differences, but variations in religion, gender, urban vs. rural backgrounds, and educational experiences. The national population projections indicate that the US population is becoming more diverse by race and Hispanic origin.

Another factor impacting the number and type of workers available is immigration. The overall increase in the number of immigrants and the shift in proportions of different ethnic groups may lead to increased competition among these groups. Areas of conflict include: job competition, public benefits, and differentiation within each minority community.

Because of the demographic trends of an aging population and lower birth rates, there will be a shortage of traditional entry level workers between the ages of 16-24 as we move into the 21st century. At the same time, corporate downsizing, early retirement programs, and the overall aging of the population will result in additional older workers being available.

The labor market participation rate of women has increased from 34% in the 1950's to 46% in 1993. There are many reasons for this shift including: the high inflation rate of the early 1980's and high taxes resulting in the need for the two income family, increased opportunities for women due to overall expansion of jobs, and increased numbers of women completing college and entering professional and graduate schools. Other reasons include the impact of the 1960's & 1970's civil rights laws prohibiting discrimination against women in compensation and employment, the Pregnancy Discrimination Act of 1978 and the Family and Medical Leave Act of 1993.

Unions were established to give workers the opportunity to bargain collectively and so improve wages and working conditions. Today, many of the reforms sought by unions have been enacted into law. In addition, exploitation of the workforce is much more difficult due to increased worker mobility as the result of the proliferation of the automobile. In the mid-1950's, 35% of the nonagricultural workforce was in labor unions. This had dropped to 23% by 1980 and in 1994 it was less than 15%. A number of laws have been passed regulating various aspects of labor union formation, operation, and the activities of employers and employees. The most important laws are the *Wagner Act* and the *Taft-Hartley Act*.

The concept of *affirmative action* is that organizations should take actions to remedy situations where there is an under-representation of certain minority employees. Affirmative action has been very controversial. However, racial and other forms of discrimination are still present in American society and business.

Social security is basically a pay-as-you-go system with taxes from current workers being transferred to retirees. Any surplus of taxes over payments is used to purchase government bonds. As more and more baby boomers swell the retirement ranks, there will be fewer and fewer workers per retiree. Its been estimated that the ratio of workers to retirees will fall to 2 to 1. Existing social security tax rates cannot support the large retiree population.

Virtually every aspect of employment practice is regulated to some extent. These include the selection process, compensation and benefits, training, and employee behavior on the job. If the actions and policies of a company do not support the laws in these areas, the government may bring suit, levy fines, and require compliance with the law. In 1980, an Amendment to the 1964 Civil Rights Act was passed which prohibited Sexual Harassment in the Workplace. Guidelines were issued and enforced by the EEOC. The Americans with Disabilities Act (ADA) was signed into law in 1990 as a bi-partisan effort. The ADA was passed to extend protections against discrimination to the 15 million workers with disabilities in the public and private sectors.

In order to compete effectively for the best employees, most firms find it necessary to offer some type of medical benefits. Corporate Wellness Programs are strategies to reduce the cost of medical care by avoiding injuries and illness. It is often necessary for both parents to work to meet the needs of the family. Child care makes it possible to return to work full-time rather than resign or work part time. Alternative work arrangements include flextime, four-day work week, and telecommuting. These arrangements provide alternative ways to balance work and family life for both full-time and part-time employees.

Companies must deal with issues of employee behavior, especially when it may endanger customers or other employees. Abuse of drugs or alcohol and smoking in the workplace are two examples of areas which must be dealt with fairly and effectively.

Questions

1. How can firms best deal with the diversity of the workplace that is occurring now and in the future?

2. Should legal immigration into the US be continued?

3. Is it ethical for companies to hire illegal immigrants?

4. Why are women's wages less than men's?

5. The only growth in labor unions in recent years has been in the public sector. Why has this occurred?

6. Should Affirmative Action be abolished? What can companies do to reduce or eliminate racial and ethnic discrimination in the workplace?

7. What should be done to solve the impending social security crisis?

8. Should the ADA be changed? If so, what should be done with it?

Key Concepts

diversity in the workforce

older workforce

glass ceiling

right-to work laws

affirmative action

reverse discrimination

means testing of benefits

sexual harassment

corporate wellness programs

flextime

four-day work week

telecommuting

Case Analysis: Discrimination and Texaco
"The Two Faces of Texaco,"
by Kurt Eichenwald

Michael Moccio knew exactly what to do when a complaint of racial discrimination landed on his desk at Texaco Inc.

A manager in the oil giant's Denver office, Mr. Moccio had read the company's equal-opportunity policies and guidelines on proper conduct toward other employees. So when Mary Devorce, a black accountant in that office, filed a complaint with the Government in 1991, contending she had been subjected to racism at Texaco, Mr. Moccio was ready.

First he assured Ms. Devorce that, despite the complaint, her job was safe. He told her that Texaco would treat her fairly. To demonstrate the company's concern, Mr. Moccio even offered her new duties that would remove her from the situation she found discriminatory.

It was all going exactly as it should. Then Mr. Moccio, who is white, called his supervisor, Jim Woolly, a white assistant controller in Houston. He filled in his boss on the complaint and described how he had handled it.

Mr. Wooly was not impressed, according to a sworn affidavit by Mr. Moccio.

"I'd fire her black ass," Mr. Woolly responded. When Mr. Moccio protested that Texaco could not dismiss someone for contending she was victim of discrimination — a move that saved Ms. Devorce's job — Mr. Woolly shrugged it off.

I guess we treat niggers differently down here," he replied, according to the affidavit, filed in a Federal discrimination suit.

An there, for Texaco, lies the grim conundrum. The antidiscrimination policies are in place. The channels for complaint are in place. The surveys in which employees can gripe anonymously to management about what needs improvement are in place.

But the array of principles and policies can often be impotent, largely because midlevel or senior managers operate by their own rules — with almost no corporate oversight.

The equal opportunity system at Texaco, the nation's 14th-largest corporation, has come under the microscope after the disclosure last week that senior company executives, in secretly recorded conversations, plotted to destroy documents demanded in the discrimination suit, and used racial epithets in discussing black employees.

But the explosive tapes are a window on a bigger problem. Thousands of pages of sealed court records obtained by the New York Times, as well as Government documents, corporate records and sworn depositions, portray a company that says all the right things but that has done far too little to insure they have meaning.

The documents, filed in the discrimination suit, which was brought by Texaco employees, reflect an equal-opportunity program without teeth. For example, responsibility for meeting equal-opportunity obligations at the company is pushed down to more than three dozen company divisions, but senior Texaco executives impose no oversight on those divisions to insure that the lower-level executives abide by Federal regulations.

And unlike many other companies, Texaco does not audit the performance of the divisions to make sure company practices like employee-performance reviews are not unfairly derailing the careers of minority-group employees. Instead, the company relies on audits conducted by the government every few years on each division.

The documents also show that Texaco has a long way to go in promoting members of minority groups and in assuring that its workplace is free of hurtful racism:

- African-Americans make up some 12 percent of the United States population, but of the 873 executives at Texaco who make more than $106,000 annually — only .6 or .7 percent — are black. And while the number of executives in the highest pay grade has grown 44 percent over the last four years, to 49, not a single black person has held such a job.

- A Labor Department audit this year of an important Texaco division found that employees who were members of minority groups had to wait far longer for promotions and were far less likely to receive evaluations that would help them in their careers. Last May the agency ordered Texaco to compensate the minority-group employees for lost wages and to revise the appraisal system, which is used throughout the company.

- Scores of Texaco's minority-group employees contend in the court papers that they were subjected to racially hostile behavior but did not report the infractions for fear of losing their jobs.

"Deficiencies in the affirmative-action programs suggest that Texaco is not committed to insuring comprehensive, facility by facility, compliance with the company's affirmative-action responsibilities," wrote Leonard J. Bierman, former acting director of the Federal agency that monitors affirmative-action programs of Federal contractors like Texaco. His comments were in a confidential report on behalf of the plaintiffs in the discrimination suit. Because of those deficiencies, "Texaco cannot determine whether its affirmative-action programs achieve their goals or whether the company's policies and practices are having an adverse impact on African-Americans."

The problems at Texaco reflect the slow and bumpy development of equal employment opportunity for minority groups at companies everywhere. To date, there has been widespread success in hiring. But now, as at Texaco, comes the next challenge—that of moving those employees into senior management and assuring that the growing number of minority-group employees are treated fairly and with respect.

The executives' slurs caught on tape—like "black jelly beans" and "niggers" raise troubling questions. Were these the words of renegade, Texaco Executives—including the former treasurer—who had abandoned the company's self-proclaimed values? Or was this the unvarnished voice of Texaco's true corporate culture finally being heard?

"The tapes really do raise some profound questions about the integrity of Texaco's commitment to equal opportunity," said Wade Henderson, the executive director of the Leadership Conference on Civil Rights, an umbrella group of 180 organizations. "With the litigation and the tapes, serious questions emerge about whether this is an isolated incident or something far deeper."

Over the last week, Peter I. Bijur, Texaco's chairman and chief executive only since July, has repeatedly stepped before the cameras and the press to express horror at the blatant racism captured on the tapes.

Those recorded words "are statements that represent attitudes we hoped and wished had long ago disappeared entirely from the landscape of our country—and certainly from our company," Mr. Bijur said at a news conference last week. "We believe unequivocally it is utterly reprehensible to deny another human of his or her self-respect and dignity because of race, color, religion or sex.

Mr. Bijur has also announced that the company intends to shake up its diversity and equal-opportunity programs from top to bottom. A board committee has been charged with reviewing them, and a special consultant has been brought in to review the company's policies and insure that minority-group workers are treated fairly.

No doubt, many of Texaco's top executives and many of the company's 19,000 employees in this country are also horrified by the behavior of some of their colleagues. And the company has, in fact, stepped up its hiring and promotion of women and members of minority groups.

But critics of the company say the tapes are merely the most overt sign of a long running problem, and that Texaco still has far to go.

"Top management says this was a deplorable aberration, but Texaco's employees tell us they see prejudice around them all the time," said Timothy Smith, the executive director of the Interfaith Center on Corporate Responsibility, a group of socially concerned investors that has been pressuring Texaco to address discrimination for years.

Source: *The New York Times*, Sunday, November 10, 1996, Section 3, pp. 1, 10. Reprinted with permission.

Texaco's Response

Press releases beginning with Peter Bijur's letter to employees on 11/4/96 when the story was first released in the New York Times.

To All Texaco Employees:

This is a very sad day for Texaco. The *New York Times* today printed an article about new allegations in a pending employment discrimination lawsuit against Texaco. These allegations claim that some current and former employees in the Harrison Finance Department made offensive and derogatory racial and religious comments concerning the company's employees. The allegations also concern possible concealment or destruction of documents related to the lawsuit.

I am deeply angered and saddened at the allegations contained in the article. If true, they are in direct violation of Texaco's long-standing core values and principles concerning respect for the individual and ethical behavior. My personal commitment to you is to intensify our efforts to eliminate this behavior from the workplace. No matter how good our policies are, they are only as good as the people that implement them. This is the responsibility of each and every one of us. The actions of any one individual reflect upon all of us; therefore, we are accountable to each other for the highest ethical and moral standards. We all have worked hard to make Texaco a company we can be proud of. None of us should permit anyone to detract from our commitment to maintain a work environment which is free from discrimination and allows every employee to develop to the utmost of their capabilities.

Texaco has retained outside counsel to immediately conduct an independent investigation to determine whether these allegations are true. If the company finds that the alleged misconduct occurred, immediate disciplinary action will be taken against the employees involved. This action could include termination of employment.

Texaco's reputation depends on the honesty, integrity and good judgment of us all. Misconduct such as that alleged, and the failure by any employee to report such behavior, will not be tolerated. Let there be no mistake: there is no place for this kind of misconduct at Texaco.

Sincerely,

Peter I. Bijur, CEO

Statement by Peter I. Bijur, November 6, 1996

I told our employees on Monday, my personal commitment is to intensify our efforts to eliminate forever this kind of behavior from our workplace. To that end, I am also announcing the following steps:

One – senior executives from Texaco will visit every major company location in the U.S. to meet with our people. Their mission will be to apologize to them for the embarrassment and humiliation this has created. We want them to understand both our personal embarrassment and our firm resolve to ensure that nothing like this ever happens again at Texaco.

Two – we will gather employees together immediately to refocus on our core values and on what we each need to do to create a workplace free of intolerance. It will be a time of reflection and a time for taking personal accountability for actions and attitudes.

Three – we are expanding our diversity learning experience to include all employees, in addition to our managers and supervisors. This two-day seminar, in which I have already participated, along with the senior officers of the company, focuses on both the intent and the impact of personal behavior on peers, teams and the organization overall.

Four – we will reemphasize the critical importance of our confidential Ethics Hotline as a vital tool for reporting any behavior – any behavior – that violates our core values, policies or the law. Calls may be made anonymously, 24 hours a day, seven days a week. We are extending this service to a broader list of countries outside of the U.S.

Fifth – I have today asked Judge A. Leon Higgenbotham of the New York law firm of Paul, Weiss, Rifkind, Wharton & Garrison to work side by side with us to assure that the company's human relationship policies and practices are consistent with the highest standard of respect for the individual and to assure that the company treats all its employees with fundamental fairness.

Sixth – we are also creating a special committee of our Board of Directors, to be headed by John Brademas, President Emeritus of New York University. This committee will be charged with reviewing our company's diversity programs in their entirety – at every level within our company.

Texaco Statement Following Meetings with African-American Leaders

The following are remarks by Peter I. Bijur following his meetings with Kweisi Mfume, Head of the NAACP at the NAACP's headquarters in Baltimore; and with Rev. Jesse Jackson, Rainbow Coalition; Rev. Al Sharpton; Rev Franklin Richardson; Nancy Ware, Executive Director, Rainbow Coalition; Ernie Prince, Regional Director, National Urban League; Dennis Walcott, Regional Director, Westchester Urban League; Hazel Dukes, Executive Director of NY State NAACP; Yuri Tadesse, Rainbow Coalition; and Chi Chi Williams, Rainbow Coalition/Operation Push at Texaco's corporate offices in White Plains, NY

Statement by Peter I. Bijur
Chairman and CEO, Texaco Inc.
November 12, 1996

These discussions have been a significant help to Texaco, and I'm gratified that these leaders have been able to make time to join with us.

"I'm gratified because Texaco is facing a difficult, but vital challenge. It's broader than a single lawsuit, larger than any taped conversation. In any organization of 27,000 people worldwide, unfortunately, there are bound to be people with unacceptable attitudes toward race, gender and religion. Our goal is to eradicate this kind of thinking wherever and however it is found in our company. And our challenge is to make Texaco a company of limitless opportunity for all men and women.

"I've already announced a number of steps to start us on this mission and we are exploring still others. We are reaching out, in meetings like today's, for ideas and perspectives that will help Texaco succeed in our mission of becoming a model of diversity and workplace equality.

"As I also said in the discussions, it is essential to this urgent mission that Texaco and African American leaders work together to help solve the problems we face as a company—which, after all, echo the problems faced in society as a whole. Discrimination will be extinguished only if we tackle it together—only if we join in a unified, common effort.

"We also want to broaden economic access to Texaco for minority firms, and increase the positive impact our investments can have in the minority community. In areas such as hiring and promotion, in professional services such as advertising, banking, investment management, accounting, legal and others, in wholesale and retail station ownership and other areas, the counsel of the leaders I have met with today and others can help Texaco establish a track record of progress in which we can all take pride.

"Together, I believe we can take Texaco into the 21st Century as a model of diversity. We can make Texaco a company of limitless opportunity. We can make Texaco a leader in according respect to every man and woman. This *must* happen; I am determined to do this; and with the help of those we met with today, we can make serious, positive changes for every member of the Texaco family.

Texaco Announces Settlement in Class Action Lawsuit

Texaco Inc. today announced it has reached an Agreement in Principle to settle the *Roberts v. Texaco* class action lawsuit, brought in 1994 on behalf of a class of approximately 1,400 individuals, comprised of all current and certain former African American employees.

Under the settlement, which was described to the Court, Texaco agreed to:

- Provide a payment to the plaintiff-class in the amount of $115 million, along with a one-time salary increase of about 11 percent for current employees of the plaintiff-class, effective January 1, 1997;
- Create an Equality and Tolerance Task Force which will be charged with determining potential improvements to Texaco's human resources programs, as well as helping to monitor the progress being made in those programs (three members of the Task Force to be appointed by the plaintiffs, three members by Texaco and a mutually agreed-upon chairperson);
- Adopt and implement company wide diversity and sensitivity, mentoring, and ombuds programs;
- Consider nationwide job posting of more senior positions than are currently posted; and
- Monitor its performance on the programs and initiatives provided for under the settlement agreement.

Case Questions

1. Is the situation at Texaco unique or is racial discrimination a problem in many firms?

2. What could Texaco have done to avoid this situation?

3. Does a monetary settlement exonerate Texaco from its past discriminatory policies?

4. Do you think the program Texaco has developed will reduce discrimination and lead to more diversity in its managerial positions?

5. Should these policies apply to all minorities at Texaco?

6. Did Texaco act in a socially responsible manner?

7. Did Texaco act in an ethical manner?

References

American Civil Liberties Union Briefing Paper Number 17.

Bolick, Clint, *The Affirmative Action Fraud: Can We Restore the American Civil Rights Vision,* Washington, D.C., Cato Institute, 1996.

Bovard, James, "The Disabilities Act's Parade of Absurdities." *The Wall Street Journal*, June 22, 1995, p. A14.

Calmes, Jackie "Wall Street Quietly Promotes Social Security Overhaul." *The Wall Street Journal,* December 3, 1996, p. A22.

Cascio, Wayne F., *Costing Human Resources: The Financial Impact of Behavior in Organizations*, Belmont, CA: Wadsworth, Inc., 1982.

Caudron, Shari, "US West Finds Strength in Diversity," *Personnel Journal* Vol 71, No. 3, March, 1992, 49-54.

Corley, Nobert H., Reed, O. Lee, Shedd, Peter J. S., Morehead, Jere U., *The Legal and Regulatory Environment of Business*, 10th edition, New York: McGraw Hill. 1996.

Craver, Charles B., "The American Labor Movement in the Year 2000," *Business Horizons*, Volume 36, Number 6, November-December, 1993, 64-69.

Day, Jennifer Cheeseman, "National Population Projections," US Census Bureau, 1996.

Dworkin, Terry Morehead, "Harassment in the 1990s," *Business Horizons,* March-April, 1993, 52-57.

Equal Employment Opportunity Commission, *Guidelines on Discrimination on the Basis of Sex*, Washington, DC, November 10, 1980.

Ferrara, Peter J, "The New Politics of Social Security." *The Wall Street Journal*, February 4, 1996, p. A14.

Ford, Robert C. and McLaughlin, Frank, "Questions and Answers about Telecommuting Programs," *Business Horizons*, May-June, 1995.

Genetski, Robert, "Privatize Social Security." *The Wall Street Journal*, May 21, 1993, p. A12.

Glass Ceiling Commission, U.S. Department of Labor, 1996.

Hodgetts, Richard M. and Kroeck, K. Galen, *Personnel and Human Resource Management*, New York: The Dryden Press, 1992.

Hudgins, Edward L., "Handicapping Freedom: The Americans with Disabilities Act," *Regulation—The CATO Review of Business and Government*, Number 2, 1995, 67-76

Keish, Karen S. and Stroh, Linda K., "Flextime: Myth or Reality," *Business Horizons*, Volume 37, Number 5, Sept-Oct, 1994, 51-55.

Kohl, John P., and Greenlaw, Paul S., "The Americans with Disabilities Act of 1990: Implications for Managers," *Sloan Management Review*, Spring, 1992, 87-90.

McNaught, William and Barth, Michael C., "Are Older Workers 'Good Buys'?—A Case Study of Days Inn of America," *Sloan Management Review*, Spring, 1992, 53-63.

McQuarrie, Fiona A. E. "Telecommuting: Who really Benefits?" *Business Horizons*, Nov-Dec, 1994.

Platz, Donald L., "Supporting Employees Who are Parents: Worksite Child-Rearing Program," *Business Horizons*, March/April, 1995, 81-82.

Schuck, Peter, "The Evolving Civil Rights Movement: Old Civil Rights and New Immigration," *Current*, January 1994.

Snavely, Kay, "Managing Conflict Over the Perceived Progress of Working Women," *Business Horizons*, Volume 36, Number 2, March-April, 1993, 17-21.

Solomon, Charlene Marmer, "Unlock the Potential of Older Workers," *Personnel Journal*, Vol. 74, No. 10, October, 1995, 56-66.

Stead, Bette Ann, "Worksite Health Programs: A Significant Cost-Cutting Approach," *Business Horizons*, November-December, 1994, 73-77.

Stuart, Peggy, "Employees Launch ESL Tutoring at the Workplace," *Personnel Journal*, Vol 73, No. 11, Nov, 1994, 49-54.

Thacker, Rebecca A., "Innovative Steps to Take in Sexual Harassment Prevention," *Business Horizons*, Volume 37, Number 1, January-February, 1994, 29-32.

U.S. Bureau of Labor Statistics, News, USDL 92-491, August 4, 1992.

U.S. Immigration and Naturalization Service, "Immigration to the United States in Fiscal Year 1995: Characteristics of Legal Immigrants," 1996.

CHAPTER 10

IMPACT OF NEW TECHNOLOGY ON THE WORKPLACE

Over the past few decades, the pace of technological change has increased at a phenomenal rate. Computers have changed from being curiosities at scientific institutions to the common place, found in homes as well as industry. Robot technology has moved from science fiction to reality as firms use these tools in production and distribution. Space technology and bioengineering have already resulted in many industrial applications, and most likely will provide many additional changes in production processes as well as the development of whole new products in the future.

Because of the technological changes that have already occurred and will occur in the future, technology is becoming an extremely important force in the external environment of business. Today's manager must keep abreast of changes in technology that result in new products and processes being developed. Adaptation of this technology may be necessary to remain competitive in the U.S. as well as in international markets. Technological change also has broad societal implications which affect business both directly and indirectly.

In a survey of 101 American companies, five out of six saw technological innovation as their main engine of growth ("American Industry Rediscovers Innovation," 1980). Along with an increased rate of innovation they saw three new systems industries developing from new technology. These are production systems utilizing robotics and computer-assisted design and manufacturing, administrative systems composed of the office of the future, and household systems combining entertainment and education with electronic banking and shopping, control of home appliances, lighting, and heating/air conditioning units. Thus, whether in the plant, office or home, technology is an important force shaping future jobs, tasks, products and processes.

By the mid-1990's many of these technologies were available to consumers and business. The price of computers dropped dramatically during the 1980's and 90's, and CD ROM books are sold at many bookstores. The Internet, dubbed the information superhighway, became available to home computer users and businesses in addition to the original availability through the government and universities. The electronic age arrived, with all its benefits and costs.

This chapter is not designed to provide a detailed understanding of the inner workings of computers, robots, etc. Rather, its purpose is to explore the important societal changes, economic developments, and public policy issues which have resulted from technological change. These social, economic, and public policy issues will then be related to business and the functions of management. In order to do this, a brief history of technological change will be presented. Related changes occurring in society in general and the public policy issues which have developed will be identified. The technological environment will be related to the other major elements of the external environment and the implications of technological change on the manager will be enumerated.

Major Technological Breakthroughs

Technology can be defined as "a process of extending human capability, and thus may include tools, techniques, products, processes, and methods" (Cravens, Hills, and Woodruff, 1976). The key to understanding technology and its impact on society lies in this definition. By extending human capability, technological change has resulted in increased production and standards of living. However, technological change has also resulted in social, political and economic change, not all of which has been beneficial. There have been a few major technological breakthroughs in recent history which have affected social, political, legal, and economic developments (Rothwell, 1981). An understanding of these breakthroughs, and the societal changes which they brought, can provide useful insights into what today's technological change may bring.

<u>Steam Power</u> signaled the beginnings of the industrial revolution. Prior to the development of the steam engine, industry relied on the harnessing of water power as a source of energy. The steam engine allowed movement of factories away from water sources. Along with this movement came a variety of other social and economic changes.

Steam power helped to facilitate the gradual movement of the economy from an agricultural to a manufacturing base. Prior to the advent of the industrial revolution, most work was performed either on farms or at home by craftsmen. The craftsmen were replaced by factories. Instead of working at home, employees of steam-powered factories worked there instead. The large factories required a large labor force that lived in close proximity to work. Thus, urban areas began to develop. In 1790, five percent of the population lived in cities with a population of 2,500 or greater. By 1860, 19.7 percent of the people lived in the cities.

As productivity increased, factory wages also moved up, increasing the purchasing power of the average worker. In addition, the development of the factory allowed the production of low-cost, standardized products to meet new consumer demand. Because of a relative shortage of skilled labor in the early 1800's, American industrialists used labor economically but were extravagant in their use of raw materials. Managerial methods of standardization of goods, interchangeability of parts, and division of labor were common by the 1830's (Hughes, 1983).

Railroads followed the development of steam power and the beginning of industrialization. Building of the railroads was done during the late 1800's through the joint efforts of government, a large immigrant labor force, and American entrepreneurs. Thus, completion of 351,767 miles of track by 1910 represented political, economic and social forces operating together. Railroads also were the first industry to be under the control of the Interstate Commerce Commission, signaling the beginning of government regulation of industry.

Movement of people and businesses to central cities was facilitated by the railroad network. The number of towns with a population over 2500 increased to 2262 by 1910, and over 45% of the population resided in these cities. The benefits to industries locating in close proximity to each other and to transportation centers outweighed the problems of large urban areas (such as pollution and other externalities).

The railroads also provided a major impetus to the settlement of the west and midwest. The fertile plains states were developed in part due to the railroads. Without railroad transportation, it was difficult and expensive to ship agricultural products to the east and to foreign markets. Railroad transportation lowered the cost of shipping agricultural commodities, making farming in the plains states commercially feasible.

The street railways and commuter rail lines that developed in the cities at approximately the same time as the intercity rail network expanded the residential possibilities of city workers. No longer was it necessary to live within walking distance of work. The railways allowed suburbs to develop, and the movement out of the central city began.

Electrical Power produced a wide variety of far-reaching changes in business and in the home. Not only did electricity change production techniques but its use also resulted in changes in the characteristics of factories and their locations. In steam-driven plants, economy and efficiency in the transmission of power required that machines be crowded around one main drive shaft in a multi-story structure. This arrangement was not necessary in electrical-driven plants. Assembly lines located in sprawling one-story facilities became feasible. Such facilities required a great deal of land which was available and cheap in suburban locations. Thus, electrical power was one of the factors contributing to the location of industry in the suburbs.

Electricity was a contributing factor in expanding the optimal size of manufacturing establishments, as well as increasing productivity. In 1870, the average manufacturing establishment was operated by eight people, adding $6,000 per year to the value of raw materials. By 1914, the typical plant was operated by 28 people and added $50,000 per year to the value of raw materials (Russell, 1964).

Electrical power permitted the development of a vast array of household products including toasters, refrigerators, washing machines, electric lights, air conditioners, blenders, mixers, etc. Electricity also provides the power source for the electronic equipment that proliferates today in both homes and industry.

The Internal Combustion Engine further increased the mobility of the American public. No longer were people confined to neighborhoods within close proximity to their homes. The automobile allowed the further development of suburbs, contributed to the movement of factories out of the central city, and later, was a factor in the development of suburban shopping malls and entertainment centers.

Whole new transportation industries also developed. The trucking and airline industries developed rapidly beginning in the 1920's along with the highway construction and oil industries.

The internal combustion engine also affected agriculture as mechanization on the farm became commonplace. Mechanization of agriculture had two distinct impacts. In the 1920's it involved the substitution of machines for animal power. After 1940, the main effect was to bring a sharp reduction in the amount of labor needed per unit of output (Davis, 1972). This increased productivity resulted in a dramatic movement of population from rural to urban locations.

The Semiconductor and related microelectronic technology is the most recent breakthrough. The transistor was developed by Bell Laboratories in 1947 by Walter Brittain, John Bardeen and William Shockley. In 1951 Western Electric licensed transistor technology to other firms and in 1954 Texas Instruments began the production of silicon transistors.

The technology was further developed as firms began producing integrated circuits which expand the number of functions contained on one "chip." This miniaturization process resulted in the development of microprocessors which form the "brain" of personal computers, robots, and many other consumer and industrial goods (Kimberly & Miles, 1981).

Throughout this period, prices have dropped and the variety and capacity of these products have increased dramatically, opening up the world of electronics and computers to small businesses and individuals. This trend is continuing, with possible impact on social patterns, educational requirements, economic trends, and future government regulation.

Two other technological breakthroughs deserve mention. The development of interchangeable parts was an American innovation which eliminated the dependence of manufacturing on handcrafting skills. This development set the stage for the assembly line production that began with Henry Ford in 1914. The telephone was a significant breakthrough which influenced office locations. Prior to the telephone, businesses had to place offices in close proximity to buyers and suppliers, which usually meant a downtown location. The telephone allowed business to be conducted at a distance, permitting suburban office locations. Thus, the telephone was an important factor contributing to the movement of offices out of central cities.

Overall Impacts of Technological Change

Taken together, the major technological breakthroughs and other tools, techniques, processes and methods which have been developed over time have had a variety of impacts on business, the economy, individuals, and the social system. Some of the more important impacts are shown in Table 10.1.

Table 10.1. Overall Impacts of Technological Change

1. Increase in Productivity of the Workforce
2. Increase in Standard of Living
3. Change in the Composition of Output
4. Decline in the Importance of Agriculture
5. Increase in Urbanization
6. Decline in the Work Week
7. Increase in Labor Participation Rates of Women
8. Mass Production with Limited Customizing
9. Change in Production Techniques
10. Growth of Suburbanization

Figure 1

By far, the most important impacts concern increases in productivity and living standards. Quantitative studies of historical changes in productivity and incomes have found that no more than 15 percent of the rise over time in per capita income in the United States could be explained by increases in capital per worker (Davis, 1972). The other 85 percent most likely came from changes in technology. An example is agriculture. In Figure 10.1 is shown output per acre and per man hour in agriculture from 1840 to 1960. The expansive growth in productivity shown in the figure began in 1940 as mechanization was substituted for labor and as the use of chemicals, fertilizer and eventually genetics and biochemistry became common.

Another impact concerns the effect of technology on the composition of output. Technological change results in new products being produced and new uses for these products. It is interesting to look at the ten largest industries in the United States in 1860 and 1960. These are shown in Tables 10.2 and 10.3. In the tables are shown the industries by employment and value added (which is the additional value added to raw materials by the production process). Value added per worker can be used as a measure of the productivity of the workplace. Not only do none of the top ten 1860 industries appear in 1960, but also, overall value added per worker has increased 24-fold for all manufacturing.

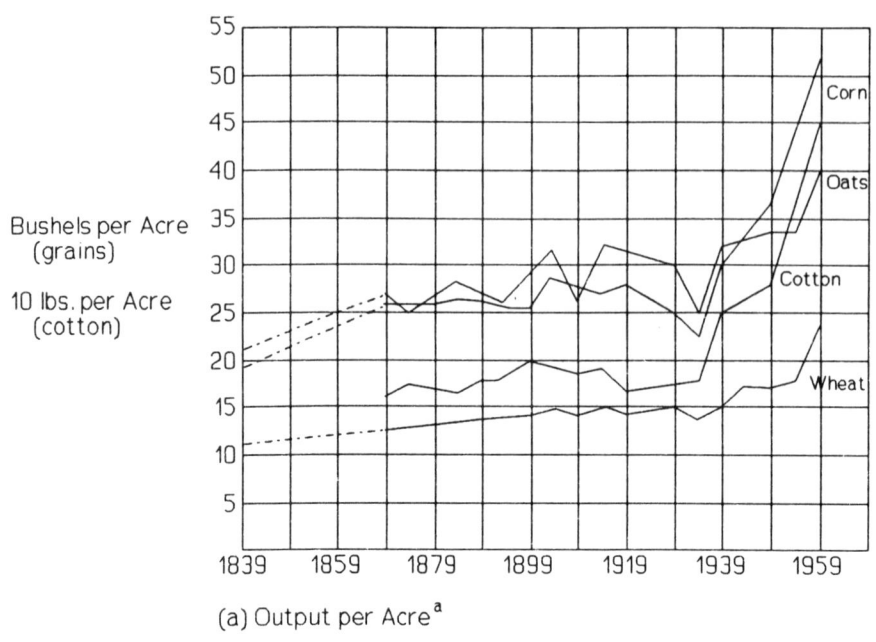

(a) Output per Acre[a]

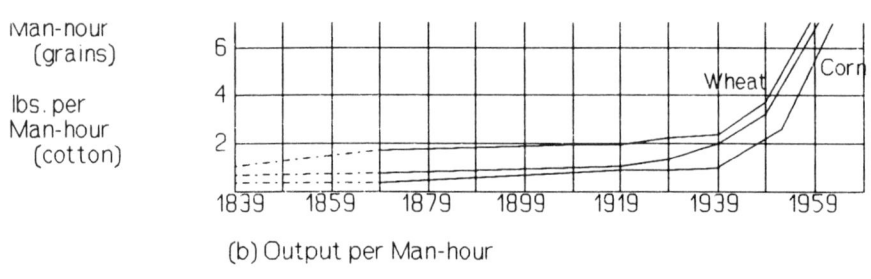

(b) Output per Man-hour

[a] Estimated trend, 1839-1869, and at five-year intervals thereafter.

Source: Davis, Lance E., et. al., *American Economic Growth: An Economists History of the United States,* Harper & Row, New York, 1972, p. 374.

Figure 10.1. Output Per Acre and Per Man-Hour in the Major Crops, 1840–1960

Table 10.2. The Ten Largest Industries in 1860

	Value Added (millions of dollars) (1)	Employment (thousands of workers) (2)	Value Added per Worker (thousands of dollars) (3)
Cotton goods	55	115	.48
Lumber	54	76	.71
Boots and shoes	49	123	.40
Flour and meal	40	28	1.43
Men's clothing	37	115	.32
Iron	36	50	.72
Machinery	33	41	.81
Woolen goods	25	61	.41
Carriages and wagons	24	37	.65
Leather	23	23	1.00
All manufacturing	815	1474	.55

Source: U.S. Bureau of the Census, *Census of the United States:* 1860, vol. 3, U.S. Government Printing Office, Washington, D.C., 1861, pp. 733–742.

While some of the 1860 industries have all but disappeared, others such as boots and shoes, leather, cotton goods and lumber are still produced. These industries are quite small in comparison to other manufacturing today. This is because consumers spend more of their incomes on other goods. There has been a massive decline in the proportion of overall consumer budgets spent on food and other necessities over the past 150 years. Increased incomes are not all spent on increased consumption of existing products. Some is spent on the consumption of new products.

Mechanization and other technological changes in agriculture have brought about sharp reductions in the amount of labor needed to produce food. In 1840, 63 percent of the labor force was involved in agricultural production. In 1960, only 8 percent of the workforce produced agricultural products (Davis, 1972). In 1992, less than 1% of those employed listed their occupation as farmers (U.S. Bureau of Labor Statistics, 1993).

Table 10.3. The Ten Largest Industries in 1960

	Value Added (millions of dollars) (1)	Employment (thousands of workers) (2)	Value Added per Worker (thousands of dollars) (3)
Nonelectrical machinery	14.38	1,012	14.2
Electrical machinery	13.07	950	13.8
Motor vehicles	10.12	571	17.8
Steel	7.69	504	15.2
Aircraft	6.45	410	15.7
Basic chemicals	5.10	161	31.7
Beverages	3.20	116	27.8
Dairy products	3.17	134	23.6
Structural metal products	2.93	239	12.3
Newspapers	2.92	160	18.3
All manufacturing	163.57	12,185	13.4

Source: U.S. Bureau of the Census, *Survey of Manufacturers, 1959 and 1960*. U.S. Government Printing Office, 1962, Washington, D.C., pp. 28–47.

The loss in agricultural job opportunities, especially after 1940, provided a tremendous economic stimulus for migration out of rural areas into urban places. Urban growth continued at a rapid pace since then, as can be seen in Table 10.4. The increase in urbanization required greater government involvement in the economy. Provision of public goods and services such as roads, sewer systems, schools, and fire and police protection were required. At the same time, the need to tax urban residents and businesses arose. Thus, the political and legal sectors increased in importance along with the movement to the city.

Some of the increased income resulting from technological change was spent in the form of increased leisure time. Thus, the workweek declined to 40 hours with the passage of wage and hour laws.

Technological change also resulted in increased labor force participation rates of women. The labor-saving devices and products developed for home use such as automatic washing machines and clothes dryers, dishwashers, microwave ovens, permanent press clothes and frozen foods, freed women from many household chores and reduced the time required to do others. This "free" time was utilized by women in a productive way through entry into the labor force.

Table 10.4. Urban Growth in the United States, 1790–1980, Places of 2500 or More

Year	Number of Cities	Population (thousands)	Population Growth per Decade (percent)	Percent of Total Population
1790	24	202		5.1
1800	33	322	59.9	6.1
1810	46	525	63.0	7.2
1820	61	693	31.9	7.2
1830	90	1,127	62.6	8.8
1840	131	1,845	63.7	10.8
1850	236	3,544	92.1	15.3
1860	392	6,216	75.4	19.8
1870	663	9,902	59.3	25.7
1880	939	14,130	42.7	28.2
1890	1,348	22,106	56.5	35.1
1900	1,737	30,160	36.4	39.7
1910	2,262	41,999	39.3	45.7
1920	2,722	54,158	29.0	51.2
1930	3,165	68,955	27.3	56.2
1940	3,464	74,424	7.9	56.5
1950	4,054	89,749	20.6	59.6
1960*	5,445	114,728	27.8	64.0
1970*	6,435	133,412	16.3	65.7
1980*	7,749	153,128	14.8	67.6

Source: U.S. Bureau of the Census, *Census of Population: 1960*, vol. 1. *Characteristics of the Population*, U.S. Government Printing Office, Washington, D.C., 1961, Part A, pp. 1-14, 1-15. Table 8, and *Census of Population: 1980*, vol. 1. *Characteristics of the Population*, U.S. Government Printing Office, Washington, D.C., 1983, Chapter A, Part 1, p. 37, Table 5.

*New census definition of urban place.

The changes in production techniques resulted in reduced manufacturing costs. In addition, mass production with limited customizing required a change in consumer habits. The tailor-made suit gave way to the "ready-made" suit. The handcrafted, one-of-a-kind item became a rarity, replaced by low-cost mass production goods. The manner in which goods were produced changed drastically over time. Gone were the craftsmen, replaced by assembly lines, electrical machinery, and sprawling production facilities.

Finally, technological change not only affected the growth of urban areas, but also the growth of suburbs as well. Both plants and offices began to move to suburban locations. Along with this movement of business came people, both from the city and from rural areas.

As can be seen from this discussion, for over 150 years, technology has had a major impact on industry, transportation, the cities, and individual lifestyles. Society today differs greatly from that of 150 years ago. These changes were caused in part by the technological changes which occurred during that time. Today, the pace of technological change appears to be increasing as new innovations are being adapted for use in the factory, the office and the home. The social changes that are occurring might be of greater significance than those of the past.

Automation in the Factory

Substitution of capital for labor has taken place since industrialization began in the early 1800's. British workers, known as Luddites, smashed machines being introduced in the textile industry at that time. Fear of massive unemployment of workers who had been replaced by machines and associated economic crises were their concerns. These same fears are expressed today by those who predict that automation and computers will replace human workers.

The word "robot" was derived from the Czech word for forced labor and was popularized by K. Capek in a broadway play entitled "Rossum's Universal Robots" in 1921 (Whaley, 1982). Industrial robots were developed in the U.S., and in 1961 General Motors installed a Unimation robot. In 1968, Cincinnati Milacron began developing robots although they did not begin selling them until 1977. By 1982, IBM, General Electric, Bendix, General Motors and Westinghouse (which had purchased Unimation) entered the industrial robot market (Dodd, 1981; Ingrassia & Darlin, 1983). Like other "high-tech" industries, numerous small firms have entered the field, often with specialized products seeking a narrow market segment.

Robots can increase productivity when they are used for appropriate functions such as repetitive manual operations, including spot welding and painting, materials handling, and certain applications in quality control. As yet, robots do not begin to approach the sophistication of R2D2 or C3PO, nor do they "do windows."

By the end of the 1980's, U.S. manufacturers had discovered that automation alone would not increase productivity. A combination of "new production methods, imaginative management, a more cooperative work climate, and some of the latest computer-controlled equipment" (Winter, 1987) were needed to reach new productivity and quality goals. Other alternatives such as small work teams or production cells responsible for manufacturing and quality control, gain-sharing programs which share cost savings with employees, and re-engineering and work redesign began to be used. All of these programs integrate automation to one degree or another into the production process. They are commonplace in today's factories.

Automation in the Office

Until recently, clerical workers have seen only a few technological changes since the late 1800's. The typewriter (first produced in large quantities in 1874), the mimeograph, the dictaphone and the photocopier were the most important technological changes in the office. In fact, the white-collar area has seen relatively little capital investment and has had relatively low productivity in the past (Lehrer, 1983).

Today, the same technology which has allowed robotics to be used in the factory has brought the computer into the office. Business now is attempting to increase the output per worker in the office as well as on the shop floor. Today's office worker must be able to use voice-mail, electronic-mail, and personal computer programs including word processing, spreadsheets, and graphics programs. All of these technical applications combine to reduce the need for the traditional secretary or receptionist. Further innovations in communications through electronic networks will reduce the need for a physical office at all. Some workers will be able to do their jobs in an "anytime/anyplace office," also referred to as the virtual office (Johansen & Swigart, 1994).

The price of small business computers has been steadily dropping and these machines are becoming commonplace in both offices and homes. These computers can be used to communicate with other computers, facilitate electronic mail and develop decision support systems. They can also be used in applications specific to one user or business. This has resulted in changes in the world of data processing, with the move from large computers operated by technical specialists and data processing managers to interconnected networks of computers operated by the end users.

There have been and continue to be changes in the organizational structures, control processes, economics, and external forces impacting the office. How these changes will affect the white-collar worker is a question only time can answer.

Future Changes Resulting from Shifts in Technology

The technological changes which are occurring today will have a broad range of industrial, societal and economic effects in the future. Many of these effects will have significant consequences on the way in which business in conducted. The full effects are not known with certainty. However, current trends in technological change and an understanding of the impacts of technology in the past provide guidance as to what these effects might be.

1. *The structure of the labor market will change.* Just as technological change in the past reduced the demand for skilled craftsmen and agricultural workers, the technological changes occurring today will have a significant impact on the types of jobs available.

In the factory, many blue-collar workers are being replaced by robots and other computer-assisted machines. This has resulted in a reduction in traditional factory jobs. Those jobs remaining will require higher and/or new skills, continuous training and restraining, and an increased demand for scientific and professional knowledge. These changes are not occurring overnight, however, due to the need to amortize old equipment, traditional managerial practices, and possible union or worker resistance.

In the office there has been relatively little capital investment in the past. The electronic office is changing that and reflects an increased interest of business in white-collar productivity. The use of microprocessors affects the jobs of everyone from receptionists to managers. Although these workers may not necessarily be replaced, increased output will require less need to expand the office workforce and may result in middle managers and specialists who previously gathered data becoming "extra baggage."

The corporate downsizing that took place during the late 1980's and early '90's was facilitated by technology. Many middle management jobs that were eliminated in these downsizing efforts involved communication of corporate policy to lower level workers as well as supervision. E-mail, voice mail, faxes, and networking allowed top management to communicate directly to workers without the need for mid-level managers. Employee empowerment, in which the remainder of the middle managers's job was done by the worker, obviated the need for this job.

The service sector in general is the place where a large proportion of the growth in new jobs has occurred. In 1973 there were 20 million people employed in manufacturing compared to 13 million in the service industries. By 1991, 29.5 million were in services with only 18 million in manufacturing.[1] Salaries are generally lower in the service sector than in manufacturing and the skills are different.

The change in the composition of jobs can be seen by projections made by the U.S. Department of Labor of the percentage growth in employment by occupation from 1992–2002. The estimated highest growth occupations are shown in Table 10.5. As can be seen from the table, noticeably absent are the traditional blue-collar jobs in manufacturing, transportation and mining.

Of the top ten high growth occupations (as seen in Table 10.5), three are in the computer or electronic communications industries, five are in the health care industry, one is in the human services area, and one is a legal assistant. The health care occupations are either relatively low paying home care aide positions or are in the occupational and physical therapy areas which require high levels of specialized education. These occupations reflect the demands of new technology as well as changing demographics and the aging population in the United States.

As shown in Table 10.6, the ten jobs declining at the fastest rate are in the traditional communications or railroad installation area, mainframe computer operators, shoe manufacturing industry, and telephone operators. These changes reflect the new technology being utilized in the communications industry, the move from mainframes to microcomputers, the widespread use of voice mail, e-mail, and direct dialing, and the movement of some industries (e.g., shoe manufacturing) offshore.

---

[1] Source: U.S. Bureau of the Census.

Table 10.5. Top Ten High Growth Occupations (Percent Change)

Occupation	Projected Percent Growth in Employment, 1992–2005
Home Health Aides	138.1
Human Services Workers	135.9
Personal and Home Care Aides	129.8
Computer Engineers and Scientists	111.9
Systems Analysts	110.1
Physical and Corrective Therapy Assistants and Aides	92.7
Physical Therapists	88.0
Paralegals	86.1
Occupational Therapy Assistants and Aides	78.1
Electronic Pagination Systems Workers	77.9

Source: U.S. Bureau of Labor Statistics, *Monthly Labor Review*, November, 1993, p. 411.

Table 10.6. Ten Fastest Declining Occupations (Percent Change)

Occupation	Projected Percent Decline in Employment 1992–2005
Frame Wirers, Central Office	−75.3
Signal or Track Switch Maintainers	−74.6
Peripheral EDP Equipment Operators	−60.2
Directory Assistance Operators	−50.6
Central Office Operators	−50.3
Station Installers and Repairers, Telephone	−50.3
Portable Machine Cutters	−40.1
Computer Operators, Except Peripheral Equipment	−39.3
Shoe Sewing Machine Operators	−38.4
Central Office and PBX Installers and Repairers	−35.6

Source: U.S. Bureau of Labor Statistics, *Monthly Labor Review*, November, 1993, p. 411.

2. The shift in demand from traditional manufacturing jobs will lead to a high level of structural unemployment. This type of unemployment results from a mismatch between job requirements and the skills of the unemployed. With the labor market changing and traditional blue-collar jobs in manufacturing becoming fewer relative to high technology jobs and low-paid, service-type occupations, workers displaced by technology may face difficulties in obtaining comparable employment. Their skills will no longer match the requirements of the mix of available jobs. In order to find employment, displaced workers may have to be retrained for high technology occupations or accept lower wage, service sector jobs.

Retraining, however, is not without its problems. Some workers may find it difficult to make the transition from a blue-collar to a white-collar environment. Along with job skills, there are a whole set of social skills needed to be employed in an office setting. Some workers may be unable to acquire these skills.

Some high technology occupations, such as automated equipment repair technician, still would be carried out in a blue-collar environment. However, some workers may not have the capability of being retrained. Some workers may be too old and set in their ways, others may experience difficulties in learning new skills. The transition from an emphasis on manual skills to an emphasis on mental skills may not be possible for some.

For those workers not able to be retrained, all that may be left are the low-paid, service sector jobs. Many may not be willing to accept the reduction in income entailed by employment in this sector. Others, such as skilled blue-collar workers displaced by technology, may resent the lower status of some of the jobs, in addition to the lower pay.

Previous technological change mainly involved substitution of machines for unskilled labor. Manual labor jobs were still plentiful, and workers could transfer to other occupations without extreme difficulty. This is no longer the case. In both the factory and the office, jobs require mental as well as mechanical skills. No longer is typing the prerequisite for an entry level office job. Instead, knowledge of word processing and spreadsheet programs as well as experience using a variety of equipment is required. Success in the future includes continual learning to keep abreast of the changing technology found in today's organizations.

3. *An increased importance will be placed on education as a determinant of wages and incomes.* During the 50's, 60's and 70's, the wages of semi-skilled workers in the factory rose faster than any other group. In fact, "the more skill or knowledge a job requires, the less its real income has risen" (Drucker, 1983). The resulting devaluation of education resulted in less incentive for the public to support high quality schools. As the new technology continues to be adopted, however, knowledge will be the determinant of productivity and the economic rewards for education has increased along with public pressure for high quality educational systems. In fact, corporations are now supporting local public schools to try to insure the future workforce will be appropriately trained.

4. *Changes in production techniques will affect the structure of industry.* The use of automation will provide a competitive edge to companies which adopt this technology. This is especially true in industries where labor costs are very large. Because the breakeven point for factories using automation may be reduced, these companies will have a greater level of recession resistance. Plants which are not used to full capacity can still make a profit. For example, one Japanese plant breaks even at 30% capacity with the aid of robots (Ohmae, 1982).

Changes in technology may also reduce barriers to enter an industry. Small companies will be able to enter industries in which they were previously banned by shortages of skilled labor. The continual decline in the cost of microcomputers also allows small firms to enter some businesses such as publishing.

As computer-assisted manufacturing and design processes become more flexible, manufacturers may be able to retool easily and meet varying customer specifications. Small batch production runs may become feasible. Although parts may remain interchangeable, design changes may occur rapidly, and customer specifications may be more economically met. Thus, the standardization required of assembly line production methods may give way to a greater degree of customizing.

5. *The home will become a workplace for more individuals.* Just as the industrial revolution moved the worker from the home to the factory, the electronic revolution will allow movement back. People whose job involves interaction via phone lines to customers, suppliers and computers no longer will have to be located in any particular place. Thus, sales personnel, stockbrokers, lawyers, consultants, and computer

programmers can be distributed geographically with little impact on their "clients." This trend opens up questions regarding supervision and performance appraisal and provides new flexibility to the workers themselves.

In 1995 it was estimated that about 10 million people telecommute full time or part time (Carlton, 1995) and by the year 2000 it will be 25 million. One of the reasons for this is the dramatic decrease in the cost and increased availability of home office equipment. In addition, there are continuous pressures to reduce overhead costs such as office space that is only occasionally used. However, telecommuting is not compatible with the typical organizational culture which requires at least some level of supervision and control. Also, not all employees like to work alone, and issues of communication with peers and alienation from the work group must be considered. Thus, telecommuting may be appropriate part of the time or on specific types of projects.

6. *Industrial locations may shift as new technology is adopted.* Movement to areas where cheap, unskilled labor is available such as Mexico and Asian countries may slow down. This is because investment in new technology may reduce the benefits of low labor cost locations. As computers and robots are substituted for labor, management can choose plant sites in order to minimize transportation and distribution costs rather than labor costs. Workers in these plants of the future must have higher knowledge and skills. If retraining of unskilled labor is not possible in underdeveloped countries, then a shift back to the U.S. of industries such as what has happened to semiconductors is possible.

7. *The composition of output will change.* Little growth is expected in the traditional manufacturing areas of radio and television, household appliances, and metal working. Motor vehicle manufacturing will increase slightly, but increased pressures from foreign competition and high labor costs have moved this industry rapidly toward the adoption of robots and higher productivity and quality. The manufacturing of electronic components and computers will increase, since automation has made it cost effective to bring this industry back into the United States from offshore sites. The major increases will come in the service sector, such as insurance, banking and printing and publishing. Such major changes in the relative positions of American industries provide an indication of the changes in the composition of output that may occur.

Some of the predicted changes in the composition of output can be seen in Figure 10.2. As can be seen in the table, in the period 1989–1991, manufacturing has lost the most jobs, while the service industries have gained the most employment. These trends continued well into the decade of the 1990's.

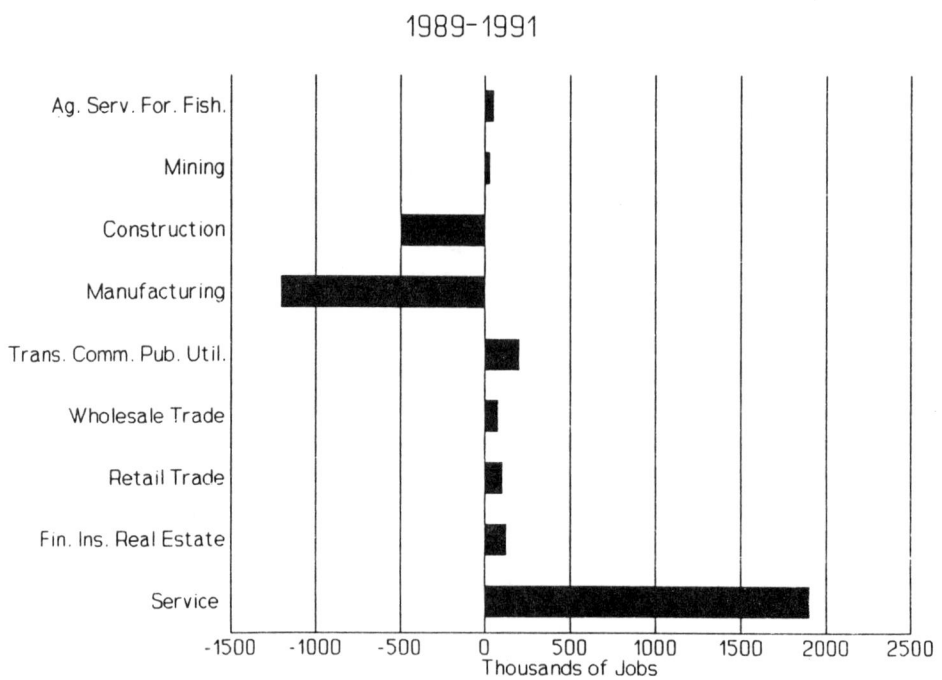

Figure 10.2. Net Job Growth/Decline in the United States by Industry Division

Source: U.S. Bureau of the Census

8. *New technology will affect productivity, incomes and living standards.* If the past is a useful guide to the impact of today's technological change, then it seems clear that the new technology will result in increased productivity of the workforce, and thus increased incomes and living standards in general. However, several nagging questions exist concerning the impact of new technology.

One question concerns unemployment. Automation is eliminating manufacturing jobs at the same time that computers and new communication equipment are reducing the need for white-collar office employees. Technology is thus replacing human intelligence as well as manual labor. Some analysts thus argue that it may not be possible to be retrained for white-collar jobs, since these are being eliminated too.

Others ask whether there will ever be enough jobs to go around. For example, the Japanese are attempting to develop a plant which will operate without any human operators. Suppose all human work is replaced by machines, who will get paid? The one worker who flipped the switch would be highly productive, but how about the rest of the workforce? What would they do?

Fears of unemployment caused by automation are expressed by many in organized labor, similar to the fears expressed by the Luddites over 150 years ago. For example, the International Association of Machinists and Aerospace Workers has urged Congress to adopt a "Workers Technology Bill of Rights." This proposal would declare that new technology would not be used so as to decrease jobs or Americans' standard of living (Neikirk and Madigan, 1982).

On the other side of the issue concerning productivity and incomes, it is argued that new technology is beneficial and will result in increased incomes and living standards. This line of reasoning holds that technological change will result in increased productivity of the workforce, which will in turn cause a decrease in the prices of goods and services produced with the aid of robots and computers. Income will be freed up to be spent on other goods and services. New goods will be produced and whole new industries will be created. These new industries will serve as a powerful job creation mechanism.

This argument says that even those workers who must accept low skill, service-type occupations will benefit. Their real incomes will increase as the cost of many of the goods and services which they purchase decreases. In addition, the demand for their services will also rise, in part caused by additional discretionary consumer income being spent in the service sector.

This argument holds that the "naysayers" are examining technological change using a static analysis that merely assumes that the same goods and services will be produced with the use of less labor. The static analysis ignores the dynamic changes in the economy that will be driven by new technology.

History, of course, decidedly favors this side of the argument. Technological change has resulted in increased standards of living over time. It is likely that current technological change will also increase incomes. The main problem of technological change concerns the distribution of its effects. There will be both gainers and losers.

The gainers will include the workers that become more productive. Since wages are related to the value of a worker's production, increased productivity will result in increased wages. Consumers in general will also benefit as the real cost of many goods and services is reduced.

The losers will be the displaced workers who cannot be retrained and are forced to take low paying jobs in the service sector. This group could be a substantial portion of the population. Some government action may be required to assure that the economy continues to expand and creates new jobs so as to keep this group as small as possible. In addition, programs for dealing with displaced workers may also be required. Thus, it may be necessary to place greater reliance on the public sector to mitigate the adverse effects of technological change. In the next section, several proposals for public sector action will be analyzed.

Public Policy and New Technology

A variety of public programs have been suggested to deal with the adverse effects of technological change. Most deal with the problem of structural unemployment, which may become even more acute in the years ahead.

One approach is federal funding of a massive job retraining program for displaced workers. Some proposals would levy a special automation tax, the proceeds of which would be used for retraining purposes. Such retraining efforts have already begun through programs such as the Job Training Partnership Act, which provides several billion dollars each year to support a variety of business-operated training and retraining assistance for displaced workers.

The public policy debate concerns whether the public sector should be involved in retraining efforts at all, and if so, at what level of funding. If public sector funding expands to a large national program, the government must be able to foresee the skills that would be in demand in the future. This is because retraining must ultimately result in employment for the trainees. Retraining is already being done in the private sector. Companies which install automation and electronic equipment often find it cost-effective to retrain existing workers. Unions also have addressed this issue in their contract negotiations, and many unions such as the United Auto Workers and the Communication Workers of America give retraining high priority.

Another approach to dealing with structural unemployment is to attempt to spread the existing work over more workers. Two proposals to spread the work are reducing the workweek from 40 to 35 hours and worksharing.

Reducing the workweek is a way to create a demand for more workers to produce the same level of output. Unions often try to increase the amount of paid time off, and this is essentially what occurs under this proposal. However, the cost of goods would go up since total compensation would stay the same. This could result in an increased rate of inflation and diminished international competitiveness. On the other hand, one way of spending the increased productivity of the workforce is in increased leisure time rather than increased amounts of goods and services. Reducing the workweek could be viewed as one means of spending the gains from technological change.

Worksharing is a proposal which can take two forms. First, two people may do one job. The overall number of people employed increases, and such arrangements often meet the specific needs of workers who want to work part-time. Coordination and job design are important in such cases, however, and some special arrangements may be needed regarding benefits such as insurance and holidays.

Second, worksharing may mean that all employee hours are reduced rather than some employees being laid off. This form of worksharing is similar to reducing the workweek. For example, the hours of 100 employees may be reduced by 20% rather than 20 people being laid off. This plan has been implemented in Arizona, California, and Oregon where partial unemployment compensation payments are allowed to help make up some of the lost wages (Klein, 1983).

Both reducing the workweek and worksharing can be accomplished with or without public sector action. A 35-hour workweek can be negotiated through individual union contracts and phased in on an industry by industry basis. However, firms which do not adopt a shorter workweek, because they are non-union or because negotiations with particular locals do not include a reduction in hours worked, may be at a competitive advantage to those who do. This provides an economic disincentive to those firms who would like to shorten the workweek. Thus, public sector action may be required to implement such a proposal. Worksharing has been implemented successfully by a variety of firms without public sector involvement. However, public policy changes may be required to encourage such programs through tax incentives, partial unemployment compensation, etc.

Another program that has been suggested is to create public service jobs for the structurally unemployed. In this program, displaced workers would be given employment in the public sector doing jobs that had previously not been filled because of lack of funds. Such jobs may also involve a retraining component as well, so that workers can eventually move into private sector employment.

Public sector jobs programs have been attempted in the past. The Civilian Conservation Corps (CCC) of the Depression and the CETA programs of the 1970's are the most visible examples. These programs, however, have had mixed success. While the CCC has generally been given high marks for employing urban youth, and at the same time improving parks and wilderness resources, other programs have not fared as well.

Public sector jobs can easily degenerate into make-work jobs in which the workers do very little productive activity and learn even less. Public sector jobs programs can easily become nothing more than disguised welfare programs. However, if job skills are obtained by the workers, and additional public services are produced, public sector jobs programs may be preferable to expanded welfare programs.

Another area of public policy involvement is primary and secondary education. The new technology requires emphasis on math and science skills to meet the demands of the computer age. This change in emphasis has resulted in computer labs replacing the language labs of the 1960's and 1970's. The pressure on quality of education may also result in changes in teacher qualifications and evaluation. Students from schools where state-of-the-art computers are available will have an advantage over those without access to this equipment. A further split between have and have-not school districts may follow. This split will be exacerbated by the fact that approximately 25% of the households with incomes over $25,000 had home computers in 1993 while only 14% of families with less than $25,000 income had them (Carlton, 1995).

Public policy may also involve government regulation. As offices and factories continue to install computer terminals and robots, new safety and health standards may be needed. Already present in some European countries, the employer in the U.S. must recognize the possibility of these actions.

Relationship to the Major Elements of the External Environment of Business

Table 10.7 reviews the major elements of the external business environment. Not every business is impacted by all of these factors, but they represent a starting point in what is often called an "environmental scanning" effort. Environmental scanning was defined in Chapter 1 as an attempt of business managers (often strategic planners) to determine what variables are most likely to impact the firm now and in the foreseeable future. In the United States today, there are many factors which are elements of the external environment that interact to determine the types of technological changes which occur as well as the rate at which they take place.

Government regulation of markets, of the workplace, human resource management, energy prices and distribution, and of the physical environment have become some of the most important elements with respect to technology. Many regulations provide incentives for the development and implementation of new technology (this is sometimes called technological forcing). Mileage standards, for example, have required the development of new automobile technology. Large investments have been made in safety equipment, energy conservation measures, and pollution controls over the past decade. Whether or not these expenditures meet societal (or practical) goals, the regulations which required them certainly have impacted the rate and direction of technological development.

Labor markets have been affected by technology. Emphasis on retraining, job security, required advanced notice of layoffs and plant closings, and alternatives such as shorter workweeks and job sharing are often advocated. White-collar workers are seen as a source of new

Table 10.7. Major Elements of the External Environment of Business

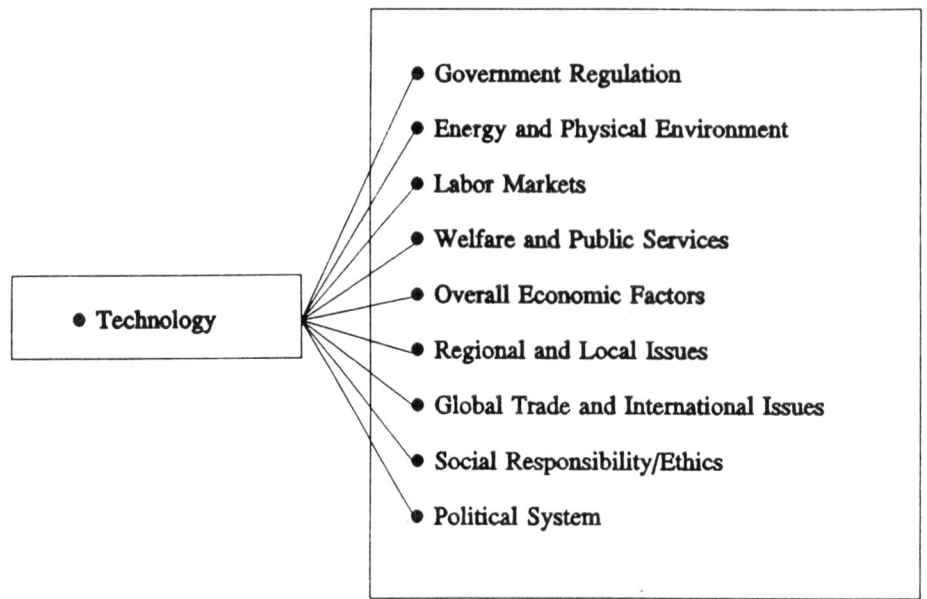

members by many unions. The future of the unions as well as of industry is related to the growth of technology.

Government services have been stretched to their limit as a result of high unemployment levels due in part to the changing structure of traditional industries. In addition to unemployment compensation, however, government may also be asked to provide money for retraining efforts needed to move traditional workers into new high-tech jobs.

Economic factors such as price changes (inflation or deflation), interest rates, and unemployment are all interrelated with changes in technology. Many economists predict unemployment will stay high in part due to the change in the types of jobs available, automation in the factory and office, and international competition. High interest rates reduce the amount of capital available for investment in R&D or new equipment, which can impact technological growth and adaptation. The state of the economy thus has a crucial impact on the technological environment.

Regional and local issues include movement of business from one area of the country to another. Many communities are avidly trying to attract high-tech firms as a panacea for their economic problems. Only a few appear to be successful, however. One criterion seems to be the availability of university facilities and talent as well as a location which attracts engineers, programmers, and scientists.

International competition has increased considerably over the past decade. Rather than relying on protectionism to stem the flow of foreign goods, many industries are turning to automation to increase productivity and efficiency, thus making them more competitive in the world market. Cheap foreign labor may lose some appeal as automation increases and fewer workers are needed. At some point the transportation savings plus automation savings may make it cost-effective to produce goods in the U.S. which are now being made abroad. In any case, the international scene, especially in Japan, has had a great impact on the movement of U.S. businesses to adopt new technologies.

The area of social responsibility is particularly important when it comes to the development and adoption of technology. Some people question whether moving unabated into areas such as genetic engineering is good for society. Other issues sometimes related to social responsibility and technology include plant closings when equipment becomes obsolete, and organizational responsibilities regarding retraining of workers displaced by machines.

The political system operates on all elements of the environment. Various interest groups lobby for their points of view, and those interested in promoting or deterring new technology are no exception. Arguments for restrictions on the exports of high-technology goods to certain countries, advocates of federal job programs and increased funding for education and R&D, and proposals for protection against health hazards resulting from video-display terminals have all been heard. Public policy will continue to be an important element in the development of new technology.

Thus, technology is an important element in the external environment. In addition, it impacts or is affected by all the other major elements identified. The interrelation of changes in technology with the other elements of the environment can result in powerful combinations having profound effects on the way business is conducted.

Managerial Implications

Technological change can have significant effects on the managerial functions of planning, organizing, controlling and staffing/rewarding. The manner in which these functions are performed may be changed by the increased use of robots, computers and other types of technology. The four functions of management and the eight impacts of technological change developed previously are shown in Table 10.8. The possible responses of each of the managerial functions to the various impacts are also shown in the table.

The planning function is directly impacted by the changing structure of industry, industrial location shifts, the changing composition of output and the increased productivity resulting from the new technology. As the pace of technological change increases and new production techniques are developed, those firms that adopt new innovations will have a distinct competitive edge. The planning function may have to include a "technological assessment" in which forecasts are made of which technologies will have the highest return on investment, or in some cases, which will become "standard" for the industry. For example, compatibility of microcomputers with each other may become an industry requirement.

Robotics and computer automation will make entry into many industries easier by reducing the necessity to use skilled labor. This may become a two-edged sword for many firms. Entry into other industries may become feasible. At the same time, new competitors may enter a firm's industry, greatly increasing competition and lowering returns on investment. In addition, managers may be able to take advantage of the new technological developments to lower breakeven points and increase the recession resistance of the business. Product planning may include many new models and increased use of customization.

Table 10.8. Managerial Responses to Future Impacts of Technological Change

Impacts of Technological Change	Planning	Organizing	Controlling	Staffing/Rewarding
1. Structure of the labor market will change.		1. New organizational structures developed. 2. New high-tech jobs created.	1. New performance measures needed for high-tech workers.	1. Selection and recruiting programs changed. 2. Increased competition for high-tech workers. 3. Lower wages paid unskilled workers. 4. Compensation/benefit packages need to meet new worker requirements.
2. Structural unemployment will increase.		1. Job design to avoid repetitive tasks. 2. Introduce technology to eliminate dangerous or repetitive jobs.	1. Robots measure own productivity. 2. Computers measure productivity of workers.	1. Continued focus on restraining of structurally unemployed. 2. Alter current career paths. 3. Union contract negotiations emphasize job security issues. 4. Reduced work week and worksharing viable alternatives.
3. Increasing importance of education.				1. Educational support benefits increased. 2. Compensation systems changed to reward education.

Table 10.8 (continued)
Managerial Responses to Future Impacts of Technological Change

Impacts of Technological Change	Planning	Organizing	Controlling	Staffing/Rewarding
4. Changed production techniques affect industry structure.	1. Technological assessment to maintain competitive edge. 2. Entry into other industries feasible. 3. Reduce breakeven point. 4. Emphasize ability to customize products. 5. Frequent model changes possible.	1. Create new divisions and subunits. 2. Alter chain of command.	1. Just in time production-inventory systems feasible.	
5. Movement of the workplace back to the home.		1. Develop new job and work roles. 2. Design new "flexible" structures.	1. Performance of "home" workers must be measured.	1. New policies regarding selection and compensation. 2. Increased use of flexible working hours. 3. Work site issue may be a part of union negotiations.

Table 10.8 *(continued)*
Managerial Responses to Future Impacts of Technological Change

Impacts of Technological Change	Planning	Organizing	Controlling	Staffing/Rewarding
6. Industrial location shifts.	1. Availability of skilled labor less important than transportation and distribution for plant location. 2. U.S. locations may become feasible for industries now overseas.			1. Move requires new selection and recruiting strategies. 2. Relocation programs will be needed.
7. Changing composition of output.	1. Service sector industries more desirable.		1. Better monitoring of quality of products.	
8. Increased productivity in the factory and office leading to potential changes in incomes and living standards.	1. Enter markets for leisure goods and "luxury" items.			1. Increased focus on quality of work life programs. 2. Emphasis on reducing absenteeism and turnover. 3. New incentives may be needed for worker of the future.

The industrial location shifts that may result from technological change may require changes in the planning process. Plant location decisions may primarily be determined by accessibility to transportation and distribution systems rather than by availability of cheap, unskilled labor. Planners may want to reconsider frostbelt locations in the U.S. as opposed to locating plants overseas. The plant location decision must be carefully thought out to include the impact of technological change in the decision-making process.

As the composition of output changes, and consumers spend increased incomes on new products and services, even the high sales growth products of today may reach the saturation-maturity stage quickly. Growth-oriented companies need to undertake research and development efforts that assure a constant flow of new products on the marketplace. If the pace of technological change continues to accelerate, many products will become technologically obsolete. Research and development is also needed to assure that the latest technology is incorporated into new product offerings. In addition, the service sector will house the high growth industries of the future. Entry into service industries should be considered much more desirable. Finally, the planning function must consider the increased leisure time and demand for luxury goods which may result from the productivity gains of the new technology. "Leisure" goods and "luxury" items may increase in importance in the marketplace of the future.

The organizing function is affected by technological change through the effect on labor, changed production techniques and the possible movement of some jobs to the home. As the labor market changes, and the demand for high-tech workers increases, while the need for unskilled factory workers declines, new organizational structures will be needed. These must be flexible and allow communication among many work groups. Fishnet organization structures have been suggested as well as virtual organizations made up of individuals and teams working from a variety of locations (Johansen & Swigart, 1994).

Of critical importance in adapting new technology in both the plant and office is to design jobs to minimize boredom and enhance job characteristics. If robots and computers take the best jobs and the workforce is left with only tedious jobs that robots cannot do, then the likelihood of worker acceptance of the new technology will be reduced. On the other hand, if dangerous jobs or those that are tedious or boring are given to robots and the retrained workers used as "masters of robots," then employees may take great pride in the "steel collar" workers under them (Ohmae, 1982). Worker acceptance and productivity may be greatly enhanced.

Finally, the organizing function will be affected by a changing industrial structure and the tendency for jobs to move to the home. New divisions and subunits may be created and the chain of command may need to be altered. New job and work roles must be developed for home workers since direct supervision may not be possible. New flexible organizational structures which incorporate the telecommuter into the system will need to be designed.

The controlling function is affected by the changing structure of the labor market, increases in structural unemployment, changing industry structure, the movement of the workplace back to the home, and the changing composition of output. As the number of high tech workers increases, new performance measures must be developed and managers trained in their utilization.

Productivity levels may also be measured directly by robots and office computers. The number of units assembled or moved can be counted by the robot's "brain," and the robots can also be used for quality control. The computer can also be programmed to measure the number of calls answered and the length of each call in a catalogue or credit card phone operation. This continuous monitoring of performance may help managers determine productivity levels, but may be resented by employees, leading to attempts to sabotage the system or may result in poor morale. Thus, monitoring systems must be designed to reduce any negative impacts.

Inventory control also may change with the application of computers for "just in time" production methods. Here, the suppliers must deliver raw materials very close to the time when they will be used in the production process. This system is being adopted by a variety of companies and may involve relocation of suppliers to sites close to the manufacturer as well as increased requirements for on-time delivery of high-quality materials.

Movement of workers back to the home changes the way in which their performance must be measured. Since it is no longer possible to supervise these workers directly, it may be necessary to use the computer to keep track of their performance (as described above) or to evaluate the actual output such as programs completed or reports written. The traditional notion of punching in and out on a time clock will have to be replaced by more flexible performance measures focusing on expected outcomes.

Finally, the changing composition of output will require better monitoring of the quality of products. As more and more products are produced by a given manufacturer, the complexity of quality control processes may increase. Also, an increase in small batch processing for customized products will require continuous attention to the quality of output.

The human resource manager in charge of the staffing/rewarding function must adapt to almost all of the trends identified. The changing labor market requires new recruiting and selection strategies to meet the competition for high-tech workers. Compensation and benefit packages may need evaluating since current salaries may be too low or too high for the new labor market. Also, the new high-tech workers may desire a different "package" of benefits than the traditional blue-collar worker.

Structural unemployment is one of the major issues facing managers in the future. Continued emphasis on retraining by both the private and public sectors is likely. In addition, people who had been following a particular career path (e.g., from apprentice to welder) may suddenly find future advancement closed to them. Advancement may require a shift to a new type of work entirely, or retraining for related jobs such as robot technicians. In addition, job security and retraining may become major issues in future labor negotiations. Other proposals offered to offset the impact of structural unemployment are the reduced workweek and some type of worksharing. All of these proposals, if implemented, will directly affect the human resource manager since each involves modifications to compensation and benefit programs as well as recruitment, selection and layoff strategies.

As education increases in importance, companies may begin offering more educational benefits. This may include tuition reimbursement and a variety of continuing education programs. Compensation systems may also be altered to reward educational achievement to a greater degree than presently.

An increasing number of employees working at home may require increased use of flexible hours, new compensation policies, and revised selection strategies. It may be that individuals who desire the social interaction of the workplace will not be comfortable working at home. In addition, the issue of work in the home may appear as a negotiating issue as more workers move away from the office. This may impact future labor negotiations.

As more industries change locations in response to technological change, the human resource manager may need to alter the selection and recruiting strategies of the firm. In addition, relocation programs and policies will have to be developed for employees the company expects to move. As more and more households have two workers, the relocation process may become more complex.

The increased productivity brought by technology may also lead to changes in income and living standards. Workers may value leisure more than previously, and absenteeism and turnover may increase. Thus, a greater emphasis on programs to reduce this behavior may be necessary. Associated with this change in attitude is an increasing emphasis on improving the quality of the work environment.

The new technology can thus have a profound impact on the managerial functions of planning, organizing, controlling and staffing/rewarding. Carefully thought-out managerial responses to technological change can enhance the productivity, efficiency and profitability of business. Managers must learn how to harness the technology of the future since the gains to both business and society in general may be substantial.

Summary

In this chapter, the role of technology in the external environment of business was explored. Major technological breakthroughs since the industrial revolution and the overall impacts on business, the economy, individuals and the social system were examined. These previous impacts provide important clues as to what changes future technology may bring.

Technological change occurring both in the plant and the office were discussed and a set of probable impacts developed. The impacts will affect labor, industry and society in general. Structural unemployment was seen as one of the biggest problems which may result from new technology. A variety of public policy alternatives to deal with the adverse effects of technological change were examined and the relationship of technology to the other elements of the external environment was explored. Finally, the implications of technological change on the managerial functions of planning, organizing, controlling and staffing/rewarding and possible managerial responses were enumerated.

Review Questions

1. Which technological breakthroughs contributed to each of the impacts of technological change?

2. What might be the ten largest industries in the year 2010?

3. Compare the capabilities of the human worker versus a robot. Which tasks are best performed by each?

4. Describe the most important future changes resulting from shifts in technology.

5. Will technological change guarantee increases in productivity and income for everyone?

6. Evaluate the advantages and disadvantages of major government involvement in retraining, reducing the workweek, worksharing, and special public sector jobs programs.

7. How does technology combine with other elements of the environment to affect business?

8. Describe how technological change will affect the managerial functions of planning, organizing, controlling, and staffing/rewarding.

Key Concepts

technology

robotics

electronic office

structural unemployment

value added

worksharing

high-tech jobs

telecommuter

Luddites

Case Analysis: Home Work—Mountain Climbers
Telluride, Colorado
by Jim Carlton

Lee Taylor is huddled over his Compaq DeskPro computer, poised to punch a button that will zap a draft of a 40-page technical presentation to a colleague.

The transmission will head east through an Internet routing center in Denver before racing over mountains and deserts to the colleague's personal computer in Santa Clara, Calif. But Mr. Taylor, a software technical writer, will pay only pennies in Internet access fees and nothing in phone charges, because he can send it to a local internet hub built by the town of Telluride.

Once the draft is on its way, he pauses to gaze out the window of his home office at a mountain stream gurgling past pines and aspens. "It's better than the Dumpster I used to look at" from his former office in Silicon Valley, says Mr. Taylor, 37 years old, padding around his cedar-frame home in socks as jazz wafts from a stereo.

This is telecommuting, Telluride style. The quaint mountain hamlet is a pioneer in ways to make working from home as practical as possible. Community leaders decided in early 1993 to set up the local Internet hub, called InfoZone, allowing telecommuters like Mr. Taylor to send data around the world with just a local phone call (something that's routine in big cities but rare in the boonies). They have also persuaded a computer company to let the town participate in the test of wireless networking. And a few have grandiose dreams of building a whole development of teleworkers. Jack Nilles, a Los Angeles author of a book on the subject, says. "Telluride is doing as much" as any community to facilitate telecommuting.

The Telluride experience holds lessons for the rest of the U.S. About 10 million Americans now telecommute from their homes, and an additional 15 million are expected to do so within the next five years. The growth has two roots: Advances in computers and other electronic equipment are making it easier to work outside the office, and many companies are finding that telecommuters deliver greater productivity at lower cost.

companies are finding that telecommuters deliver greater productivity at lower cost.

Standing in the way of more rapid growth, though, are old-fangled phone connections between home and office. Most residences aren't yet plugged into data pipelines big enough to handle the voluminous multimedia files that can shoot through the networks of big corporations. This usually precludes, among other things, the personal contact that hooking into a video-conference would give telecommuters. And some smaller cities and towns—including, until a few years ago, Telluride—lack even the basics for connecting to cyberspace.

Individuals can make some improvements on their own. But only a few diehard techies are lacing their homes with computer-networking hookups and replacing overloaded analog phone wire with higher-capacity digital copper lines, or still-higher-capacity fiber-optic lines. Most people don't even go to the trouble of buying the equipment and software necessary for a slow connection to the World Wide Web, the graphical portion of the Internet.

But some communities, hoping to spur their local economies by attracting telecommuters, are upgrading service themselves. As Telluride did, Santa Monica, Calif., plans to build its own local Internet hub. In Modesto, Calif., a developer is building homes with fiber-optic phone lines. And some towns in Nebraska are hooking up to fiber-optic networks to provide community "fiber rooms" for video-conferencing and faster telecommuting for residents.

No More Party Lines

Telluride has come a long way from just five years ago, when all telephones here were still on analog party lines and lightning strikes caused power surges that fried computer modems. To enable locals to telecommute, the community, led by a nonprofit research outfit called the Telluride Institute, has made the most of existing technology: digital copper phone lines and the local Internet hub. That provides people living here, in a glacial canyon beneath the towering peaks of Colorado's San Juan range, with the same level of service and ease of Net access as most big-city dwellers.

"It's like training wheels on the information highway," says Richard Lowenberg, program director of the institute.

Telluride, of course, isn't perfectly wired just yet. A fiber-optic line has been extended into town from Montrose, 65 miles away, but no locals are yet shelling out to have the line connected to their homes. So, telecommuters don't yet have phone links that can handle massive multimedia files (though such connections are at least possible now). And the town's rugged setting takes a toll: Electricity regularly goes out when, say a beaver chews into a power line. Experienced telecommuters keep battery packs on hand to avoid losing data.

Telluride has a wild and woolly past that gives no hint of its information-age emergence. Once a mining boomtown that attracted brothels, saloons and the likes of Butch Cassidy, who robbed a local bank, Telluride became almost a ghost town after gold and silver prices collapsed during the Depression. The population sank to 300 from a peak of 5,000.

The town's savior was a California investor named Joseph Zoline, who bought up much of 13,319-foot Palmyra Peak and opened the Telluride Ski Resort in 1972. Skiers began flocking here, and for year-round appeal, local officials starting summer festivals celebrating everything from wine to mushrooms to "Nothing," as one event is called.

Visitors smitten by Telluride's magnificent scenery began buying second homes in the area, sparking a real-estate boom that's only now letting up. A vacant town lot goes for $250,000 today, up from $30,000 a decade ago. Hollywood stars joined the rush, including Tom Cruise, and the town's upscale makeup came to be reflected in new Thai, French, and sushi restaurants.

Soon, some skiers and second-home buyers began deciding they didn't want to leave. They opened the era of the telecommuter. "The visuals are what get you on this place," says David Hoffman, a Chicago Lawyer who in 1982 became one of the first local telecommuters.

The Dark Ages

Back then, telecommuting was a nightmare. Mr. Hoffman remembers having to travel to Montrose to copy documents on a case and then walk the files across the street to have them shipped to Chicago by air. His law firm eventually folded, leaving him to work as a local lawyer.

Mr. Lowenberg, the Telluride Institute official, began tackling those logistical problems. An artist, designer and land planner from California, he saw telecommuting as a way to diversify the town's economy beyond tourism and real estate. Starting in 1990, he led efforts to pressure the local telephone company, US West Communications, to replace the analog party lines with private digital lines. It did so two years later.

He also helped persuade the company, a unit of Denver-based US West, Inc., to run the fiber-optic trunk line here so locals could tap into it. The company will connect residences to the town's fiber loop at no charge, but people have to pay to have trenches dug for the last leg to their homes; so far, no one has been willing.

But the digital lines alone made it technically possible for Telluride to hook into the Internet. There was just one problem: The closest Internet connection was in Denver, and that meant high long-distance charges for any meaningful use. Some people were paying $50 a month just to peruse e-mail. "It wasn't practical for us," says Peter Spencer, who recently gave up a telecommuting consultant's job to run a small newspaper nearby.

The solution, Mr. Lowenberg figured, was an Internet hub for Telluride. He applied for assistance for the Colorado Advanced Technology Institute, a state agency. It provided $130,000 in technical support and equipment to create the hub, called InfoZone, in early 1993. The equipment included a high-performance computer server for handling world-wide Internet traffic to and from Telluride, and a smaller server to accommodate a community bulletin board. For townspeople, all Internet access would require only a local call.

Before Mr. Lowenberg could get InfoZone up and running, he ran into a low-tech problem: His institute's headquarters building, a century-old warehouse in the center of town, lacked extra phone lines needed for the servers. For nine months, InfoZone operated out of the local elementary school, until US West could add more lines at the institute. (US West officials say it took so long to install the lines because of Colorado's overall rapid growth.)

Windfall From Apple

Around that time, Mr. Lowenberg got an unexpected boost. Apple Computer, Inc., having heard of Telluride's telecommunications forays, offered to donate eight Macintosh computers to deploy in public buildings around town. They were put in the library, medical center, schools, and even the Steaming Bean coffee shop. At all these locations, as well as from home and office computers, people could cruise the Net.

InfoZone was an overnight sensation. One-third of Telluride's 1,500 residents signed on for Internet accounts, perhaps the highest percentage in the country for a non-university town. Telecommuters like Mr. Taylor now found it cheaper to send documents on the Internet than by overnight mail.

Catherine Sellman, a 23-year-old environmental engineer, says she chose to telecommute from Telluride to her office in Washington, D.C., last October, in part, because Internet access was so good. "I always wanted to live in a place like this, but I didn't want to be a ski bum," says Ms.Sellman, who wanders into the Steaming Bean one recent snowy morning on a break from her Toshiba laptop. Besides working, she partakes in some of Telluride's special joys, like riding the lift from downtown for some lunchtime skiing. "I've learned how to snowboard," she adds.

Telluride's technology has also connected locals. The community bulletin board has discussion groups on everything from hiking and rock climbing to philosophy and politics. "A lot of people you know by a wave, you start to find out about their thoughts," says Art Goodtimes, arts editor of the Telluride Times-Journal. Some high-school students have also started an underground paper on-line, recently lampooning California Gov. Pete Wilson's anti-immigration stance as a police-state mentality. Mr. Lowenberg welcomes the free expression, except when some teens spouted obscenities over the Net. "We had to kick two off," he says.

It isn't high-tech heaven. Mr. Taylor, a heavier user than most, finds even the current setup agonizingly slow at times. A maker of CD-ROM programs, he says he once found it faster to drive a 30-minute video product to a customer 12 miles from his canyon home than to send it over the wire. "It was a glorious afternoon, so I'm not complaining," he says.

Pie in the Sky?

One technology related project still on the drawing board after years of planning is Skyfield, the would-be telecommuting village. Skyfield was dreamed up in 1985 by Pam Zoline, daughter of the local ski mogul, and her husband, John Lifton, a British-born architect. The Liftons, who had recruited Mr. Lowenberg to the Telluride Institute, shared many of his ideas for the town's future. They envisioned Skyfield as a mecca for a type of worker they called "information independents."

They also added a social element: They intended the community to address a growing disparity between rich and poor and the rising cost of housing, which forced many locals to move out.

Skyfield would be situated on 620 acres of pristine meadow lands owned by Mr. Zoline, providing everything from affordable condominiums to million-dollar homes—all wired with fiber-pitch cables to transmit data at far faster speeds than traditional phone lines, says Mr. Lifton.

The Liftons drew up a town plan and obtained initial approval from San Miguel County officials. But the months they thought it would take to start the project turned into years, and today ground is still unbroken. Mr. Lifton says the project has been delayed because it was ahead of its time. Others say he has trouble lining up financing. While conceding it will cost much more to build Skyfield than first envisioned, he says he has some investors lined up and hopes to close a deal soon.

Going Wireless

But even without Skyfield, Telluride has moved far toward the Liftons' vision. And now that the town is pretty well wired, it will soon begin going wireless. Through his contacts at Apple, Mr. Lowenberg says, he learned that a Palo Alto, Calif., company called Tetherless Access Ltd. was about to pick one more city to test a wireless service that it says lets personal computer users ship data around the world. The service combines special routing software and a radio modem to send data out over the airwaves to transmission "nodes," similar to cellular phone towers. Tetherless says the wireless networking package is being tested before being shipped this summer.

Mr. Lowenberg says he called Tetherless, which had already picked test sites in California, Mexico and Brazil. The company was glad to sign up Telluride. "Telluride is a progressive community," says Charles Brown, the company's president. The wireless network was installed last month on PCs in some of Telluride's public buildings, and will also be available to telecomuters who want to pay for the service.

With data capacity roughly double that of non-fiber phone lines, Mr. Lowenberg says, the wireless network could be a boon to "power" users such as Mr. Taylor (though it won't carry as much data as a fiber line, which has about four times the capacity of copper lines). And the wireless network, he says, could help connect some telecommuters doing business over cellular phones from cabins so remote, they don't even have telephone lines.

This wireless service can transmit data at roughly 10 times the speed of cellular analog modems, Tetherless officials say, and lets users transmit from as far as 20 miles from a node, compared with only about five miles from a cellular tower.

The service won't come cheap, though. The software and modem will cost about $5,000, plus monthly fees of as much as $200.

Bigger Pipelines

For power users, Telluride also wants to work with US West or another phone company to improve the capacity of its wired phone network, perhaps through a digital switching technology called frame relay, or ISDN, a digital network that operates at up to 128,000 bits, or units of data, a second (equal to about 15 pages of typewritten text). Mr. Lowenberg says Telluride is also talking with its cable company, Telluride Cablevision, about selecting the town to test new set-top boxes that relay data through televisions over existing cable lines.

All the great technology in the world won't solve two remaining drawbacks to telecommuting from Telluride. Situated at an altitude of about 9,000 feet, the town in the winter has snowfall so incessant that its airport is closed much of the time, forcing telecommuters who need to make business trips to drive an hour or so to Montrose. The other problem is a stronger form of the sense of isolation that can afflict telecommuters everywhere.

Still, says Mr. Hoffman, the lawyer, "as long as you're willing to give up the critical ideas you get from your buddy in the men's room, you can telecommute."

Source: *The Wall Street Journal*, June 19, 1995, page R30. Reprinted with permission.

Case Questions

1. What are the benefits of telecommuting from Telluride for the telecommuter? What are the negative factors which must be considered?

2. What technological advances make telecommuting from Telluride feasible?

3. How might being connected to the Internet impact the townspeople of Telluride? What are both positive and negative impacts?

4. What factors mitigate for and against the planned community of Skyfield?

5. Is Telluride the prototype of the future?

6. What adjustments must managers make to incorporate telecommuters into their organization?

References

Alexander, Charles P., "The New Economy," *Time*, May 30, 1983, pp. 62–70.

"American Industry Rediscovers Innovation," *The Economist*, July 5, 1980.

Barnes, Kathleen, "Government Program Supports On-the Job-Training," *HRFOCUS*, June, 1994, pp. 12–13.

Brittain, Jack W., and Freeman, John H., "Organizational Proliferation and Density Dependent Selection." In John R. Kimberley and Robert H. Miles, eds., *The Organizational Life Cycle*, Jossey-Bass Publishers, San Francisco, 1981, pp. 291–338.

Carlton, Jim. "Down to Business: The Home Office is Quickly Becoming Less Expensive and More Sophisticated," *The Wall Street Journal*, June 19, 1995, p. R32.

Cravens, David W., Hills, Gerald E., and Woodruff, Robert B., *Marketing and Decision Making: Concepts and Strategies*, Richard D. Irwin, Homewood, Illinois, 1976.

Davis, Lance W., et al., *American Economic Growth: An Economist's History of the United States*, Harper & Row, New York, 1972.

Dodd, John, "Robots: The New 'Steel Collar' Workers," *Personnel Journal*, September, 1981, 688–695.

Drucker, Peter F., "Quality Education: The New Growth Area," *Wall Street Journal*, July 19, 1983, p. 24.

Hughes, Jonathan, *American Economic History*, Scott, Foresman and Company, Glenview, Illinois, 1983.

Ingrassia, Paul, and Darlin, Damon, "Cincinnati Milacron, Mainly a Metal-Bender, Now is a Robot Maker," *Wall Street Journal*, April 7, 1983, pp. 1, 19.

Johansen, Robert & Swigart, Rob, *Upsizing the Individual in the Downsized Organization*, Reading, Massachusetts: Addison-Wesley Publishing Company, 1994.

Klein, Haywood, "Interest Grows in Worksharing, Which Lets Concerns Cut Workweeks to Avoid Layoffs," *Wall Street Journal*, April 7, 1983, p. 27.

Lehrer, Robert N., *White Collar Productivity*, McGraw-Hill Book Company, New York, 1983.

Neikirk, Bill and Madigan, Charles, "High-tech's Big Fear: Too Many Lost Jobs," *Chicago Tribune*, November 30, 1982, p. 10.

Ohmae, Kenichi, "Steel Collar Workers: The Lessons from Japan," *Wall Street Journal*, February 16, 1982.

Rothwell, Roy, "Technology, Structural Change, and Manufacturing Employment," *OMEGA*, 9 (1981), 229–245.

Russell, Robert R., *A History of the American Economic System*, Appleton-Century-Crafts, New York, 1964.

U.S. Bureau of Labor Statistics, *Monthly Labor Review*, November, 1993.

Whaley, George L., "The Impact of Robotics Technology Upon Human Resource Management," *Personnel Administrator*, September, 1982.

Winter, Ralph E., "Upgrading of Factories Replaces the Concept of Total Automation," *Wall Street Journal*, November 30, 1987, pp. 1, 8.

SUBJECT INDEX

Affirmative Action	424–427
American Civil Liberties Union (ACLU)	425
American Trucking Association	129–134
Americans with Disabilities Act	434–436
Authoritarian Socialism	40, 42
Authoritarian Socialism, in Poland	77–82
AVCO Financial Services	411
Black Fury	420
Brown vs. The Board of Education of Topeka	104, 424
Cartels	373–374
Clayton Act	388–391
Committee for Economic Development	4
Communism	40, 42
Consolidation Movement	106–107
Consumer Products Safety Commission (CPSC)	11, 263–265
Contestable Markets	374–375
Controlling	7–8
Corporate governance	152–154
Cost of Living Adjustment (COLA)	18
Council of Economic Advisors	3
Cross Impact Analysis	71–72
Delphi Technique	69
Demand	
curve	46, 47
definition	43
determinants	44–46
Democratic Socialism	40–42
Department of Commerce	98, 100
Deregulation	273–277
Diversity	409–412
Drug and Alcohol Abuse	442
Economic Goals	62–63
Economic Systems, types of	40–43
Energy	
and Physical Environment	12–13
future oil prices	309–314
government policy and	300–309

Environmental Protection Agency (EPA)	13, 101
Environmental Scanning	66–73
information sources	69–71
Equal Employment Opportunities Commission (EEOC)	11, 424
Equal Job Opportunity	423–424
Ethical egoism	187–189
Ethical relativism	186–187
Ethics	20–21, 34, 38–39, 185–214
concepts	185–193
definition	184
dilemmas	197–205
tests	194–197
Executive Branch	98–102
External Environment	
and management functions	8–10
definition	1
Model of Change	33–39
why study	4–5
Externalities	87–88
Family and Medical Leave Act	415
Federal Anti-Trust Laws	384–393
Federal Communications Commission (FCC)	11
Federal Energy Regulatory Commission (FERC)	11
Federal Grants in Aid	105–106
Federal Trade Commission	392
Fiscal policy	91
Flextime	440
Food and Drug Administration (FDA)	258–260
Free Enterprise System	42–43
GATT	19
Glass Ceiling Commission	418
Government Regulation	10–12
alternatives	272–282
benefits and costs	269–272
consumer movement	256–265
employment practices	432–437
Interest Group Theory	243
methods of	245–247
Public Interest Theory	240–243

Government Regulation (cont.)	
scope of	228–240
traditional regulation	250–256
typology	247–249
Government, structure of	98–104
Herfindahl-Hirschman Index (HHI)	383–384
Home Work-Telluride, CO	494–501
Immigration	14, 412–414
Industrial concentration ratios	379–383
Industrial policy	92
Inflation	17–18, 59
Interstate Commerce Commission (ICC)	10, 27, 129–130, 247, 250–256
Invisible Hand	55
Joint supply	89
Judicial Branch	103–104
Labor Laws	421
Labor Unions	418–421
Laissez Faire Capitalism	40, 41
Legislative Branch	102–103
Management Functions, see also Planning, Organizing, Controlling, Staffing/Rewarding	5–9
Manville Corporation	289–296
Marginal Cost	
curve	49–51, 364
definition	49
Marginal revenue, definition	364
Market Equilibrium	51–54
Market Power, sources of	375–379
Market System	34, 37–65
McDonald's ReHIREment Program	414
Medical and Life Insurance	437
Medicare	430–432
Merger, Union Pacific-Southern Pacific	400–407
Minimum Wage	14
Modern Mixed Economy	40, 41
Monetary policy	91

Monopoly	364–367
Consumer's Surplus	365, 366
Deadweight Loss	365, 367
efficiency effect	366
Producer's Surplus	365, 367
redistributional effect	366
Social Waste	365, 368–370
Munn vs. Illinois	251
National Association of the Advancement of Colored People (NAACP)	423
National economic planning	92
National Highway Traffic Safety Administration (NHTSA)	260–263
Non-exclusion	88–89
North American Free Trade Agreement (NAFTA)	19
Occidental Petroleum Corporation	2
Occupational Safety and Health Administration (OSHA)	11
Occupational Safety and Health Regulation (OSHA)	265–268
Office of Federal Contract Compliance (OFCP)	11
Office of Federal Contract Compliance Programs (OFCCP)	424
Older Workforce	414–416
Oligopoly	370–374
Organization of Petroleum Exporting Countries (OPEC)	13, 59, 312–314, 373
Organizing	6–7
Physical Environment	
acid rain	340–342
alternative approaches	332–340
benefits and costs of policy	327–332
environmental goals	315–321
federal environmental policy	321–326
hazardous wastes	342–343
Planning	5–6
Playskool Inc.	175–180
Polaroid	216–223
Political Action Committees (PAC)	118, 120–122

Political System	21, 34, 36–37
definition	85
impacting	116–123
policy formulation process	111–116
political process	109–110
proposals for reform	124–125
Pregnancy Discrimination Act of 1978	415
Prices, role of	56–62
Private sector vs. Public sector	97–98
Professional Air Traffic Controllers Organization (PATCO)	14
Profits	54
Public Policy Process	107–116
Public sector	
adjustments for externalities	87–88
and economic growth	91–92
income inequality	90–91
legal foundations	86–87
problems of	92–97
provision of public goods	88–90
role of	85–86
vs. Private sector	97–98
Pullman Standard	3, 26–29
Railway Labor Act	423
Reaganomics	17
Scenario Method	69
Securities and Exchange Commission (SEC)	11
Sexual Harrassment	432–434
Sherman Act	385–388
Smoking	442–443
Social Responsibility	20–21, 34, 38–39
and controlling	167–170
and organizational structure	165–167
and societal elements	156–162
arguments against	146–148
arguments for	142–145
definition	138–140
model	148–171
primary involvement	141
secondary involvement	141
social action model	164

Social Security	17, 427–430
Societal Elements	34, 35–36
Staffing/Rewarding	8
Supply	
curve	48, 50–51
definition	48
determinants	48
Taft-Hartley Act or Labor-Management Relations Act	421–423
Technology	15–16
and external environment	481–483
and management functions	484–491
automation	468–470
future changes	470–478
major breakthroughs	459–462
overall impact	462–468
public policy and	478–481
Telecommuting	440–442
Texaco	447–455
Transfer payments	90
Underlying Forces	34–35, 409–414
Unemployment Insurance	437
Union Carbide	349–359
Unions	13–14
US West	411
Utilitarianism	189–193
Wabash Railway Co. vs. Illinois	251
Wagner Act or National Labor Relations Act	421–423
Wealth of Nations	55
Welfare	16–17
Wellness Programs	438, 439
Whistleblowing	199–201
Workers Compensation	437
Working Women	415–418, 439–442

NAME INDEX

Aaker, D. A.	70, 73, 83
Ackerman, R. A.	165, 181
Adams, Walter	385, 407
Aldag, R. J.	143, 163, 164, 181
Alexander, Charles P.	503
Alpern, K. D.	204, 224
Aplin, J. C.	119, 135
Barmeier, R. E.	68, 83
Barnes, Kathleen	503
Barth, Michael C.	414, 456
Baskin, Otis	296
Beauchamp, Tom L.	188, 189, 191, 193, 223, 224
Bleeke, Joel	284, 285, 297
Bok, S.	199, 224
Bolick, Clint	455
Bovard, James	436, 455
Bowen, H. R.	138, 181
Bowie, N. E.	188, 189, 191, 193, 210, 224
Bowman, E. H.	139, 143, 145, 181
Brenner, S. N.	206, 210, 224
Brittain, Jack W.	503
Brown, Clarence J.	281, 297
Buchholz, Rogene A.	3, 30, 184, 224
Burke, Jack	406
Burkhead, J.	96, 135
Butler, R. M.	134
Calmes, Jackie	455
Carlton, Jim	475, 494, 503
Carr, A. Z.	204, 224
Carroll, A. B.	193, 206, 224
Cascio, Wayne F.	443, 455
Case, Karl E.	40, 83
Case, Stuart	257
Caudron, Shari	411, 455
Chan, Marjorie	218, 221
Chapman, R. S.	134
Chatov, R.	224
Cochran, P. L.	145, 181
Conte, C.	135
Corley, Nobert H.	415, 455

Corley, Robert N.	384, 387, 389, 407
Cravens, David W.	459, 503
Craver, Charles B.	456
Cressey, D. R.	207, 224
Darlin, Damon	468, 503
Davidson, Joe	374, 407
Davis, Keith	135, 184, 225
Davis, Lance W.	463–465, 503
Day, Jennifer Cheeseman	410, 456
DeGeorge, Richard	217
Dill, W. R.	153, 181
Dodd, John	468, 503
Dolbeare, K. M.	108, 135
Dorfman, John R.	29
Drucker, P. F.	96, 135, 474, 503
Dworkin, Terry Morehead	434, 456
Dye, T. R.	108, 135
Eichenwald, Kurt	447
Fair, Ray C.	40, 83
Ferrara, Peter J.	456
Ford, Robert C.	440–441, 456
Forrester, J. W.	35, 83
Fox, T. G.	96, 135
Frederick, William C.	135, 184, 225
Freeman, John H.	503
Freeman, R. E.	150, 181
Friedlander, Ann	271, 297
Friedman, Milton	20, 30, 59, 86, 94, 135, 138, 147, 181, 188, 265, 272–273, 277, 297
Friedman, R.	59, 83, 86, 94, 135, 265, 272–273, 277, 297
Fulmer, R. M.	22, 30
Gabel, H. Landis	219, 222
Garvin, David A.	278, 279, 297
Genetski, Robert	428, 456
Grant, J. H.	66, 83
Green, Mark	297
Greenhouse, Steven	180
Greenlaw, Paul S.	435, 456
Greer, Douglas F.	268, 297

Gruley, Bryan	394, 407
Gujarati, Damodar	228, 230–235, 247, 279, 297
Guzzardi, W., Jr.	119, 135
Haire, M.	139, 143, 145, 181
Halal, W. E.	151, 181
Heald, M.	181
Healy, Robert E.	272, 297
Hegarty, W. H.	119, 135
Henderson, V. E.	195, 225
Hills, Gerald E.	459, 503
Hilton, George	297
Hodgetts, Richard M.	456
Hoffman, W. M.	184, 187, 189, 190, 193, 224–225
Holland, J. W.	96, 135
Hooker, M.	225
Horrel, Muriel	218
House, R. J.	22, 31
Houser, George M.	222
Hudgins, Edward L.	456
Hughes, Jonathan	460, 503
Ingrassia, Paul	468, 503
Jackson, B.	121, 136
Jackson, D. W.	143, 163, 164, 181
James, G. G.	199, 200, 225
Johansen, Robert	469, 488, 504
Johnson, H. L.	143, 181
Johnston, J.	68, 83
Jones, Barry	281, 298
Jones, C.	30
Jones, L. R.	298
Jones, Thomas M.	2, 20, 30, 142, 182
Kant, Immanuel	191–193
Keish, Karen S.	456
Kennedy, J. F.	136
King, W. R.	66, 83
Klein, Haywood	479, 504
Kohl, John P.	435, 456
Kolko, Gabriel	247, 298
Kotler, Philip	257, 298
Kroeck, K. Galen	456
Kudla, R. J.	22, 30

LaForge, J. M.	22, 30
Lance, Burt	198–199
Lanzillotti, Robert F.	376, 377, 407
Lee, L. W.	243, 298
Lehrer, Robert N.	469, 504
Linowes, D. F.	168, 169, 181
Machalaba, D.	134
Madigan, Charles	477, 504
McConnell, C. R.	40, 83, 135
McGuire, J. W.	138, 181
McKenzie, R. B.	136
McLaughlin, Frank	440–441, 456
McNaught, William	414, 456
McQarrrie, Fiona A. E.	441, 457
Mintzberg, H.	143, 146, 147–148, 181
Mitnick, Barry M.	283, 298
Molander, E. A.	206, 210, 224
Moore, J. M.	184, 187, 189, 190, 193, 207, 224–225
Morehead, Jere U.	455
Murray, E. A., Jr.	165, 181
Nader, Ralph	257, 377
Neikirk, Bill	477, 504
Niskanen, W. A., Jr.	96, 136
Noah, Timothy	267, 298
Ohmae, Kenichi	474, 489, 504
Okun, A. M.	62, 83
Page, Clarence	180
Pastin, M.	225
Pattan, J. E.	197, 225
Pindyck, Robert S.	68, 83
Platz, Donald L.	439–440, 457
Posner, Richard A.	242, 247, 298
Post, James E.	20, 30, 66, 67, 84, 108, 135, 136, 139–141, 148, 160, 182, 184, 225
Preston, Lee E.	20, 30, 31, 66, 67, 83, 84, 108, 136, 139–141, 148, 182
Purcell, T. V.	211, 225

Rapporteur, Clyde	30
Reed, D. L.	150, 181
Reed, O. Lee	384, 387, 389, 407, 455
Ricklefs, R.	225
Rothwell, Roy	459, 504
Rubinfeld, Daniel L.	68, 83
Rue, L. W.	22, 30
Russell, Robert R.	461, 504
Samuelson, P. A.	40, 84
Sapp, Richard W.	22, 30
Scherer, F. M.	373, 407
Schlink, F. J.	257
Schuck, Peter	412, 457
Seidler, L. J.	167, 168, 181
Seiler, Robert E.	22, 30
Sethi, S. P.	160, 181
Shedd, Peter J.	384, 387, 389, 407, 455
Sinclair, Upton	257
Smith, Adam	55, 188
Snavely, Kay	418, 457
Solomon, Charlene Marmer	415, 457
Sparkman, David	406
Starling, Grover	272, 296, 298
Stead, Bette Ann	438, 457
Steiner, George A.	2, 30, 218
Steiner, John	218, 221
Stigler, George J.	243, 298
Stoffels, John D.	6, 31
Stroh, Linda K.	456
Stuart, Peggy	412, 457
Sturdivant, F. D.	151, 181
Suzman, C. L.	217–221
Swigart, Rob	469, 488, 504
Tamarkin, Bob	29
Thacker, Rebecca A.	434, 457
Thompson, Fred	281, 298
Thune, S. W.	22, 31
Thurow, L. C.	136
Tombari, H. A.	69, 84, 108, 136

Verma, Dharmendra T.	217, 222, 223
Vogel, David	218, 222
Warner, Daniel M.	386, 389, 407
Warren, Melinda	298
Watzman, Norman	297
Weber, J.	211, 225
Weidenbaum, Murray L.	2, 3, 31, 119, 136, 230–235, 247, 248, 249, 298
Whaley, George L.	468, 504
Wilson, G. T.	200, 225
Wilson, Gary S.	374, 407
Winter, Ralph E.	469, 504
Wood, D. R., Jr.	22, 31
Wood, R. A.	145, 181
Woodruff, Robert B.	459, 503
Woutat, D.	135
Zentner, R. D.	69, 84